Sport, Culture and History

In addition to being an internationally recognised pioneer of sports history, Brian Stoddart has also been a leading thinker and influence in the field. That influence has crossed several areas of history, sociology, business, politics and media aspects of sports studies, and has drawn deeply upon his own training in Asian studies. His work has been characterised by cross-disciplinary work from the outset, and has encompassed some very different geographical areas as well as crossing from academic outlets to media commentary. As a result, his influential work has appeared in many different locations, and it has been difficult for a wide variety of readers to access it fully and easily. This volume draws together, in the one place for the first time, some of his most important academic and journalistic work. Importantly, the pieces are drawn together by an intellectual/autobiographical commentary that locates each piece in a wider social and cultural framework.

This book was previously published as a special issue of *Sport in Society*.

Professor Brian Stoddart is Deputy Vice-Chancellor (Research) at La Trobe University in Australia, and has long been recognised as a leading international authority on sports culture. He has published widely on Australian sport, sport in the British Empire, golf history and cricket, especially that of the Caribbean.

Sport in the Global Society
General Editors: J.A. Mangan and Boria Majumdar

Sport, Culture and History
Region, Nation and Globe

Sport in the Global Society

General Editors: J.A. Mangan and Boria Majumdar

As Robert Hands in The Times recently observed the growth of sports studies in recent years has been considerable. This unique series with over one hundred volumes in the last decade has played its part. Politically, culturally, emotionally and aesthetically, sport is a major force in the modern world. Its impact will grow as the world embraces ever more tightly the contemporary secular trinity: the English language, technology and sport. Sport in the Global Society will continue to record sport's phenomenal progress across the world stage.

Other Titles in the Series

Sport, Culture and History

Region, Nation and Globe

Brian Stoddart

Routledge
Taylor & Francis Group

LONDON AND NEW YORK

First published 2008 by Routledge
2 Park Square, Milton Park, Abingdon, Oxon, OX14 4RN

Simultaneously published in the USA and Canada by Routledge
270 Madison Ave, New York NY 10016

Routledge is an imprint of the Taylor & Francis Group, an informa business

Transferred to Digital Printing 2009

Typeset in Minion 10.5/13pt by the Alden Group, OxfordShire

British Library Cataloguing in Publication Data
A catalogue record for this book is available from the British Library

ISBN 10: 0-415-42079-2 (hbk)
ISBN 10: 0-415-49566-0 (pbk)

ISBN 13: 978-0-415-42079-2 (hbk)
ISBN 13: 978-0-415-49566-0 (pbk)

CONTENTS

Series Editors' Foreword
J.A. Mangan and Boria Majumdar

SPORT IN THE GLOBAL SOCIETY was launched in the late nineties. It now has over one hundred volumes. Until recently an odd myopia characterised academia with regard to sport. The global *groves of academe* remained essentially Cartesian in inclination. They favoured a mind/body dichotomy: thus the study of ideas was acceptable; the study of sport was not. All that has now changed. Sport is now incorporated, intelligently, within debate about *inter alia* ideologies, power, stratification, mobility and inequality. The reason is simple. In the modern world sport is everywhere: it is as ubiquitous as war. E.J. Hobsbawm, the Marxist historian, once called it the one of the most significant of the new manifestations of late nineteenth century Europe. Today it is one of the most significant manifestations of the twenty-first century world. Such is its power, politically, culturally, economically, spiritually and aesthetically, that sport beckons the academic more persuasively than ever- to borrow, and refocus, an expression of the radical historian Peter Gay- 'to explore its familiar terrain and to wrest new interpretations from its inexhaustible materials'. As a subject for inquiry, it is replete, as he remarked of history, with profound 'questions unanswered and for that matter questions unasked'.

Sport seduces the teeming 'global village'; it is the new opiate of the masses; it is one of the great modern experiences; its attraction astonishes only the recluse; its appeal spans the globe. Without exaggeration, sport is a mirror in which nations, communities, men and women now see themselves. That reflection is sometimes bright, sometimes dark, sometimes distorted, sometimes magnified. This metaphorical mirror is a source of mass exhilaration and depression, security and insecurity, pride and humiliation, bonding and alienation. Sport, for many, has replaced religion as a source of emotional catharsis and spiritual passion, and for many, since it is among the earliest of memorable childhood experiences, it infiltrates memory, shapes enthusiasms, serves fantasies. To co-opt Gay again: it blends memory and desire.

Sport, in addition, can be a lens through which to scrutinise major themes in the political and social sciences: democracy and despotism and the great associated movements of socialism, fascism, communism and capitalism as well as political cohesion and confrontation, social reform and social stability.

The story of modern sport is the story of the modern world-in microcosm; a modern global tapestry permanently being woven. Furthermore, nationalist and imperialist, philosopher and politician, radical and conservative have all sought in sport a manifestation of national identity, status and superiority.

Finally, for countless millions sport is the personal pursuit of ambition, assertion, well-being and enjoyment.

For all the above reasons, sport demands the attention of the academic. *Sport in the Global Society* is a response.

J.A. Mangan
Boria Majumdar

Series Editors
Sport in the Global Society

Preface

It must have been fun because, as in common with all 'Baby Boomer' colleagues, it seems impossible that I am old enough to gather a collection of essays covering a quarter of a century. Yet here we are. The bad news is that this resembles 'having a great career behind me'. The good is that sports culture study is now so extensive that it warrants a reflection upon where it has (or has not) been for at least one early participant, so as to provide some sort of reflection on its evolutionary stage.

That is no a claim that I am at the intellectual forefront or that I have been a major driver for sports history and its nuances; far from it. The collection simply outlines how one history-trained New Zealander journeyed into Sportsworld, where that journey went and why it produced what it did. Every person on the same voyage has his or her version, and all versions reveal ways still to be taken.

I assembled this project during 2005, writing with this section and the linking commentaries in many places: at home looking over the Victorian countryside; on planes going to or from meetings in Australia, India, Europe and elsewhere; or in hotel rooms in those and other places as the intellectual world for which I joined the universities clashed with the strategic world of university management into which I put myself several years ago. To quote Gareth Evans when, as Australian Attorney-General, he sent an air force plane over Tasmania to photograph a contentious site: 'It seemed like a good idea at the time!' The commentaries, unlike most of the essays, were written in a post-9/11 as well as a post-Bali world, and during an ongoing Iraqi invasion which meant, for Australians and their friends, interrogation of a supposedly new-strength Australian-American official alliance alongside an expressed desire to get closer to the 'new' powers of China and India as well as continuing dialogue with oil-wealthy jurisdictions. For those accustomed to the Anglo-Australian alliance there was one feature missing from the George W. Bush-John W. Howard mutual admiration society: cricket. Howard struggled to find sporting analogies that could smooth discourse with a highly America-centred Bush whose world view, to many outside the United States, has always seemed spectacularly uninformed about cultural patterns let alone traditions and thinking elsewhere around the globe. Inside Australia, universities struggled with ideological changes wrought by a Howard government marked by a utilitarian, functionalist approach to higher education with the responsible Minister declaring war on what he termed 'cappucino' courses, including those on sport. Twenty-five years earlier the drive was to create culturally insightful sports and other courses that checked the mass passion pulse; now it was to eliminate such insights because they were socially unproductive.

Some in my generation, and even in subsequent ones, might recognize the reflective impulse here – in a career made by writing about sport there arrives a moment that questions whether the endeavour is socially, even morally, justifiable. How can you write and think about sport when millions die in a tsunami (and you remember the hundreds of thousands who died in tidal waves that swept through one of your fieldwork sites, but who went unremembered because instant global television did not exist then); when indigenous populations in your country and others are little better off than a hundred years earlier; when homeless people tramp streets everywhere in increasing numbers; when HIV/AIDS and avian flu hover as the new Black Death; when child labour and abuse are increasing not declining; when institutions like the Church stand revealed as fallible as the rest of us; when savagery (some sponsored by our own leaders) stalks the globe; when the French dispossessed take to the streets in frightening frustration; and when too many Western quarters conflate 'Islam' to a demonized, one-dimensional category in fashion similar to their Crusader representatives almost a thousand years earlier? In short, is the cappucino minister not right in believing that some things are trivial?

Well, no. We now know, more than ever after years of accumulating work, that for millions of people sport *means* something, ranging from the mundane to the serious: from people taking a day off work to recover from their favourite team's latest loss, to nations spending billions because they believe staging the Olympics signifies something to other nations as well as themselves. In India and Pakistan, cricket might have helped avert yet another shooting war as they puzzled over why they still contest Kashmir almost sixty years after Partition. In 2005, Lance Armstrong inspired many with his historic seventh consecutive Tour De France win, perhaps the one American that year idolized as much in Europe as his President was despised. Much was read deeply into a 'revival of England' theme through a national cricket team beating Australia for the first time in almost twenty years. Increasing numbers of black players in South African rugby and cricket teams reminded us how central sport was to the struggle for freedom and equality. And over the 25 years a stream of works has detailed the cultural importance of sport in global life and politics; the rising intersection of sport and the media and, by extension, the business world; the complex place of sport in gender relations, gender expression and body culture; and much, much more.

This is a world of cultural understanding, working out how others think and acknowledging the stark fact that, for many, a team's fate carries more significance than a far-off war, national politics, the economy or famine. The cappuccino Minister might dislike it, but this is a central part of the modern life of the mind where what people *believe* to be true is as important as what *is* true. That Minister would dismiss film studies and related work if he followed his logic and that, of course, makes the point. Sport is increasingly significant globally and, more than ever, we must understand it – without forgetting that it occurs inside and alongside social concerns of wider moment.

Over the twenty-five years in producing these essays I have enjoyed the support of many, many people: to all of them I express my deep thanks for their humour, tolerance, insight, encouragement, information and support. They know who they are, but some I must mention especially.

Ian Catanach was the University of Canterbury teacher who set me on the scholarly path, now the friend seen too rarely but never absent. Though I became a trained teacher, he showed me the power of the teacher in university life, and whenever I have rewritten the promotion rules for one or other of my institutions Ian has always been in my mind: he should have been a professor. He was the hardest marker ever known. When, late in my undergraduate and Honours years, I began to pick up As from some, I never did with Ian − a B++? was as close as I ever got, but it seemed better than an A. His standards were set very high, and that has stayed with me. He typifies the time when New Zealand exported educated talent as much as any other commodity, and I was a beneficiary.

Ken McPherson is my longest standing close friend (saying now 'my oldest friend' raises issues neither of us would have considered years ago), and he has taught me as much about life as about the mind. His insights into history and cultures have always inspired me as have his observations on art, antiques, places and people. We have witnessed each other's trials, tribulations and triumphs, mutual advice and support always present. Ken worked and continues to work on the concept of the Indian Ocean in much the same way as I did on sport and, so, has had the similar exhilaration of doing something really new matched by the constant struggle to justify the enterprise. He succeeded despite many obstacles, and I count myself fortunate to have him as a friend.

Peter Reeves saved my doctoral thesis on India, then supported my professional move from South Asia, his great and abiding intellectual passion, to sport. Peter, for his students, has always been the great 'Rivz Sahib', the man of ideas and conviction and intellect and drive and bloody-minded commitment. He retains a ferocity of political view undiluted by whatever permutations of 'New Labor' might have swung in and out of view. His commitment to equality is unrivalled.

Robin Jeffrey started life as a Canadian sports journalist then became an Indianist, so he and I crossed the Rubicon in opposite directions, as it were. He alerted me to Roger Kahn's *The Boys of Summer*, a turning point for me. That book is an American equivalent of C.L.R. James's *Beyond The Boundary*, and further convinced me that insightful and important work on sport was possible. It was delightful, briefly, to be back working with Robin at La Trobe, enriched by his enthusiasm for India and learning, before he was snared by the Australian National University to become the Director of the Research School of Pacific and Asian Studies, a justly deserved post.

Patricia Vertinsky became a great friend in my Vancouver days, and has remained such. Like all of us in some form or another, she is a driven person who believes strongly in what she does, works hard to achieve that and does not understand why others do not behave similarly. I admire that, as I admire the intellectual curiosity that has taken her in many different directions on her own journey, and as I admire her warmth as a person as well as the major professional contributions she has made to furthering the field.

Boria Majumdar is a generational revelation. The title of this work, as South Asianists will recognize, is a play on that given to a collection of essays edited by Anthony Low, *Soundings In South Asian History*, that set much of the debate in the study of modern India. A later collection was dubbed by insiders as 'Son of Soundings', and Boria is sort of like that: a man allowed to write, as a Rhodes Scholar, an Oxford DPhil on the social history of Indian cricket, something unthinkable twenty-five years ago. His enthusiasm has driven this present collection and other recent works, so I am grateful to him for reminding me why I enjoyed 'doing' sport so much in the first place.

My brothers Lindsay and Ian may be surprised to find themselves here. We grew up apart in that I was older and at university before they left primary school. They had to cope, at too young an age, with the ageing and passing of our parents. Their lives have taken very different tacks to mine, helping me keep things in perspective. Lindsay still lives with his family in the town where we grew up, and that reminds me constantly of my personal history. He lives up the road from one of my classmates at Ashburton High School, and still my good friend, Lyn Macdonald who became a teacher at the successor school – that, too, reminds me how lucky I was to be educated in New Zealand when education was truly valued. Lindsay was a much better cricketer than me, and remains an informant on sporting matters in New Zealand, and in recent times we have satisfyingly watched matches together in Melbourne. Ian is one of those people who can do anything and, with his family, shifted to Western Australia where he still lives, running a grape harvesting business which was a million miles from his mind back in Ashburton. He followed an opportunity, and is a constant reminder to me of just how important is that quality of adventure. Hockey was his sport, played with a passion and skill that awed many and scared some. Like me, he loves it when the ABs win, especially against Australia – who ever doubted the power of sport as a national identifier – and the ambition is to watch one of those together. I admire them both for who they are and what they have achieved, and for the insights they have given me.

Friends and colleagues at La Trobe have provided a stimulating environment within which to think about this collection and its reflections. Vice-Chancellor Michael Osborne has been among the last of the scholar-leaders and is a great friend, while Bob Goddard, Paul Richardson and Denise Kirkpatrick have been (without their necessarily knowing it) influential in my thinking about much of this while we got on with the business of strategic thinking! Researchers so divergent as Nick Hoogenraad, Peter Dyson, Leann Tilley, Marilyn Anderson, John Carroll, Robert Manne, David de Vaus, Peter Beilharz, Dick Freadman, Sue Thomas, Judy Brett, Joe Camilleri, Malcolm Rimmer and many others who make up the vibrant La Trobe scene have given me more inspiration than I have had in years. Above all Cathy Besliev, my wonderful Executive Assistant, has provided more assistance and support than I should ever expect.

Sandi, Kirsten and Laura have shared so much of the journey, tolerated the time given to work, shaken their heads at over-commitment as much as at my unfathomable despair and exultation as the All Blacks or West Indies lose/win, asked the obvious question 'why', reminded me that there are other things in life, introduced me to all forms of new technology, shared my enthusiasm for new places, and enriched my life and existence.

Brain Stoddart
'Serlkirk'
9 November 2005

Cricket's Imperial Crisis: The 1932–33 MCC Tour of Australia

Introduction

Between 1970 and 1975 I was preoccupied with India while playing cricket for University of Western Australia (UWA) teams (during a period when Australian player John Inverarity led the club; and one of my opening bat partners was Geoff Gallop who went to Oxford as a Rhodes Scholar and later became Premier of Western Australia) and, later, with Nedlands. Games with those clubs told me more about social attitudes expressed via sport. University teams were considered elitist because access to university then was still a social elite privilege, especially so at UWA, while Nedlands and Dalkeith were and remain Perth establishment bastion suburbs. One memorable match involved a UWA team playing in a far-off suburb where ethnic communities predominated and the contest was fierce – our exit from the ground was blocked and a physical encounter seemed inevitable with our opponents thinking us privileged snobs who should be taught a lesson. This was sharper than my New Zealand experience. The 'West' also had a love-hate relationship with the rest of Australia (referred to as 'the Eastern States') expressed powerfully through cricket and Australian football – before the transformation of the Victorian Football League into the Australian Football League, Western Australia resented the recruitment of Perth footballers by Melbourne clubs.

Academically, I was investigating a small part of the rise of Indian nationalism and the drive to independence from Great Britain in 1947. Archival work in Delhi, Hyderabad and Madras and fieldwork elsewhere in present day Tamilnadu and Andhra Pradesh (a long way from Ashburton) was supplemented by wide reading with a staple being daily editions of the great Madras (now Chennai) newspaper, *The Hindu*. Reading all editions from the 1920s and the 1930s, and current editions while living there, it occurred that as the Raj left India politically but not culturally in 1947 sports and games, especially cricket, were an important marker.

That realization was augmented daily. At one point in Hyderabad (still a favourite city) I lived opposite a huge *maidan* where hundreds of kids and men came out daily for organized or spontaneous cricket matches. When lined up in banks or railway stations, someone would discover I was a Kiwi/Australian and invite me to coach or play for some team or another – it was assumed I was a cricketer. My first visit to Chennai coincided with Tony Lewis' MCC tour, and a huge crowd gathered in Mount Road to watch a ball-by-ball scoreboard record first test progress in far-off Delhi. Imagery, style and crowd behaviour differed from that in which I had grown up, but Indian cricket clearly meant as much socially as for James in the Caribbean and me in New Zealand.

I was interested now in sport as cultural power, imperialism and colonialism (including colonial response), sport as social interaction, and sport as metaphor for social expression. This was accentuated by reading Gramsci, Edward Said's *Orientalism* and John Berger's *Ways of Seeing* among many other things. I was steeped in cricket history, living in Australia, experiencing cricket with different patterns in different cultural settings, and encouraged by works such as Jim Walvin's *The People's Game* suggesting sport could be part of the 'new' social history.

During 1975–76 I taught in a UWA Australian social history first-year course designed by Tom Stannage, who encouraged me to mount mini-courses on sport. Interested in the social dimensions of the 1930s economic depression, that led me back to the 1932–33 MCC tour because it had everything: an imperialist villain in MCC captain Douglas Jardine; an English manager who hailed from the West Indies; the great Aussie hero in Sir Donald Bradman; an Australian headmasterly captain who played the game by the English code book; an Indian prince; an English fast bowler emerged from the Yorkshire coalmines; English amateurs; a touch of class prejudice, and so it went.

I began assembling the story in standard fashion: the secondary literature from all sides, the newspapers and cricket magazines, and a first tilt at the archives and personal materials as well as contacting survivors. The story got interesting. Most English survivors would not speak to me, despite the lapse of almost 50 years. The Australian Cricket Board archives were almost bare, and while a file was catalogue-listed in the Australian Archives it had disappeared. However, I unearthed a diary kept by the then British Trade Commissioner in Canberra, confirming the matter was discussed in official political circles. It recorded that Sir Alexander Hore-Ruthven had much to say as Governor in South Australia, and that led to the South Australian archives.

The essay reproduced here first appeared at the inaugural *Sporting Traditions* conference convened by Richard Cashman and Michael McKernan. That conference laid the foundations for sports history in Australia and brought together for the first time many of the names that would recur. By then, though, the Bodyline story had become deeper.

Encouraged by the materials, I applied to the Australian Research Grants Committee (ARGC) for funding to support further investigation in England. The grant came through but an Australian Labor Party Senator, who later became Finance Minister, asked a parliamentary question suggesting such grants were unproductive, misguided and ill-applied. The question created a round of media interviews and public scrutiny continued for some time. During 2005, ironically, I was appointed to the Quality and Scrutiny group within the ARGC's successor body, the Australian

Research Council, overseeing the fitness of grants recommended to a Minister as skeptical about humanities and social science grants as my interrogator from the other side of politics.

The research in England was fascinating. I spent a day with G.O. Allen who made it clear he had no time for Jardine or the tactics employed – many years later he donated some letters to the New South Wales archives. In Scotland I met Douglas Jardine's daughter and discovered a man much, much deeper than anyone had imagined. While many English survivors would not talk, Bill Bowes did, recounting the pain the tour had inflicted upon him and his colleagues. At the MCC I was told that some correspondence existed but was unavailable, and last time I asked it was still in that state.

In 1984 Ric Sissons and I published jointly a work reviewed warmly by John Arlott, among others, and that led to my involvement as historical advisor for the Kennedy-Miller company in Australia (best known for the Mad Max films) on their drama series, *Bodyline*, that upset many British viewers who thought it a blatant attack on the British sense of fair play.

This first foray, then, taught me a great deal: the traditional materials of history did exist for sport, there was a great media and public interest, and that sport would be a controversial area of investigation.

* * * * *

On 18 January 1933, during the third test match of the 1932–33 England-Australia cricket series, the Australian Cricket Board of Control dispatched this telegram from Adelaide to the committee of the Marylebone Cricket Club in London:

> Body-line bowling assumed such proportions as to menace best interests of game, making protection of body by batsmen the main consideration, and causing intensely bitter feelings between players, as well as injury. In our opinion it is unsportsmanlike, and unless stopped at once is likely to upset the friendly relations existing between Australia and England.

The remainder of the English tour came close to being cancelled during the next three weeks. Discussions and negotiations were held at the highest political and diplomatic levels in both England and Australia. A fierce debate raged in the press and on radio in both countries. Similarly, bodyline was a major topic of conversation wherever people met in all walks of life. Had the tour been called off, sporting relations between England and Australia would definitely have been damaged. More seriously, the wider imperial links which bound the two countries might also have been affected. One British diplomat, at least, feared that cricket's entry 'into the scope of diplomacy' could well have had extremely serious political consequences.[1]

The controversy arose from a new form of bowling attack developed by the English team. It was an adaptation of leg theory, which had been practised in England for some years by county bowlers attempting to restrict the high scoring that had become common since the First World War. However, its initial description of *fast leg theory* was replaced by *bodyline* after Australian journalists such as Jack Worrall, Hugh Buggy and Ray Robinson used the word to economize on their cables to England. A fast bowler pitched the ball well short of the batsman on or outside the line of leg stump. When the ball reached the batsman it was travelling towards his chest or head at speeds up to 145 kilometres an hour. Numerous fielders were placed on the leg side so that if the batsman tried to step inside the line of flight and hit the ball he would risk being caught. Most batsmen preferred to duck underneath the delivery or scramble out of its way, but because the ball was bowled so quickly, a number of them were inevitably struck painful blows. The pace of the delivery was both the new feature of, and the key to, this attack, and the MCC team contained four of the finest fast bowlers of that era: Harold Larwood, Bill Bowes, Bill Voce and G.O. Allen, the Australian-born amateur, had all finished well towards the top of the 1932 English county averages – Larwood, in fact, topped those averages by taking 203 wickets at an average of 12.9 runs per wicket.[2] There was little respite then, for Australian batsmen confronted by these bowlers and their new methods.

The bodyline controversy has been interpreted hitherto almost entirely within its playing context, with hapless Australian batsmen beset by ruthless English bowlers. There is, of course, considerable validity in that approach, but it does not fully explain the bitterness with which the 1932–33 tour is remembered even now. Two aspects of cricket history suggest that an account based upon the broad context of English and Australian society, and upon the nature of the Anglo–Australian relationship, during the early 1930s will yield a more satisfying explanation.[3]

Firstly, every tour undertaken by England or Australia since 1877, when official test matches began, had been marked by some controversy. During a late-nineteenth-century match between England and New South Wales, for example, the Sydney crowd invaded the playing field, upset by an umpiring decision against a local player. In 1912 the sensations began even before the Australian team left for England. Almost half the players originally selected refused to tour because the newly formed Board of Control overruled their choice of manager. During the Australian tour of England in 1921, English batsmen were unable to cope with the sheer pace of Macdonald and Gregory, much to the consternation of English crowds who often questioned the legitimacy of the attack.[4] The important point to be made here, however, is that none of these controversies went beyond their sporting contexts; they were purely cricketing issues. Bodyline, on the other hand, spread beyond the sporting arena to create enmity between England and Australia in a variety of social circles: governments, cricket administrators, players, the cricketing public and the general public. This unprecedented development suggests strongly that non-cricketing conditions contributed to the crisis.[5]

The second aspect of cricket history important here certainly had strong social connotations, especially in the context of the early 1930s. That was cricket's considerable imperial significance. Throughout the British Empire, the game was widely regarded for its role in maintaining imperial unity and keeping good temper between nations. In India, Africa, the West Indies, Australia, New Zealand, even

Canada and Hong Kong, cricket symbolized the cultural hegemony of British social values and their successful transfer from generation to generation throughout the Empire. In the imperial vocabulary, 'to play cricket' meant more than participation in a mere game; it was the embodiment of British fair play, justice and sportsmanship. Cricket displayed throughout the Empire the continuity and organization of British social traditions. Changes to the laws of the game, for example, were made only after full reflection upon their possible consequences, and they emanated solely from the MCC, which symbolized British authority in such matters. Cricket's social standards, too, were strictly maintained. The rigid separation of 'amateurs' and 'professionals', which lasted into the 1960s, was the most spectacular but by no means the only example of this. This social role of cricket was taken especially seriously in the outposts of Empire where 'progress' was measured essentially by success in British terms against British standards maintained in British institutions. Sport was as important a yardstick as politics or economics in this measuring process, and cricket was undoubtedly considered the most important form of imperial sports activity.[6]

Viewed in this cultural context, the Australian charge that the English team played in an 'unsportsmanlike' manner becomes more than a sporting bubble, for it challenged the imperial tradition that Britain set the standards for civilized social behaviour. The charge was serious enough in its own terms. But it assumed even greater significance because it occurred during the economic depression of the early 1930s when imperial relations generally underwent what was probably their most stringent test ever. That is, events on Australian cricket fields helped confirm a popular impression that accustomed social order and organization was about to be radically transformed. For at the beginning of the MCC tour, cricket was one of the few social institutions in both countries apparently untouched by the all-prevailing social crisis. By the end of the tour however, it was clear that even so strong and traditional a cultural prop as cricket had not escaped the social turmoil. For many people, consequently, a protest against bodyline was a protest against the wider social changes impinging upon their lives.

In England, the press reported the 1932 cricket season as 'one of the brightest and most inspiring' in county championship history. Yorkshire won its sixteenth championship, while Sussex won praise for playing cricket 'as it should be played by those who love it because it is a game and yet calls for the same strenuous energy and concentration as if it were a business'. The widely regarded importance of cricket in encouraging social discipline and normality was implicit in this review and in accounts of the MCC's departure for Australia. A 'huge and enthusiastic crowd' saw the players off from St Pancras Station, and all the way to the ship at Tilbury people 'assembled at every station, women waved from back gardens, and men stopped working on their allotments'. As the Observer put it, cricket was not everybody's game, but it was everybody's news. Socially, England seemed its normal self in cricket terms.[7]

But the touring side left an England vastly different from that left by any previous team. The period from September 1932 to January 1933 – which coincided almost exactly with the tour programme – marked the depths of the economic depression in Great Britain. At least 25 per cent of the workforce was unemployed, and bankruptcies rose by 12 per cent between 1930 and 1932. The middle classes, for whom cricket was a great passion, felt these figures suggested that the established bases of their social position were breaking up, and that they were consequently vulnerable to pressure from sections of the community normally kept in check. Crimes without violence against property, for example, rose by over 60 per cent between 1930 and 1933. Thieves were created by unemployment, it was argued, and constituted 'a greater menace than usual to those who are loyal to the laws of social fellowship and "play the game" the game of good faith and mutual trust which makes English life the most free from shadows that any race of men have ever lived'.[8] In that climate, British authorities acted quickly to curb threats to fair play and social order, qualities maintained so much through discipline in sports in general and cricket in particular.

As the English players sailed for Australia, a Lancashire weavers' union official appeared in court accused of inciting fellow workers to resist strike, breaking attempts by mill officials following a wage dispute. In Birkenhead, near Liverpool, numerous unemployed workers were arrested during widespread rioting. Police considered that the night of looting and stone-throwing was inspired by 'Communists' active among the unemployed. 'Communists' were also thought responsible for an attack on a newly elected Conservative MP after the declaration of a by-election poll in London. On the Broomhead Moors near Sheffield, gamekeepers employed by local land-owners clashed with members of the Ramblers' Rights Movement who walked on property traditionally administered as part of the Yorkshire county estates. In the midst of this widespread social tension and change, then, it was reassuring for the middle classes to see Herbert Sutcliffe, the Yorkshire professional, going off to Australia with a cricket bat which he promised to get autographed for the son of Lord Harewood of Yorkshire. Cricket, at least, retained its social stability and ordered hierarchy in the midst of otherwise worrying social alterations.[9]

When they landed at Fremantle in Western Australia, the MCC players found themselves in as socially fragile a situation as the one they had left. In Western Australia, an emergency bill to place a special 41/2d in the pound tax (to help alleviate the economic crisis raised by the Depression) was being guided through its final parliamentary stages. At least 29 per cent of the national workforce was unemployed, with the figure being as high as 34 per cent in some states. Even those who were employed were feeling the pinch economically, for the fall in real wages far outstripped the decline in retail prices. As in England, there were fears that this economic dislocation was contributing to the breakdown of social order. A Communist Party organizer was on trial in Sydney for having incited unemployed workers to join his organization. There were riots in New South Wales following the implementation of compulsory questionnaires for those seeking unemployment assistance. In Perth, women's organizations opposed legislation aimed at liberalizing gambling laws. Such liberalization, they argued, might prove momentarily expedient in boosting government revenue, but in the long term it would set an 'anti-social and uneconomic' example for future generations. The *West Australian* lamented that the necessity of a city campaign against vandalism demonstrated 'the failure of discipline in school and home'.[10]

Just as in England, then, an MCC tour was welcomed by many Australians as an assurance that not all traditions and standards had disappeared. It reminded Australians that they were part of a wider social organization in which they had always found comfort, both material and psychological. As one Western Australian politician declared at the MCC's first official reception in Australia: 'We look upon these visits as a powerful influence in cementing the bonds of Empire. In that respect they are, I think, second only to the influence of Australian soldiers in the Great War. Australia is part of the British Empire, and its people are of the same stock as those of England.'[11]

The tour, in fact, assumed considerable importance in the matter of Empire by taking place at a time when imperial relationships in general, and those between Great Britain and Australia in particular, faced numerous pressures. As in Canada and New Zealand, it was widely believed by Australians that Britain's repudiation of the gold standard had contributed substantially to colonial economic depression. These misgivings were then deepened by Sir Otto Niemeyer's criticisms of the Australian economy, and by the Ottawa Agreement on tariff and trade conditions which was popularly thought to favour Britain rather than her satellites. In Australia, these economic tensions were heightened by changes in the political relationship with Great Britain. The 1931 Statute of Westminster was supposed to have altered Britain's constitutional role in Australia; yet this was followed very shortly by Governor Sir Philip Game's dismissal of J.T. Lang's New South Wales government. All this political and economic disquiet bearing upon the imperial structure was underlined in India, the very heart of the Empire, where widespread unrest was regarded apprehensively by its imperial partners who felt, perhaps, that it symbolized the imminent breakdown of longstanding British sovereignty in many parts of the world.[12]

An interesting feature of the Indian case was that it demonstrated the importance of cricket in its colonial context. When an MCC team to tour India was announced in 1931, Indian cricket authorities complained that they were being sent a second-rate side. The implication was that, just as in politics, India was being treated badly in cricket by the British. Lord Willingdon, viceroy of India and an old English county player, realized that there were potential political dangers in this discontent. Cricket administrators in India came exclusively from the social groups upon whom the British relied for much of their political support in the subcontinent. Willingdon therefore smoothed the matter over diplomatically in the midst of political problems which, on the surface, appeared to be far more pressing than any cricket concerns. Against this general background, then, the MCC tour of Australia took on an even greater imperial significance than usual, and its progress was monitored closely throughout the Empire.[13]

The tour opened in Perth with matches against Western Australia and an invitation team that included Don Bradman.[14] He failed in both innings on a damp wicket, but there was no bodyline bowling involved. The MCC then beat South Australia and

Victoria convincingly, again without short-pitched bowling. Bodyline made its first appearance in Melbourne against another invitation team. Bradman fared badly, falling to Harold Larwood in both innings, moving away from the flying deliveries and playing them unorthodoxly. Australian captain Bill Woodfull, playing more correctly, took the first of many heavy body blows he was to receive in the following weeks. Larwood was rested for the New South Wales match, but Bradman and Jack Fingleton, another test player, still looked most uncomfortable against the short-pitched bowling of left-hander Bill Voce.

In this build-up to the first test in Sydney, the three players who held the key to the bodyline theory and controversy had already emerged. The fortunes and on-field actions of Bradman, Larwood, and Douglas Jardine, the English captain, held widespread public attention for weeks. Music hall songs were even written about the battle in which they were joined.[15] But their personalities were important for more than their cricketing aspects. Each demonstrated to a widely attentive and largely resentful audience of administrators and spectators that in cricket, just as in society generally, important conventions and traditions were undergoing major changes.

Donald George Bradman was born the son of a carpenter in Cootamundra, New South Wales, in 1908 and later moved with his family to Bowral.[16] He scored heavily in local cricket matches from the age of 12; centuries were regular, double and triple centuries not uncommon. By the age of 18 he had attracted the attention of the New South Wales selectors, even though he was a country player with no experience on turf wickets. He was given a trial in Sydney, the selectors were impressed, and, through a system of cricket patronage, he entered Sydney grade cricket. During the 1927–28 season he played regularly for New South Wales, scoring a century on debut and finishing with an average of forty-six. A good performance against the touring MCC side in the following season gained him selection for the first test. Australia was ground into submission in that match, and Bradman failed. Dropped for the second test, he was recalled for the third to make 79 and 112, while he scored another century in the fifth test. Another successful domestic season followed, and he was a natural selection for the 1930 tour of England. In that year, at the age of 22, Bradman turned on the most phenomenal scoring feats ever seen in the cricket world. He sustained his form over a whole English summer to score 2,960 runs in all games at an astonishing average of 98. His test record was even more spectacular: 974 runs in seven innings at an average of 139. Even so Australia won the series only by two matches to one with two drawn. Bradman clearly made the difference between the sides, and most commentators argue that his success in 1930 marked the real birth of bodyline, as English cricket sought to nullify the genius of the 'boy from Bowral'.

Because of this success, and at least partly because of the social conditions in which it was achieved, Bradman became a new kind of Australian sports personality. In confounding the view that Australian cricketers were strictly amateurs, he turned sports success to commercial advantage in the midst of general economic distress and, in so doing, challenged the authority and values traditionally possessed by Australian cricket administrators. While on tour in England he wrote a book which was serialised in the press; one-third of his tour bonus was subsequently withheld by the Board of Control, which argued that he had contravened a contract clause that forbade players from writing about matches in which they were involved. This did not diminish Bradman's public popularity. Fingleton recalls how Bradman left the rest of the Australian team in Perth after the 1930 tour to undertake a triumphal overland journey. Some players did not take kindly to this, arguing that Bradman's commercial commitments were so great during the tour that the only time they saw him was when he went out to bat. This commercial image was consolidated late in 1931 when he signed a joint contract with a newspaper, a radio station and a sports goods organization. At the beginning of the next season the Board of Control told Bradman that he could not play and write, and for a while it seemed that he would not play against Jardine's side. That he did so suggests that cricket's new commercial aspect was a powerful one in an age of economic stress, and that a new state had been reached in player-administrator relationships.[17]

Douglas Robert Jardine marked a similarly new change in the traditional conventions of English captaincy. He was an amateur, like all English captains until the early 1950s, but he was an amateur who looked and played like a professional. This was in direct contrast to the affable, outward-going, 'the-game's-the-thing' characters who were his predecessors in Australia, notably A.P.F. Chapman who had captained the 1928–29 team. Jardine was born in Bombay in 1900, and the family name was well known in India. His grandfather had been a judge of the Allahabad High Court in north India, and his uncle was a senior member of the Indian Political Service, which handled British relations with the Indian princely states. Jardine's father was educated at Balliol College, Oxford, played cricket for Oxford University, and became advocate-general of the Bombay presidency after a career at the Bombay bar. Two other Jardines occupied major positions in the Bombay legal profession. Douglas Jardine was an only child, so the sense of tradition and independence created in this colonial climate would have impressed itself upon him. Independence and aloofness were certainly a mark of his character. While at Horris Hill, an English preparatory school with a tradition of good cricket coaching, he was said to have corrected his coach on a technical matter by referring him to a basic coaching manual. Herbert Sutcliffe wrote later that he had spent a lot of time with Jardine during the 1928–29 tour, yet knew him as little at the end as he had done at the beginning. Sutcliffe thought Jardine 'a queer devil' at that stage, but gradually came to regard him as 'one of the greatest men' he had ever met.[18]

By the time Jardine went from Winchester to New College Oxford, he was an established player with a string of fine performances to his credit. In 1921 he scored 96 not out for Oxford against the Australian touring side before the match was called off early. Some writers have argued that Jardine never forgot the incident, and that thereafter his inherent tough-mindedness became even more pronounced when playing against Australia. He left Oxford with a degree in 1923 and, while playing for Surrey, qualified as a solicitor by 1926. Selected for the 1928–9 MCC tour, he discovered Australian crowd behaviour, something to which he never became reconciled and which seemed to strengthen his resolve when playing Australia. He led a team to India in 1931 and was then chosen to lead the team to Australia in 1932–33. His leadership experience was limited, but his attitude towards the game clearly impressed the selectors. On hearing that Jardine had been appointed captain of England, an old schoolmaster of his at Winchester is reported to have said, 'Well, we shall win the Ashes – but we may lose a Dominion'.[19]

Harold Larwood played a crucial role in that prophecy. In the five test matches he bowled 220 overs (more than any other bowler), took thirty-three wickets (Allen, with twenty-one was the next most successful) at an average of nineteen runs per wicket. Of English bowlers who have toured Australia since Larwood, only Frank Tyson in 1954–55 and John Snow in 1970–71 have approached his record of the 1932–33 tour, a performance that ranks as one of the greatest fast-bowling feats of all time. Larwood was the archetypal English professional fast bowler. Born in Nuncargate Nottinghamshire, he began his working life in the local coal-mines at the age of 14. His cricket was learned initially from his father, who captained the colliery side. An old English player who lived near by thought Larwood showed promise and recommended him to the county authorities. By 1924, when he was still not 20, Larwood had played for the county, and by 1926 he was playing for England. He toured Australia in 1928–29 and enjoyed some success, but in England in 1930 he suffered at the hands of Bradman, as did all English bowlers that year. On his own report, however, Larwood did learn in 1930 that Bradman did not like short-pitched deliveries; between 1930 and 1932 he improved his accuracy so that he could direct such an attack to a carefully placed field. In so doing, he initiated a cricket revolution in which the fast bowler was no longer subservient to batsmen as he had been throughout the 1920s because of the perfect pitches which encouraged very high scoring. Much of the bodyline controversy consequently revolved around what the *Manchester Guardian* called 'the contrast between the revolutionary and the classical idea', a clash between old and new conventions of cricket behaviour.[20]

These key figures did not meet in the first test, for Bradman was unable to play because of illness. England won easily, Larwood bowling forty-nine overs in the match to take a total of ten wickets for 124 runs. Only Stan McCabe, who scored 187 not out, played Larwood effectively; all the other Australian batsmen succumbed to the bodyline attack. Criticism of the English bowling methods became so vehement that an English newspaper writer accused Australian journalists of inflaming public opinion. The Board of Control was to meet in Melbourne during the second test, and there were reports that the MCC committee would be asked to impose restraints upon its team's tactics.[21]

Jardine and his fellow selectors, however, were so convinced of bodyline's success that they played their four fast bowlers in the Melbourne test and did not carry a slow bowler. The decision seemed vindicated when Bradman was bowled first ball, playing wildly at a bouncer from Bill Bowes. Bowes wrote later that the crowd was stupefied. Bradman walked off the field amid a silence that would have been a 'theatrical producer's triumph.' But the other Australian batsmen batted on a wicket that was too slow for the English fast bowlers; the Australian bowlers then worked hard and Australia took a first innings lead. Only Bradman played well in Australia's second innings, scoring a magnificent 103 not out in 183 minutes which took Australia to 191. England again fell to the Australian bowlers, and Australia won the match. But this squaring of the series did not ease the tension completely; Larwood was booed on numerous occasions when batsmen were hit. The *Argus* reassured itself and its readers that 'cricket is a grand old game, no matter what may have been done to it by those who sublimate it and call the result Test cricket'.[22] Changes in the conventions of cricket, and all that they represented, clearly rested uneasily with most of the Australian press and public.

The scene shifted to Adelaide for the third test. Interest was so high that special trains carried three times the normal number of passengers from Melbourne to the South Australian capital, where the Englishmen became unpopular before the match even began. Upset by the behaviour of a youthful crowd at practice sessions, Jardine had the ground closed to spectators. The *Sydney Morning Herald* hoped that such unpleasantness would not prevent the game from being 'played in the tradition and the spirit that have made it what it is – the true embodiment of British sport and fairplay'.[23]

England batted first and made 341 after being four for 30 at an early stage. Australia began batting on the Saturday afternoon, and, 'vehement protests followed when Woodfull was hit' over the heart by a lifting delivery from Larwood. Numerous 'hostile demonstrations' followed when other batsmen ducked under similar deliveries. Newspaper reports read over the Sunday rest day ensured that a record crowd thronged the Adelaide Oval when play resumed on Monday. The atmosphere, tense from the outset, erupted when Australian wicket-keeper Bert Oldfield glanced a short-pitched ball from his bat into his face. One English observer felt that 'if some impetuous member of the crowd had set himself up as leader any number would have followed him over the fence with unimaginable results'. Jack Hobbs, one of England's greatest-ever batsmen, who was covering the tour for a London newspaper, said later that he had left the ground worn out by the noise of the crowd in a demonstration which an experienced Australian observer agreed was 'remarkably hostile'. Police armed with batons and automatic pistols were said to have been sent to the ground for fear of an imminent full-scale disturbance.[24]

Australian crowd behaviour had bothered English touring teams for many years, mainly because Australian spectators shouted advice of all kinds to players during the course of the game. This was very different from the demure atmosphere that generally surrounded English cricket grounds. 'Barracking', as it was known, had emerged in Australia at least as early as the 1890s, and one self-confessed exponent of the art estimated that by the 1930s it was practised by at least 70 per cent of Australian cricket spectators. But although barracking alarmed many Englishmen, it contained an element of social control that matched English crowd behaviour. Participation was almost entirely verbal, invasions of the pitch being almost unknown, and apparent ill-feeling rarely outlasted the duration of the game. One spectator in Adelaide, for example, gave vent to his anger with Jardine by shouting during a drinks break, 'don't give him a drink! Let the bastard die of thirst!' Such emotional outlets perhaps lessened the danger of physical violence breaking out. On an earlier tour, Herbert Sutcliffe endured the jibes of a Brisbane crowd for four days and was then delighted by some well-known barrackers who presented him with tobacco pipes as a memento.[25]

In 1932−33, however, there was a sharper edge to this normally abrasive but relatively ordered crowd participation, and it may be linked to the underlying social and economic conditions. The crowds were bigger than ever before. Record attendances were set on nearly every ground, and a world record for cricket match attendance was set during the Melbourne test. Spectators went to great lengths to be assured of a good vantage point. In Melbourne, for example, the first enthusiasts reached the gates at 5.30 a.m. on the first morning; many people ate breakfast outside the ground, and an hour before the gates opened a twelve-wide queue was over quarter of a mile long. Many of these people were thought to have attended the cricket at least partly to unburden themselves of the wider pressures bearing upon them. One correspondent thought that Australian spectators needed, more than ever before, to identify with a standard of excellence attained by a champion so that they might reassert some of their general social confidence. Harold Larwood thought that many people were at the grounds in anticipation of an Australian victory which might provide hope and encouragement in the face of unemployment and dole queues. Jack Fingleton explained much of Bradman's public popularity in similar terms; to see Bradman succeed was to see Australia triumph in the face of adversity.[26]

But it is easier to evoke the size and atmosphere of those crowds than to analyse their composition. It is unwise, for example, to assume that they were 'middle class' simply because, given the depressed economy, it was relatively costly to attend the matches. People were prepared to pay to see the cricket because they thought it would offer them some degree of psychological comfort and a good deal of entertainment. One Melbourne man, though he could 'ill-afford' to do so, paid eight shillings for two stand seats so that he might take his wife to the cricket and give her a day's entertainment. People like him paid almost £70,000 in gate takings at the five tests, and the Argus calculated that for admission, transport and refreshments the Melbourne crowd spent at least £40,000 to watch the second test.[27]

It seems sensible to suggest, then, that the crowds probably reflected fairly closely the general social mix of Australian society. A number of observers confirmed this by drawing social distinctions between people who sat in members' stands and those who watched from the 'outer'. But the important point here was that both sections reacted angrily to English tactics during the really fiery moments of bodyline, particularly in Adelaide. In a time of Australian stress, there was a degree of social cohesion and identity perhaps unmatched in any other social situation of the time. Nevertheless, the one constant feature of the crowds was their very complexity. By the end of the tour, for example, many people went to see bodyline bowled, were vocally disappointed when it was not produced immediately, and then reacted bitterly when it did make an appearance.[28]

But as England dominated then won the Adelaide test, bodyline spread its effects beyond the playing arena and the crowds to the administrators and politicians who were as much concerned with its underlying social significance and issues as with its purely cricketing aspects. The press reflected something of this trend. One English writer felt that Larwood had made a battlefield of the Adelaide Oval, that the 'morality' of his bowling was in question; it was 'not cricket' and might have political and economic repercussions. *The Times* felt that 'any breach in the mutual good will and friendliness between the players of the two countries which have survived the ordeal of many a desperate encounter over the period of more than half a century would be a cricketing disaster of the first magnitude'.[29] One Australian writer argued that cricket, like the established social order, was being ruined by the 'Philistines of a ruthless modern age' for whom sporting encounters were 'grim international encounters in which everything is staked upon the prowess of a few chosen champions'. Spectators who so 'lost their perspective and their sense of humour as to attempt to control the tactics and deflect the fortunes of the game by angry advice', and who 'roared continuously from behind the fence', were the sporting equivalents of mobs that roamed both England and Australia.[30] None felt the force of this incipient cricketing and social breakdown more keenly than the game's administrators in Australia and England.

The mixed reaction that greeted the 18 January telegram in Australia reflected the public's divided attitude towards the Board of Control. Since its formal creation in 1912, the Board's short history had been as much marked by federal-states' rights questions as the wider political federation movement which had partly encouraged its appearance. To assert its position, the Board elaborated an authoritarian air which made it unpopular with states' associations and players; the 1912 controversy over the Australian touring team, mentioned earlier, was just the first of many. One cricket-minded New South Wales politician, for example, painted the Board as an oligarchy which from its inception had assumed powers 'incompatible with the prosperity of Australian cricket and players'.[31]

The choice of the word *oligarchy* was important for there was a popular view that the Board, besides being politically authoritarian, was socially unrepresentative of Australian cricketers and their communities. The *Bulletin*, for example, felt that bodyline's most distressing feature was that Australians who had 'no use for the Board or its works may be mistaken for small-minded people who attach exaggerated importance to cricket matches'. The *Bulletin* missed the real point in one way; many Australians, besides members of the Board, did attach considerable importance to cricket matches, especially those against England. One Australian cricket writer pointed out shrewdly that 'Marylebone, and the spirit of cricket, have probably stood higher in this faraway land than, perhaps, in England'.[32] That was because cricket, including its organization and administration, helped determine the progress and place of Australia within the Empire.

For the people who administered Australian cricket, success in running such a British institution as cricket determined their social status as much as success in economic or political spheres. And the importance of that cricket status was increasing rather than diminishing by the early 1930s. The *Australian Cricketer* made the interesting point that before the First World War there had been no need for people to parade their social status by travelling from Melbourne to Adelaide to watch test cricket, unlike the early 1933 situation.[33] An analysis of the Board's membership supports the view that cricket was a major feature of the colonial aristocracy's benchmark. Further, it suggests that the 1932–33 crisis resulted at least partly from that group's desire to preserve tradition against commercialism and revolutionary tactics which smacked of the undesirable changes it perceived in society more generally.

In 1932–33 there were thirteen men on the Board: three each from New South Wales, Victoria and South Australia; two from Queensland, and one each from Western Australia and Tasmania. These men shared a common social heritage, an above-average education, and a commercial/professional background.[34] One of the New South Wales members, for example, traced his ancestry to an infantry officer of the New South Wales Regiment who arrived at Sydney in 1792. Similarly, the Western Australian representative descended from families that had been among that state's early colonists. At least half of the Board's members had been educated at prestigious private schools; and many had proceeded to a university education, particularly for the professions there were at least four lawyers and two medical practitioners among them. There were, besides, two stock exchange members, a pastoral agent, the managing director of a timber company, and a bread company director. Their membership of the Board invariably followed a lengthy spell in state cricket administration, where their positions in some part resulted from their social and occupational status. Few of them had playing experience in first-class cricket. Two examples help demonstrate what cricket meant socially to these people and, indirectly, why bodyline upset them.

Dr Allen William David Robertson, chairman of the Board, exemplified the role of cricket as a medium for upward social mobility. Born in 1867 in Deniliquin, on the Victoria-New South Wales border, where his father ran a general store, he was orphaned at an early age and went to Melbourne in the care of an aunt. He worked first in a warehouse and was then apprenticed to a chemist for whom he worked in a number of Victorian country towns. During his time in the country, Robertson qualified for entrance to the University of Melbourne, where he began studying medicine part-time, eventually graduating at the age of 36. He worked in private practice in Melbourne besides holding various hospital posts. Capitalizing on his professional standing, he formed a business partnership with other doctors and developed property in the heart of Melbourne. The social mobility which augmented this economic success stemmed from his involvement with the University Cricket Club. Robertson was appointed as its president in 1914; five years later he became a Victorian representative on the Board of Control, and he became its chairman in 1930.[35]

William Charles Bull, on the other hand, saw cricket from a more established position in Australian society. His father had been born in Liverpool, New South Wales, about 1840; along with his brothers he trained for the legal profession in Sydney and, after serving in local government, sat in the New South Wales parliament in the late nineteenth century. His son was born in 1881 and educated at Sydney Grammar before qualifying as a solicitor in 1909 and joining his uncle's law firm. Like his father, he quickly became a prominent member of the New South Wales Cricket Association (which held many of its meetings in his uncle's office), rising through its executive ranks and becoming a New South Wales representative on the Board of Control in 1925.[36]

These men identified solidly with the British and imperial traditions of cricket. In that sense, their telegram to the MCC was as much a plea as a demand for protection of the game and all that it had come to represent socially for them by the 1930s. Incidentally, their views were clearly shared by at least some Australian players. Woodfull himself wrote later that cricket 'is of such world renown, and is so finely British, that it rests with all cricketers, and especially, of course, first-class cricketers, to hold its good name dear'. It was a measure of the Board's apprehension about general change, then, that its hasty wording of the 18 January telegram accused the English team of 'unsportsmanlike' play, a charge that cut at the heart of British sporting and social traditions. A more judicious cable might have won the Board greater sympathy from the MCC, but the imperial cricket authority could not ignore such an accusation from a colonial subordinate. As *The Times* suggested, neither the MCC nor England could tolerate such a charge: 'It is inconceivable that a cricketer of Jardine's standing, chosen by the MCC to captain an English side, would ever dream of allowing or ordering the bowlers under his command to practice any system of cricket that, in the time-honoured English phrase, is not cricket.'[37] The MCC, a pre-eminent English social institution whose formation predated the foundation of Australia, met the charge with the full weight of its social and political power.

There were, for example, numerous important peers of the realm on the MCC committee, among them Hampden (first title created in 1307), Buccleuch (1663), Dartmouth (1711), Hawke (1776) and Lucan (1795). Then there was Sir Francis Lacey, a lawyer who married into the aristocracy and served as MCC secretary between 1898 and 1926; his knowledge of cricket politics was second to none. Wider politics were also presented. Lord Ullswater was an eminent lawyer who served in parliament between 1883 and 1921, acting as Speaker in the House of Commons for sixteen years. Sir Stanley Jackson had played cricket for Yorkshire, been financial secretary to the War Office in the early 1920s and chairman of the Unionist Party in the mid-1920s before becoming governor of Bengal in 1927, a post he held until 1932 – he was clearly accustomed to dealing with imperial crises of all kinds. Viscount Bridgeman had served as home secretary and first lord of the Admiralty during the 1920s, and had been MCC president in 1931. Sir Kynaston Studd, lord mayor of London in 1928–29, had spent a lifetime in City politics.[38] These last three, along with Lord Lewisham, who was the current MCC president, formed a formidable deputation to the Dominions Office at the height of the crisis.

The MCC committee did not fail those of its supporters who favoured a hard line towards the Australian Board of Control. 'We, the Marylebone Cricket Club, deplore your cable message and deprecate the opinion that there has been unsportsmanlike play. We have the fullest confidence in our captain, team and managers, and are convinced that they would do nothing to infringe the laws of cricket or the spirit of the game. We have no evidence that our confidence is misplaced. Much as we regret the accidents to Woodfull and Oldfield, we understand that in neither case was the bowler to blame. If the Board wishes to propose a new law or rule it shall receive our careful consideration in due course. We hope that the situation is not now as serious as your cable appears to indicate, but if it is such as to jeopardise the good relations between England and Australian cricketers, and you consider it desirable to cancel the remainder of the programme, we would consent with great reluctance.'[39] In its political sense, it was a document worthy of Whitehall.

The situation was so fluid by the end of January that the future of the tour was by no means clear. Some sections of the press felt that the Board had been soundly defeated by its imperial master; others that the MCC had been, as the British generally were in political and economic matters, typically condescending towards a member of the Empire worthy of better treatment. The Board of Control met to reconsider the matter. A long discussion produced a more conciliatory telegram which, however, still did not withdraw the word unsportsmanlike. By that stage, there were rumours that the Australian prime minister had spoken to his London representative about the crisis.[40] The MCC, alarmed by the charge that it had undermined a tradition of sportsmanship upon which much of the imperial ethos was based, had already sought diplomatic assistance in its dealings with the Board.

In fact, E.T. Crutchley, the British government's representative in Australia, was so concerned by the possible damage being done to imperial relations by the controversy that he took the initiative and asked the MCC managers for their interpretation of it.[41] Their reply, which reached him on 1 February, claimed that the situation had been inflamed unnecessarily by the Board's initial telegram. On the same day he received from the managers a telegram prompted by the Board's second telegram to the MCC committee. Crutchley was asked to use his 'influence' and have the word unsportsmanlike withdrawn, or the rest of the tour was likely to be cancelled. The British government's representative telephoned J.A. Lyons, the Australian prime minister, whose first comment was: 'It looks as though we are leading two opposing armies'. Both men viewed the situation very seriously from the imperial angle. The British representative stressed 'that the cancellation of the tour would be a very grave thing, for Australia especially, just when feeling was so good'. This clearly referred to an improvement in Anglo-Australian relations in wake of the political and economic difficulties of recent years. Lyons telephoned Dr Robertson to convey 'the importance of the matter from the national point of view'.

Neither side was anxious to yield ground in the bargaining that followed. Lyons, for example, wanted to know what 'gesture' the MCC would make in return for the withdrawal of the word unsportsmanlike. On the basis of information received from the English management, Crutchley replied that the field placings might possibly be modified. Robertson, too, clearly wanted an assurance about a 'gesture', for the prime minister later asked Crutchley for confirmation about the altered field placings. At that point the English management adopted a hard line, declaring that they would not bargain about the withdrawal of the 'obnoxious' word. They were clearly seeking an unconditional Australian surrender. At this level, cricket events were only the superficial manifestations of wider social, political and economic considerations concerning the future status of the imperial relationship. Had negotiations broken down and the tour been cancelled, the popular view would have been that the MCC had contravened those conventions of 'fairplay and sportsmanship' upon which much of imperial life was based; consequently, incalculable psychological damage might have been done to Anglo-Australian and wider imperial ties.

It was only on the eve of the fourth test in Brisbane that the crisis was averted. There were reports that the MCC team was virtually on strike and would not play the match unless the offending word was withdrawn by the Board of Control. In London a special MCC subcommittee followed up Crutchley's work by calling on the secretary of state for the dominions, J.H. Thomas, who denied that their visit had any political connotations. They had, he said, merely wanted to use the diplomatic communications system to establish rapid contact with Australian authorities. But the fact that an earlier caller to discuss the cricket situation was the governor of South Australia, Sir Alexander Hore-Ruthven, suggests that the MCC visit was more important than Thomas admitted. The demands made by the MCC throughout this official and non-official activity in England and Australia were met in time to save the fourth test when the Board of Control signalled: 'We do not regard the sportsmanship of your team as being in question... We join heartily with you in hoping that the remaining Tests will be played with the traditional good feeling.'[42]

England won the fourth test, and the series, and the tour reached a tired end in a situation from which the tension was never really removed. A real crisis had been avoided, but not without cost to the personal feelings of Englishmen and Australians about each other at all levels in society. Crutchley reported that on a visit to his Canberra club at the conclusion of the affair, 'Everyone I spoke to with one exception was quite frantically against present practice and the hated word... cropped up, with temper, in quite unexpected quarters'. In another very different social situation an English-born university student, listening to the radio broadcast of the third test with some friends in Tasmania, supported the MCC players. His friends became so cool towards him, to the point of not speaking, that he packed his bags to leave their home. Only at the last moment did they ask him to stay.[43]

In purely cricketing terms the events of 1932–33 were dramatically stirring; memories of them remain vivid for those involved directly as players and for those who watched. The bodyline tour's importance in cricket history is that it constituted a major stage in the evolution of the game. Short-pitched bowling had appeared before the early 1930s without becoming a cricketing convention. By breaking the tradition that batsmen should be protected from such tactics, bodyline established a new role for fast bowlers. The cricketing and public acceptability of 'bouncers' as bowled by Miller and Lindwall, Tyson and Trueman, Hall and Griffiths, Lillee and Thomson, and the rest since the Second World War has derived in many ways from the tactics employed by Harold Larwood and his colleagues. After bodyline, unlike before it, batsmen could never anticipate with certainty that fast bowlers would invariably pitch the ball up to them.

But cricket history alone does not explain the full significance of the bodyline tour which, more than most sports events, became a matter for widespread public concern and comment. Cricket's imperial significance, the fragility of Anglo–Australian relations, and the social ravages of the economic depression combined to give the on-field events a sharper edge than might normally have been the case. For most people in the early 1930s, life was a series of abnormalities which created uncertainty about the future. In that context, the 1932–33 tour was initially regarded as a reassurance that not all the accustomed traditions of national and imperial life had been upset, and that social change might not be so widespread as feared initially. When the tour turned sour, it was a sure indication that all aspects of life had been altered drastically by the bewildering social, economic and political changes of the early 1930s.

Reactions to that realization revolved around the relationships exhibited between Englishmen and Australians at all levels in society, manifested in different ways in different circles. The series was an unfriendly one for the English and Australian players: few of them met socially off the field, a rare occurrence in Anglo-Australian cricket. Cricket administrators in both countries pondered the prospect of a future without England-Australia test cricket; each group considered the other primarily responsible for damaging a major imperial cultural institution. Politicians and diplomats, already grappling with difficult issues in dispute between the two countries, wondered how these cricketing developments might further complicate official relations between England and Australia. For the Australian public, seeking assurances of social normality and sporting success to counteract social failure, bodyline bowling was simply one more example of Great Britain adversely effecting Australian life in the early 1930s. Alternatively, the British public generally regarded complaints about the MCC tour as yet another example of Australian social immaturity, a condition that had to be remedied with firm action.

Yet what remains most important, perhaps, is not that Australian and English relationships were threatened by the bodyline controversy, but that they survived it. The friendly receptions given to Harold Larwood when he emigrated to Australia in 1950, and to Douglas Jardine when he re-visited Australia shortly before his death in 1957, serve as at least one testimony to that social and cultural continuity. That the links and continuities survived is a tribute not only to the inherent strength of the traditional Anglo-Australian connection, but also to the international power of cricket as a culturally unifying institution.

Notes

[1] The telegram was reproduced in most newspapers of the time and in most books written about the tour. The following books raise the point briefly: Bolton, *Britain's Legacy Overseas*, 64; Alexander, *Australia Since Federation*, 109; Robertson, '1930–1939', 449; Crowley, *Modern Australia in Documents*, 525. The following are among the more popular accounts of the tour: Blythe, *The Age of Illusion: England in the Twenties and Thirties*, Chap. 7; Graves and Hodge, *The Long Weekend*, 290–1; Kisch, *Australian Landfall*, final chapter; Crutchley, Diary, 1 Feb. 1933; Petrie, 'Sport and Politics'.

[2] Space precludes a full discussion of the origins of bodyline, but, as with the tour itself, there are numerous interpretations; some Buggy papers are held by the La Trobe Library in Melbourne, but they contain no references to the tour, though Harold Larwood and Kevin Perkins note in *The Larwood Story* that Buggy made a collection of cricket material available to them. The county averages may be seen in *Cricketer*, Spring Annual 1933, 36.

[3] For example, Sir Robert Menzies' foreword and Sir Donald Bradman's introduction to Swanton, *Swanton in Australia with M.C.C.*, 12, 16. For a fascinating journalistic attempt to put the Brooklyn Dodgers baseball team of the early 1950s into the context of American society, see Kahn, *The Boys of Summer*.

[4] Darling, *Test Tussles*, 58–61 and Mason, *Warwick Armstrong's Australians*.

[5] Professor Inglis impressed upon me the importance of this point.

[6] This subject warrants considerable investigation, but for the purposes of this essay see Hawke, *Recollections and Reminiscences* and Warner, *Long Innings*. For some colonial perspectives, see James, *Beyond A Boundary* and Mandle, 'Cricket and Australian Nationalism'.

[7] Roy Webber, *County Cricket Championship*; *The Times*, 31 Aug., 19 Sept. 1932; *Observer*, 18 Sept. 1932.

[8] Figures calculated from Tables 96, 125 and 205, *Statistical Abstracts for the United Kingdom for Each of the Years 1913 and 1923 to 1936* (London: HMSO, 1938). For background to the period, see Aldcroft, *The Inter War Economy*; Lloyd, *Empire to Welfare State*; *Observer*, 11 Sept. 1932. For some aspects of social history, see Stevenson, *Social Conditions in Britain*; Heinemann and Branson, *Britain in the 1930s*.

[9] *Manchester Guardian*, 17 and 19 Sept. 1932; *The Times*, 19 and 20 Sept. 1932. Sutcliffe later led the players' support for Jardine; see Harris, *Jardine Justified*, 24.

[10] *West Australian*, 19 and 26 Oct. l932; *Official Yearbook of the Commonwealth of Australia*, 1933, 743; ibid., 1936, 523–43; Bolton, *A Fine Country to Starve In*.

[11] *West Australian*, 19 Oct. 1932.

[12] See Drummond, *British Economic Policy*, part 1, Ch.3; and especially W.F. Mandle, 'Sir Otto Niemeyer'. Ratification of the statute caused considerable discussion in Australia; for example: Commonwealth of Australia, Parliamentary Debates, vol.131, 193 1, 4500 29 for something of Senate concern over the statute, see Sir Keith Officer Papers, Interview Transcript, series 2, box 7, Australian National Library; Foott, *Dismissal of a Premier*; Morrison, 'Dominions Office Correspondence'. For a general view of the Indian situation at this time, see Brown, *Gandhi and Civil Disobedience*; Moore, *The Crisis of Indian Unity*.

[13] Hammond, *Cricket My World*, 101; Harry Pichanik wrote from Rhodesia, for example, 'You would no doubt be surprised to see how keenly cricket enthusiasts are following the progress of the M.C.C. tour': *Australian Cricketer*, 1 March 1933, 97.

[14] The following two paragraphs are based upon tour book and daily newspaper accounts.

[15] Larwood, *Body Line?*, 72–3. One England player thought Australian cricketers received more attention than film stars or politicians; Wyatt, *Three Straight Sticks*, 87.

[16] Bradman, *My Cricketing Life*; Mayes, *Bradman*.

[17] Fingleton, *Cricket Crisis*, 50; *Bulletin*, 18 Jan. 1933.

[18] Robertson-Glasgow, *46, Not Out*, 104–5; Sutcliffe, *For England and Yorkshire*, 117.

[19] See Warner, *Lord's 1787–1945*, 206–7. The selectors' role in the development of bodyline was clearly an important one. T.A. Higson, for example, had a reputation for being tough minded with an intense will to win. See Kay, *A History of County Cricket*, 124–6, quoted in Swanton, *Sort of A Cricket Person*, 69. The biographical details for the Jardine family are gathered from *Who's Who?*, *Who Was Who?*, and *Dictionary of National Biography*. For some of Jardine's attitudes towards cricket, see his *Cricket*.

[20] Larwood and Perkins, *The Larwood Story*, Mason, *Sing All A Green Willow*, 69–75; Larwood, *Body Line?*, 15–16; Oldfield, *Behind the Wicket*, 199; *Manchester Guardian*, 3 Jan. 1933; Maclaren, *Cricket Old and New*, 25.

[21] *Observer*, 18 Dec. 1932. Some English players shared this view, Brown, *Cricket Musketeer*, 102; *Sydney Morning Herald*, 29 Dec. 1932.

[22] Bowes, *Express Deliveries*, 106–7; *Argus*, 2 Jan. 1933.

[23] Jardine's account appears in his *In Quest of the Ashes*, 126. See also Crutchley Diary, 14 Jan. 1933; *Sydney Morning Herald*, 13 Jan. 1933.

[24] *The Times*, 16 Jan. 1933; *Argus*, 16 and 17 Jan. 1933; *Sydney Morning Herald*, 17 Jan. 1933; Oldfield, *Behind the Wicket*, 202; Harris, *Jardine Justified*, 10, Wyatt, *Three Straight Sticks*, 97; Hobbs, *The Fight for the Ashes*, 120.

[25] Mandle, 'Pommy Bastards and Damned Yankees'; Corrie, *The Barracker at Bay*, 5. For an indication of what little has been done on the behaviour of sports crowds, see Smith, 'Sport and Collective Violence'; Kippax, *Anti Body-line*, 45; Hele and Whitington, *Bodyline Umpire*, 155; Jardine, *In Quest of the Ashes*, 140; Sutcliffe, *For England and Yorkshire*, 41–2.

[26] *Manchester Guardian*, 2 Jan. 1933; *Daily Herald*, 2 Jan. 1933; *Argus*, 3 Jan. 1933; *Australian Cricketer*, 1 Dec. 1932; Larwood and Perkins, *The Larwood Story*, 94; Fingleton, *Cricket Crisis*, 28.

[27] 'Disgusted' in *Argus*, 2 Jan. 1933; Victorian Cricket Association, *Annual Report 1932–33*, 21; Mailey, *And Then Came Larwood*; Wilmot, *Defending the Ashes 1932–1933*, 58; *Argus*, 4 Jan. 1933.

[28] For example: Larwood, *Body Line?*, 84; Kippax, *Anti Body-Line*, 27; Wilmot, *Defending the Ashes*, 255; Mailey, *And Then Came Larwood*, 105.

[29] *Manchester Guardian*, 16 Jan. l933; *The Times*, 19 Jan. 1933; however Mailey, *And Then Came Larwood*, 94 denied that there were wider political, social or economic ramifications to these cricketing events.

[30] *Argus*, 21 Jan. 1933; the *Australian Cricketer*, 1 Dec. 1932, argued that this was the age of 'Big Cricket'.

[31] *Sydney Morning Herald*, 20 Jan. 1933, *Argus*, 21 Jan. 1933; *West Australian*, 19 Jan. 1933. For example, see the quarrel between the Melbourne Cricket Club and the New South Wales Cricket Association reported in *Sydney Morning Herald*, 15 May l906: Wilmot, *Defending the Ashes*, 58; *Sydney Morning Herald*, 2 Jan. 1933.

[32] *Bulletin*, 25 Jan. 1933; *Australian Cricketer*, 1 Feb. 1933.

[33] *Australian Cricketer*, 1 March 1933.

[34] The following information has been gathered from scattered sources.

[35] *Australian Encyclopaedia*, 1958 edn, vol.7, 465–6. For some views on sport and social mobility, see: Loy, 'The Study of Sport and Social Mobility'; Luschen, 'Social Stratification and Social Mobility among Young Sportsmen'; Gruneau, 'Sport, Social Differentiation, and Social Inequality'.

[36] *Who's Who in Australia*; *Sydney Morning Herald*, 16 and 17 May 1906.

[37] Woodfull, *Cricket*, 2; There were only three board members in Adelaide when the decision was taken to send the telegram; *The Times*, 19 Jan. 1933; C. Stewart Caine, editor of the authoritative *John Wisden's Cricketers' Almanak 1933*, 307, used almost exactly the same expression. *Daily Herald*, 19 Jan. 1933, carried a more indignant report.

[38] *Who's Who?* and *Who Was Who?*

[39] This telegram was widely reported in the daily press. Sydney J. Southerton, editor of Wisden's for 1934, noted contentedly that the MCC 'never lost their grip of the situation' (332).

[40] *Daily Herald*, 24 and 26 Jan. 1933; S.H.D. Rowe (Western Australian member of the Board) in *Sydney Morning Herald*, 25 Jan. 1933; 'The Sporting English'?, 23–4. This telegram may be found in the daily press of 1 and 2 Feb. 1933; *Bulletin*, 1 Feb. 1933.

[41] The next two paragraphs are based upon Crutchley Diary for 1, 2 and 4 Feb. 1933; and on Crutchley to P.F. Warner, 2 Feb. 1933; Warner to Crutchley, 6 Feb. 1933; Crutchley to Warner, 10 Feb. 1933.

[42] *Daily Herald*, 3 Feb. l933; *Argus*, 3 Feb. 1933; *The Times*, 3 Feb. 1933; Warner to Crutchley, 6 Feb. 1933; *Manchester Guardian*, 3 Feb. 1933; *Bulletin*, 8 Feb. 1933; Thomas, *My Story*, 293; Swanton, *Sort of a Cricket Person*, 77. This telegram may be seen in the daily press.

[43] See tour book and press accounts. Swanton, *Sort Of A Cricket Person*, 77–8, and Wisden's, 1934, 328–31, outline some of bodyline's complications for the 1934 Australian tour of England, which was in doubt for some time. See also Stirling, *Lord Bruce*, 16 for an indication of Australian political reactions in London. Crutchley to Warner, 10 Feb. l933; McInnes, *Humping My Bluey*, 142–4.

References

Aldcroft, D. H. *The Inter War Economy: Britain 1919–1939*. London: Batsford, 1970.

Alexander, F. *Australia Since Federation*. Melbourne: Nelson, 1967.

Australian Encyclopaedia. Sydney: Augus and Robertson, 1958.

Blythe, R. *The Age of Illusion: England in the Twenties and Thirties*. Harmondsworth: Penguin, 1964.

Bolton, G. C. *A Fine Country to Starve In*. Perth: University of Western Australia Press, 1972.

Bolton, G. *Britain's Legacy Overseas*. London: Oxford University Press, 1973.

Bowes, B. *Express Deliveries*, London: Stanley Paul, nd.

Bradman, D. *My Cricketing Life*. London: Stanley Paul, nd.

Brown, F. *Cricket Musketeer*. London: Kaye, 1954.

Brown, J. M. *Ghandi and Civil Disobedience: The Mahatma in Indian Politics, 1928–1934*. Cambridge: Cambridge University Press, 1977.

Corrie, R. T. *The Barracker at Bay: An Outspoken Reply to Bodyline*. Melbourne: Keating Wood, 1933.

Crowley, F. K., ed. *Modern Australia in Documents*. Vol.1. Melbourne: Wren, 1973.

Darling, D. K. *Test Tussles on and Off the Field*. Hobart: the author, 1970.

Drummond, I. M. *British Economic Policy and the Empire 1919–1939*. London: Allen and Unwin, 1972.

Fingleton, J. H. *Cricket Crisis*. Melbourne: Cassell, 1946.

Foott, B. *Dismissal of a Premier: The Philip Game Papers*. Sydney: Morgan, 1968.

Graves, R. and A. Hodge. *The Long Weekend*. New York: MacMillan, 1941.

Gruneau, R. S. "Sport, Social Differentiation, and Social Inequality." In *Sport and Social Order: Contributions to the Sociology of Sport*, edited by D. W. Ball and J. W. Loy. Reading, MA: Addison-Wesley, 1975.

Hammond, W. R. *Cricket My World*, London: Stanley Paul, nd.

Harris, B. *Jardine Justified: The Truth About the Ashes*. London: Chapman and Hall, 1933.

Hawke, Lord. *Recollections and Reminiscences*. London: Williams and Norgate, 1924.

Heinemann, N. and M. Branson. *Britain in the 1930s*. London: Heinemann, 1973.

Hele, R. S. and G. Whittington. *Whittington and Grorge. Bodyline Umpire*. Adelaide: Rigby, 1974.

Hobbs, J. B. *The Fight for the Ashes*. London: Harrap, 1933.

James, C. L. R. *Beyond a Boundary*. London: Hutchinson, 1969.

Jardine, D. *Quest of the Ashes*. London: Hutchinson, 1933.

Jardine, D. *Cricket*. London: Dent, 1936.

Kahn, R. *The Boys of Summer*. New York: Harper and Row, 1972.

Kay, J. *A History of County Cricket . . . Lancashire*. London: Sportsman's Book Club, 1974.

Kippax, A. *Anti Body-Line*. Sydney: Sydney and Melbourne Publishing Co., 1933.

Kisch, E. *Australian Landfall*. Melbourne: MacMillan, 1969.

Larwood, H. *Body Line?* London: Elkin Mathews and Marrot, 1933.

Larwood, H. and K. Perkins. *The Larwood Story*. London: Allen, 1965.

Lloyd, T. O. *Empire to Welfare State*. New York: Oxford University Press, 1970.

Loy, J. W. "The Study of Sport and Social Mobility." In *Sociology of Sport*, edited by G. S. Kenyon. Chicago: Athletic Institute, 1969.

Luschen, G. "Social Stratification and Social Mobility among Young Sportsmen." In *Sport, Culture, and Society*, edited by J. W. Loy and G. S. Kenyon. London: Macmillan, 1969.

McInnes, G. *Humping My Bluey*. London: Hamish Hamilton, 1966.

Maclaren, A. C. *Cricket Old and New*. London: Longmans Green, 1924.

Mailey, A. *And Then Came Larwood*. Bodley Head, 1933.

Mandle, W. F. "Cricket and Australian Nationalism in the Nineteenth Century." *Journal of the Royal Historical Society* 59, no. 4 (1973): 225–46.

Mandle, W. F. "Pommy Bastards and Damned Yankees: Sport and Australian Nationalism." In *Going It Alone: Australian National Identity in the Twentieth Century*, edited by W. F. Mandle. Harmondsworth: Penguin, 1977.

Mandle, W. F. "Sir Otto Niemeyer: Catalyst of Australia's Depression Debate." In *Going It Alone: Australian National Identity in the Twentieth Century*, edited by W. F. Mandle. Harmondsworth: Penguin, 1977.

Mason, R. *Sing All a Green Willow*. London: Epworth, 1967.

Mason, R. *Warwick Armstrong's Australians*. London: Epworth, 1971.

Mayes, A. G. *Bradman*. Sydney: Angus and Robertson, 1948.

Moore, R. J. *The Crisis of Indian Unity 1917–1940*. Oxford: Oxford University Press, 1974.

Morrisson, A. S. "Dominions Office Correspondence on the New South Wales Constitutional Crisis 1930–1932." *Journal of the Royal Australian Historical Society* 6, no. 5 (1976).

Official Yearbook of the Commonwealth of Australia. Canberra: Commonwealth Bureau of Census and Statistics, 1933.

Official Yearbook of the Commonwealth of Australia. Canberra: Commonwealth Bureau of Census and Statistics, 1936.

Oldfield, W. A. *Behind the Wicket: My Cricketing Reminiscences*. London: Hutchinson, 1938.

Petrie, B. M. "Sport and Politics." In *Sport and Social Order: Contributions to the Sociology of Sport*, edited by D. W. Ball and JW. Loy. Reading, MA: Addison-Wesley, 1975.

Robertson, J. R. "1930–1939." In *A New Histroy of Australia*, edited by F. K. Crowley. Melbourne: Heinemann, 1974.

Robertson-Glasgow, R. C. *46, Not Out*. London: Hollis and Carter, 1948.

Smith, M. D. "Sport and Collective Violence." In *Sport and Social Order: Contributions to the Sociology of Sport*, edited by D. W. Ball and J. W. Loy. Reading, MA: Addison-Wesley, 1975.

Stevenson, J. *Social Conditions in Britain between the Wars*. Harmondsworth: Penguin, 1977.

Stirling, A. *Lord Bruce: The London Years*. Melbourne: Hawthorn, 1974.

Sutcliffe, H. *For England and Yorkshire*. London: Arnold, 1935.

Swanton, E. W. *Sort of a Cricket Person*. London: Fontana, 1974.

Swanton, E. W. *Swanton in Australia with the M.C.C.* London: Fontana, 1976.

'The Sporting English?' From Front Line to Bodyline: A Commentary from a 'Man in the Street. Sydney: Macquarie Head Press, nd.

Thomas, J. H. *My Story*. London: Hutchinson, 1937.
Warner, Sir Pelham. *Long Innings*. London: Harrap, 1951.
Warner, Sir Pelham. *Lord's 1787–1945*. London: White Lion, 1974.
Wilmot, R. W. E. *Defending the Ashes 1932–1933*. Melbourne: Robertson and Mullens, 1933.
Woodfull, W. M. *Cricket*. London: Pitman, 1936.
Wyatt, R. E. S. *Three Straigh't Sticks*. London: Stanley Paul, 1951.

Sport and Society 1890–1940: A Foray

Introduction

Tom Stannage was responsible for this piece, too. Returning to the UWA History Department from Cambridge, he began commissioning writers for a comprehensive history of Western Australia and, as a former leading Australian Rules footballer, he was alive to the role of sport so invited me into the project. It was another fascinating journey into the historical record, uncovering a local sporting press dating from the later nineteenth century to supplement the relatively limited (from a sports standpoint) standard press. Bill Mandle, Australia's principal sports history pioneer, revealed the sporting dimensions of papers like *Bell's Life,* the *Sportsman* and the *Town and Country Journal,* but there was scarce use of the localized sporting press. Indeed, there was no serious work on Australian local or regional sporting experiences, although Wray Vamplew was beginning a similar piece on Adelaide.

This Western Australian work helped me formulate a view of sport as a determinant of cultural and social outlook and attitude. Most sociological commentary then saw sport as a reflection of patterns seen in more 'normal' social domains. In the United States, Jack Berryman influentially posited sports history that way – a social practice within which behaviour patterns mirrored those displayed in other life settings.

The patterns began to appear differently to me. Having examined the role of power in social performance in India, I envisaged sport and its organizations as a power source whereby people without access to that commodity ordinarily could exercise great authority. Something of that view appeared in the Bodyline analysis, with the inner workings of the MCC and the Australian Cricket Board of Control revealing reified attitudes. Sport looked a force for conservatism rather than change, so explaining odd inclusion and exclusion patterns. The most notable case concerned women, but the same applied to Australia's indigenous population and ethnic communities. Conservative views about such groups were pronounced in sport, even when older patterns were weakening elsewhere in contemporary life.

The work also identified possible concerns about sports culture investigations. The Western Australian Turf Club provided access to its records. That was important because the WATC was among *the* Perth social institutions with membership keenly sought, zealously screened and highly prized. My access was negotiated carefully by officials, but not for reasons I had imagined. They were concerned I might publicize long forgotten cases of corrupt jockey behaviour, betting scandals, horse doping and similar matters. These were all on display in the records and I read them with interest, but the historically explosive materials lay elsewhere and officials had no concern about them. The materials relating to membership were highly revealing, the WATC record of admissions a touchstone to Western Australian elite acceptability and ranking. During the economic depression, bankrupt graziers and pastoralists were admitted to membership while prosperous publicans and trades people were not, at a time when the WATC was financially vulnerable. Here was a clear mark of distinction as Pierre Bourdieu might have noted: I was reading him avidly.

Similarly, a 1940s royal commission into harness racing contained great detail about how the industry worked (or did not work), confirming a sports world that was no superficial entity or trivial pursuit but one with nuance, tension, high stakes financially and psychologically, rivalry, intrigue and even enmity.

There were two lessons here. First, there was the danger of sport as social history being diverted by sport as 'games' history. With the WATC, it would have been easy to dwell upon the racing scandals and ignore the major social role played by sport in Western Australia. It is not that an 'inside' Australian racing history is unimportant – far from it, as Richard Waterhouse demonstrates – but that story is a real rather than sensationalist one.

Second, a wider reading of history and other disciplines was essential in discerning the deeper meanings of sport. The sports materials alone would neither expose the full meaning nor impress disciplinary colleagues about the potential of the sub-field. This was particularly important in Australia. It would be simplistic to argue a clear dichotomy in the Australian approach, but two distinct patterns were surfacing. One came from history departments in the central figures of Bill Mandle and Ian Turner. Each man had a different historical position (Mandle a Whig traditionalist, Turner the 'new' social historian) as well as an ideological one (Mandle read Marx then rejected Marxism, Turner was clearly on the Left), but both employed conventional historical analysis and boundaries. The second group was more complex and came from physical education/kinesiology backgrounds with Max Howell (ex-Australian rugby union international trained first in kinesiology and later in history from a physical education standpoint) and Ian Jobling (University of Alberta-trained Australian) prominent figures along with Ray Crawford (English and England-trained in physical education).

These two groups, independently, started work on sports history research and met formally at the first 'Sporting Traditions' conference in 1977, leading to the publication of *Sport in History* in 1979. There was tension between the groups initially, even if great friendships developed. Put crudely, the 'historians' thought the 'physeders' antiquarian or hagiographical or both, while 'physeders' (probably correctly) considered the historians arrogant interlopers. At one meeting convened by Ray Crawford in 1978 the tension approached enmity, and looking back now at the papers it is easy to see why.

Along with this field complexity, Tom Stannage's book produced the usual issues surrounding contested legitimacy in different spheres of intellectual and academic life.

Tom ran seminars where writers presented their work to team members. At one session a writer on Western Australian literature declared that sport should not be included. My revenge was to suggest Lucy Walker be declared the leading WA writer and be included alongside obscure people who circulated limited and unpublished works. Lucy Walker was a WA writer who sold millions of copies of Mills & Boon novels in their earlier forms, so the idea was received coolly. A few years later, as Dean of Communication in Canberra, I helped create the first short course for aspirant Mills & Boon writers.

＊ ＊ ＊ ＊ ＊

In his celebrated work, The Astonished Muse, Reuel Denney wrote:

> Australia leads the world in the degree to which its sports interests and sports organizations reflect the total social and political ideals of the nation. Sport in Australia is virtually the invisible government of an egalitarian semi-socialistic community based on generations of lower-middle-class immigration from the old country. The development of mass sports and spectacle sports is not out of balance with the development of individual sports, and there is no professional-amateur friction to speak of. Any Australian in sport is believed by his countrymen to be a sort of gentleman to begin with, deserving all the support he can get from the rest of the gentlemen, even if it amounts to providing him with a welfare state and fringe benefits. All this results in part from the ethnic and linguistic consistency of the Australian population, which in turn creates the image of a whole social group going up the social scale altogether.[1]

This Arcadian view of Australian sports and sportsmen coincides with the opinions most Australians have about themselves, and incorporates the attitudes held by most contemporary sports historians and sociologists about the contribution of sport towards shaping modern western industrial societies. Many Australians consider their society an egalitarian one in which social advancement and advantage is open to all. As part of that view, they consider themselves to have access to all forms of organized sport, and that they are therefore 'sportsmen' in some sense of the word. Their view of sport in Australia simply reflects their general views about society, as Denney suggests.

This 'mirror image' view of sport in society also dominates the academic study of sport in its historical and sociological settings, both in Australia and elsewhere. W.F. Mandle, for example, argues that late-nineteenth-century cricket material reveals a similar explanation for the growth of Australian nationalism as do the works of political and economic historians.[2] James Walvin claims little more than that the growth of soccer reflects the growth of modern British society.[3] Eldon Snyder and Elmer Spreitzer, in an overview of sports sociology, conclude that 'sport is a social institution which interfaces with, and reflects, many dimensions of social life'.[4] Charles Page, in one of the best summations of sports sociology to date, reaches a similar conclusion.[5]

These restricted claims essentially emerge from a widely held view that the investigation of sport is academically unrespectable. As Norbert Elias and Harry

Edwards point out, this comes from a modern western tradition which separates intellectual and physical education when the two might be linked quite closely.[6] Academics venturing into what is considered the field of physical education, therefore, have been regarded as intellectual inferiors by their peers. One sports historian, for example, has argued that his colleagues could not associate with social historians because the latter thought sport unworthy of academic research.[7] Because of these constraints, the 'reflective' view has become dominant with sports sociologists and historians anxious to justify their work in terms familiar to potentially antagonistic academics. Theoretical constructs which ascribe more formative roles to sport in the processes of modern society have not been encouraged.[8]

This study, however, suggests that organized sport in Perth helped establish important, lasting social structures, traditions and relationships during an important phase in the city's historical development. This is not to deny entirely the presence of the 'reflective' element, but to argue that the study of sport might be approached more positively. In that regard, the work is founded upon two interrelated concepts. First, it is informed by Antonio Gramsci's theory that the civil hegemony of any dominant social group stems as much from the general acceptance of that group's cultural values as from its political and economic values.[9] Second, sport has played an increasingly important role in Australian popular culture from at least the middle of the nineteenth century, stimulated by the greater amounts of leisure time steadily made available to all social groups since then.[10] A consequent increase in organized sport, then, has placed greater emphasis on the social values inherent in, and conveyed by, such sport. It is argued here that between 1890 and 1940 organized sport in Perth did not just reflect general social developments, but helped shape and sustain the city's social structure, as well as relationships within it.

Evidence for this argument is drawn mainly from three periods of different social stress in Perth between 1890 and 1940. In the early 1890s, frenetic social and economic growth reached the city after more than fifty years of measured development. This accelerated growth placed pressure on the values, conventions and structures established to that point. During the First World War, similarly, Perth faced many changes to its social beliefs and organization, not all of which met with the approval of all sections of society. Then, the economic depression of the early 1930s challenged many established social views, and raised both prospects and fears of widespread change. Through all this, the role of organized sport in aiding or resisting social change was considerable in a number of these areas: social status, community identity, social values, social mobility, social organization as represented in the place of women, and the political value of sport.

As Geoffrey Bolton points out, Western Australia's initial growth was directed by an aspirant 'colonial gentry' whose values matched those of the British ruling classes.[11] Because social and economic growth was so slow until the late 1880s these values – based principally upon beliefs in property, capital and birth – were entrenched in colonial society, consolidated as much by cultural as by political precepts. While a full discussion of this early social formation is impossible here, it is significant that the first sport institutionalized in Perth was horse racing. Founded in 1852, the Western Australian Turf Club was modelled on the Jockey Club in England and quickly became a major social organization governed principally by men of property and status.[12] The growth of the 1890s, however, marked the beginning of a challenge to the dominance of those transplanted cultural standards; and that challenge holds the key to the 1890–1940 period. In 1890 the granting of full parliamentary government to Western Australia coincided with the flood of the gold rushes which set the colony's economy apart from those elsewhere in Australia during a generally depressed period.[13] As the following table shows, the population changed radically within a few years, then developed steadily.

An important feature of this change was its rapidity. From being an almost 'face-to-face' society before 1890, Perth was rapidly transformed into a major capital city.[14] Much of the new population was centred in Perth itself which became a more than usually dominant political, economic, social and residential capital. The population widened from its pre-1890 British character to one which embraced people born elsewhere in Australia as well as elsewhere in the world. As an urbanized and industrialized community arose to complement the pastoral and agricultural sector which had dominated the pre-1890 economy, so specialized commercial and professional service groups emerged. These new groups provided new sources of capital and property, thereby altering the social fabric developed since the foundation of the city. These changes, then, confronted the dominant values of the colonial gentry and its descendants; between 1890 and 1940 the reshaping of cultural values was a major part of the city's experience.

This general growth was matched by a growth in organized sport. There were only a few sports competitions organized systematically by 1890. Racing was conducted in the city almost every week, while cricket and football authorities arranged fixtures among a restricted number of teams. But even there the organization was likely to be minimal. Half of the 1889–90 cricket season elapsed before the Metropolitan Cricket Club held its annual meeting. When it did, the players decided not to play matches away from their home ground.[15] Other sports held competition events, but they were conducted irregularly. Rowing and cycling were among the most important, with athletics meetings also being arranged. Until 1890 the cultural and social values deemed important in Perth society had their main expression in racing, which was often combined with picnics and other recreational leisure activities. Organized

Table 1 Western Australian population change, 1890–1940

Year	Population	Year	Population
1885	35,000		
1890	45,000	1920	331,000
1895	101,000	1930	432,000
1905	250,000	1938	467,000

competitive sport had been less important and served both restricted purposes and a restricted clientele. Cricket was played mainly among the small number of government servants in the city, while football was concentrated in the fledgling industrial working class.

By 1895 sports organization, like the population, had increased dramatically. Eight cricket teams were organized into competitions based in Fremantle and Perth. The Turf Club's domination over racing was being challenged by private company proprietary racing clubs which established new tracks. Perth's first tennis club was being formed, while the Fremantle Rowing Club was about to build a substantial pavilion.[16] New sports were appearing. A polo match played between Coolgardie and Perth teams demonstrated the continuing importance of imported values and cultures; most of the players came from important colonial families.[17] By the turn of the century there were regular competitions in cycling, lacrosse, tennis, swimming, athletics, golf, boxing, wrestling, rugby union, soccer and other sports.

As growth steadied during the first thirty years of the twentieth century, so did organized sport. Racing was firmly established as a subculture by the 1920s and the press published regular lists of the leading jockeys and trainers. The Lacrosse Association had at least 245 players organized into a fifteen-team competition.[18] Newer clubs were joining established competitions; for example, the Claremont-Cottesloe Football Club was admitted to the football league, while University won a place in the Western Australian Cricket Association pennant competition.[19] King's Park Tennis Club facilities won praise from touring international players.[20] Interstate football and cricket fixtures were established on a regular basis.[21] Facilities were improved in a number of sports. Many golfers, for example, joined the new Lake Karrinyup club built on the outskirts of the city and destined to become a leading sport and social institution.[22]

The changing role of sport in conveying social values was implicit in this development. While established values were maintained through the older sporting institutions, changes in those values were frequently expressed through sport by newer social groups. As a result, few sporting clubs escaped being allocated or taking a particular social status.

The Western Australian Turf Club was and remains the most socially prestigious sporting institution in Perth. Set up as it was on the English model, its members were mostly from the colonial gentry who dominated politics, pastoralism and the social pages in the newspapers.[23] In 1890, for example, its officials included Dr Edward Scott, an English-born medical doctor who set up practice in Perth during 1875. He threw himself into the colony's public life, serving in the unreformed Legislative Council from 1886–90, and then in the new Council from 1890–93. By 1890 he was also in the middle of a three-year term as mayor. Scott was closely connected to the city's leading families and his second marriage was to a member of the Sholl family, which had extensive pastoral and commercial interests. The Sholls were well represented in the Turf Club in 1890. Robert Frederick Sholl was colonial born and established himself as a pastoralist in the north-west, later buying into a number of city businesses. He, too, served in the old Council from 1886–90; then in the new Assembly from 1890–97, and again in the Council from 1904–09. His pastoralist brother, R.A. Sholl, was also a prominent member of the Turf Club. George Leake was born in Perth, his lawyer father having come to the colony in 1833. He was called to the Bar in 1880 and became a leading lawyer as well as a political activist, becoming premier of the state in 1901–02. His wife was the daughter of Sir Archibald Burt, the chief justice and founder of a leading legal family. M.F.A. Canning was born in England and arrived in Perth to manage a branch of the Bank of New South Wales. Four years later he founded the Western Australian Mortgage and Agency Company which handled pastoral business.

These men demonstrated how social, economic and political power came together in the Turf Club. If they were born in the colony, they came mostly from founding families whose values had shaped the society. If they were not from established colonial families, then they shared the colonial gentry's aspirations by identifying with its social and economic interests. They were frequently organized by marriage into tight social networks which gave the Turf Club an added air of exclusiveness. This social prominence and cohesiveness gave the club a reputation for exercising extreme care in choosing its members. The complaint that the Turf Club was more difficult to enter than parliament was heard frequently between 1890 and 1940.[24]

For the pattern of Turf Club membership continued almost unchanged until 1940, with its offices held by prominent public men and supported by members chosen carefully. During the 1920s, for example, the chairman was E.H. Lee Steere who was also president of the Pastoralists' Association and of the Weld, the city's most exclusive private club.[25] The Lee Steeres were leading members of the colonial gentry. Their ancestral home, reputedly since the Norman Conquest, was Jayes in Surrey. Lee Steere's grandfather was a Conservative member of the House of Commons from 1870 until his death in 1890. Lee Steere's father, the third of five sons, went to Western Australia during its early days to fulfil the social and landed aspirations restricted by his position as a younger son in England. Once in the colony he became a leading pastoralist, public figure and member of the principal social institutions like the Turf and Weld Clubs. Men like Lee Steere chose their fellows carefully. During the early years of the depression, when club finances were shaky, there was no thought that membership criteria might be relaxed to provide an additional source of revenue. Many established members dropped out during the period, their replacements being chosen largely on status grounds rather than on income.[26] Throughout the period, then, the club maintained its social exclusiveness and its cultural standards which were those of the colonial gentry and, therefore, expected to be accepted by the community at large.

These standards and values were most visible publicly at the club's annual race meetings held over Christmas and New Year. While the Perth Cup and the Derby were undeniably major races, the meetings' main functions were social, an opportunity to gauge the progress of the state against the yardstick established by the colonial gentry. While the members mingled in the private areas of the club, consolidating their ties and interests, out on the public sections the general public absorbed the atmosphere created by their social superiors. In 1890, for example, the 'sporting fraternity' patronized the meetings with its usual enthusiasm.[27] By 'sporting fraternity' was meant the members of the club, especially the pastoralists who made a pilgrimage to the meetings from the far corners of the state. Racing was the sport, for it symbolized the power of the colonial elite. As the *West Australian* pointed out, the Turf Club was not just a mere private association – it was an institution of social and commercial importance whose fortunes were of importance to those who desired the state to progress.[28] In 1929, similarly, a 'big social gathering' watched the New Zealand-bred Jemidar set a Perth Cup race record. The victory was thought to symbolize the solidarity of Western Australian society, because the owner and trainer had fought side by side in the 44th Battalion during the First World War.[29] The Turf Club, then, was thought to promote social values by which the state's development might best be guided. The social status of its membership, therefore, was highly prized and jealously guarded.

This social monopoly of racing was so strong that it contributed directly to the appearance of another horse-sport, trotting, fostered mainly by small to medium businessmen who emerged in the city in significant numbers late in the nineteenth century. The earliest contests were match races between horses used to pull carts for these inner-city businessmen. But trotting developed so quickly that by 1914 regular night racing was conducted under lights.[30] The sport employed standard bred horses which were less expensive to buy than racing thoroughbreds, so even modest businessmen could maintain teams of horses rather than just one animal.

James Brennan was the dominant figure in Perth trotting until the early 1930s when his business closed under the impact of the economic depression.[31] He took advantage of the 1890s boom to open one of Perth's first department stores, and then expanded his activities to the goldfields. He was a major business figure in the city for three decades, but lacked the necessary social status to become a leading figure in the racing world. From the 1890s onwards he worked single-mindedly to develop trotting among people of a similar social station and he, more than anyone else, promoted trotting as the 'People's Sport' in direct opposition to the exclusiveness of racing.[32] For a long time the major promoters of trotting, and the leading owners, were drapers, butchers, chemists, hotel proprietors, bootmakers and people of similar occupations.[33] It was noted as late as 1932, for example, that butchers had always been successful owners in the sport.[34] These people moved quickly to establish a subculture of trotting, employing professional trainer-drivers to manage their teams, a replication of one mark of racing status. The Kersleys, for example, one of Perth's leading trotting families, came to the city in the early 1920s to take advantage of the boom after experience in the sport in three states.[35] Other trainer-drivers took similar advantage of the drive by the businessmen to establish a status by way of a new sport.[36] Trotting, in short, was one of the major avenues by which a growing social group expressed its identity and solidarity.

Cricket organization was important in the consolidation of the dominant social group's cultural values, particularly in socializing people who aspired rather than belonged to the original colonial gentry. The Western Australian Cricket Association was formed in the mid-1880s and, until the turn of the century, J.C.H. James was probably its most important president.[37] Born the son of a Berkshire clergyman in 1841, James was educated at Rugby and Oxford before being called to the Bar in 1866. In 1875 he arrived in Western Australia as the first commissioner of land titles. He was subsequently raised to the bench, but a technical breach in his qualifications prevented his elevation to the highest judicial offices. James cemented his connections with the colonial gentry in two ways: by marrying into the Clifton family whose kinship network connected many important colonial families; and by working with it socially through sports organizations. Not only was he important in the Cricket Association, but held office in cycling, rowing and athletic organizations as well.

An analysis of James's committee members reveals how the established and aspirant gentry mixed socially to fortify the prevailing cultural values.[38] Dr Scott, so prominent in the Turf Club, was a vice-president of the Cricket Association. E. Sholl, one of Scott's in-laws, was a member of the committee. R.E. Bush, another vice-president, was also tied to Scott by kinship. Bush was born into a Bristol military family in 1855, and arrived in Western Australia in 1878. He explored the Gascoyne region in the north-west of the state, and took up the Clifton Downs station which ran 11,000 cattle and 100,000 sheep. By 1890 he was a leading pastoralist and served in the Legislative Council between 1890 and 1893. His second marriage was to Scott's daughter. E.F. Darlot, another of the vice-presidents, also came from outside the colony to establish himself as a leading member of the gentry. Born in New South Wales in 1860, Darlot arrived in Western Australia at the age of 18 and in 1881 was appointed by his father to manage a station in the Murchison district. By the 1890s he and his brother controlled a number of important properties which gained them political office and social power. The Darlots were especially active in encouraging the growth of dominant cultural values among young people through sport – the Darlot Cup is still contested by the cricket elevens of Perth's leading private schools. The association's trustees completed the social pattern. One was John Forrest, who ended his life as Lord Forrest. He was one of Western Australia's leading pioneers and one of its greatest politicians who, consequently, possessed wide social connections and authority. The Honourable J.G.H. Amherst was the fifth son of the second Earl of Amherst. Like many other younger sons of the nobility, Amherst initially sought his career as a colonial servant. Between 1881 and 1883 he was private secretary to the Governor of Fiji; then from 1885 until 1889 he was private secretary to the governor of Western Australia, Sir Frederick Broome. Amherst then stayed in Perth as an important member of the social elite, and had small property interests. George Parker, the third trustee, came from one of the colony's most important political and legal families which had been among the earliest pioneers. The tight social network demonstrated here established a conservative ruling group in Perth cricket, their values based on those of the social groups who dominated English county clubs.[39]

Moreover they placed as much, if not greater, importance upon sport as a vehicle for conveying social values as did their English counterparts.[40]

The social importance of cricket was perhaps best demonstrated in 1890 when the association gained control of the ground in East Perth from which it still operates.[41] The association sent a deputation, led by James and Parker, to discuss with Governor Broome the possibility of gaining a site. Broome clearly approved for he authorized Forrest, who happened to be commissioner of lands, to issue a 999-year lease for the East Perth land. Forrest then became a trustee. At the association meeting which ratified this arrangement it was agreed that the committee to control the ground should not only understand the values of cricket but possess business aptitude. That combination of values was the colonial gentry's benchmark.

Of all the early organized sports in Perth, tennis was most clearly concerned with the social aspects of the game and its value in strengthening links between people of particular social categories. At the conclusion of a tournament late in 1894 it was suggested that a club be formed. Those who had experienced clubs in England, it was reported, knew the important place those institutions occupied in social life.[42] They also provided 'friendly rivalry' and, presumably, gentle exercise. By April 1895 a circular was being sent to leading citizens seeking the formation of a tennis club, and this was its message:

> the co-operation of the leading residents of Perth has been invited to form a club, such as exists in England and in the other colonies, not only to provide healthful and desirable exercise for both ladies and gentlemen, but also to furnish that which is absolutely lacking in Perth – a place of general resort where members can readily meet their friends.[43]

The purpose, composition and objectives of this club were clearly more concerned with social values than sport. Among the promoters of the club were Justice E.A. Stone, puisne judge of the Supreme Court and member of an influential colonial family; A.C. Willis, who was local manager of the Union Bank of Australia; and A.K. Money, local organizer for the Australian Mutual Providence insurance company.[44] Tennis was an important social activity for the emergent commercial-financial community and its service associates, as the Fremantle Tennis Club example demonstrates. It was formed early in 1895 and was restricted to thirty members.[45] That may have been partly conditioned by available facilities, but it was also a sign of social restrictiveness. Among the foundation officials were H.F. Brandon, Fremantle manager of the Bank of Australasia; W.R. Hodge, chief accountant for the Western Australian Bank in Fremantle; J. Bassett, a Fremantle broker and agent; and R.M. Walker, principal of one of Perth's most important accounting firms.[46]

Officials in Australian Rules football, on the other hand, came from more commercial and less professional backgrounds; and they also identified strongly with their local communities.[47] D.K. Congdon, for example, spent most of his life in Fremantle as a businessman with deep interests in the Fremantle Football Club around the turn of the century. One of his colleagues, L.P, Alexander, ran an import agency at the port. John Hardwick, treasurer to the Metropolitan Football Club during the 1890s, accumulated capital as a saddler and bootmaker to move into the real estate business. E.L. Wilson, secretary-treasurer for the West Perth Football Club during the same period, was also a real estate agent. His advertising was dominated by his sporting connections, and he donated trophies to many clubs. R.H. Barrett, the West Perth president of 1895, was a city businessman with Stock Exchange interests. These men differed substantially in social terms from their administrative counterparts in racing, cricket and tennis.

It is evident, then, that the control of many sports organizations in Perth was inspired as much by social considerations as by the love of sport itself. Sport offered a major opportunity for social groups to consolidate and extend their values, and this became increasingly important with the growing complexity of society. The form and substance of those social values was not always agreed upon universally, but if the evidence relating to violence and gambling in sport is to be believed then social order was a major objective.

Football, Australian style, was and remains the sport most readily connected with violence by the general public. The game appeared in Perth in the late 1870s and was turned into a regular competitive sport towards the end of the 1880s.[48] From its earliest point it was marked by physical clashes between both players and spectators; and that characteristic made it the focal point for considerable public concern throughout the period 1890–1940. The root of this concern, it appears, was the interpretation that physical violence in a sports setting indicated tensions and dislocations in the society generally.[49] That is, it was regarded as a breakdown of the cultural values most cherished by the colonial gentry.

During the 1890 football season a number of incidents raised fears about the level of violence abroad in society. Early in the season the Metropolitan club met Fremantle in a match at Perth, and the home club's supporters allowed their enthusiasm to run wild. When Fremantle scored, the proceedings were disrupted 'by the hooting and yelling crowds of barrackers who had invaded the grounds. Followed by dogs they occasionally joined in the game.' The Metropolitan players then became over-enthusiastic, 'but the Fremantle men never do things by halves' and the game became extremely rough.[50] The authorities were alarmed by this and when Fremantle returned to Perth the following week to play the Rovers, two mounted troopers patrolled the ground to keep the peace, on and off the field.[51] When the Rovers played a return match in Fremantle later in the season, Fremantle supporters paid off some old scores and the match was marred by 'the disgraceful conduct of a number of juvenile larrikins who congregated at the pavilion steps, and greeted the Rovers with hoots and yells, and even went so far as to strike several of the visitors with their hats'.[52]

Football commentators and the public deplored this behaviour and advocated stringent measures to eliminate it. At least some of their concern stemmed from the apparent disappearance of traditional football values and controls. One writer noted that in earlier times the players had helped control the crowds, both by refusing to resort to violence themselves and by discouraging it among their supporters.[53] The former Perth player W.H. James was cited as an example. This was significant, because James was connected with the colonial gentry in an interesting way.[54] Born in Perth in 1863, he later became the stepson of George Randell, who came to Perth in 1850 and set up a successful river ferry company. Randell became a successful municipal and state politician, finishing his career as colonial secretary and minister for education. James capitalized on this start brilliantly by becoming an articled clerk to George Leake, the lawyer-politician who was active in the Turf Club and a member of a leading colonial family. After a spell in England, James was called to the Western Australian Bar in 1888. He became a leading city lawyer, entered parliament in 1894, became premier between 1902–04, and was knighted for his services to the state. Although something of a social renegade, James's reported actions in quelling football disturbances, therefore, were consistent with at least some of the social values exhibited by the groups with which he had to mix. That the football writer thought such people less in evidence may be taken as an indication of fears that their values were now less authoritative.

Similar fears, about the growth of violence indicating a loss of social values, appeared during the 1895 football season. Concern was expressed at the league's annual meeting about the degree of violence witnessed during the 1894 season; but the introduction of enclosed grounds in 1895 did little to improve the situation.[55] By the end of May the *West Australian* was calling for stronger action against rough play, on the grounds that it was killing healthy sport.[56] Despite these and other pleas the season ended on a low note when the final match between Fremantle and Rovers turned into one of the roughest matches on record.[57] Feelings ran high from the outset, and a large section of the crowd invaded the ground late in the game when a Fremantle player felled an opponent behind the play. There were reports that the Fremantle team had been instructed to play roughly, the implication being that premeditated violence was abroad.

The consequences revealed something of the general concern about such violence, for the Fremantle player whose actions provoked the crowd invasion was charged with assault by the police. In sentencing him to a £5 fine or 14 days in jail, the judge remarked that he was alarmed by the amount of verbal and physical violence induced among the general public by football affiliations.[58] One of the witnesses against the player was George Parker, the trustee for the Cricket Association and member of the colonial gentry. Parker was later responsible for a resolution which banned the Fremantle player from the cricket ground for life.[59] The police action, the judge's remarks and Parker's involvement suggest that there was amongst the ruling group a fear that their cultural values as expressed through sport faced a challenge that had to be met head on.

Concern about the social implications of football violence surfaced again during the economic depression of the early 1930s when there were widespread fears about general social disintegration.[60] The possibilities were pointed to in a 1929 season match between Claremont and East Perth. Perth Oval, the East Perth ground, had a reputation for producing crowd demonstrations, and the club's committee was anxious to improve that image.[61] But at the conclusion of this match a large section of the crowd rushed the umpire and subjected him to a stream of verbal abuse, though physical violence was prevented.[62] Other matches on the same day were characterized by flying fists and elbows. One reporter, at least, thought these alarming developments, even in a naturally rugged game like football.[63] After a particularly rough match during the 1932 season, the South Fremantle captain-coach collapsed and died. The following Saturday, an East Perth versus West Perth match produced two serious incidents, numerous occasions when the ball was the least of the players' concerns, and a 'disgraceful scene' involving several players.[64] This violence provoked demands for greater controls over the game.[65] The implication was that if the football authorities could not control violence, then it might be a sign that violence could break out under stress on a wider scale.

The interesting point is not so much that football produced violence, but that the violence it did produce neither assumed widespread social significance nor passed completely out of control. Sports violence remains little investigated, although some evidence suggests that such violence has a cathartic social effect which controls indiscriminate social violence in modern industrialized societies.[66] Geoffrey Bolton argues that view in his work on Perth during the early 1930s.[67] But the Western Australian example also suggests that football authorities were anxious not to transgress the sports cultural values established by the colonial gentry. Relatively few members of the dominant social class moved in football circles, yet their values were observed strictly. The football league, for example, supported George Parker's proposal for a life ban on the East Fremantle player convicted of assault.[68] The views of people like Walter James were widely respected by football authorities.[69] The authorities clearly agreed that some football incidents warranted police action to control undesirable demonstrations. Football officials frequently expressed fears that anti-social behaviour would cause the game to lose support. All these actions, it may be argued, constituted attempts to adhere to values established by a socially dominant group and accepted by the general public in the belief that it would ensure continued social order.

Football was not, of course, the only sport which incited violence among its players and supporters. Reports on other sports demonstrated similar public concern about the social implications of sports behaviour. In 1890, for example, it was thought a matter of note that 'not even a single fight or the spectacle of a drunken man disturbed the general harmony' of the Turf Club's main race day of the autumn carnival.[70] On the eve of the First World War some prominence was given to a brawl which broke out at the Literary Institute during a billiards match in which one player breached convention by potting his opponent's ball.[71] By the late 1920s some observers were alarmed by the expectations of violence displayed by spectators. Many boxing and wrestling matches ended in disturbances with spectators protesting about refereeing decisions.[72] One reporter thought the crowd at a world middleweight wrestling title bout seethed with the spirit of gladiatorial Rome as fights and scuffles broke out in the stands.[73]

These fears, like those about football, sprang from a concern to preserve public order. Again, the main point is probably that the violence was never widespread and rarely went beyond the confines of the sporting arena. Indeed, by the 1930s there were interesting comments that violence at boxing and wrestling bouts was more ritual than actual. Crowds went along, it was argued, for entertainment and adopted violent attitudes which helped them release frustrations about the wider economic and social tensions.[74] In 1934, for example, one wrestling crowd 'rose to a man and expressed its disapproval' of the manhandling suffered by one performer.[75] As with football crowds, this cathartic social drama served, in part at least, a positive social function in maintaining order within the context of generally accepted behavioural standards.

Attitudes towards gambling, another great Australian passion, also demonstrated widespread concern with the maintenance of social order and ranking. As elsewhere in Australia, gambling appeared early in Perth, and by 1890 was associated with almost all sports: wrestling, boxing, billiards, football, cricket, cycling and athletics, to name a few. At the 1895 annual meeting of the football league, for example, it was reported that delegates' betting habits complicated decisions about disputed matches.[76] The debate about the morality of gambling had begun, and ranged over many issues. But it is important to note in passing, at least, that part of it concerned the division between amateur and professional which had implications for the conventions and standards adumbrated by the colonial gentry. In 1890, for example, the gentry-dominated Western Australian Athletic Club resolved 'Any person who has not run for public money since the Proclamation of Responsible Government in Western Australia shall be eligible as a member of the club'.[77]

That was in a period when two 'leading amateurs' could meet in a billiards match for £25 a side and individual transactions with spectators.[78] The discussion of gambling involved changing views about sport as business or leisure, with consequences both for the acceptance of the dominant social group's values and for the general ordering of society. The main brunt of the debate, of course, was carried by horse-racing whose intimate connections with gambling were long established.

Official investigations about the connection between racing and gambling were opened at least as early as the 1890s with parliamentary attempts to regulate bookmakers' activities.[79] This caused at least one interesting court case when a bookmaker was charged with accepting a bet from the postmaster general who was a prominent member of the Turf Club.[80] The general lines of the argument about gambling were drawn here: did totalizators encourage betting among social groups which might not bet otherwise; and should betting be permitted off the racecourses? In 1895, for example, the West Australian's editorialist argued that the working class was induced to bet indiscriminately so that the racing clubs could benefit economically.[81]

A 1905 parliamentary Select Committee into racing revealed many impressions about how social order and ordering were affected by gambling.[82] A police officer estimated that 250 to 300 people lived by racing alone in Perth, and that it cost society at least £500 per week to keep them. A retired horse breeder claimed that gambling was spreading; schoolboys everywhere, he argued, had a cigarette in their mouths and talked about betting. Another detective reported that during 1904 eight men had embezzled £22,000 between them for their racing activities. The president of the Perth Chamber of Commerce claimed that city merchants were badly hit by gamblers who could not meet their everyday bills. The president of the Turf Club countered that smalltime gamblers utilized the totalizators and lost only small amounts. But critics of gambling pointed to the Turf Club secretary's evidence which reported that £900,000 had passed through the on-course totalizators during 1904.

Similar evidence was presented during another Select Committee hearing in 1915 and, as in 1905, the social implications were clear.[83] A strongly held view argued that the working classes should have only restricted access to gambling facilities, because they were socially ill-equipped to handle such financial management.[84] The people who controlled horses and the racing establishment, on the other hand, could cope with it. In that sense, there was to be a general acceptance of the dominant class values, but not equal access to the activities through which one section of those values was consolidated. That explains something of the racing authorities' ambivalent attitudes towards bookmakers – there was no guarantee that the bookmakers would observe the social conventions which, in the authorities' view, should surround gambling. It was much easier to control the totalizator, a machine, than the bookmakers. These efforts to restrict the general availability of gambling became most pronounced during the economic depression.

From the middle of 1929 onwards a campaign was organized jointly by the police and the Turf Club to eliminate illegal off-course betting. The general argument was that gambling off the course away from the horses meant the activity was not a legitimate sport, and that illegal gambling attracted inappropriate social groups and so impeded general economic recovery. This view was taken up by many newspapers which highlighted such cases as the bank teller who stole almost £600 from his employers of thirteen years. A heavy punter, he made up to £500 per race meeting until his luck changed and he became heavily indebted to his bookmaker.[85] The newspapers ran in-depth reports on life in the numerous illegal off-course betting shops which dotted the inner city, especially, it was said, in the industrial areas.[86] That was a clear reference to the supposed working-class basis of off-course betting.

The campaign continued throughout the depression years, in conjunction with attacks on other forms of gambling.[87] Turf Club officials locked public gates on the courses, withheld odds, fed out misleading information, altered starting times unexpectedly and changed the order of races, all to prevent prestarting time information reaching the illegal operators in the city. Off-course bookmakers reportedly established a fighting fund to protect their interests.[88] But by early 1931 the police were effecting a high number of arrests, often in amusing circumstances.[89] Estimated figures for the amount of money handled by illegal bookmakers ranged as high as £20,000 per week, so in its economic context the battle was not insignificant.[90] Overall, however, the campaign bore strong marks of an attempt to reassert a set of values promoted by the dominant social group through its racing connections, with the economic depression providing both motive and opportunity. To control off-course betting meant stopping the slide away from those values by which the community had been long guided. Views about social change, therefore, were never far from discussions about the organization of sport in Perth, as suggested by the evidence concerning the rise of speedway and the changing role of women in sport.

Born during the mid-1920s in Maitland, New South Wales, speedway was introduced to Perth by Johnny Hoskins, who later went to England and became 'Mr Speedway' there until the early 1970s. The sport was a product of the new technological revolution of the twentieth century, and of the forces of cultural diffusion which turned bicycle riding into a sport during an earlier age.[91] It was an instant success. Late in 1928 the Claremont Speedway Company was establishing with a working capital of £20,000.[92] One of the directors was M.S. Brooking, state road race motorcycle champion and founder of a major motor-vehicle business. As many as 20,000 people crammed Claremont speedway weekly to watch the racing, making the sport one of the most spectator-oriented in the city.[93] Besides the racing there were side attractions, such as a fireworks display which depicted the sinking of the Emden by HMAS Sydney.[94]

These characteristics set speedway right outside the established structure of organized sport in Perth. It demonstrated, for example, the need to incorporate a new technology into the sporting framework, and no traditional sports authorities were in a position to do so. Then, the composition of the crowds indicated the rise of a new social group whose recreational and sporting needs were not catered for by traditional outlets. This new 'skilled technological' group, as it might be called, would not be accommodated easily into the system of values so long established in the city's sportsworld. The entrepreneurs for this new group and the technology, like Hoskins and Brooking, raised the spectre of increasing professionalism in sport. So, too, did many of the riders; both antagonized the establishment views generally accepted by Perth society.

Of all the early Perth riders, Sig Schlam demonstrated the characteristics and possibilities of speedway.[95] He was approximately 21 years old when competitive speedway began in Perth, and had learned to ride motorcycles in South Africa and on the goldfields where he was brought up. As a salesman-mechanic in a Perth motorcycle business, he soon drifted into the sport. Although a very small man he displayed a natural talent for riding round small dirt tracks at high speed; so at the end of his first Perth season he went to England to ride for one of the professional teams springing up there.

These professional teams, incidentally, grew very quickly – a young Perth motor mechanic who earned £2 per week before the Depression saved over £1,000 from a year's riding in England during the Depression.[96] This degree of professionalism was little accepted in Perth. By the time Schlam returned to Perth for the 1928–29 season he was one of the best riders in the world. In the next two seasons he won local and Australian championships, and was much in demand as a promoter of different brands of motorcycle. But he was to demonstrate the tragic side of the sport, too. Just after the beginning of the 1930–31 season he died, at the age of 24, in a race crash.

This meteoric career provided all the elements attacked by the opponents of speedway: commercialism and professionalism in sport; unduly spectacular social mobility for successful professional sportsmen; and an apparent cheapening of human life for the entertainment of a section of society unsatisfied by traditional sporting forms. There was an implicit fear here that this new sporting form could damage the values established in sport by those traditional sports activities upon which social life generally was so much based. Predictably, most of the organized opposition worked from the point that no sport in which young men constantly risked death could be morally justified.

The first Claremont fatality occurred on New Year's Eve 1928 when an 18-year-old rider fell during a race. Barely two months later another young man died, and public discontent grew.[97] One report attacked the speedway on the grounds that it was simply to make money for the promoters; that it encouraged young and inexperienced riders; and that it encouraged recklessness on the roads generally at a time when fatalities were already alarmingly high.[98] One clergyman watched a speedway meeting and was appalled by what he thought a gamble with death.[99] An annual conference of the Methodist Church of Western Australia debated the issue at length, and the promoters were asked to make riding conditions as safe as possible.[100]

Speedway authorities countered the criticism by stressing those aspects of the sport which seemed compatible with established values, but their themes were not well chosen. First, they argued, speedway riders needed to be extremely fit and alert, so they led exemplary lives, eschewing liquor in particular. This could only upgrade the state's moral and material condition on which social and economic progress was based.[101] Then, they went on, speedway eliminated a lot of the evils of modern life. It encouraged the 'democratic Australian outlook' because 'favouritism, social-standing, wire-pulling and such measures cut no ice on the speedway'.[102] They sought no betting facilities, because they wanted a 'clean, manly sport'.[103] The speedway enthusiasts, then, saw the need to defend their sport within the framework of dominant social values. But at least two of their arguments cut across some of those values, so speedway won over few of its critics.

The frailty of these arguments, in fact, was revealed indirectly in a struggle for the administrative control of speedway. By the beginning of the 1930–31 season there were two rival tracks. The original Claremont track was controlled by the Claremont Speedway Syndicate and initially supported by the West Australian Track Riders Union (an indicative name). It was opposed by Perth Speedways Ltd, which built a new track on the Western Australian Cricket Association ground, a home of sporting conservatism. The new body received official blessing from the Western Australian Motor Cycling Association which controlled all motorcycle clubs in the state, and which was affiliated to the Australian ruling authority. Significantly, the association was spoken for by M.S. Brooking, who had helped set up Claremont but who now, it seems, had decided to go with an apparently more powerful group. The battle, then, was largely about the impact of rules, authority and institutionalization in a vigorous new sporting form. Speedway riders in the union held out briefly but many soon went over to Perth Speedways whose proceedings were opened by Attorney-General T.A.L. Davey, a sure sign of social acceptance. It was on the new track, in his second appearance there, that Sig Schlam died. Even the radical and egalitarian speedway, then, found it difficult to escape institutional conventionality, and it was a number of years before racing returned to Claremont.[104]

The role of women in organized sport, however, presented an ongoing prospect of social change not being accepted universally.[105] Sport in Perth, as in Australia, was male-dominated between 1890 and 1940; attempts by women to change that met with suspicion and resistance, so that only towards the end of the period did women have a reasonable choice of sports available to them. During 1895, for example, Melbourne reports noted that women had taken up football. This was an 'absurd' development, wrote a Perth commentator, which typified unwelcome social change eroding areas of male exclusiveness in all aspects of life.[106] This segregation of the sexes resurfaced during the First World War over the question of mixed bathing, a social reform accepted only gradually:

> If a modest girl or matron can't go to the baths without the risk of being mauled about or insulted in her hearing by dirty-minded poltroons who ought to be at the war there will have to be some restriction of mixed bathing.[107]

The real concern was not so much that women were being insulted, but that undesirable social change placed them in situations where they risked insult.

The First World War produced many changes of that kind. As women became increasingly involved in the work place and assumed roles previously reserved for men, they began to express much of their new freedom through sport.[108] Billiard saloons, for example, have until very recently been treated as unsuitable places for women. But in 1915 a women's billiards tournament attracted over forty young women who raised a lot of money for patriotic funds. The women, a reporter noted carefully, were all most charming and entirely above reproach.[109] These changes were accepted only reluctantly, and most male observers preferred to see them as an unfortunate and temporary consequence of the war. Women appeared in crowds at boxing and wrestling bouts where their presence always occasioned comment – twenty-round prize fights were not places for women, it was argued on numerous occasions.[110] Again, not so much a care for women's sensibilities as a concern for their appearance in unaccustomed social situations, and the implications of that.

Similar concerns appeared during the 1920s and 1930s. Not long after speedway opened in Perth, for example, an Englishwoman named Fay Taylor appeared as a rider at Claremont speedway. The speedway crowd and the general public reacted differently. Speedway supporters mainly noted her inability to compete on equal terms with men, but accepted her as a person interested in motorcycle racing. The general public regarded her as a blatant example of the flapper age in which all social conventions relating to women were being shattered.[111] Speedway attracted substantial criticism in that regard. One complainant, for example, thought it disgraceful that the speedway authorities should run a beauty contest in which young women were paraded on the pillion seats of motorcycles, winking at and displaying their figures to all the young men whom they passed.[112] In 1930 a smartly dressed woman cricketer walking through the city moved one reporter to comment that domestic duties were 'a mere sideline with many of our modern day maidens'.[113] They needed 'a sound talking to by their parents', according to another observer.[114] A golf writer complained that his life was quite miserable enough without having to report 'the misdeeds of the high-heel brigade who gouge holes in our greens and make nightmares of our fairways'.[115]

Sport, then, was a major social instrument for keeping women in their ascribed places. Nowhere was this more the case than in racing, the national sport. Women were acceptable in the members' stands, but only as guests or appendages of men. Such women rarely placed bets; if they gambled, then a male carried out the necessary transactions. On the public sections of racecourses women were treated as even more inferior beings. At the parliamentary racing inquiries of 1905 and 1915 it was argued that many women on the flat were prostitutes in search of business. Those who were not prostitutes were simply interested in backing winners; their language and demeanour were quite unacceptable.[116] Any racing reform that might possibly encourage more women to attend meetings was considered only reluctantly. The male dominance of racing symbolized the male dominance of sport generally, and any change had implications for the ordering of wider society.

But women were not the only group to experience the use of sport to maintain the social status quo. For example, Reuel Denney's view about unrestricted upward social mobility through sport, a view shared by many Australians, is not entirely supported by the Perth evidence. What emerges, rather, is the use of sports connections to promote or consolidate position within social groups; the boundaries between groups were rarely crossed. Sport reinforced the boundaries, if anything, so that individuals seeking mobility knew the heights to which they might aspire. James Brennan, a pioneer of Perth trotting, did not attempt to move into racing circles but concentrated upon his social and economic peers; Sig Schlam, the speedway rider, established himself within the confines of the 'skilled technological' group; cricket administrators were not often found in football administrative circles where there were different social bases. The example of A.J. Diamond demonstrates many of the possibilities and boundaries of social mobility through sport in Perth.

Arthur James Diamond was a businessman who arrived in Fremantle from South Australia in 1885 and built a public life almost entirely on the strength of his sporting connections.[117] His business interests centred on his customs and shipping agency company, from which he branched into areas such as the wholesale liquor trade. Revivifying and running the Perth Chamber of Commerce underpinned those interests for him. The lynchpin of his sports organization network was the Fremantle Football Club of which he was president by 1890. Diamond was probably the most important of the businessmen who ran the club, which he represented on the football league for many years. He revived the fortunes of the Fremantle Cricket Club in 1890; and later led the Cricket Association of Western Australia (Fremantle) against the established Western Australian Cricket Association following a disagreement over fixtures and grounds. Another important connection came from his position on the committee of the Fremantle Rowing Association. Diamond was instrumental in securing for the club a favourable land lease from the government on which to build a permanent pavilion. Beyond that, his formal or informal support for Fremantle sports organizations was guaranteed; for example, he was one of the businessmen who sought to establish a racing club in the area.

The strong Fremantle connection was important, for Diamond turned his local prominence to political use. In 1889 he led the organization of the Fremantle Lumpers' Association among waterfront workers. At the union's first anniversary meeting he reported, as president, to his members that he had urged his commercial colleagues to employ only union labour; and that he was establishing links with labour organizations elsewhere in Australia.[118] The Fremantle Football Club drew many players from the wharf labourers, so Diamond was strongly placed. He also drew upon sports contacts in his role as president of the Fremantle Liberal Association, the interests of which reflected his own: the protection of local industries and the implementation of a land tax, which suited him and his business colleagues in the cricket and football clubs; manhood suffrage and the abolition of qualifications for entrance to the lower house of parliament, which suited his supporters on the wharves and in the football fraternity.[119] Diamond spoke for both interests, for example, when he criticized the extent of Asian immigration during the mid-1890s.[120] His sports contacts, then, were influential in shaping his public career, which culminated in a Legislative Assembly seat held from 1901 until his death in 1906.

It is important to note, too, that Diamond was not atypical. T.H. Marshall, for example, was a soft drink manufacturer and hotel proprietor whose career was associated with, and similar to, Diamond's. Marshall was secretary to both the Lumpers' Association and the Liberal Association; he served on the Rowing Club Committee, and was closely involved with a number of other Fremantle sports organizations, particularly the Football Club. He was mentioned as a possible politician in 1890, then gained a Legislative Council seat in 1894 which was declared vacant two years later when he went bankrupt.[121]

Diamond and Marshall demonstrated the possible extent of social mobility through sport. Both worked within a strictly defined geographical region, and within distinct social groups. Although their formal sports links were clearly important, the informal networks they built around them were probably more important. There was no suggestion that they could, or wanted to, break through those social and cultural boundaries into new or alternative public and political fields. The cultural standards established in Perth allowed only restricted social mobility.[122]

They were probably not the first and certainly not the last public figures in Perth to test the strengths and limitations of sport links. Sir Walter James was one premier who maintained his football links to advantage; Jack Scaddan was another. A Labor politician, Scaddan was renowned as a recruiting officer for the Subiaco Football Club, and he placed great social importance on football. In 1914, for example, he declared that the military authorities 'recognized that football was of great importance in producing men of nerve and courage'.[123] J.J. Kenneally, federal president of the Australian Labor Party from 1928 until 1936 and member of the Legislative Assembly between 1927 and 1936, was a leading East Perth Football Club official for many years. During the 1920s he was influential in improving the club's public image, on and off the field. H.W. Mann, a former detective whose tasks had included overseeing racing, was a member of the Legislative Council between 1921 and 1933 and very prominent in football circles. At the beginning of each season during the 1920s Scaddan, Kenneally and Mann were the guest speakers at numerous club functions. Alex Clydesdale based his political career more directly on organized sport.[124] A plumber by trade he turned to managing racing concerns. While in the Western Australian parliament for most of the inter-war period, he maintained interests in at least two proprietary racing clubs until they were taken over by the Turf Club. When the Western Australian Lotteries Commission was set up during the 1930s, Clydesdale turned to his racing experience and became its first chairman. Again, these men all capitalized upon their sporting links, both formal and informal, to promote their public careers. Like Diamond and Marshall, they worked within prescribed boundaries and established values.

Sports connections with politics were not just important to politicians; their sports constituents frequently considered themselves to have power as political units. In 1930, for example, Fremantle Golf Club members claimed to have unseated a Labor member at the state elections. They claimed that the Labor member thought they would not cast votes because polling day was also the club's opening day. But they went to the polls early and voted for a new man – he was a member of the powerful Parker legal family, so long important in the city's public and sporting life; a Gallipoli veteran and a member of the Turf Club.[125] He was clearly an establishment figure thoroughly approved of by the Fremantle Golf Club members. The important point is not so much whether or not they did upset the election, but that they thought of themselves as a corporate sports group capable of influencing a political situation.

Indeed, 1920s golfers were given to statements supporting established political and cultural values. After the 1929 federal election one golfing reporter wrote, 'yesterday, as on every weekend ... the idle rich played their effeminate game of golf, seemingly unconcerned, unaffected by the fact that tomorrow we shall have Labor governments in Commonwealth and State alike!'[126]

When the site of the Cottesloe Golf Club was changed in 1931, one report read:

> The old course served the purpose for many happy years, but with the advent of Bolshevism, and its sister creeds, the profiteering golfer received scant sympathy or courtesy from certain sections of the local community, who did not hold with golfers

or any other blokes who walked about in garments which resembled the underwear of mid-Victorian ladies.[127]

The tone of these pieces is semi-serious, perhaps, but they reveal something of the golfers' visions about themselves as a recognizable and influential political community. The connections forged on the golf course involved the discussion of prevailing social values and the consequences of change.

Between 1890 and 1940, organized sports played a central role in the establishment and maintenance of a code of social and cultural values accepted by most people in Perth society. During the 1890s, when social change was rapid, sport was thought to provide a bulwark against undue change. Breaches of convention were regarded askance. One contestant in a cycle match race was reprimanded by officials and crowd for taking unfair advantage of an opponent.[128] Two cricketers who thought themselves above the selectors were reprimanded.[129] During the First World War sport was thought to have been instrumental in producing fine soldiers who would also produce a fine society.[130]

Throughout the depression there was a prevailing sense that if the fabric and conventions of sport could survive then so could society generally.[131] More thematically, sport played a major part in the containment and release of violence in Western Australian society; women owed much of their restricted social life to the values enforced by organized and male-dominated sport; individuals could climb up the social ladder, but only as high as the rungs allowed them by their cultural training and perceptions. Organized sport played an important role in encouraging group identities and typologies; and it enabled those groups to demonstrate their identities to similar groups. In all this, organized sport helped shape society, and did not always simply reflect developments established in political and economic spheres. The acceptance of established values lay at the heart of all this, for any organized sport which appeared to break ranks was considered with disfavour, as the speedway promoters discovered. Opposition to changes in sports forms and values was rooted in fears of general social change. So it is appropriate, perhaps, to close with the inimitable 'Miss Gossip', society columnist for a sports newspaper which in the 1930s represented the rump of the colonial gentry, the proponents of so many of Perth's cultural standards. She expressed dissatisfaction with the deteriorating standards of one of the city's major 'amateur' social occasions:

> Then the bookies, and the bootmakers and the wholesale butchers began making money. Nowadays the Animal Ball has quite a second elevenish smack about it. Times change with bank balances, of course, and new generations whom you know not rise up to step into the shoes part worn and ancient seeming... the dull and uninteresting crowd inspired me with no sense other than boredom.[132]

'Miss Gossip' may have been bored, and alarmed by the arrival of new social groups; perhaps, on the other hand, she should have been surprised not by the extent of change but that any change at all had occurred.

Notes

[1] Denney, *The Astonished Muse*, 127.

[2] Mandle, 'Cricket and Australian Nationalism', 225–46; also reprinted in Jacques and Pavia (eds), *Sport in Australia*, 46–72. For some aspects of the 'egalitarian' view, see *Hoskins Weekly and Speedway News*, 5 Nov. 1927, 15; *WA-Sportsman*, 26 March 1915, 3f–g.

[3] Walvin, *The People's Game*. Brailsford, *Sport and Society* displays similar attitudes; Voight, *America Through Baseball*, provides a classic expression of this view in the American context.

[4] Snyder and Spreitzer, 'Sociology of Sport: an Overview', 9–34.

[5] Page, 'Pervasive Sociological Themes in the Study of Sport', 14–37. The most recent and comprehensive account of sports sociology is Loy, McPherson and Kenyan, *Sport and Social Systems*.

[6] Elias, Foreword, xi–xiii; Edwards, *Sociology of Sport*, 6–7. There is an awkward discussion of this point in Chapter 3 of Inglis, *The Name of the Game*.

[7] Berryman, 'Sport History as Social History?', 65–73.

[8] Edwards, *Sociology of Sport*, and Gruneau, 'Sport, Social Differentiation and Social Inequality', 121–84, are two limited exceptions to this. Lasch, 'The Corruption of Sports', 24–30, argues that modern society has shaped modern sport, not vice versa. Geertz, 'Deep Play: Notes on the Balinese Cockfight', 1–37, reaches a more balanced view: 'In the cockfight, then, the Balinese forms and discovers his temperament and his society's temper at the same time' (p.28), For the varying nature of recent offerings in the field, see: Inglis, *The Name of the Game*; Walvin, *Leisure and Society*; Guttmann, *From Ritual to Record*.

[9] Gramscian literature is expanding rapidly; but a convenient account is Joll, *Gramsci*.

[10] For the general background to Australian sport, see Inglis, *Sport and Pastimes in Australia*, and Dunstan, *Sports*. For a general introduction to leisure in this sense, see Marrus (ed.), *The Emergence of Leisure*, and Parker, *The Sociology of Leisure*. English examples of this point may be followed in Dobbs, *Edwardians at Play*, Meller, *Leisure and the Changing City*, and Bailey, *Leisure and Class in Victorian England*. During the 1890s in Perth, the Eight Hours Movement planned specifically for increased leisure; see *West Australian* 25 Jan. 1890, 5d; 28 Jan. 1890, 3f; and 30 Jan. 1890, 2h–i.

[11] Bolton, 'The Idea of a Colonial Gentry', 307–28.

[12] For a brief history of the Turf Club, see *W.A. Turf Club Centenary, 1852–1952*. The English story is well told in Vamplew, *The Turf*; also Rodrigo, *The Racing Game*. For a world survey, see Longrigg, *The History of Horse Racing*.

[13] The general history is recounted in Crowley, *Australia's Western Third*.

[14] The history of Perth is best followed in Stannage, *The People of Perth*. The following discuss North American links between city change and organized sport: Reiss, 'The Baseball Magnate and Urban Politics in the Progressive Era: 1885–1920', 41–62; Jobling, 'Urbanization and Sport in Canada, 1867–1900', 65–72; Freedman, 'The Baseball Fad in Chicago, 1865–1870', 42–64.

[15] *West Australian*, 5 May 1890, 3c.

[16] Ibid. 19 Dec. 1894, 3c–d; 21 Dec. 1894, 3b.

[17] Ibid. 14 Jan. 1895, 6c; also 20 Feb. 1929, 6f. For some aspects of the ruling class and colonial roles of polo generally, see Dale, *Polo Past and Present* and *Polo of Home and Abroad*; de Lisle, *Polo in India*; and Stoddart, 'A Ruling Passion: Polo in British India'.

[18] *West Australian*, 9 March 1929, 15d. The general growth of racing is best followed through the Western Australian Racing Calendar issues 1890– ; and the West Australian Turf Club *Annual Reports*.

[19] *West Australian*, 15c (report of Claremont's third Annual Meeting); and *Sunday Times*, 14 Sept. 1930, 3i.

[20] *West Australian*, 5 Feb. 1929, 12d.

[21] Ibid. March 1929, 16c.

[22] Ibid. 27 March 1929, 7c, by which time the club had 262 members.

[23] The following paragraph is based on scattered newspaper and biographical sources. The main biographical indexes are Kimberly, *History of West Australia*; Battye (ed.), *The Cyclopedia of Western Australia*; Colless, *Men of Western Australia*; Bolton and Mozley, *The Western Australian Legislature, 1870–1930*. The Turf Club committee for 1890 is in the *West Australian*, 6 May 1890, 2d–e; also Western Australian Racing Calendar issues for 1890.

[24] *Report of the Select Committee of the Legislative Assembly to Inquire into the Alleged Surfeit of Horse-Racing, Parliamentary Papers Western Australia, 1905*, Session 1, A2 (1905 Report), 23; *Report of the Joint Select Committees of the Legislative Council and Legislative Assembly appointed to consider the question of Horse-racing and Matters Connected Therewith, with a view to the subsequent Introduction Providing for the Control of Such Matters, Parliamentary Papers Western Australia*, 1915, 11, A3 (1915 Report), 55; *Sunday Times*, 22 Sept. 1914, l8d; *Groper*, 31 Jan. 1932, 15.

[25] Collected from scattered biographical sources.

[26] Based on a reading of Western Australian Turf Club Committee Minute Books, May 1927–Jan. 1931; Feb. 1931–Jan. 1935. For example: 16 Oct. 1929, 388; 27 Nov. 1929, 406; 11 Dec. 1929, 42.

[27] *West Australian*, 26 Jan. 1890, 3e.

[28] Ibid., 30 April 1890, 2h–i. For a much later expression of a similar sentiment, Sunday Times, 7 April 1935, 5. A comparative view of the race meeting as a social pilgrimage may be seen in Buckland, Sketches of Social Life in India, 62–76.

[29] *West Australian*, 2 Jan. 1929, 9g–h; 6 Jan, 1929, 31d.

[30] See James Brennan's evidence, 1915 Report, 17–23; 'Report of the Royal Commissioner Appointed to Inquire into the Administration, Conduct and Control of the Sport of Trotting in the State of Western Australia', Parliamentary Papers Western Australia, 1946, 11, no.12; History of Trotting In the State of Western Australia; People's Heritage (Perth, n.d.); Western Australian Trotting Journal, 3 June 1915, 2.

[31] From scattered biographical sources.

[32] For example: *W.A. Sportsman*, 16 April 1915, ld–g; 23 April 1915, 3c–e.

[33] See Brennan's evidence, 1915 Report, 21.

[34] *W.A. Sporting Record*, 30 June 1932, 5.

[35] *Sunday Times*, 17 May 1931, 5d.

[36] See the reports on A. Sheahan, C. Clarke, L. Walton and C. Coulson: *Sunday Times*, 8 Feb. 1931, 6f; 15 Feb. 1931, 5e; 1 March 1931, 6c; 15 March 1931, 6e.

[37] There is a convenient sketch in *Australian Dictionary of Biography*, Vol, IV, 468–9.

[38] The Cricket Association Committee list may be seen in the *West Australian*, 12 June 1890, 3f. Biographies from scattered sources.

[39] A number of English county cricket histories bear out this point: Duckworth, *The Story of Warwickshire Cricket*, and Kay, *A History of County Cricket* are two examples. Some general indications of the English position may be seen in Brookes, *English Cricket*.

[40] This aspect of Australian cricket administration was to be demonstrated most spectacularly during the 1932–33 season. See Stoddart, 'Cricket's Imperial Crisis'. For general background, see Best, *Mid-Victorian Britain, 1851–75*, esp. Parts 3 and 4; Mandle, 'Games People Played'.

[41] The following paragraph is based on the *West Australian*, 24 Feb. 1890, 3h, and 20 June 1890, 3g. Forrest later granted funds for improvements to the grounds, despite opposition from some of his staff: Premier's Dept. 1558/1896.

[42] *West Australian*, 21 Dec. 1894, 3b. The general tennis background may be followed in Grimsley, *Tennis: Its History, People and Events*.

[43] *West Australian*, 8 April 1895, 3b.

[44] Biographies from scattered sources.

[45] *West Australian*, 23 Feb. 1895, 3b.

[46] Biographies from scattered sources.

[47] Ibid. For the development of Australian Rules football, see Turner, 'The Emergence of Aussie Rules'.

[48] Orr, 'History of Football', and Halcombe, 'A Report on the Development of Sport in Western Australia'.

[49] For a modern development of this point, see Taylor, 'Soccer Consciousness and Soccer Hooliganism'; and 'Football Mad'.

[50] *West Australian*, 17 June 1890, 3c.

[51] Ibid. 23 June 1890, 3f.

[52] Ibid. 25 Aug. 1890, 3g–h.

[53] Ibid.

[54] A convenient sketch is Hunt, 'Sir Walter James: the Social Reformer'.

[55] *West Australian*, 30 April 1895, 3a–b; 11 May 1895, 6a.

[56] Ibid. 23 May 1895, 4e–f.

[57] Ibid. 30 Sept. 1895, 3a–b.

[58] Ibid. 2 Oct. 1895, 3b

[59] Ibid. 24 Oct. 1895, 6a–b.

[60] For the depression in Perth, see Bolton, *A Fine Country to Starve In*. A comparative view may be seen in Stevenson and Cook, *The Slump: Society and Politics During the Depression*, especially Chapter X on social disorder.

[61] See East Perth Football Club Annual Report 1919–29, Battye Library HS/592; *West Australian*, 8 June 1929, 1 Sc.

[62] *West Australian*, 17 June 1929, 14a.

[63] Ibid. 12a. For an earlier but similar report, 3 June 1929, 12a.

[64] *Sunday Times*, 9 Oct. 1932, 1c–e.

[65] Ibid., 25 Sept. 1932, 7f.

[66] For some views in this area, see Smith, 'Sport and Collective Violence'; and Atyeo, *Blood and Guts*. Some links between industrialization and sport are demonstrated in Dunning, 'Industrialization and the Incipient Modernization of Football'.

[67] Bolton, *A Fine Country to Starve In*, 115. Hobsbawm makes a similar point in *Industry and Empire*, 308.

[68] *West Australian*, 24 Oct. 1895, 6a–b.

[69] He occupied influential club and league positions throughout the 1890s.

[70] *West Australian*, 20 March, 1890, 3f–g. Some indications of general conditions for race crowds during the period may be seen in: Inspector Public Health to Chief Inspector Public Health, 13 Nov. 1902, Public Health 1376/1902; A.E. Cockram to Secretary Central Board of Health, 13 May 1903, Medical/Public Health 1961/1909; Secretary Western Australian Turf Club to Chief Inspector Central Board of Health, 3 Nov. 1908, Medical/Public Health 1585/1908; Inspector Public Health to Chief Inspector Public Health, 9 Sept. 1915 and 17 Sept. 1915, Medical/Public Health 2322/1915; Principal Architect Dept. Works and Labour to Commissioner Public Health, 14 July 1930, Medical/Public Health, 779/1930.

[71] *Sunday Times*, 7 Dec. 1913, 2e.

[72] For example: *West Australian*, 12 Jan. 1929, 16e; 23 Feb. 1929, 16c; *Sunday Times*, 25 Nov. 1934, 5b.

[73] *West Australian*, 9 March 1929, 20c. A similar image was given to a much later bout; *Sunday Times*, 12 May 1935, 6h–l.

[74] Stone, 'Wrestling – the Great American Passion Play', and Barthes, 'The World of Wrestling' in *Mythologies*, both develop this line. (Michael Robinson drew my attention to the latter

reference.) A similar point is expressed in a very different vein in Smith, *From N to Z*, Chap.15. See, too, *Sunday Times*, 4 Nov. 1934, 5 g. For a much later indication of these links between participants and spectators, see Stoddart, 'Dennis Lillee: the Sportsman'.

[75] *Sunday Times*, 26 Aug. 1934, 5d.

[76] *West Australian*, 30 April 1895, 3a–b. Gould, *On and Off the Turf in Australia*, Chap.V, indicates the extent of late-nineteenth-century Australian gambling. Bookmakers were still on Perch football grounds as late as 1903: Western Australian National Football League Committee Minutes, 8 July 1903, 123.

[77] *West Australian*, 28 Oct. 1890, 3 g. For a comparative view of amateurism and professionalism in this period, see Jones, 'Developments in Amateurism and Professionalism'.

[78] *West Australian*, 14 Sept. 1895, 6b.

[79] Ibid. 2 Jan. 1895, 4f–g.

[80] Ibid. 11 Jan. 1895, 3a–c.

[81] Ibid. 15 Jan. 1895, 4d–e.

[82] Drawn from evidence presented to the inquiry, contained in 1905 Report.

[83] See evidence in the 1915 Report.

[84] See particularly the views given by Dr F.L. Sawell, Detective-Sergeant H. Mann, H.F, Wilkinson and L.H. Darlot.

[85] *West Australian*, 18 May 1929, 17f.

[86] See, for example, Ibid. 3 June 1929, 6 g.

[87] Prize money for crossword puzzles in newspapers was banned, for example; see Premier's Dept 441/192 1 and 5. See *West Australian*, 24 June 1929, 14d.

[88] For registered bookmakers' problems with the Turf Club, see Western Australian Turf Club Committee Minutes, 5 Feb. 1931, 6. For reference to illegal operations, ibid., 28 July 1931, 73.

[89] See the various reports in Police Dept. 6555/1931. These 'periodic wars' by the police and the racing authorities were not always welcomed: *Groper*, 31 Jan. 1932, 15, and 1 Aug. 1931, 31. Much earlier official attitudes are indicated in Secretary Premier's Dept to Secretary Bunbury Race Club, 2 Sept. 1898, Premier's Dept 1182/1898.

[90] *Sunday Times*, 26 April 1931, 10e.

[91] For the cultural diffusion, see Weber, 'Gymnastics and Sports in Fin-de-Siècle France'; for some aspects of cycling in Perth, see Fitzpatrick, 'The Spectrum of Australian Bicycle Racing, 1890–1900'.

[92] *Sunday Times*, 23 Dec. 1928, 16f–g.

[93] Ibid. 6 Jan. 1929, 30a–c; 13 Jan. 1929, 33c; Hoskins Weekly and Speedway News, 17 Sept. 1927, 16.

[94] *West Australian*, 1 Jan. 1929, 8f.

[95] This sketch drawn from numerous newspaper sources.

[96] *Groper*, 30 Sept. 1932, 13–14. For earlier references to 'professionalism' in Perth sport: *West Australian*, 15 April 1895, 6b; 11 May 1895, 6a; *W.A. Sportsman*, 18 June 1915, 5d; *W.A. Amateur Sports*, 8 April 1932, 1. Also, Western Australian National Football League Committee Minutes, 9 June 1915, 78.

[97] *West Australian*, 1 Jan. 1929, 6 h; 4 March 1929, 12 g.

[98] *Sunday Times*, 10 March 1929, 7a–b.

[99] Rev. A.A. Lyons in the *West Australian*, 5 March 1929, 16f.

[100] Ibid. 6 March 1929, 13c.

[101] *Hoskins Weekly and Speedway News*, 17 Sept. 1927, 3; 1 Oct. 1927, 15; 8 Oct. 1927, 3; 18 Feb. 1928, 15.

[102] Ibid. 5 Nov. 1927, 15.

[103] Ibid. 24 March 1928, 15.

[104] This story may be followed in outline in the *West Australian*, 9 Aug. 1930, 11b; 24 Sept. 1930, 5c; 25 Sept. 1930, 6c; 27 Sept. 1930, 16d; 24 Sept. 1930, 4e; 27 Oct. 1930, 6e. I owe the general point to Margaret Brown.

[105] For a general introduction to this theme, see Chap. 5 in Talamini and Page, *Sport and Society: An Anthology*; for an Australian perspective, King, 'The Sexual Politics of Sport'; also Summers, *Damned Whores and God's Police*, 69–88.

[106] *West Australian*, 23 May 1895, 4e–f.

[107] *Sunday Times*, 5 Dec. 1915, 8 g.

[108] The general point is made by Marwick in *Deluge: British Society and the First World War*; the Australian point by Turner, '1914–1919'. This point is not accepted by all Australian feminists: Summers, *Damned Whores and God's Police*, 380–8.

[109] *Sunday Times*, 28 Nov. 1915, 1 l.

[110] For example, Ibid. 14 March 1915, 19e.

[111] See *West Australian*, 4 Jan. 1929, 12f; 10 Jan. 1929.

[112] *Hoskins Weekly and Speedway News*, 24 Sept. 1927, 15.

[113] *Sunday Times*, 2 Nov. 1930, 5f.

[114] *Hoskins Weekly and Speedway News*, 24 Sept, 1927, 15.

[115] *W.A. Amateur Sports*, 13 Aug. 1931, 2.

[116] See evidence of M. McDonald, J.M. Farrell and Detective Mann in 1905 Report; and that of Detective Sergeant Mann in 1915 Report. For a newspaper comment on women and gambling, *W.A. Sportsman*, 22 Jan. 1915, 1 f–g; also Secretary Fremantle Women's Service Guild to Premier, 24 Nov. 1920, Premier's Dept 414/1921.

[117] This biography drawn mainly from scattered newspaper references.

[118] *West Australian*, 7 July 1890, 36. For one study of connections between sport, business and politics see Reiss, 'The Baseball Magnate and Urban Politics in the Progressive Era'.

[119] *West Australian*, 1 Aug. 1890, 3c–d.

[120] Ibid. 27 April 1895, 3a–b.

[121] References drawn from scattered sources.

[122] Metcalfe, 'Organized Sport and Social Stratification in Montreal', reaches similar conclusions. A similar story is also told by Wettan and Willis, 'Social Stratification In the New York Athletic Club'; and 'Social Stratification in the New York City Athletic Clubs'.

[123] *West Australian*, 10 Aug. 1914, 5d–e; also *Sunday Times*, 25 July 1915, 2c. Scaddan was also implicated in the battle for the control of speedway.

[124] Sketches of Kenneally, Mann and Clydesdale drawn from scattered sources. The political ramifications of Australian sports clubs are touched on by Cunneen, 'The Rugby War'. In the same volume, Mandle makes out a solid cast of sport and politics in the Irish context, 'Sport as Politics'. See also Parsons, 'The Birth of the Dragons' (unpublished paper). For the connections between sport and politics in very different societies, see Hardy, 'Politicians, Promoters, and the Rise of Sport'; Cameron, *Porphyrius the Charioteer*, and *Circus Factions*.

[125] *Sunday Times*, 29 April 1930, 2 g. The club had just been awarded the honorific 'Royal'; for reasons, see Premier to Governor, 10 Dec. 1929, Premier's Dept 520/1928. The confirmation of the decision may be seen in Dominions Office file DO 35/384/J0758, Public Records Office, London.

[126] *Sunday Times*, 20 Oct. 1929, 4 g.

[127] *W.A. Amateur Sports*, 10 July 1931, 2,

[128] *West Australian*, 10 March 1890, 3 h.

[129] Ibid. 6 April 1895, 3a.

[130] *W.A. Sportsman*, 26 March 1915, 3f–g; *West Australian*, 23 Nov. 1914, 5h–i. McKernan, 'Sport, War and Society', makes this point frequently.

[131] For example, Richard Halliday's comments in *Sunday Times*, 16 Dec. 1928, 35a–i; 21 June 1931, 3 g; 6 Aug. 1933, lc–d; 31 Dec. 1933, 1 a–e.

[132] *W.A. Amateur Sports*, 16 July 1931, 1.

References

Australian Dictionary of Biography vol IV, edited by D. Pike. Melbourne: MUP, 1970.

Western Australian Trotting Journal, 3, (1915): 2.

History of Trotting in the State of Western Australia. Perth [n.d.].

People's Heritage. Perth [n.d.].

W.A. Turf Club Centenary, 1852–1952. Perth, 1952.

Atyeo, D. *Blood and Guts: Violence in Sports*. Melbourne: Paddington Press, 1979.

Bailey, P. *Leisure and Class in Victorian England: Rational Recreation and the Quest for Control 1830–1885*. London: Routledge and Paul, 1978.

Barthes, R. In *Mythologies*. Edited by Roland Barthes, translated by Annette Lavers. New York: Hill and Wang, 1972.

Battye, J. S. *The Cyclopedia of Western Australia*. 2 vols. Adelaide: Hussey and Gillingham 1912–13.

Berryman, J. W. "Sport History as Social History?" *Quest* 20 (1973): 65–73.

Best, G. *Mid-Victorian Britain 1851–75*. London: Weidenfeld and Nicolson, 1973.

Bolton, G. C. "The Idea of a Colonial Gentry." *Historical Studies* 51 (1968): 307–28.

Bolton G. C. *A Fine Country to Starve In*. Perth: University of Western Australia Press, 1972.

Bolton, G. C. and A. Mozley, *The Western Australian Legislature 1870–1930*. Canberra: Australian National University, 1961.

Brailsford, D. *Sport and Society: Elizabeth to Anne*. London, Toronto: Routledge & K. Paul/University of Toronto Press, 1969.

Brennan, J. "Report of the Royal Commissioner Appointed to Inquire in to the Administration, Conduct, and Control of the Sport of Trotting in the State of Western Australia." 17–23, 1915. Parliamentary Papers Western Australia 11 no. 12 (1946).

Brookes, C. *English Cricket: The Game and Its Players through the Ages*. London: Weidenfeld and Nicolson, 1978.

Buckland, C. T. *Sketches of Social Life in India*. London: W.H. Allen, 1884.

Colless, V. H. *Men of Western Australia*. Perth: 1937.

Cameron, A. *Porphyrius the Charioteer*. Oxford: Oxford University Press, 1973.

Cameron, A. *Circus Factions: Blues and Greens at Rome and Byzantium*. Oxford: Oxford University Press, 1976.

Crowley, F. K. *Australia's Western Third: A History of Western Australia*. Melbourne: Heinemann, 1970.

Cunneen, C. "The Rugby War: The Early History of Rugby League in N.S.W., 1907–1915" In *Sport in History*, edited by R. Cashman and M. McKernen. Brisbane: University of Queensland Press, 1979.

Dale, T. F. *Polo Past and Present*. London: Offices of Country Life, 1905.

Dale, T. F. *Polo of Home and Abroad*. London, 1915.

de Lisle, H. D. B. *Polo in India*. Bombay: Thacker, 1907.

Denney, R. *The Astonished Muse*. Chicago: University of Chicago Press, 1957.

Dobbs, B. *Edwardians at Play: Sport 1890–1914*. London: Pelham, 1973.

Duckworth, L. *The Story of Warwickshire Cricket*. London: Stanley Paul, 1974.

Dunning, E. "Industrialization and the Incipient Modernization of Football: A Study in Historical Sociology." *Stadion* 1 (1975): 103–39.

Dunstan, K. *Sports*. Melbourne: Cassell, 1973.

Edwards, H. *Sociology of Sport*. Homewood, IL: Dorsey Press, 1973.

Elias, N. "Foreward." In *The Sociology of Sport: A Selection of Readings*, edited by E. Dunning. London: Frank Cass, 1971.

Fitzpatrick, J. "The Spectrum of Australian Bicycle Racing, 1800–1900." In *Sport in History*, edited by R. Cashman and M. McKernen. Brisbane: University of Queensland Press, 1979.

Freedman, S. "The Baseball Fad in Chicago, 1865–1870: An Exploration of Sport in the Nineteenth-Century City." *Journal of Sport History* 5, no. 2 (1978): 42–64.

Geertz, C. "Deep Play: Notes on the Balinese Cockfight." *Daedalus* 101, no. 1 (1972): 1–37.

Gould, N. *On and Off the Turf in Australia*. London: Routledge, 1895.

Grimsley, W. *Tennis: Its History, People and Events*. Englewood Cliffs, NJ: Prentice-Hall, 1971.

Gruneau, R. S. "Sport, Social Differentiation, and Social Inequality." In *Sport and Social Order: Contributions to the Sociology of Sport*, edited by D. W. Ball and J. W. Loy. Reading, MA: Addison-Wesley, 1975.

Guttmann, A. *From Ritual to Record: The Nature of Modern Sports*. New York: Columbia University Press, 1978.

Halcombe, R. "A Report on the Development of Sport in Western Australia." HS/816: Battye Library.

Hardy, S. "Politicians, Promoters, and the Rise of Sport: The Case of Ancient Greece and Rome." *Canadian Journal of the History of Sport and Physical Education* 8, no. 1 (1977): 1–37.

Hobsbawm, E. J. *Industry and Empire*. Harmondsworth: Penguin, 1976.

Hunt, L. "Sir Walter James: The Social Reformer." In *Westralian Portraits*, edited by L. Hunt. Nedlands: University of Western Australia Press, 1979, pp. 111–9.

Inglis, F. *The Name of the Game: Sport and Society*. London: Heinemann, 1977.

Inglis, G. *Sport and Pastimes in Australia*. London: Methuen & Co, 1912.

Jacques, T. D. and G. R. Pavia. *Sport in Australia*. Sydney: McGraw-Hill Book Company, 1976.

Jobling, I. F. "Urbanization and Sport in Canada, 1867–1900." In *Canadian Sport: Sociological Perspectives*, edited by R. S. Gruneau, J. O. Albinson, and D. Mills. Ontario: Addison-Wesley, 1976.

Joll, J. *Gramsci*. London: Fontana, 1977.

Jones, K. O. "Developments in Amateurism and Professionalism in Early Twentieth Century Canadian Sport." *Journal of Sport History* 2, no. 1 (1975): 29–40.

Kay, J. *A History of County Cricket . . . Lancashire*. London: Sportsman's Book Club, 1974.

Kimberly, W. K. *History of West Australia: A Narrative of Her Past, with Biographies of Her Leading Men*. Melbourne: FW Niven and Co., 1897.

King, H. "The Sexual Politics of Sport." In *Sport in History*, edited by R. Cashman and M. McKernen. Brisbane: University of Queensland Press, 1979.

Lasch, C. "The Corruption of Sports." *New York Review of Books*, April (1977): 24–30.

Longrigg, R. *The History of Horse Racing*. New York: Stein and Day, 1972.

Loy, J. W., B. D. McPherson, and G. Kenyan. *Sport and Social Systems: A Guide to the Analysis, Problems, and Literature*. Reading, MA: Addison-Wesley, 1978.

McKernan, M. "Sport, War and Society: Australia, 1914–1918." In *Sport in History*, edited by R. Cashman and M. McKernen. Brisbane: University of Queensland Press, 1979.

Mandle, W. F. "Cricket and Australian Nationalism in the Nineteenth Century." *Journal of the Royal Australian Historical Society* 59, no. 4 (1973): 225–46.

Mandle, W. F. "Games People Played: Cricket and Football in England and Victoria in the Late Nineteenth Century." *Historical Studies* 60 (1973): 511–35.

Mandle, W. F. "Sport as Politics: The Gaelic Athletic Association 1884–1916." In *Sport in History*, edited by R. Cashman and M. McKernen. Brisbane: University of Queensland Press, 1979.

Marrus, M. R., ed. *The Emergence of Leisure*. New York: Harper and Row, 1974.

Marwick, A. *Deluge: British Society and the First World War*. London: Bodley Head, 1973.

Meller, H. E. *Leisure and the Changing City 1870–1914*. London: Routledge and Paul, 1976.

Metcalfe, A. "Organized Sport and Social Stratification in Montreal, 1840–1901." In *Canadian Sport: Sociological Perspectives*, edited by R. S. Gruneau, J. O. Albinson, and D. Mills. Ontario: Addison-Wesley, 1976, pp. 78–97.

Orr, W. R. "History of Football." HS/720: Battye Library.

Page, C. H. "Pervasive Sociological Themes in the Study of Sport." In *Sport and Society: An Anthology*, edited by J. T. Talamini and C. H. Page. Boston: Little Brown, 1973.

Parker, S. *The Sociology of Leisure*. London: International Publications Service, 1976.

Parsons, T. O. "The Birth of the Dragons: The St. George District Rugby League Football Club in the 1920s." (unpublished paper).

Reiss, S. A. "The Baseball Magnate and Urban Politics in the Progressive Era: 1885–1920." *Journal of Sport History* 1, no. 1 (1974): 41–62.

Rodrigo, R. *The Racing Game: A History of Flat Racing*. London: The Sportsman's Book Club, 1960.

Smith, M. D. "Sport and Collective Violence." In *Sport and Social Order: Contributions to the Sociology of Sport*, edited by D. W. Ball and J. W. Loy. Reading, MA: Addison-Wesley, 1975.

Smith, N. V. *From N to Z: A Humorous Study of New Zealand*. Wellington: Hicks Smith & Wright, 1947.

Snyder, E. E. and E. Spreitzer. "Sociology of Sport: An Overview." In *Sport and Social Order: Contributions to the Sociology of Sport*, edited by D. W. Ball and J. W. Loy. Reading, MA: Addison-Wesley, 1975.

Stannage, C. T. *The People of Perth*. Perth: Perth City Council, 1979.

Stevenson, J. and C. Cook. *The Slump: Society and Politics During the Depression*. London: Cape, 1977.

Stoddart, B. "Cricket's Imperial Crisis: The 1932–33 M.C.C. Tour in Australia." In *Sport in History*, edited by R. Cashman and M. McKernen. Brisbane: University of Queensland Press, 1979.

Stoddart, B. "Dennis Lillee: The Sportsman." In *Westralian Portraits*, edited by Lyall Hunt. Nedlands: University of Western Australia Press, 1979.

Stoddart, B. "A Ruling Passion: Polo in British India." *Hemisphere*, Sept–Oct (1979).

Stone, G. P. "Wrestling – the Great American Passion Play." In *The Sociology of Sport: A Selection of Readings*, edited by E. Dunning. London: Frank Cass, 1971.

Summers, A. *Damned Whores and God's Police: The Colonization of Women in Australia*. Ringwood, Vic: Penguin, 1975.

Taylor, I. "Football Mad: A Speculative Sociology of Football Hooliganism." In *The Sociology of Sport: A Selection of Readings*, edited by E. Dunning. London: Frank Cass, 1971.

Taylor, I. "Soccer Consciousness and Soccer Hooliganism." In *Images of Deviance*, edited by S. Cohen. Harmondsworth: Penguin, 1977.

Turner, I. "1914–1919." In *A New History of Australia*, edited by F. K. Crowley. Melbourne: Heinemann, 1974.

Turner, I. "The Emergence of Aussie Rules." In *Sport in History*, edited by R. Cashman and M. McKernen. Brisbane: University of Queensland Press, 1979.

Vamplew, W. *The Turf: A Social and Economic History of Horse Racing*. London: Allen Lane, 1976.

Voight, D. Q. *America through Baseball*. Chicago: Nelson-Hall, 1976.

Walvin, J. *Leisure and Society 1830–1950*. London: Longwood, 1978.

Walvin, J. *The People's Game: A Social History of British Football*. London: Allen Lane, 1975.

Weber, E. "Gymnastics and Sports in Fin-De-Siècle France: Opium of the Classes?" *American Historical Review* 76, no.1 (1971): 70–98.

Wettan, R. and J. Willis. "Social Stratification in the New York Athletic Club: A Preliminary Analysis of the Impact of the Club on Amateur Sport in Late Nineteenth Century America." *Canadian Journal of the History of Sport and Physical Education* 7, no. 1 (1976): 41–53.

Wettan, R. and Willis, J. "Social Stratification in the New York City Athletic Clubs 1865–1915." *Journal of Sport History* 3, no. 1 (1976): 45–63.

Illusion or Reality: Aspects of Contemporary Australian Sport

Introduction

Looking back, this was a dry run for the *Saturday Afternoon Fever* framework, that book appearing three years later. Additionally, it was my first 'public intellectual' works, taking academic ideas into the public arena for consideration by the population at large. It was an approach unpopular with the sports fraternity, then and now substantially skeptical of anyone scrutinizing its world, and with the wider cultural one which, publicly at least, dismissed sport as having any meaning. As the piece shows, sports analysis already emphasized critical theory with analysts like Jean-Marie Brohm and Christopher Lasch excoriating sport from vastly different standpoints.

Increased public debate about sport was needed to support the efforts of Bill Mandle and Colin Tatz, especially in an institution where the programmes I taught were to educate Australian Institute of Sport elite athletes. Several coaches disliked their charges being distracted from sport by education, especially by history and sociology courses where key social assumptions about sport were challenged. Several early students suddenly discovered training sessions scheduled exactly across university classes: they had to choose. Some coaches were more positive, among them Patrick Hunt who was not only a basketball coach but also a student who encouraged his players to get better educated. (As coach of the Canberra Cannons NBL side, Patrick had me accompany the team on a Melbourne road trip so that I experienced the game from 'the inside', giving me greater appreciation of life as an elite player.)

One story demonstrates the vast changes that have occurred inside Australian universities. This was 'pre-Dawkins' (a reference to the 1989–90 actions of the Labor government that abolished the binary system of Colleges of Advanced Education and universities), well before the present 'Nelson Reforms' under which the Liberal-National conservative government has widened free market principles within the university sector. When asked to become sports editor by the leading Canberra commercial radio station I was initially refused permission by my Principal, a retired Sudan Civil Service member with little if any feel for universities – among his tricks, a promotion committee would beaver away for months, he would receive its report then release his proclamations (invariably at odds with committee findings) just after he had left on his annual long visit to England and his private interests which included a biscuit factory, it emerged. The radio station manager pointed out that my institution would receive $5,000 worth of free advertising weekly, a huge figure then, but the Principal explicitly demanded the institution not be named! Universities now spend vast sums and time engineering such arrangements, and the federal government demands that academics 'engage' with their constituencies. As I write this, a national committee is working out how to measure and reward 'public intellectuals' like the stellar group of La Trobe colleagues for whom I now have great admiration, including Robert Manne, John Carroll, Joe Camilleri (not he of the Falcons, Black Sorrows and Bakelite Radio fame), Judy Brett, Robin Jeffrey and Dennis Altman – they do what academics should do, and what I started doing for sport back then in the early 1980s.

That combination of antagonistic coaches and unsympathetic leaders led to one of my best pieces, published under the pseudonym of Howard Kirk. Academic novel devotees will recognize the central character from Malcolm Bradbury's *The History Man*, one of my favourite novels among many in the *genre* by Bradbury, David Lodge, J.I.M. Stewart (aka Michael Innes), and all the rest. Given that name, and the fact that sections in the long essay (in *Inside Canberra*, reviewing Australian Institute of Sport progress) were all subtitled from *Alice In Wonderland*, I reckoned someone would work out the author. The piece was warts and all, critical of and analytical about how taxpayer dollars were being spent, so it stirred considerable interest in sportsworld and the Australian Institute of Sport (AIS). One colleague reported that AIS personnel narrowed suspects to three including me, but she assured them it could not possibly be me because of the Alice references!

The academic novel has sustained me through hard times because in surviving the modern university, a strongly developed sense of humour is the first requirement on the position description. As C.P. Snow showed so well in the 'Strangers And Brothers' series, the academic world is a stressed one that mixes intelligence, ambition, cruelty, ego, shallowness, self-absorption and self-interest in with insight, commitment, self-belief, forgiveness, depth, hardship and self-defence. It is a heady mix.

On my bookshelves is an early copy of that wonderful little essay by F.A.M. Cornford entitled *Academica Cosmographica*, a guide to the young person (man, inevitably, in the early twentieth century when it was written) commencing academic life. J.H. Hexter's *The History Primer*, more specifically, and Henry Rosovsky more generally (in his *The University: An Owner's Manual*) later built upon Cornford to reveal a world of paradox: a place committed to building knowledge and insight but resisting change and innovation; a place preaching collegiality but practicing rampant individualism; a place emphasizing learning but enshrining bureaucracy; a place extolling teaching but rewarding research; a place hating governments but loving committees; and a place arguing equity but reifying inequality. Helping pioneer sports culture and navigate all this was and remains a fascinating exercise for all who take it on.

'Illusion or Reality' starts from a premise that sport is deeply embedded in, formed by and forming of any culture within which it finds itself, and sets the tone for *Saturday Afternoon Fever* (SAF) by starting from the present and working back into the past to explain how things became the way they are. Given that mix, early on I began describing what I do as 'sports culture' rather than sports history or sociology, a prime reason being the boundary crossing I have found necessary to get adequate explanation. That is not the path taken by all or many, but it is has helped me do what I set out to do.

* * * * *.

It was appropriate, if saddening and divisive, that Australia entered the 1980s with a vitriolic debate about whether or not to attend the Moscow Games. That debate followed the equally sharp controversy aroused by World Series Cricket during the late 1970s. During these upheavals, many Australians for the first time in their lives were forced to question the social roles of a most revered institution – organized sport. Was it simply a flippant activity peripheral to the mainstream of life; or did it have a more fundamental significance? Should Australia recognize the mix of sport and politics? And, if she did, should she enter the world of honest professionalism as opposed to dishonest 'shamateurism', thereby sanctioning sport as a major creative force in the Australian social makeup and image? The discussion of these and similar questions has been superficial and simplistic, stereotyped to the point of bigotry.

One group, represented mostly by professional sportspersons, has no doubt that Australian sport must become fully professional. First, the group argues, if Australia is to remain competitive internationally then she must adopt international attitudes which mean paying international performers. This might be likened to a 'Domino Theory' of international sport. Second, sport now constitutes a major section of the Australian entertainment industry, giving pleasure to countless people. Therefore just as musicians, artists, dancers and television stars are paid handsomely, so, too, should sport stars be. The basis for this view is that sport is quite naturally a work category.

The opponents of the first group range from journalists like Keith Dunstan to academics like Colin Tatz. Professional sport, they argue, becomes too much the opiate of the masses and destroys the fundamental goodness of games. The pursuit of the dollar contributes to the disappearance of inconvenient conventions and rules, even though the conventions and rules might be lynchpins of the games' behaviour. Money means mania, according to these critics, because it stresses undue competitiveness which leads to excessive on-field violence with consequences among partisan spectators. Social divisiveness, then, might just as easily spring from sport as from politics. Here Australian critics point to similarities between the divisions created by the 1975 sacking of Whitlam and Fraser's involvement in the 1980 Olympic debate.

These are bald characterizations, perhaps even exaggerated. Nonetheless, they contain the essential elements of the debate concerning the future of Australian sport and its social functions. Significantly the underlying philosophies rest upon a series of value judgments which do not allow the debate to proceed along more than 'either/or', 'black or white' lines. Even more significantly, the opposing groups hold many of those value judgements in common.

The most limiting obstacle to the serious study of sport in many modern societies has been the view that sport counts for very little in the progress of those communities. In this view 'progress', of course, is, by definition a desirable and cumulative objective. Curiously enough the major, albeit unintentional, contributors to the view have been serious and scholarly writers on play and games. For example, Johann Huizinga's classic *Homo Ludens* can be used by Colin Tatz to argue that play is simply the suspension of unfortunate reality. Tatz can also use Roger Caillois' *Man, Play and Games* to say essentially the same thing. Sport should not be serious. American left-wing commentator Christopher Lasch argues the same line when discussing the increasing trivialization of sport by modern society, itself increasingly trivial. One need not be a raging Marxist to see that the argument is related to 'progress' as measured by productivity. Sport does not contribute to the development of community as do politics and industry, therefore it should not be accorded equal rights as an area of serious investigation or, of course, serious social investment.

In different ways, then, our contending critics proceed from the same philosophical assumptions. The pro-professionalists see sport essentially as entertainment, an escape from the realities of life such as that found in reading fiction, watching films or listening to music. They want more money to promote the escape. Only at that point do they part company with their opponents who see that the promotion of professional sport will destroy, not foster, the suspension of reality.

The need now, clearly, is to re-examine the underlying assumptions to determine whether or not they are valid in Australian conditions. If they are not, then the debate about the future form of Australian sport might be encouraged into a more profitable direction, and some of the current issues about professionalism, sponsorship and commentary might reveal new aspects of both problem and promise.

Considered historically, it is difficult to see that Australian sport has ever been about the suspension of reality. Especially so if by the 'suspension of reality' is meant the complete escape from the current issues of life. As many international observers have now pointed out, fairs, festivals and crowds which take on apparently chaotic, anonymous and 'escapist' appearances more often than not confront reality more vigorously than normal. With the normal social constrictions relaxed, participants can adopt the approach to problems of reality which they would ideally like to see employed. In that sense, 'escapism' provides a major key to the serious business of life.

Sport has always been a serious business in Australian life at local, national and international levels. Visiting observers have frequently commented on this. Jack Hobbs made the point on his first MCC tour early this century; Reuel Denny made a similar if more academic judgment nearly fifty years later. A number of points are necessary here. First, many important Australian athletes sprang from their occupational pursuits. Later nineteenth century scullers invariably began their careers by being occupied in water transport of some description. Similarly, Australia's champion axemen emerged from the milling industries all over Australia. Renowned cyclists, too, sprang from another communications industry: a vital one, in fact, as Jim Fitzpatrick has demonstrated. This emergence was not a simple one-way process in which elite performers reaped the benefit of their skills without promoting the industry whence they came. As each of these sports developed, so did the efficiency of the equipment employed both by sportsmen and workers. Boats and bicycles became lighter and faster; axes became better designed. And, it might be argued, this trend continues. As fuel crises mount, the return to the bicycle continues and it is to an increasingly efficient bicycle. As the timber industry develops so does the search for better equipment which produces new sports, involving power saws for example. So the pattern continues. Similarly, whatever else the critics of motor-racing might say there is little doubt that much of the automobile safety we now enjoy springs from developments on the track.

Second, sport has always been associated with measuring social progress (as Bill Mandle points out). Moreover, it has always been popularly regarded as a contributor to social progress. This is a long way from its 'progress' role ascribed by the bulk of its critics. 'Social progress' itself takes many forms in sport as the following examples show. From the inception of Australian rules football, many matches were more class warfare than sport. This was especially marked in Melbourne, as revealed in the Vagabond Papers (James, 1969) – a North Melbourne versus Carlton game of the 1870s was a classic. But all centres where the game was played revealed similar characteristics. In Western Australia during the 1890s, for example, many matches between Perth and Fremantle clubs were punctuated by violence. All these matches, no matter their locale, were fought (often literally) between teams who shared some sort of class feeling within themselves and against their opponents. The same has been the background in other football codes and in cricket. Many cricket clubs, for example, save their toughest performances for matches against University sides. The social attitudes revealed in those games often rival those observed by the Vagabond in Melbourne football of the 1870s. It is difficult to see how this situation equates with the 'suspension of reality' delineated by Huizinga, Caillois and their Australian supporters. This was social progress by the increasing delineation of class lines among clubs formed along community lines.

The role of sport in ethnic communities adds another aspect to the question of progress. In Australia the field is almost untouched by investigation, but some features are clear. First, many players of ethnic descent have used sport consciously to gain acceptance within traditional Australian society. While Ockers might disparage 'foreigners' in other areas of life, they will respect success in sport. VFL football, as so often, provides the best examples. Teams there are replete with Yugoslav, Italian, Dutch and even White Russian names. While 'wog' might still be a pejorative term in society at large, when Carlton fans nickname a player 'Superwog' it takes on a quite different connotation. The same is beginning to happen in cricket with first-class players being openly of Austrian and Sri Lankan descent, unlike an earlier period when a player of Yugoslav origins felt it necessary to Anglicize his name. In both Australian football and cricket, many 'ethnic' players have turned to games not theirs traditionally in order to gain social acceptance.

The other side of ethnic football shows, too, that it is far from illusory in its social significance. Australian soccer clubs have invariably carried ethnic ties and names – Tricolore, Olympic, Helas, Azzurri, Croatia, Dalmatinacs and Athena, to name a few. Almost as invariably these clubs have carried the social banner for the communities backing them, especially as soccer is the major 'European' game with a large Australian following. Such clubs often proved the rallying point for communities which felt their cohesiveness threatened by immigration policies or social attitudes. Football kept them together, often promoting fear amongst 'Anglo-Saxon Australian' groups which saw cohesiveness as antisocial. Far from being light-hearted or escapist, this sport has always been socially serious.

Internationally, this serious quality of Australian sport has always been visible. Playing cricket against England has been and continues to be one of the most serious enterprises any Australian can engage upon. Even now, when few of Australia's international interests lie with Great Britain, to win against England is to reaffirm Australia's emergence from colonial status. A dominant art, literature and music will take a lot longer to appear, but cricket is enough to illustrate Australia's self-reliance and independence. Little wonder, then, that cricket has occasionally become warfare as in 1879, 1932–33, 1946–47, 1970–71 and 1974–75, to name just the more obvious moments. This has spilled over into other international contests. Rugby League had its 'Battle of Brisbane' in the 1930s and another infamous match in Sydney twenty years later. Australian Rugby Union remembers with bitterness the treatment handed out to Ken Catchpole by the New Zealand All Blacks, and with pride the 1978 Brisbane test against Wales, one of the roughest Union matches on record. All these contests had a sense, for players and spectators, of international importance which went beyond the confines of the playing arenas.

The merit of these three examples is that they reveal sport in Australian society as a constant, organic and creative force. To argue that modern trends in Australian sport depart from a traditional play element, then, is simplistic in the extreme. Sport in Australia has never been escapist in the sense in which that word is normally used. It follows, then, that the principles upon which the debate about the patterns of future Australian sport have been based are far too narrow, perhaps even beside the point. What is required is an analysis of key areas of the debate to assess if and how they will alter the serious role of sport in Australian social reality.

Television has been the chief target for the opponents of increased professionalism in Australian sport. Their arguments run something like this. Television lies in the hands of a few promoters who use sport as a vehicle to attract advertising. The advertisers want their products shown to the best advantage, and apply pressure to have the game concerned altered to attract the largest possible viewing audience. That trivializes the game to the point of sensationalism, attracts ignorant crowds, may promote unrest, and generally degrades the game to the status of another consumer product. Again, this is essentially the Christopher Lasch line, echoed by many observers outside the United States, and there may be something to it. But before it can be accepted totally, two general questions should be considered.

The theory essentially ignores why television and advertising are so interested in sport. The answer, consistent with earlier argument, is that sport is of serious concern to a considerable proportion of the Australian public. So television and the advertising industry need sport as much as vice versa. This factor has been overlooked almost entirely by Australian observers. Yet realization of it helps explain a number of otherwise puzzling occurrences – why should television networks vie for international rights to athletics, soccer, boxing and cricket contests; why should the Australian Cricket Board hold out so strongly against Kerry Packer then apparently give in so quietly? The key issue is simply the constant struggle between promoter and provider concerning who secures the best terms.

Then, to say that television and sponsorship trivializes the game does a serious disservice to both players and spectators. Australian sporting crowds are widely regarded as amongst the most knowledgeable in the world. In a sense, World Series Cricket reflected that. Huge crowds were predicted for its first season, yet did not eventuate. Too much of the cricket seemed too artificial for too many people. A score of close to 450 on the first day of a 'test' in Perth attracted very few spectators; it was scored on a ridiculously easy wicket with ridiculously short boundaries. On a neighbouring ground, supposedly weak Australian and Indian teams played before enthusiastic and knowledgeable crowds. After that season, Packer cricket was forced to shed many of its sensationalist trappings which did not accord with the values of the Australian spectator.

Alternatively, where the changes necessary for television needs were sensible and creative, they became quite acceptable to crowds and players. Perhaps the best example is the fielding circle introduced to one-day cricket matches. Fielding captains were limited in the number of players they might place in deep fielding positions. This reduced the incidence of negative play in games designed to provide attacking cricket. Traditionalists who scoffed at its initial appearance changed their attitudes when its positive features became marked.

Similar caveats might be entered on discussions about the supposed links between sensationalism and violence, argued to emerge from sport being trivialized. There is considerable evidence to suggest that the increased professionalism brought about by television and sponsorship has curbed the incidence of violence. Simple indications are the proliferation of tribunals, player associations, codes of ethics and increased powers to referees and umpires. Less simple to gauge is the inferential evidence. For example, fewer incidents of player violence seem now to be shown on television replays; and even in live telecasts less attention is given to such incidents. To play up this sensationalism is not in the interests of the promoter; a product must not be associated with anti-social elements.

But, the anti-professionalists would say, does not television create crowd unrest? Another popular catchcry, certainly; but, again, one with another side to it. Critics like Lasch claim that the appearance of placards and banners at matches promotes sensationalism and, thereby, unrest. That quite misses the significance of those cultural artefacts. Australia has had 'barrackers' since at least the later nineteenth century, and many of them have underscored the reality (as opposed to illusion) of sport. At first the voice was enough. The crowd at the ground constituted the main audience, with newspaper readers aided by the reporter. With the advent of radio, the serious barracker needed to be near a broadcasting point. Television is visual, so banners are required to get the message across, and many of them show a firm grip on reality. One theme with a lot of variations during 1978 and 1979 concerned the bearded similarities of the Ayatollah Khomeini and England cricket captain Mike Brearley – it may be doubted whether sensation-seeking, violent-minded crowds would have displayed so keen an interest in international politics. Similarly, one Leeds test crowd showed its social preoccupation – 'Geoff Boycott – Yorkshire Ripper', a reference to a local multiple killer not then apprehended. A Leeds United football crowd derisively chanted '12 nil, 12 nil' during a police appeal for help in locating 'The Ripper'. To the crowd, the score was a sad indictment of police inefficiency because, at that point, twelve women had been murdered. While at one level the banner and the chant were 'trivial', at another they were visual displays of public discontent conveyed in non-violent fashion. The 'Len Pascoe for Premier' sort of banners similarly reveal a thoughtful awareness of issues beyond the field; this may be the only way the banner-wavers feel it possible for them to make their views known on a wider scale. (The 1982 Victorian election campaign showed a realization of this: the Labor Party had behind-the-posts signs erected at one VFL 'Match of the Day' to read 'V John Cain'. Politics were definitely abroad among that crowd.) The superficial criticism of this activity denies the crowd creativity which undoubtedly exists. One 1980 Carlton banner read 'Carlton are [sic] Atomic' – 'Yes', commented a Fitzroy supporter, 'they keep bombing out'. It may be argued, then, that this creativity simply continues that established in earlier years by using a new technological form which is servant rather than master of the supposedly easily-misled sports crowds.

This points immediately to one area of great need in Australian sport. While radio commentary has frequently produced good performers, television sport has never come to terms with itself. The role and significance of professional sport in Australia can only be conveyed by professional television commentary. It will not be served by such gems as 'Whoever stays in front will win this race' and 'that was a brand new record never set before', both heard during the 1980 Olympics; not to mention the 'Here is a Rugby League score for those of you who do not want to hear it' message carried on a 1982 ABC-TV report in Sydney. Much of the visual and deeper significance at modern matches (of banners, say) escapes these commentators. We need the educated talents of a John Arlott who once referred to an Australian wicketkeeper as 'the prehensile Tallon – all [talons] are prehensile'. Similarly, Australia needs more sports journalists like Jack Fingleton whose work always reflected a close relationship between sport and the concerns of the community which supports it, especially in the political sphere. Fingleton came closest to describing the real importance of Don Bradman to the Australian people. An expatriate like Sinclair Robieson, who can describe a rugby referee as signalling a penalty with all the authority of von Karajan conducting the Berlin Philharmonic, is also badly needed. For sport in Australia, or anywhere else for that matter, is not something to be studied in isolation from the other issues of life. It is very much part of them.

The structure of future Australian sport will be built upon foundations established during the nineteenth century. There will be continuity, not the dysfunction feared by so many critics. There will be change, obviously, but it need be no more cataclysmic than such past changes as enclosing racecourses, inventing points posts, introducing radio broadcasts or permitting 'open' tennis. All seemed revolutionary in their time, but none provoked a revolution. Ritual festivals in Australian sport will remain. One newspaper report on the 1980 Melbourne Cup bemoaned that the day was degenerating into a fake folk festival with people in fancy dress. Once more, that is too superficial a view. Anthropologists and historians alike now point to apparently antisocial festivals like Mardi Gras as having distinct social functions in the area of tension relief. Like other racing cups, and for that matter Show Days in Australia, the Melbourne Cup has always had an importance beyond mere racing. For example, marriage alliances amongst pastoral families were often arranged during cup meetings; business and political concerns were frequently discussed at the same time.

VFL finals and England-versus-Australia cricket tests will continue to draw large crowds, despite the pressure of television. Examples from around the world, in fact, show that where a sport begins television coverage it will quickly draw both larger gates and actual participation. Soccer has been a prime example in Australia, as has golf, another indication that television will not destroy sport as we know it. This is because going to a VFL final or to a test match is a far greater personal, even spiritual experience than watching either event on television. The time and context of play, for the spectator in this case, is no less unreal than the world beyond the arena gates. If anything, the reality of the outside is heightened.

Australia will promote professionalism in all areas of sport, not simply at the playing level, although it will be there that the most obvious impact will be made. There are already people who make their living out of sport, so future development (like the creation of degree courses in Sports Studies and the establishment of the Australian Institute of Sport) will merely accentuate a process already begun. For many players that will help solve many problems, not the least being a present taxation problem created by the income of wages or salary plus a healthy part-time income from sport. The new professionalism will relieve sportspeople of the necessity to have occupations other than their sport. Those players will have access to far better professionally trained coaches and administrators than they do presently. Their activities will be understood and described by informed and trained commentators. Their business affairs will be guided by specialist lawyers and accountants. In short, there will be a fully-fledged industry. It is at that point, possibly, that the critics of increased professionalism will weigh in most heavily. That industry, they would argue, will be exploitative and parasitic, returning nothing in social terms. But need that necessarily be the case?

In pure economic terms, the immediate costs of professional sport will be only a small portion of the leisure industry which it will help continue to develop. That industry is substantial now, and will grow as the population expends more time and energy out of the workplace and home. As golf proved in America during the 1960s and tennis worldwide during the 1970s, growth rates beyond the professional ranks can be phenomenal, to the point of being considerable components in national economics. Equipment, clothing, coaching, centres, resorts and publications all produce employment and investment opportunities. Orthodox left-wing critics, like Jean-Marie Brohm, of course, see this as simply another manifestation of the parasitic capitalist state, with many of them pointing to sport as being the one area where Eastern European regimes got their Marxist-Leninist theories wrong. Once more, the superficial reading of that position masks some of the lessons to be learned and which, in fact, Australia is already beginning to learn. Any society with aspirations to produce a population which makes maximum social use of leisure, especially in seeking fitness and preventive health, needs both an elite and a mass aspect which will have mutually beneficial effects. As the East German experience described by Doug Gilbert so clearly reveals, the mass programme will incidentally produce high-performance athletes who will then by deed and example encourage others to go through the same process. With efficient coaching, competent administration and sufficient resources, the process will become self-sustaining. So instead of just being a miniscule elite, the professional, sports group will be an integral part of a worthwhile social system.

Certainly, television and advertising will do very well out of this; but it might be a small social price to pay if the number of participants in football, netball, soccer, golf, tennis and cricket (to name a few) continue to grow as they have done in recent years. Especially so if the conventions and the aesthetics of sport are maintained as, by and large, it might be expected that they will. If that is the case, and television improves its educative function in sport by informing more viewers about those qualities, then Australia need not be badly placed.

All that having been said, there is probably one area in which Australia will learn most – sport and politics. Hunter S. Thompson was one of Richard Nixon's most trenchant critics and allowed that disastrous President just one credit: the man was a highly informed observer of professional football. It was, Thompson claimed, the only area in which Nixon came close to that section of America he professed to understand, the silent majority.

In a country so historically devoted to sport and where politicians deem it so important to be identified with major sports clubs, it seems inexplicable that in Australia the increasing modern link between sport and politics could be denied for so long. It has taken the 1980 Olympic issue to reveal to Australia the power of the sport-politics nexus. And even then, the lessons of that confrontation seem all but forgotten in the aftermath of the Games. The boycott that seemed so all-important at the time has faded practically into oblivion.

Yet, curiously enough, Australia has had excellent examples upon which to ponder in this area. The 1936 Olympics caused a great stir throughout Europe, and controversy in America where Jewish athletes were dropped from the team to go to Berlin. Australian attitudes at the time, it seems, were that it had nothing to do with us. Just four years earlier, during the tumultuous Bodyline cricket tour, the Australian government had learned how sport might be closely associated with politics. As host of the 1956 Olympic Games, Melbourne witnessed the ferocious Russia-versus-Hungary 'Blood

In The Pool' water polo match, a symbolic re-enactment of the struggle occasioned when Russia invaded Hungary earlier in the year. But before 1980 the most difficult political consideration undoubtedly concerned sporting ties with South Africa.

The international sporting boycott of South Africa developed steadily during the 1960s, most particularly among black nations. Like her near neighbour New Zealand, Australia professed no interest in the matter, imagining that she could maintain a special and privileged position. As the former British 'White Dominions' the three shared rugby union and cricket passions – those, it was thought, were beyond politics. But the 1971 rugby union tour of Australia by South Africa changed all that. Amidst the demonstrations, police actions, riots, arrests, declarations of civil emergencies and smoke bombs which marked the tour, Australians generally, it might be argued, were more amazed than the outside world at what was happening. The internal political policies of another nation were being challenged on Australian sports fields. Since then Australian sports links with South Africa have been cautious if not firmly resolved. The letter of international agreement is observed if the spirit is not convincingly embraced.

By 1980, Australia knew that the politics of race and ideology were firmly stamped on sport: and there should be the knowledge that the stamp will, if anything, become more indelible. It might, for example become more difficult for Australia to criticize the politics of Third World nations yet at the same time maintain direct sporting links with them. Similarly, Australia should not be surprised by any political difficulties ranged against her by nations whose sports objectives she has criticized. For the position is clear: sport in the international political world – for both goodwill and ill will – carries an ever-increasing importance, and the benefits of that cannot be taken to the exclusion of the disadvantages.

This brings us full circle to the question of fundamental principle. Australia faces a decision about whether or not she wishes to be a major sporting nation in terms of internal achievement and international power. There are increasing signs that the decision will be taken in the affirmative. But that decision should not be taken without a full appreciation of the sporting heritage with which Australia has to work. The choice cannot be decided on a simplistic notion of whether or not 'degradation of sport' will occur. Like the Balinese cockfight, as analyzed by Clifford Geertz, Australian sport forms, as much as reflects, the nation's character.

Postscript

Since this essay was written, developments within Australian sport confirm many of the original assessments and emphasize just how rapidly changes are occurring, often without public awareness. The areas of commercialism and politics provide just some of the revealing examples.

One business estimate was that the six leading spectator and participant sports in Australia would attract at least $200,000,000 worth of sponsorship and endorsements during 1981. Those providing that money would spend as much again ensuring that their product came across well in associated advertising. Ward's Transport group put up over

$1,000,000 to support the Sydney Swans Australian football team for a three year period. When asked what return the group would get, the VFL marketing manager claimed that the team's Sydney launch alone was worth $250,000 in 'free' advertising. During 1982 the McDonald's fast-food chain announced a $750,000 sponsorship of the Australian Soccer Federation, again for three years. Electronics giant Sanyo also announced a major underwriting during 1982. The Australian Amateur Athletics Association would receive $30,000 directly; $100,000 would go towards the Commonwealth Games effort in Brisbane; and the Games would also receive $150,000 worth of video monitoring equipment. It is now, then, a truism to say that sport is big business.

And as the Sydney Swans case demonstrates, business is beginning to have an enormous impact upon sport. Hitherto known as South Melbourne Football Club, the Swans were transplanted onto the Sydney Cricket Ground by the VFL, but only after a bitter faction fight within the South Melbourne camp. While the major reason given publicly for the shift concerned the spreading of the Australian football message, the overwhelming pressure was economic. An unsuccessful club in terms of results, South Melbourne attracted little television and advertising attention. By playing in Sydney on Sundays, it gained instant television attention and revenue back in Melbourne. Other clubs in need of propping up were soon mentioned as candidates for similar action – during the 1982 season Footscray were constantly mentioned as candidates for Surfer's Paradise. One football joke had the disastrously unsuccessful Collingwood side shifting to the Philippines to become the 'Manila Folders'. Economic necessity and increased commercialization, then, is already changing the traditional face of at least one major sport.

This comes through, too, in the new electronic scoreboards at VFL Park and the Melbourne Cricket Ground. Giant television and advertising screens, they have the capacity for action replays. At present the replays extend beyond the restart of play. It will not be long before the restart will be delayed, basically to provide new advertising opportunities. So Australian football, which has long prided itself on its rapid and constant pace, will be on the way towards the American example where one hour of football takes almost three hours to complete. American football needed advertising. Now advertising largely dictates its pattern of play.

If these are new developments for Australia, then recent political events are more in the nature of reminders. When the New Zealand government argued that the 1977 Gleneagles Agreement did not force it to cancel the 1981 Springbok tour, the 1982 Commonwealth Games in Brisbane were placed in direct jeopardy. Black African nations threatened a boycott of the Games if New Zealand athletes were allowed to compete. The Australian government, mindful of its relatively high standing in Africa, worked very hard both directly and indirectly to have the New Zealand government alter its decision. While Australian official representatives in Wellington pressed hard formally, semi-official documents like the Department of Foreign Affairs' Backgrounder carried hardliner articles against apartheid in sport.

In the event the tour proceeded, with disastrous social results and a nasty election campaign for New Zealand. Australia almost escaped but not entirely unscathed.

Some African nations criticized the government for not taking firmer action, and it was well into 1982 before the British Commonwealth Games Federation reached a compromise which might allow Black African attendance in Brisbane.

Public concern was surprisingly low, with little media coverage or discussion. Despite Moscow, there was still a considerable 'it couldn't happen to us' attitude. That persisted even when the Prime Minister and the Queensland Premier adopted quite different postures over the problem. The politics of sport, then, flourish and grow more complex.

Very slowly, an awareness is growing that sport is an integral, influencing institution in Australian life, as a fitting finale to this note confirms. The New South Wales Rugby League, not normally considered a progressive body, during 1981–82 commissioned quite sophisticated social surveys to analyze the true roots of its attendance patterns and economic prospects. The bulk of its supporters were found to be stranded geographically far away from the majority of its clubs. On that basis, the League began drawing tentative plans for organizational reform. Such reconsideration of social position will become a regular feature of Australian sport.

Acknowledgement

The author thanks Sandi Bell for her wonderful assistance during the preparation of this essay.

References

Brohm, J.-M. *Sport: A Prison of Measured Time*. London: Ink Links, 1976.

Caillois, R. *Man, Play and Games*. New York: Free Press, 1961.

Cashman, R. and M. McKernan, eds. *Sport in History*. Brisbane: University of Queensland Press, 1979.

Cashman, R. and M. McKernan, eds. *Sport: Money, Morality and the Media*. Sydney: University of New South Wales Press, 1981.

Denny, R. *The Astonished Muse*. Chicago: University of Chicago Press, 1957.

Dunstan, K. *Sports*. Melbourne: Cassell, 1973.

Fitzpatrick, J. *The Bicycle in the Bush*. Melbourne: Oxford University Press, 1981.

Geertz, C. "Deep Play: Notes on the Balinese Cockfight." *Daedalus* 101, no. 1 (1972).

Gilbert, D. *The Miracle Machine*. New York: Coward, McGann and Geoghan, 1980.

Guttman, A. *From Ritual to Record: The Nature of Modern Sports*. New York: University of Columbia Press, 1978.

Huizinga, J. *Homo Ludens: A Study of the Play Element in Culture*. London: Temple Smith, 1970.

James, J. S. *The Vagabond Papers*. Melbourne: Melbourne University Press, 1969.

Lasch, C. *The Culture of Narcissism: American Life in an Age of Diminishing Returns*. New York: Norton, 1979.

Mandle, W. F. *Winners Can Laugh: Sport and Society*. Ringwood: Penguin, 1974.

Mandle, W. F. *Going It Alone: Australia's National Identity in the Twentieth Century*. Ringwood: Allen Lane, 1978.

Stoddart, B. "Sport and Society, 1890–1940: A Foray." In *A New History of Western Australia*, edited by C. T. Stannage. Perth: University of Western Australia Press, 1981.

Tatz, C. "The Degradation of Sport." *Weekend Australian*, 25–26 Oct. (1980).

Thompson, H. S. *The Great Shark Hunt: Strange Tales from a Strange Time*. London: Picador, 1979.

Cricket, Social Formation and Cultural Continuity in Barbados: A Preliminary Ethnohistory

Introduction

Inevitably, I ended up writing West Indies. Remembering those Ashburton backyard days, decoding James, playing cricket in different places, observing the South Asian passion and working on Bodyline, Caribbean cricket obviously had special meaning. I read all I could, especially Orlando Patterson's seminal piece, and the sense of significance intensified. Some false starts delayed my physical arrival there, though, and they illustrated some early sports historians' professional travails.

The Indian experience said fieldwork was essential, but the Caribbean was and remains a difficult place to access easily from Australia. In 1977 I joined the WA Institute of Technology (now Curtin University of Technology) to teach social science, and after three years was eligible for study leave (sabbatical, that hangover from days colonial when progress and improvement could come only from a visit 'Home'), so I applied to visit the Caribbean to investigate the social history of cricket there. The study leave committee was troubled because the project looked more like fun than work (in truth, it was both) and was it academic? Application versions multiplied, questioning intensified, and the frustration was such that I contemplated leaving the academy for journalism.

Then came the offer to join Bill Mandle at the Canberra College of Advanced Education (CAE) (now the University of Canberra) where he created the Centre for Sports Studies to support educationally the new Australian Institute of Sport. Bill was *the* sports history *guru*, so anyone with a claim in the field applied and fortunately I won out. Bill made me a full-time 'sports' person, and his commitment ensured the future study of Australian sports culture. An extraordinary character now retired from his sports work some way back, he made it possible for all of us, and for me in particular. Physically towering with blazing eyes, mercurial intellect and unpredictable temperament, Bill was an enigma to many. A working-class kid from Barrow-in-Furness who made it on scholarship to Pembroke College, Oxford, Bill worked in Adelaide and New Zealand before arriving at the Australian National

University where he was Reader in History before transferring to the CAE for complex reasons.

I met Bill at the 1977 conference where he was the central figure, the only person who had really published on sport, and he had endured his own problems with the history establishment in placing those pieces. Soon after, I invited him to a Perth conference where upon arrival he opened his suitcase to reveal a VB beer six-pack – he thought it unavailable! Mandle stories are legion. At one early *Sporting Traditions* conference he declared that two men in suits were from ASIO (the Australian Security and Intelligence Organization) tracking a speaker – they were in fact accountants intrigued by the idea of a sports conference. Bill was in the press constantly and, after a typical piece attacking rugby league, I found him anxiously on the watch for a league fan intent on coming to Canberra from Sydney to kill Mandle. Bill would convene Faculty executive meetings in his office then, when an argument arose, get up from his chair and leave the room. He discussed one of his marriage breakups in detail live on radio. In 1991 I succeeded Bill as Dean after his 'spend it until they say stop' management approach indebted the Faculty and forced University managers to move him out – it cut Bill deeply and our relationship was never really the same after.

He remains one of the most powerful minds I have ever encountered: a conservative with a deeply considered position who could still support the likes of me with vastly different ideas, scathing though he was of theory and cultural studies – committed to the Newman university view, he could still pioneer Sports Studies because he believed in knowledge and curiosity. He forced people to think intellectually about sport. In all the time I worked with him it was never dull and frequently 'on the edge'.

After three years in Canberra I was again eligible for study leave and revived the Caribbean claim. Yet another committee had problems with it, aided by the aforementioned College Principal who was a very long way from Bill Mandle's insights and innovations. After several attempts approval arrived, I put all my leave together, added unpaid leave, and went to Barbados for a year to research the game's history and play my last competitive cricket season.

By then, I had read a great deal of anthropology, particularly social anthropology and ethnography from people such as Clifford Geertz through to George Marcus via Victor Turner and on further to (in my view) historical anthropologists such as Greg Dening and Marshall Sahlins. It seemed to me that much of sport was about anthropology in that it involved cultural transformation/preservation and social practice as adaptation. The film *Trobriand Cricket* made a big impression on me, and I had started to collect some excellent materials on Samoan cricket (that would appear in a chapter on 'Other Cultures' that I had in the book Keith Sandiford and I edited, *The Imperial Game*). Given that, I approached the Caribbean work with an even more anthropological stance than I had done with my doctoral work on India, testimony to the fact that we can learn by experience.

So, early in 1984, we flew into Sir Grantley Adams International Airport at Bridgetown and Sandi remarked, 'Well, you have finally made it'. It was to be one of the best years of my life because so many things happened and I learned so much. Above all, my work was welcomed and appreciated for the first time. My great friend Woodville Marshall, Professor of History at the Cave Hill Campus of the University of the West Indies, commented at our first meeting that 'they' were glad I was there to research a cricket history to which they were too close. It was a sobering moment, but it made the journey to that point all the more worthwhile.

* * * * *

Just 166 miles square and the most windward of the Caribbean islands, Barbados has long possessed a reputation for being culturally and economically dominated by the production of sugar, and for being a 'Little England'.[1] The two circumstances are inextricably connected. Barbados was a British colony from 1627 until the coming of political independence in 1966, and for all that time its level of prosperity was determined by fluctuations in the sugar industry. To some extent it still is, despite the encouragement of mass tourism since the 1960s. During the long colonial period the social organization geared to produce the sugar wealth was based upon British concepts of economic ordering, political power and social distancing between elaborately defined caste categories. This social order was founded in the period from the 1650s until 1838, during which time Barbados derived its wealth from a slave-based economy organized in a plantation system. The owners were either British-based absentees or descended from British stock; the labour force was African or of African descent. Middle level management was largely white, as was the commercial trading sector, although in both a small mulatto element had appeared by the late eighteenth century. After the final emancipation of the slaves in 1838, the legal relationship between these groups might have altered but the social one did not – British law, British custom, British social conventions and British culture continued to direct the island's development. The results are intriguing. On an island with a population now exceeding 250,000 and a per square mile density of over 1,200, the 97 per cent of the community descended from African slaves are located in a cultural construct established by white arbiters whose descendants now comprise less than 3 per cent of the population.

The present legislative system, political parties, educational structure, Anglican religion and the English language itself (or, at least, a distinctive form of it) are all tangible products of this long British heritage as they are in a number of other non-white majority, post-colonial settings. But unlike those other settings, in Barbados it is cricket, that most English of games, which is the most striking and influential benchmark and cultural monument to the British social influence.[2] Barbados is renowned as the most prolific per capita producer of top flight players in the world and Bajans, wherever found, are persistently and passionately devoted to the playing of and talking about cricket. This is quite unlike the situation elsewhere as in, say, India where only a tiny percentage of the population based in relatively few centres and concentrated in a restricted number of social communities displays a passionate devotion to cricket.[3] In Barbados cricket is not so much a game which inspires enthusiasm as a cultural institution, a way of life in itself.

This deep social reach may be illustrated briefly in a number of ways. From the late nineteenth century until well into the twentieth, and even now on special occasions, shops, offices and schools were closed while important matches were in progress. From at least the turn of the twentieth century, citizens would identify themselves by their playing or supporting connections with a cricket club, as in 'Spartan man', for example. When responsible government came to Barbados in 1954, the swearing-in ceremony had to be rescheduled so as to avoid a clash with an important match. Independence itself, in 1966, was celebrated with a special cricket game. Cricket is still a constant subject of conversation in rumshops, the workplace, the streets, homes, parties and on buses, while a match anywhere on the island will draw spectators from those passing by. Even visitors from other cricketing cultures, let alone those from non-playing areas such as North America, are overwhelmed at the extent of Barbadians' devotion to the game. Because of that deep attachment, then, an analysis of cricket's social dimensions and history necessarily becomes an investigation into the inner workings of Barbadian society as a whole.

This preliminary sketch of the relationship between cricket and its Barbadian social setting is based upon 1985 fieldwork which employed two main research strategies.[4] The first involved social history methods in investigating archival, institutional and private materials, surveying primary and secondary sources in both empirical and theoretical areas, as well as conducting extensive oral history sessions. The second strategy was ethnographic, principally through playing membership in a club participating in the major Barbadian domestic cricket competition. That membership (which according to one former Barbadian and West Indian cricketer meant 'living' rather than 'studying' the game) facilitated access to players, administrators, clubs and club life, cricket supporters, sports journalists, cricket folklore and the social practices of cricket in many different Barbadian contexts. The essay, then, analyses the centrality of cricket in Barbadian life in light of the game's history on the island, but begins with some necessary and fundamental observations about the cultural context in which the game developed there.

Debate concerning the precise nature of Barbadian social structure and 'culture' has swung largely upon whether or not its evolution has been influenced most by British, African or Creole emphases.[5] It is not an abstract debate because any positions adopted have a strong bearing upon prevailing attitudes towards class, colour and politics. One conventional wisdom, for example, has it that since at least 1966 blacks have dominated political life in the island and whites the economy.[6] While this economic pattern and associated social patterns have begun to change recently, they still retain some validity. Such retentions have reinforced popular beliefs in the existence of separate, carefully delineated and vigorously defended social circles defined by colour, economic standing and status. Supporters of the Creolisation theory, however, have emphasized the steady emergence of a hybrid culture created jointly by blacks, whites and mulattos, thereby softening the idea of separate cultural circles. Important and interesting though these analyses are, they oversimplify or even ignore a more complex cultural condition in which cricket figures prominently.

It may be argued that two general and competing cultures have co-existed in Barbados until well into the twentieth century.[7] One was British-originated and identified historically with that white ruling class which dominated plantation ownership and commercial activity. From at least the beginning of the nineteenth century, if not earlier, these ruling whites gained considerable support from better-off, free blacks and mulattos who sought advancement, limited though it was, in the island's white-dominated social and economic hierarchy. As early as 1837, for example, many elementary schoolteachers were blacks who not only taught an English classical curriculum but also strongly upheld its attendant cultural values and behavioural attitudes.[8] Despite the small and steadily declining numbers of whites, then, their cultural practices from an early point gained considerable credibility as a result of its support by sections of the non-white community seeking an accommodation with the ruling order.

In distinction, and essentially in opposition to this, a folk culture persisted strongly within the black majority descended from African slaves. This folk culture was maintained through such practices as bush medicine, obeah (known more popularly and inaccurately as black magic), tuk band music (employing distinctly African rhythms and African-descended instruments such as drums and whistles), community dances and festivals.[9] These practices were essentially both a rejection of white culture and the defence of a black one, thereby establishing a considerable tension between the two.

The strengths of this folk culture, and the potential depth of the tension, were best revealed in the attacks made upon it by the ruling white order and its non-white supporters. For a considerable period after emancipation the police, the judiciary, the church and the educational system attempted to wipe out obeah and folk music in an effort to incorporate the black majority within the ruling culture.[10] These enforcing agencies were themselves part of a system of social coercion established by the plantocracy-controlled legislative bodies in order to replace the forms of authority held previously in the little political worlds of the individual plantations. A most important strand here was the 1840 master and servant legislation which turned chattel slaves into estate-tied wage slaves. But there also arose the police force, the militia and a range of incarceratory institutions (such as jails and asylums) designed to bring former slaves under direct state jurisdiction.[11] 'Undesirable' social elements became defined as vagrants, petty thieves, the insane and the poor, and were consequently subjected to an increasing range of thoroughgoing state controls. The creation of central markets for meat and vegetables, for example, was not simply about 'modernizing' commodity supplies.[12] It also enhanced respect for property because by licensing dealers, state authorities sought to minimize praedial larceny (the stealing of food crops) which was directed largely against the major landholders, the former slave masters.

While coercion certainly made substantial inroads into the folk culture, on its own it proved incapable of generating servility and acquiescence among the freed black majority. In the 1860s, food riots revealed possibilities for the rejection of constituted authority. The greatest challenge to that authority came during the so-called Federation Riots in 1876 when large crowds turned out against landholders, marching on plantations in support of an English governor who was apparently seeking to break planter power.[13] In 1895 rebellious bands again marched on food crop fields, invoking in song the memories and spirit of 1876.[14] Occasions such as these created fears within the elite about potential social dislocation and a breakdown in the dependent status of the black masses. It became clear, then, that the former slavemasters now required a new form of moral authority to augment, perhaps even to replace the coercive powers which in some senses had simply replaced one form of slavery with another.

As a result, such non-coercive and largely voluntary institutions as the education system and the church were utilized to instill in the population a set of values which produced the behaviour patterns desired by the powerbrokers whose traditional social, economic and political advantages would thus go untrammelled. This was achieved by such means as a careful construction of the school curriculum and by the teachings of the numerically powerful Church of England. This created the illusion of popular access to cultural agencies, yet, in reality, maintained the structural bases of discrimination and inequality. During the second half of the nineteenth century, for example, basic educational instruction was provided for most children, but the prominent education development lay in elite secondary schools such as Harrison College and The Lodge.[15] By 1900 there were 25,000 students under instruction, but only 205 of these were in the two elite colleges which serviced the plantation and commercial elite, grooming those who would inherit the relatively few positions available in the civil service and the professions.[16] The church, too, displayed internal divisions.[17] Throughout the island's eleven parishes, which were also local government bases controlled by rectors and churchwardens, pew rents yielded positions of prestige and symbolic power to the local elites. From St Michael's Cathedral down, churches set aside specified areas for whites and blacks with the latter relegated to back rows or galleries.

Strong though these cultural institutions were in preserving the dominance of the white tradition over that of the folk while at the same time apparently accommodating a new, post-slavery social order, none were individually as powerful as cricket in creating virtually without protest a consensual Barbadian society. While the education system and the church might from time to time encounter criticisms for the reality of their discriminations as opposed to the illusion of their equality, cricket rarely if ever did, even though its practices were essentially more restrictive than those of the other agencies. While cricket apparently allowed the two cultures to meet in social unity, its organizational and participatory forms preserved the exclusiveness of those cultures more effectively and for longer than other institutions, and also maintained traditional hierarchies within the cultures. The consensual as opposed to the coercive manner in which this was achieved must be underlined because, as Ashis Nandy argues:

> Modern colonialism won its great victories not so much through its military and technological prowess as through its ability to create secular hierarchies incompatible with the traditional order. These hierarchies opened up new vistas for many, particularly for those exploited or cornered within the traditional order. To them the new order looked like – and here lay its psychological pull – the first step towards a more just and equal world.[18]

In Barbados, cricket constituted such a secular hierarchy as confirmed in two particular ways.

The first involves important theoretical literature which supports the significance of cricket as a Barbadian and Anglophone Caribbean cultural institution. In 1963 C.L.R. James emphasized the role of cricket and English literature in his personal development, arguing that the cultural code which they instilled made him quite different from his mainstream Marxist colleagues. Orlando Patterson later suggested that because of its connotations of a white colonial plantocracy and commercial domination, Caribbean people would never be 'free' until they rejected cricket. Subsequent commentators such as W.K. Marshall, St Pierre, T. Marshall and Thompson have developed aspects of this debate to explain the role of Caribbean cricket in the construction of colour relations, colonial class and post-colonial political evolution.[19] Throughout this writing runs the largely unstated themes of cultural domination, resistance and consensus. For that reason such analysis is further supported by the literature on social reproduction, cultural studies and social history derived largely from Gramsci. Briefly, work from analysts such as Gramsci, Bourdieu, Hall and Williams has confirmed the importance of cultural institutions in creating social consensus which often overrides the interests of the bulk of the community involved.[20] Cricket in Barbados was one such institution.

The second importance of cricket as a major influence in Barbadian cultural evolution centres upon the game's emergence in its modern form coinciding with the Barbadian ruling order's search for a moral authority. While the first recorded match occurred on the island early in the nineteenth century, regular games were being staged by the 1840s and Barbados played its first representative match, against British Guiana, in 1865. Given the particular needs of their political culture, the Barbadian ruling order then took up with enthusiasm that 'games revolution' which occurred in, and was transported from, Britain during the later nineteenth century.[21] Cricket gained a reputation as a game through which young people (men, mostly) might be trained for their social and occupational missions in life. Through games the middle and upper ruling classes learned respect for authority, loyalty, honesty, courage, persistence, teamwork and humility. The language of sport became a code, so that to 'play the game' meant not so much to be involved in simple physical activity as to subscribe to the social conventions and beliefs which sport symbolized. Manuals on all games were replete with advice on social etiquette and behaviour. Socializing institutions such as the public schools, universities and the established church embraced this sporting philosophy whose power underlay the life of Britain and its colonial empire by the last quarter of the nineteenth century.

It was this cultural modelling through cricket, specifically, which served as an important bridge between the two major Barbadian cultures where other institutions were not nearly so effective. Through cricket most Barbadians pledged their faith in a social system predicated upon British cultural values, British concepts of social progress, British morality codes, British behavioural standards and British attitudes towards social rankings. In so doing, Barbadians at large accepted the framework of social power elaborated by the dominant culture to replace that lost in 1838.[22] Transformation from slave-master to contract-master was acquiesced to by the former slaves who became labour servants, as were the social systems, cricket chief among them, which reproduced the patterns of inequality. For that reason, the structure of Barbadian cricket provides an important analytical starting point.

Given its small size and population, the island possesses an unusually elaborate cricket organization strongly defined by its social heritage. The Barbados Cricket Association is the senior body, incorporated by a 1933 Act of Parliament as successor to the Barbados Cricket Committee which had been established in the early 1890s to organize local competition as well as control visiting teams.[23] Then there is the Barbados Cricket League, formed in 1936 to cater for the needs of the lower and working-class black majority. Between them, these two associations now supervise in excess of 140 teams. In addition, however, there are modified cricket forms administered by such bodies as the Barbados National Softball Cricket Association and the Barbados Tapeball Cricket Association. Beyond these groups sectional bodies such as business houses, trade unions, local communities and groups of friends also organize matches on a regular competitive basis. At any given point in a competition season, there are probably in excess of 1,000 teams playing cricket on an island of 166 square miles where land is a scarce resource, a sure pointer to both the popularity and cultural importance of the game.

That popularity and importance is further revealed in the largely but not exclusively juvenile world of unstructured cricket found on beaches, waste lands, public parks and even on streets. This unstructured cricket has long provided the breeding ground for the island game and one interviewee recalled substantial sums of money resting upon the results of street matches played in one working-class village during the 1930s. That points to the necessity of qualifying the word 'unstructured' because such cricket, too, has had organized elements since the later nineteenth century, as revealed in the persistence of 'firms' and 'marble' cricket.[24] In firms, a number of boys band together to control bat and ball at the expense of other players, thereby enhancing their opportunities to develop superior skills. Marble cricket is a miniature game designed to accommodate small playing areas with participants kneeling to bat, bowl and field. Beneath this elaborate, strong and deeply respected cricket structure lie the central concerns of a dominant culture which sought the widespread acceptance of its practices and objectives as a detailed analysis of what that structure suggests.

The Barbados Cricket Committee was a self-appointed, self-constituted, self-selected and self-perpetuated group drawn from the most eminent sections of the late-nineteenth-century Barbadian elite. It was a cricketing extension of the economic and political oligarchy, dominated particularly by wealthy merchants. As the plantations fell more and more into their hands from 1900 onwards, these merchants inherited the social mores of the plantocracy which had controlled the quest for moral authority and consensual cohesion to replace political coercion. The merchants on the Committee were joined in their beliefs by others of the elite whose fortunes, directly or indirectly, depended upon sugar: business executives, lawyers, accountants, medical practitioners, senior civil servants and elite school headmasters. A significant number of members remained with the BCC from its creation to its demise, a fact which emphasizes the continuity of its cultural philosophy. Its colour remained as constant as its class – one or two mulattos appeared but it was otherwise overwhelmingly white.

By the early 1930s, however, the worldwide economic crisis had hit these sugar barons hard and many of them were unable to continue supporting cricket financially.[25] That led to the creation of a new administrative body, the Barbados Cricket Association, but not to new social attitudes because it has continued many Barbados Cricket Committee practices and traditions. Its Board of Management continues to be made up largely of business directors, company executives and managerial officers connected with trading conglomerates spawned from sugar industry concerns.[26] Service industry personnel such as lawyers and accountants are still prominent. There is still a high degree of personal continuity. In the more than fifty years since its foundation there have been just five presidents, and one secretary held his post from 1946 until well into the 1980s. Similarly, there have been just five treasurers, and numerous examples of long committee service on the Board of Management. Besides their occupational backgrounds, the majority share an elite school and often post-secondary education, and high social status. This last point is complicated by being bound up in the changing colour structure of the Association.

Until at least 1966 the management was predominantly white, and only in recent years have blacks become numerous. In 1985, of the thirteen executive officers four were white including the president, junior vice-president and secretary. This is a high proportion given the population balance between blacks and whites, emphasizing both the continuity factor and the power of cricket as an agency of minority cultural dominance. While in the past the whites and non-whites would not have mixed outside Board circles, that is no longer entirely the case because non-white members are being drawn increasingly into the wider business managerial structure where they work along with, and share many cultural values held by, whites.[27] The colour composition of the Board might have changed, that is, but the inherent cultural attitudes continue to reflect those of the old Barbados Cricket Committee because the non-white members have consistently shared with the whites an occupational, educational and social background which has preserved many of the demarcations established between different social groups during the second half of the nineteenth century. The Association management, then, is a high status, homogeneous and largely static body in terms of its composition, even though it is theoretically subject to democratic processes within a general membership which now exceeds 1,100.

The Barbados Cricket League was founded in 1936, just after the Association, but enjoyed a far sketchier heritage than that provided by the old Barbados Cricket Committee. Some short-lived bodies organized cricket outside Committee auspices at various times beginning from 1902, but there was no continuous leadership or organizational structure.[28] The League's guiding principle was to provide regular competitive cricket for poor blacks whose colour and status ruled them socially ineligible for Association teams. As a result, the League is still perceived as the 'mass' cricket organization in comparison with that of the 'elite' Association. That view is reinforced by most League teams (which far outnumber the 47 competing in the Association) having a strong country-village base unlike the Association whose teams are largely drawn from the Bridgetown city and suburban area. League administrators have come from more humble origins than their Association counterparts. J.M. (Mitchie) Hewitt, the founder, was a journalist come up the ranks; a journalist colleague of similar background served as president, and artisans were prominent in management positions.[29] A recent change has seen the President come from a senior civil service position and a higher status educational background. The League shares continuity with the Association, however. Hewitt was Secretary from 1936 until his death in 1969, while his journalist colleague served a similarly long term. On the evidence of their management composition, then, the Association and the League have occupied quite different positions in the local status system and those differences have started to soften only recently.

From the cultural viewpoint, however, there has been a distinct similarity of objective between the two bodies: to have an increasing number of players accept the cricket code of behaviour and social ethics derived from Victorian England, first laid down by the Committee and later protected by the Association. Clearly, this acceptance involves the League not initiating its own code but inculcating its members into that promoted by the senior body. From its inception, the League has demonstrated a strong concern to match the playing and non-playing standards apparently reached in the Association. Individuals and teams have been consistently punished for breaches of discipline, violations of agreed ethical codes or 'unsportsmanlike' behaviour with the yardstick standards taken over from the Association.[30] The objective has been to graduate players of lower status and caste ranking into the practices of a higher social order.

That point underlines the strong social ranking system which has dominated the evolution of Barbadian cricket, and emphasizes that equality of participation has been based upon social recognition rather than playing attainments. League successes, such as having players selected for Barbados representative teams or having a League side accepted into the Association competition, have all been interpreted as evidence of social 'improvement' or acceptance rather than as recognition of simple playing ability.[31] But perhaps the strongest evidence for this social ranking and dominant cultural power within Barbadian cricket comes from the histories of its clubs.

Until 1939 there were four major long-term teams in the dominant Association competition: Wanderers, Pickwick, Spartan and Empire. Wanderers was founded in 1877 and until independence its members, playing and general, were drawn from plantation owners, major business house proprietors, very senior civil servants and people of otherwise high social status and independent wealth.[32] Until the late 1960s its playing membership was exclusively white, and it is still considerably white. Its general membership is still noticeably white leavened by mulattos and high status blacks, and it is now the main venue for the few white players seeking to play high-class cricket.

Pickwick was formed in 1882 and its membership has constantly differed from that of Wanderers, with the exception of its whiteness.[33] Business house wage staff, plantation and factory managerial or supervisorial personnel, commercial house employees such as insurance salesmen, and lower level civil servants have traditionally characterized the Pickwick membership. It was the mid-1970s before non-whites became a significant element in that membership, and the general perception of Pickwick still focusses upon its fiercely defended white heritage. One rival club supporter remarked acidly that a former Pickwick stalwart must be 'spinning in his grave' now that the first division side is largely made up of blacks.[34] Wanderers and Pickwick, then, were rival clubs within a numerically small white minority with the rivalry based on finely wrought class and status considerations. For example, one excellent Pickwick player of the interwar period, a sugar factory manager, was once kept at work beyond the normal Saturday time by the owner of the factory who was a Wanderers supporter – the two normally had a good working relationship, but this was the occasion of a Wanderers versus Pickwick fixture.[35]

Spartan was formed in the early 1890s as the first non-white club and consisted mostly of lawyers, medical practitioners, elite schoolmasters, higher level civil servants and the few non-whites to have penetrated the managerial levels of the business, commercial and plantation worlds. Although not exclusively so, there was a significant mulatto element in Spartan.[36] Symbolically, its foundation President was a mulatto who became Barbados' first and only non-white Chief Justice until the second half of the twentieth century. Many Spartan members were involved in pre-1937 political life, and almost without exception were found in conservative rather than radical camps. Sir Grantley Adams, as he became, was a most interesting example.[37] Like C.L.R. James, Adams imbibed English cricket and culture from his schoolmaster father. He attended Harrison College and Oxford University, then became a lawyer, as well as a good enough cricketer to represent Barbados in 1924. During the 1920s he was a public critic of the fledgling radical movement, opposing its socialist tendencies. It was well into the 1930s before he moved towards a more mass-based political position, symbolized by the lending of his name to the low status Barbados Cricket League at its formation.[38] Adams became the first Chief Minister of Barbados, then Prime Minister of the shortlived West Indies Federation. He never lost his admiration for English cricket or English culture, or for Spartan and its membership which became increasingly influential in political, economic and social spheres.[39] Spartan maintained a jealous watch over that membership, a concern which led directly to the creation of Empire in 1914.

Herman Griffith, a lower middle-class black player of outstanding ability was consistently denied membership in Spartan, some of whose members with minimum status (they included a minor businessman and a professional musician) subsequently seceded to form Empire in protest.[40] Griffith established an excellent intercolonial and international career, and built around him at Empire a tightly knit group of similarly lower middle-class players. It was said that Empire men were either sanitary inspectors or elementary schoolmasters, but self-employed businessmen, minor civil servants and shop clerks were also prevalent. Like Spartan, Empire has never had a white player and few if any amongst its general membership. While the lines of social demarcation between the two clubs have blurred somewhat, members of both date that from the mid-1970s at the earliest and even now there is a sense of Spartan being drawn more from the black managerial than from lower status groups.

Several points are worth making about the social ranking of these clubs and on their relationship with ruling cultural practices. Their strong and lengthy maintenance of exclusiveness is striking. The community at large was theoretically moving towards more open social interaction from the 1890s to the 1970s through the creation of popular political parties, a widening franchise, an extension of the education system, legislation against racial discrimination and reform in landholding patterns to name a few. But these cricket clubs have been instrumental in preserving conservative and dominant patterns of caste relationships consolidated during the second half of the nineteenth century until well into the second half of the twentieth century. This was achieved largely by a high continuity of membership type, as five-yearly profiles drawn up for the clubs suggest – by 1965 they retained essentially the same types of people as they had in the 1890s.[41] That continuity was itself maintained through an oversupply of players being constantly available for a restricted number of places. Even where they fielded teams in all three Association competitive levels following the Second World War, these clubs catered for a very small percentage of the cricket-playing male population so that admission policies could maintain strict social criteria as well as playing ability. The most notable relaxation has been in the colour coding, not least because of substantial alterations to white demographics since 1966 – total numbers have fallen steadily while the cricket-playing age brackets have been undermined further by either permanent or long-term temporary emigration for educational and/or occupational reasons.

Another important element in this exclusiveness was its self-imposed or, at least, non-contested nature. None of the clubs had any rules or constitutional provisions which specified the socially acceptable dimensions of their membership.[42] Former players recall that they 'knew' which club to join; it was a tacitly accepted conventional wisdom based upon rigid social categorization.[43] Moreover, there was a recognized feeder system for these clubs. Whites and blacks might play together while at Harrison College, but upon leaving school they would 'find' themselves at Wanderers and Spartan respectively. Whites from The Lodge went to Pickwick more frequently than

Wanderers, while blacks and whites from Combermere (with its commercial educational orientation) gravitated to Empire and Pickwick. Exceptions generally proved the rule. One player recalled that in the early 1930s he was among the first Harrison College products to join Empire, largely because he was a 'poor black boy' whose education resulted from a scholarship rather than from established family wealth or status. And the first black to join Wanderers in modern times (in the late 1960s) was an ex-Lodge man with an outstanding academic and athletic record as well as a respectable social background, who went on to hold very high civil service positions. Clearly, the sociology of popular knowledge combined with careful club selection policies to maintain traditions of social differentiation until well into the post-independence period.

This rigid and persistent classification extended into all other clubs which joined the Barbados Cricket Association after 1914, and especially to the Barbados Cricket League whose membership from the outset ranged from agricultural labourers to skilled artisans and all the occupational categories between. The most obvious evidence of the low status accorded to these players concerns those who attempted to shift from League teams into the Association. Almost the only possible team available for such transfer was Empire and it guarded its ranks jealously. It might have been a black club with an underprivileged reputation but it was by no means 'poor black', so the working classes faced considerable difficulties in trying to enter Empire. One story has an Empire official altering an applicant's stated occupation from 'Ice Company employee' to 'ice vendor' – the status connotations in the change are both obvious and important. A League fast-bowling star of the Second World War period recalls that he attempted to join Empire in order to improve his cricket prospects, and was shattered to have his request denied on the grounds that he was a lowly 'messenger' for a small business and therefore socially unsuitable for the club.

Some very successful players did move from the League into the Association as early as the 1940s but they had to be exceptionally successful, show potential for adopting dominant cultural standards and be fortunate enough to strike the right circumstances. But it was really the 1970s before such players began to move in numbers and with relative ease. That change coincided with the admission of whole League teams into the Association competition with one, St. Catherine, now in First Division, and a number of others dominating lower grades. This is probably the beginning of a real change in the traditionally rigid status divisions but, even so, incoming clubs are vetted carefully for their off-field behaviour and their initial performances in that regard are monitored closely. Such clubs are still socially 'on trial' because they are perceived to differ substantially from those which have traditionally appeared in the Association. This attitude is firmly grounded in both a belief and an acceptance that quite complex social differences and venues exist within Barbados, facilitated by cultural institutions such as cricket clubs.

It is important to remember that from the immediate post-emancipation period onwards, these infinitely graded social divisions continued to be preserved in Barbados not so much by law as by social practice, as in the cricket case. From Schomburgk onwards, visitors to Barbados inevitably referred to the existence there of a greater degree of colour consciousness and discrimination than found elsewhere in the Anglophone Caribbean. Complex and close defined social levels were codified and accepted upon the twin, intersecting indicators of class and colour. Trollope reported that non-whites were never met in Barbadian 'society'. Chester thought Barbadian whites still maintained a 'strong feeling in favour of slavery'. McLellan confirmed the existence of numerous divisions based upon colour and class. Macmillan considered Barbados the most socially exclusive and conscious of the Caribbean territories. Fermor reported the existence of considerable colour prejudice. Swanton and Blackburne remarked similarly on the noticeable social distances observed in Barbados.[44] Local writers were not so prolific on the theme; many of them were more keen to accommodate the cultural elite. But the few who did comment were extremely critical as revealed in Bernard, Wickham, and Harewood.[45] The consistency of these reports indicates the deep implantation in Barbadian life of ideas about social relations based upon the cultural precepts of the minority cultural elite, and mediated by institutions such as cricket.

In the century from 1870 these deepseated and rigid views were consolidated by the intersection of economic pressure and political conservatism through which the minority elite attempted to maintain its dominant position. The sugar industry experienced some 'highs' such as the First World War boom when European beet supplies were disrupted, in the early 1930s when British imperial preference systems boosted prices, and during the 1960s when world prices reached high levels.[46] For the most part, however, the industry faced depression as in the 1890s when a British Royal Commission was necessitated, during the 1920s when a world glut forced prices very low, and the 1970s, when began a steady decline after a promising beginning.[47] In response to this pattern the Barbadian sugar aristocracy, from 1900 a coalition of the most successful and surviving members of the plantocracy together with the new businessmen planters, was moved reluctantly into changes in production systems, financing arrangements, labour relations and so-called peasant landholding patterns.[48] One major result was that living conditions for the black majority declined to such a point that by the outbreak of labour and political disturbances in 1937 they were among the worst in the region if not the Empire.[49] The long-term ruling elite held the ring through its control over the Legislative Assembly and the Executive Council, bodies whose power was untouched until the introduction of limited popular government in 1944, followed by the introduction of ministerial government in 1954, then independence in 1966.[50]

During this long period of economic and political change, cultural institutions such as formalized cricket vigorously maintained those patterns of social relationships, based upon class and colour considerations, which had been elaborated during the post-emancipation moral authority quest in order to maintain the social power of a cultural minority. As the cricket case demonstrates, cultural organizations maintained until well into the post-independence period quite elaborate systems of social discrimination which would have been unacceptable in government, civil service and commercial sectors. In 1900, for example, the Trinidad-born and Harrison-educated English cricket boss Pelham Warner argued that Caribbean cricket standards would not improve until non-whites participated without restriction. Yet as late as 1970 the Barbadian international player Charlie Griffith could still point to a high degree of colour and class prejudice in the organization of Barbadian cricket.[51] During the intervening seventy years players and spectators alike had accepted the social parameters of cricket and few challenged them. It may be argued, then, that the process of social change generally was modified by the conservative construction of voluntary institutions such as cricket. As Herman Griffith is alleged to have remarked, 'if it had not been for cricket we would have been at each others' throats'.[52]

While the sharpness of the divisions has now been blunted, the underlying attitudes are still extant. Wanderers members suggest that it took a long time to introduce non-whites to the club because of the need to preserve an atmosphere where 'talk' might be free and 'families' could be brought, so newcomers had to be vetted carefully.[53] At Kensington Oval in 1985 a match between two Donwhite teams, one representing Pickwick, saw players drift away quickly at the close of play so that in the bar just one or two non-whites mixed with perhaps thirty whites who were mostly Pickwick Club members. Changes have occurred but will take time to consolidate and some perceptions of the changes are guarded – one former international player believes that non-white players admitted to formerly all-white clubs have no voting rights.[54] There is some substance to his claim. Permeating this exclusivity and its modern residual remains is the widespread belief in all quarters that the other parties prefer it that way, whites with whites and blacks with blacks, itself a firm pointer to the power of the dual culture and of cricket as the carefully controlled bridge.

One guide to this fundamental but masked conflict lies in the history of traditional club rivalries. At first the highlight of any season was always Wanderers versus Pickwick, especially up until 1914 when Committee officials organizing fixtures would pit those teams against each other on public holidays in order to give as many people as possible a chance to observe the great clash.[55] Early crowd data are unreliable but 8–10,000 spectators were not unusual, and many who attended wore appropriate colours to identify the team of their allegiance.[56] From these matches, Pickwick particularly gained a reputation for being relentless, determined opponents, and there was always a class-based edge to the clashes, the comfortable versus the not-quite-so-comfortable. Allegiance to a team was invariably for the entirety of a player's career because of that class consideration. Just before the First World War it was reckoned a sensational moment when a former Wanderers player turned out for Pickwick against his old club.[57] It was not so much a desertion of a team as of a caste group. Although the championship significance of Wanderers versus Pickwick matches declined after 1920 and public interest declined as well, teams themselves still approached the fixtures as of old. During one match in the 1960s, for example, Pickwick players changed in their cars, refusing to enter the Wanderers' pavilion alleging that a female Wanderers supporter had spat upon a Pickwick player during the first day of the match.[58] With the increasing non-white composition of both teams the hard edge is disappearing rapidly but the spirit is remembered.

From 1915 onwards the great clash was always between Spartan and Empire, partly because of the controversial origins of Empire, partly because of the subtle colour shadings, partly because of perceived class differences and partly because of the marvellous players involved (at any point between the 1920s and the 1960s one of these matches might have seen two, three or even more international players on each of the teams). One Empire player of the early 1930s recalls the roar from his team's supporters when he went out to bat, and his silent prayer: 'Lord, let me not disappoint these people today.' Another Empire player who began early in the 1940s remembers being stopped in the streets weeks before a match against Spartan and being 'advised' by groups of well-wishers. Players of both clubs remember this spirit existing into the 1970s and even now, although club distinctions have blurred, there is still an 'atmosphere' about an Empire-Spartan match.[59]

Two points are important about this rivalry in relation to the creation of a shared culture via cricket which, in turn, had considerable significance for social relations on the island. First, the meeting of these clubs in the annual rituals of their matches helped create a general belief in the essential openness of the society; cricket, that is, provided an apparent avenue for the meeting of different colour and class groups. Pickwick, for example, had a tradition that visiting players always had their after-match drinks paid for by the club. Empire players of the inter-war years recall that at Wanderers they were always assigned to a home player after the match and looked after, even to the point of being driven home by the wealthier white players.[60] All this, of course, was a momentary suspension of the island's normal caste conditions, but one which was widely subscribed to as an indication of what people considered might be the normal Barbadian position. Second, the crowds at all these matches were overwhelmingly black, and blacks were the most avid supporters of Wanderers and Pickwick. By supporting these quite different class and colour groups, Bajans again were demonstrating support for the ideals of cricket and culture as established during the nineteenth century by the creators of the moral authority system.

This pattern has continued since the late 1960s in the form of a representative team from the Barbados Cricket League playing in the Barbados Cricket Association competition. The arrangement replaced an annual match instituted in the late 1940s between representative teams of the two competitions. Given the League's history it is not surprising that matches between its teams and those from the Association have had a fierce competitive spirit. One longtime League member recalls Mitchie Hewitt being criticized by a black Association member for attempting to give regular cricket to 'ill-behaved, ignorant working men'.[61] Matches against white teams were strongly contested, but those against the socially exclusive Spartan club were highpoints for the League and to a degree remain so. The rivalry, as with that between other major clubs is rooted very strongly in the evolution of the island's specific social relations system. League teams have a highly developed social image as having 'come from the people', and an equally developed sense of other teams having been drawn from more privileged sections of the society. It is from the history of such social rankings that emerge two other important aspects of Barbadian cricket.

One concerns the cricketer as popular hero, with the patterns of adulation charting the slow changes in Barbadian cricket. In early days the heroes were drawn from the elite white culture with the bulk of their support coming from the black majority. During the 1890s the Pickwick giant, Clifford Goodman, was idolized whether helping his club beat Wanderers or Barbados defeat visiting teams.[62] From before the First World War until the 1930s George Challenor of Wanderers, Barbados and West Indies was feted as one of the best batsmen in the world.[63] Both Goodman and Challenor symbolized the power of the dominant cultural elite. Goodman came from a plantation managerial background and, of his famous cricketing brothers, P.A. Goodman became a secondary school headmaster renowned for discipline, and G.A. Goodman became Chief Justice in the Straits Settlement following a local political career. George Challenor came from a leading merchant family and, with his brother and fellow Barbados player, became a leading businessman planter. Challenor demonstrated this social position in classic English cricket cultural style. At practice he would place money on one of the three stumps and challenge net bowlers to claim it by bowling him. On the occasions when five dollars were put up, bowlers came from everywhere in the vicinity of the Wanderers ground.[64]

It is worth recalling that the very grounds themselves, such as Wanderers, reinforced the social hierarchies elaborated among the players, their spectators and the public at large. Playing areas were invariably donated by plantation owners and, in the League especially, this established a strong patron-client relationship between those owners and the cricketers, many of whom were often employed on the estates from which the grounds were carved. Even now, many of the smaller country grounds are overlooked by plantation houses. The strength of the subsequently created loyalties to team, plantation and patron were demonstrated graphically at Wanderers and Pickwick. Their strongest black supporters came from the tenantries of the old Bay and Kensington estates, respectively, and well into the 1940s those tenantries were among the worst slums in Barbados, underlining the ability of shared cultural values to override patently obvious social and economic inequalities.

Black cricket heroes began to emerge from the time of Herman Griffith whose Empire connections provided opportunities for a caste affiliation to parallel the loyalties to localities developed within the ranks of common supporters. What the black heroes did in an important sense, however, was to justify the underlying social philosophy of cricket. By following its precepts they were thought to have 'improved' and 'succeeded', to have 'risen' from the mass. That is, they not so much symbolized a challenge to the dominant cultural elite as constituted a justification for that elite's ideology – many of the new stars were seen, significantly, not just as 'good' players but as 'good' blacks who had learned their social lessons. Many potential black stars failed to make the grade because of social rather than playing misdemeanours.[65] Two of the most significant players with this 'success' story pattern have been Everton Weekes and Gary Sobers whose representative careers began in the early 1940s and early 1950s respectively.[66] Both came from poor, underprivileged backgrounds, Weekes from the New Orleans tenantry near Kensington Oval and Sobers from the Bay land adjoining the Wanderers ground. Both acquired their skills in 'gully', school and knockabout cricket, both frequented local Association club grounds where their talents were recognized by influential members. Both played for League clubs when very young, and both were 'drafted' into socially appropriate Association teams where places were made available: Weekes was helped to join the army which had an Association team for a short while; Sobers joined the Police as a band recruit. Only their exceptional talents made this Association entry possible, and both had patronage from influential Association men. Their very rise indicates just how rigidly prescribed the system was. By their cricket talents they then made their ways in the world as professional players, and cricket has continued to ensure their upward mobility.

It is difficult to convey adequately the awe in which these men have been held by the Barbadian public. Weekes retired in the mid-1960s, Sobers in the early 1970s, yet their stature grows rather than diminishes. Sobers received a knighthood from the Queen in 1975, an achievement interpreted as the ultimate sign of ability making all things possible in an 'open' society. Men in rumshops, at cricket grounds and other gathering places refer to 'Everton' and 'Gary' as if they were personal friends which, in one sense, they are. The Sobers story was thinly veiled in a mid-1970s festival play, and he has been mentioned as a Barbadian cultural icon in a number of popular calypsos, a sure sign of social significance.[67] These men remain mass heroes even though the lifestyle and status of both is vastly removed from their humble origins. But despite the fierce pride in their achievements, their stories are considered not so much a comment on the exclusivity barriers which they had to overcome, as an indication that through cricket in Barbados anything is possible provided the right lessons are learned. While they might recall how difficult things were, Weekes and Sobers are generally philosophical and harbour few if any grudges against a social structure which determined that, in the opinion of one of them, they had to be three times better than the average white player in order to be selected.

The widespread acceptance of this cultural consensus shows up best in the cases of players who did not conform, perhaps the best example being the late Sir Frank Worrell.[68] Born in Barbados he was a cricket prodigy playing for Combermere in senior competition at the age of 12 and attracting big crowds. Before he was 20 he had established world records and later became an international star; he was the first regular black captain of West Indies, and won a knighthood before his tragically premature death from leukemia. Although hailed, Worrell was never loved uncritically by Barbadians, largely because of his outspokenness about his dissatisfaction with cricket's social structuring and its relationship with the wider cultural pattern. He made no secret of his irritation with Barbadian exclusivity and prejudice and, after a stint in Trinidad, ended up in Jamaica. Shortly before his death he criticized Barbados for trying to demonstrate its regional superiority by organizing the match against the Rest of the World XI, and his burial on the Cave Hill campus of the University of the West Indies in Barbados was not without controversy.[69] During

1985 one interviewee, a white woman, remarked acidly that Worrell should not have been buried on the island because he did not love it or accept its ways.[70] Hero status was, and to some extent still is, accorded only to those who accept without question the internal ranking scale which from the outset has marked Barbadian cricket and its consensus cultural context.

The second aspect, in addition to the role of heroes which highlights the social depth and complexity of Barbadian cricket, concerns crowd behaviour which is most instructively examined through its prominent personalities of whom three are especially important here: Brittania Bill, Flannigan and King Dyal. The three cover the history of organized cricket in the island. Brittania Bill became famous late in the nineteenth century as a black supporter of English touring teams who followed their players everywhere, carrying a Union Jack to pronounce his great loyalty.[71] His message was that England carried all before it, and that its cricket players were the epitome of civilized, gentlemanly demeanour and to whose monarch, Queen Victoria, he had pledged undying loyalty. Right up until the First World War, visiting teams were astonished by the warmth of the welcome extended by the black majority, often to the point of being embarrassed by it.[72] While this loyalty was in line with a widespread allegiance to the monarchy and especially to Queen Victoria, in cricket it found its most popular expression. In particular, such allegiance sprang from a perceived shared bond with the Barbadian elite of the nineteenth century which established loyalty to both the monarchy and cricket after emancipation in 1838 (which symbolically, of course, matched Victoria's accession). The black Barbadian majority genuinely believed that obedience to the British cultural model, of which cricket was such a focal feature, was the means by which they would progress.

Fred Flannigan dominated the inter-war period and epitomized the idolizing of white stars by black men.[73] Flannigan himself was a player of ability who earned a living, as did many lower-class players, by providing practice to members of the Association clubs. In Flannigan's case it was Wanderers for whom he became an ardent supporter, and his idol was George Challenor. One of Flannigan's most famous remarks came during an intercolonial match when a black fielder kneeled to tie a shoelace for Challenor who was batting. 'That's right', shouted Flannigan to the fielder, 'on your knees before the Lord thy God, George Challenor'.[74] It was a graphic and symbolic representation of Barbadian social relations. Challenor, in fact, paid a retainer to Flannigan who became a mascot for the Barbados team when it travelled, and Challenor was always hailed as the living symbol of what cricket and Barbados stood for. There was no equality in that cricket system, rather there was a very carefully defined sense of social ranking and distance recognized by all those who were part of it, both carried over from and reinforcing relationships in the community at large.

Dundonald Redvers Dyal, better known as the self-proclaimed 'King' Dyal, came of age in the Flannigan era and is a strong pointer to the role of cricket in linking the folk and dominant cultures.[75] The son of a master tailor, Dyal is a flamboyant character who dresses extravagantly in a society where clothing is generally conservative. During a 1985 test match he appeared in two suits within two hours, one bright lime green and the other bright red, both with matching accessories including appropriately coloured pipes and walking sticks. King Dyal's 'subjects', especially during major matches, are the patrons in the public stands drawn from the masses. But his decrees proceed from a dedication to English cricket culture and tradition, to the precepts laid down by the organizers of the Committee and their Association successors and drawn up upon the needs of the minority elite culture. King Dyal is fiercely loyal to the illusion of cricket as an apolitical social agency, thereby demonstrating its very power to mask the inequalities and prejudices which would be criticized if they appeared in any other social venue.

Brittania Bill, Flannigan and King Dyal represent more than just a passionate devotion to cricket as a game. Their allegiance is based upon an acceptance of the cultural context in which the Barbadian game evolved. Following the Victorian games model cricket was 'emblematic', as older references have it, of life and social relations.[76] Any recognizable decline in cricket standards, therefore, has ramifications for wider social concerns. This concern is particularly noticeable in the contemporary 'hailers', the major supporters and constant followers of the important clubs. An excellent example occurred during 1985 after a team in a match-winning position failed to enforce victory. A younger player had batted for a long time, unable to adapt to the match circumstances. 'If you had known something about life', advised the chief hailer in the clubhouse later, 'if you had some experience, you would have known what to do. Understand what I mean? You have to learn experience.' A few weeks earlier the same hailer observed that men who appeared in court with such folk culture nicknames as 'Tall Boy' and 'Roughhouse' were never found in cricket because cricketers knew how to behave.[77] This, too, is the direct cultural heritage of that public school cricket code adumbrated in late nineteenth-century Britain and transplanted so successfully in Barbados where its moral principles are shared by two quite different cultural traditions.

One logical extension to this ethical and behavioural code concerns discipline both on and off the field. During 1985 there was considerable public debate about the origins of a perceived decline in Barbadian cricket standards, and many critics returned to some central points: younger players were not learning discipline, especially in the schools, and club life had degenerated as a consequence.[78] Cricket clubs in Barbados are important male social centres (a further reminder of the social centrality of cricket) where at most times of the week may be found members playing cards, dominos, darts, backgammon or table tennis, discussing cricket, other sport or current affairs, drinking or organizing social activities. This process has a long history and there is a concern in many quarters for a continued high standard of social conduct. Following one relatively insignificant after-match skirmish, two senior players of one club were suspended for the bulk of the 1985 season. They were allowed into the clubhouse but their suspension from playing was deliberately severe, according to some officials, in order to curb a decline in discipline: 'Fellows have to learn how to behave in public.'[79] Earlier in the season a promising young player was criticized severely for an open display of anger after being given out in a dubious umpiring decision. The decision might have been poor, said his critics, but as in life he must learn to take the hard knocks as well as to accept decisions made by those in authority.[80]

This deep, symbolic strain permeates Barbadian cricket crowds which are recognized as amongst the most knowledgeable in the world. That helps explain two of their most noticeable characteristics. The first is a pronounced social conservatism which has given the island a far better record of crowd behaviour than most of its Caribbean counterparts. This conservatism was displayed during a 1985 test match incident in which a New Zealand player on the field lowered his trousers to treat a leg injury. A now acceptable practice elsewhere in the cricket world, this act created an air of shock in Barbados. An off-duty police inspector in the members' stand seriously suggested that the player be charged with an indictable offence. The touring team's management was required to issue a public apology for what in Barbados was widely considered as a breach of the cricket/life morality code.[81]

The second important characteristic is the utter seriousness with which spectators approach the game, almost sharing in the action itself as they urge, encourage and almost will the players to better performances. At the heart of this activity is a desire to have observed and see performed the tacitly accepted conventions and traditions of play. Those players who do so are treated with respect, those who do not receive contempt. During the 1985 test match, for example, one spectator kept repeating to the New Zealand captain, 'Howarth, you can't bowl to Vivvy [Vivian Richards] without a sweeper'. When Richards proved the point by hitting yet another boundary the spectator held out his hands as if to say 'what more can I do?' and his neighbours all agreed.[82] The New Zealand captain had ignored a basic cricket concept and so was deemed unworthy of further assistance. In club matches it is not uncommon to see fielding captains adjusting their positionings in accordance with spectator advice such as 'give me a square leg'. When such adjustments are made, batsmen are then told to 'watch that man at square leg'. Spectators and players alike are involved in a joint process through which cricket and its attendant social symbolism proceed by way of a shared set of behavioural and moral principles which themselves have deep social significance more widely.

Cricket, then, has deeply influenced the shape and character of Barbadian life since the last quarter of the nineteenth century. Far from being a mirror image of community development, the game has been a major determinant of the unique cultural relationships established in Barbados between the descendants of a minority, dominant group and a mass, subordinate community whose potential for conflict has been considerable.[83] It is not simply that cricket has provided a 'safety valve'. Rather, in Barbados the game has provided on-going connections between two quite different cultural traditions through carefully regulated social meeting points, helping to reduce areas of potential conflict. At the same time, cricket has preserved well into the twentieth century a set of social relationships established during the mid-nineteenth century and which in other arenas of social life would be considered inappropriate. In cricket Barbados has one of its most conservative social and political institutions, a perfect example of the power of culture in the face of general social, economic and political change.

Acknowledgements

The author wishes to thank the Canberra College of Advanced Education for making available the leave around which the research project was based, the University of the West Indies (Cave Hill) which elected him as Visiting Fellow in History for 1985, and all these people in Barbados who assisted the research.

Notes

[1] For the Barbados story: Schomburgk, *The History of Barbados*; Starkey, *The Economic Geography of Barbados*; Hunte, *Barbados*; Hoyos, *Barbados*; Levy, *Emancipation, Sugar and Federalism*; Beckles, *Black Rebellion in Barbados*.

[2] Hamilton, *Cricket in Barbados*, describes the growth of cricket on the island. For an analysis of the early period, see Stoddart, 'Cricket and Colonialism in the English-Speaking Caribbean Before 1914'.

[3] Cashman, *Patrons, Players and the Crowd*.

[4] The method here attempts to meet some of the points made by Cohn, 'History and Anthropology: The State of Play,'. Also, Geertz, 'Blurred Genres' in his *Local Knowledge*.

[5] Allsopp, *The Question of Barbadian Culture*; *Advocate*, 16 Sept. 1985.

[6] For an example, see the pamphlet 'The High Cost of Living' (Bridgetown: National United Movement, 1981). A long-term view is in Taylor, 'Black Labor and White Power in Post-Emancipation Barbados'.

[7] For some general insights into the analytical possibilities here, see Wilson, *Crab Antics*; Henry and Stone (eds.), *The Newer Caribbean*; Burrowes, 'African Survivals: Aspects of African Continuity in Barbadian Culture'. One very interesting view is that in Berthelot and Gaume, *Caribbean Popular Dwelling*, 9–10.

[8] Sturge and Harvey, *The West Indies in 1837*, 130–1.

[9] Specifically see Reece and Clark-Hunt (eds), *Barbados Diocesan History*, Ch.XIX; Handler and Sio, 'Barbados', 253; Johnston, *The Negro in the New World*, 225. For the wider story, Bell, *Obeah – Witchcraft in the West Indies*. For an indication of the persistence of obeah, *Advocate*, 9 July 1935, 10.

[10] For example, *An Act for the Suppression and Punishment of Vagrancy*, Laws of Barbados, No.129.

[11] For example, *An Act to Establish a Police in Bridge-Town and the Parish of St. Michael*, Laws of Barbados, No.78; *An Act to Provide for the Building of Houses of Correction, and Police Establishments*, Laws of Barbados, No.87; *An Act to Increase the Number and Efficiency of the Mounted Militia of This Island*, Laws of Barbados, No.105; *An Act for the Better Care and Protection of Lunatics*, Laws of Barbados, No.522.

[12] For example, *An Act to Regulate the Trade and Business of Butchers, and to Check and Prevent As Much As Possible the Stealing of Stock*, Laws of Barbados, No.96; *An Act to Consolidate and Amend the Several Laws of This Island Relating to the Market of Bridgetown*, Laws of Barbados, No.199; *An Act to Provide a Summary Remedy for the Prevention of Persons Holding Markets in the City of Bridgetown*, Laws of Barbados, No.395.

[13] Clarke, *The Constitutional Crisis of 1876 in Barbados*; Hamilton, *Barbados and the Confederation Question*; Belle, 'The Abortive Revolution of 1876 in Barbados'.

[14] *Barbados Herald*, 4 and 11 April 1895; *Barbados Agricultural Reporter*, 12 April 1895, 9 and 16 July 1895.

[15] The role of cricket in this area may be followed in Sandiford and Stoddart, 'Cricket and the Elite Schools in Barbados'.

[16] Barbados Blue Book, 1900, educational statistics.

[17] The best guide here is Davis, *Cross and Crown in Barbados*. For a specific example, *Barbados Times*, 25 June 1870.

[18] Nandy, *The Intimate Enemy*, ix.

[19] James, *Beyond a Boundary*. For some thoughts, see Tiffen, 'Cricket, Literature and the Politics of De-Colonisation'; Patterson. 'The Ritual of Cricket', 23–5; Marshall, 'Gary Sobers and the Brisbane Revolution'; St. Pierre, 'West Indian Cricket', Parts I and II, 7–27 and 20–35; Marshall, 'Race, Class and Cricket in Barbadian Society'; Thompson, 'How Cricket is West Indian Cricket?'

[20] Gramsci, *The Modern Prince*; Femia, *Gramsci's Political Thought*; Bourdieu, 'Sport and Social Class'; Hall, 'Cultural Studies: Two Paradigms'; Williams, *Problems in Materialism and Culture*. For some considerations, Jackson Lears, 'The Concept of Cultural Hegemony'; and Gottdiener, 'Hegemony and Mass Culture'. A stimulating view on sport is Parry, 'Hegemony and Sport'.

[21] On this general point see Mangan, *Athleticism in the Victorian and Edwardian Public School* and also his *The Games Ethic and Imperialism*.

[22] For the period, see Levy, *Emancipation, Sugar and Federalism*. For an interesting analysis of developments during that time, see Governor Robinson to Secretary of State for the Colonies, Confidential, 27 Sept. 1881, COL 211126, Barbados Archives.

[23] This section based on Gibbons (ed.), *Barbados Cricketers' Annual*, issues from 1894–95 to 1913–14; *Advocate*, 27 Oct. 1925, 5 and 28 Nov. 1931, 12; Act of Barbados, No.12 of 1933, 22 Dec. 1933.

[24] For one account of 'firms' about the turn of the century see Frank Collymore's piece in *Combermerian*, 1973–4, 15.

[25] For BCC economic difficulties, *Advocate*, 5 February 1929, 8 and 7 July 1932, 8.

[26] Based on interview material.

[27] See BCA, Report and Statement of Accounts, 1 April 1984–31 March 1985 for the recent membership, analysis based on interview material.

[28] See the foundation committee for the Frame Fond Challenge Cup Series in *Barbados Cricketers' Annual 1902–03*, 186. For the extent of later Bank Holiday cricket, *Advocate*, 2 Aug. 1932, 20. Hewitt, *The Annual Barbados League Cricketer* indicates some of the early BCL activity. Lynch, *The Barbados Book*, 166–74 conveys the flavour of a 'country' match.

[29] For Hewitt, see *Advocate*, 3 March 1969.

[30] In 1955, for example, one player was suspended for five years after removing the stumps in protest at an umpiring decision. *Advocate*, 12 Nov. 1955, 10. Earlier, in 1946, the League had attempted to head off such behaviour by initiating a series of educational talks entitled, 'What the BCL Expects of You', *Advocate*, 26 July 1946, 4.

[31] See, for example, comments which followed the selection of Gary Sobers in the 1953 West Indian touring team to India, *Advocate*, 27 Jan. 1953, 10.

[32] *Wanderers Cricket Club Centenary, 1877–1977* (Bridgetown: WCC, 1977). For a brief comparison of Wanderers and Pickwick, see Lowenthal, *West Indian Societies*, 82–3.

[33] See Hamilton, *Cricket in Barbados*; interview material drawn from Pickwick personnel.

[34] Interview material.

[35] Ibid.

[36] Ibid. Also, Barbados Cricketers Annual series.

[37] Hoyos, *Grantley Adams and the Social Revolution*.

[38] *Advocate*, 22 Oct. 1936, 12 – he was appointed Vice President.

[39] Interviewees invariably pointed to the fact that all post-independence Governors-General and Prime Ministers have been Spartan men, not to mention a preponderance of politicians and senior civil servants.

[40] For an interesting outline, see Wickham, 'Herman', *West Indies Cricket Annual, 1980*; interview material.

[41] These profiles were based upon Voters' Lists from the 1880s until the 1960s, supplemented by these biographical sources: Fraser, *The Barbados Diamond Jubilee*; Leverick, *Leverick's Directory of Barbados*; *Barbados Year Book and Who's Who* (Bridgetown: Advocate, 1934, 1951, 1964).

[42] See, for example, *Rules of the Pickwick Cricket Club*.

[43] Remainder of this paragraph and the next based upon interview material.

[44] Trollope, *The West Indies and the Spanish Main*, 215; Chester, *Transatlantic Sketches in the West Indies*, 99; McLellan, *Same Phases of Barbados Life*, 45–6, 54; Macmillan, *Warning from the West Indies*, 49; Fermor, *The Traveller's Tree*, 151; Swanton in *Advocate*, 27 July, 1960, 11; Blackburne, *Lasting Legacy*, 85–6.

[45] Bernard [Guidon Belle], *Wayside Sketches*; Wickham, *Colour Question*; Harewood, *Black Powerlessness in Barbados*.

[46] See Starkey, *Economic Geography of Barbados*, Ch.IV and Marshall, *Re Population/Environment system of Barbados in the 1930s*; *Barbados Sugar Industry Review* 15 (March 1973).

[47] *Report of the West India Royal Commission; Report of the West Indian Sugar Commission; Sugar Confidential; The Economic and Social Development of Barbados: Characteristics, Policies and Perspectives; Nation*, 18 Sept. 1985, 12.

[48] Two accounts of this process may be seen in Parris, 'Race, Inequality and Underdevelopment in Barbados' and Karch, 'The Transformation and Consolidation of the Corporate Plantation Economy in Barbados'.

[49] For some indications: 'Housing in Barbados'; 'Report on a Preliminary Housing Survey'; 'Report on a Housing Survey of Eight Slum Tenantries'. Later nineteenth century conditions may be gauged from *Report of the Commission on Poor Relief*. For the outline of political events, Hoyos, *Grantley Adams and the Social Revolution*.

[50] For comments on the process of democratization, see Hewitt, *Ten Years of Constitutional Development*. This was the same Mitchie Hewitt who founded the BCL.

[51] Warner, *Cricket In Many Climes*, West Indian section; Griffith, *Chucked Around*, 117–18.

[52] Interview material; for a similar version, Wickham, 'The First Hundred Yews', 45.

[53] Interview material.

[54] Ibid.

[55] This practice began during the 1890s.

[56] For example, Barbados Cricketers' Annual 1895–96, 71–4.

[57] Barbados Cricketers' Annual 1909–10, 47.

[58] Interview material.

[59] Ibid.

[60] Ibid.

[61] Ibid.

[62] See the reception accorded Goodman for his outstanding performances against an English touring team in 1897, *Bulletin*, 15 Jan. 1897, 8–10.

[63] After the 1923 West Indies tour of England, he was ranked among the top six batsman in the world, Wisden 1924, 422–3.

[64] Interview material.

[65] Most cricket fans in Barbados have a list of players who, though good enough, were never selected for Barbados because they could not get a 'break' given their low social status. Interview material.

[66] Based on interview material; see also Sobers, *Cricket Crusader* and Bailey, *Sir Gary*.

[67] Spencer and King, *Lost Ball – Six Runs*. Calypso examples are 'Hit It' and 'Miss Barbados', both by Gabby.

[68] For an illuminating account of the Worrell experience, see Eytle, *Frank Worrell*, in which Worrell comments on each chapter.

[69] Worrell thought the match displayed 'bigotry, vanity and insularity', *Advocate*, 2 Oct. 1966, 14.

[70] Interview material.

[71] See Warner, *Cricket in Many Climes*, 42–6; *Bulletin*, 31 Dec. 1897, 4–5.

[72] See the account by the 1895 touring English captain in Bowen, *English Cricketers in the West Indies*, 13.

[73] For one account of Flannigan's style, see Intercolonial Cricket Tournament, 1925 (Port-of-Spain: Chronicle, 1925), 8, 35.

[74] Interview material.

[75] The following section is based largely upon interview material. See also *Advocate*, 14 May 1966, 14; Ross, *Through the Caribbean*, 27–8.

[76] For example, *Bulletin*, 3 July 1899; *Advocate*, 12 Jan. 1926, 9 and 4 Jan. 1930, 12.

[77] These points drawn from observation.

[78] See the 'Cricket Crisis' series in *Sunday Sun*, 13, 20, 27 Oct. and 3, 10, 17 Nov. 1985.

[79] Interview material.

[80] Point drawn from observation.

[81] Ibid.

[82] Ibid.

[83] For the 'reflective' approach, see Berryman, 'Sport History as Social History'; for a guide to a more structural and insightful approach, Geertz, 'Deep Play'.

References

Allsopp, R. *The Question of Barbadian Culture*. Bridgetown: Bajan, 1972.

Bailey, T. *Sir Gary: A Biography*. London: Collins, 1976.

"Barbados Blue Book". Bridgetown: Government of Barbados, 1900.

Barbados Cricketers' Annual 1902–03. Bridgetown: Globe, 1903.

BCA. "Report and Statement of Accounts 1 April 1984–31 March 1985." Bridgetown: Letchworth, 1985.

Beckles, H. *Black Rebellion in Barbados: The Struggle against Slavery, 1627–1838*. Bridgetown: Antilles, 1984.

Bell, H. J. *Obeah – Witchcraft in the West Indies*. Westport: Negro Universities Press, 1970.

Belle, G. A. V. "The Abortive Revolution of 1876 in Barbados." *Journal of Caribbean History* 18 (1984): 1–34.

Bernard, G. (GuidonBelle). *Wayside Sketches: Pen-Pictures of Barbadian Life*. Bridgetown: *Advocate*, 1934.

Berryman, J. W. "Sport History as Social History." *Quest* 30 (1973): 65–73.

Berthelot, J. and M. Gaume. *Caribbean Popular Dwelling*. Guadeloup: Editions Perspectives Creoles, 1982.

Blackburne, K. *Lasting Legacy – a Story of British Colonialism*. London: Johnson, 1976.

Bourdieu, P. "Sport and Social Class." *Social Science Information* 17 (1978): 819–40.

Bowen, C. P. *English Cricketers in the West Indies*. Bridgetown: Herald, 1895.

Burrowes, A. E. "African Survivals: Aspects of African Continuity in Barbadian Culture." *Caribbean Studies Papers*. Cave Hill, 1979.

Cashman, R. *Patrons, Players and the Crowd: The Phenomenon of Indian Cricket*. Bombay: Orient Longman, 1980.

Chester, G. J. *Transatlantic Sketches in the West Indies, South America, Canada and the United States*. London: Smith Elder, 1860.

Clarke, C. P. *The Constitutional Crisis of 1876 in Barbados*. Bridgetown: Herald, 1896.

Cohn, B. S. "History and Anthropology: The State of Play." *Comparative Studies in Society and History* 22 (1980): 198–221.

Davis, K. *Cross and Crown in Barbados: Caribbean Political Religion in the Late Nineteenth Century*. Frankfurt: Lang, 1983.

Eytle, E. *Frank Worrell*. London: Sportsmans Book Club, 1965.

Femia, J. V. *Gramsci's Political Thought: Hegemony, Consciousness and the Revolutionary Process*. Oxford: Oxford University Press, 1981.

Fermor, P. L. *The Traveller's Tree: A Journey through the Caribbean Islands*. London: Murray, 1950.

Fraser, S. J. *The Barbados Diamond Jubilee Directory and General West Indian Advertiser*. Bridgetown: King, 1898.

Geertz, C. "Deep Play: Notes on the Balinese Cockfight." *Daedalus* 101 (1972): 1–37.

Geertz, C. "Blurred Genres." In *Local Knowledge*, edited by Geertz Clifford. New York: Basic, 1983.

Gibbons, J. W., ed. *Barbados Cricketers' Annual*. Bridgetow n: Globe, 1894–95 to 1913–14.

Gottdiener, M. "Hegemony and Mass Culture: A Semiotic Approach." *American Journal of Sociology* 90 (1985): 979–1001.

Gramsci, A. *The Modern Prince and Other Writings*. Translated by Louis Marks. New York: International, 1975.

Griffith, C. *Chucked Around*. London: Pelham, 1970.

Hall, S. "Cultural Studies: Two Paradigms." *Media, Culture and Society* 2 (1980): 52–72.

Hamilton, B. *Cricket in Barbados*. Bridgetown: Advocate, 1947.

Hamilton, B. *Barbados and the Confederation Question, 1871–1885*. London: HMSO, 1956.

Handler, J. S. and A. Sio. "Barbados." In *Neither Slave nor Free: The Freedom of African Descent in the Slave Societies of the New World*, edited by D. W. Greene and J. P. Cohen. Baltimore: Johns Hopkins University Press, 1972.

Harewood, L. *Black Powerlessness in Barbados*. Bridgetown: Black Star, 1968.

Henry, P. and Stone, C., eds. *The Newer Caribbean: Decolonisation, Democracy and Development*. Philadelphia: Institute for the Study of Human Institutions, 1983.

Hewitt, J. M. *The Annual Barbados League Cricketer*. Bridgetown: Cole's, 1952.

Hewitt, J. M. *Ten Years of Constitutional Development in Barbados, 1944–1954*. Bridgetown: Cole's, 1954.

"Housing in Barbados: Report of a Committee". Bridgetown: Advocate, 1943.

Hoyos, R. A. *Grantley Adams and the Social Revolution*. London: MacMillan, 1974.

Hoyos, F. A. *Barbados: A History from the Amerindians to Independence*. London: Heinemann, 1978.

Hunte, G. *Barbados*. London: Batsford, 1974.

Jackson, T. J. "The Concept of Cultural Hegemony: Problems and Possibilities." *American Historical Review* 90 (1985): 567–93.

James, C. L. R. *Beyond a Boundary*. London: Hutchinson, 1963.

Johnston, Sir Harry. *The Negro in the New World*. New York: Johnson, 1969.

Karch, C. A. "The Transformation and Consolidation of the Corporate Plantation Economy in Barbados, 1860–1977." Ph.D. Dissertation, Rutgers University, 1969.

Laws of Barbados. *An Act to Establish a Police in Bridge-Town and the Parish of St. Michael*, 78, 24 July 1834.

Laws of Barbados. *An Act to Provide for the Building of Houses of Corrections and Police Establishments*, 87, 14 Sept. 1835.

Laws of Barbados. *An Act to Regulate the Trade and Business of Butchers, and to Check and Prevent as Much as Possible the Stealing of Stock*, 96, 23 Nov. 1836.

Laws of Barbados. *An Act to Increase the Number and Efficiency of the Mounted Militia of This Island*, 105, 25 Oct. 1837.

Laws of Barbados. *An Act for the Supression and Punishment of Vagrancy*, 129, 7 Jan. 1840.

Laws of Barbados. *An Act to Consolidate and Amend the Several Laws of This Island Relating to the Market of Bridgetown*, 199, 20 Nov. 1848.

Laws of Barbados. *An Act to Provide a Summary Remedy for the Prevention of Persons Holding Markets in the City of Bridgetown*, 395, 11 Sept. 1863.

Laws of Barbados. *An Act for the Better Care and Protection of Lunatics*, 522, 24 Aug. 1872.

Leverick, P. S. *Leverick's Directory of Barbados*. Bridgetown: King, 1921.

Levy, C. *Emancipation, Sugar, and Federalism: Barbados and the West Indies, 1833–1876*. Gainesville: University of Florida Press, 1980.

Lowenthal, D. *West Indian Societies*. London: Oxford University Press, 1972.

Lynch, L. *The Barbados Book*. London: Andre Demsch, 1972.

McLellan, G. H. H. *Some Phases of Barbados Life*. Demarara: Argosy, 1909.

Macmillan, W. M. *Warning from the West Indies: A Tract for the Empire*. Harmondsworth: Penguin, 1938.

Mangan, J. A. *Athleticism in the Victorian and Edwardian Public School: The Emergence and Consolidation of an Education Ideology*. Cambridge: Cambridge University Press, 1981.

Mangan, J. A. *The Games Ethic and Imperialism*. London: Viking, 1986.

Marshall, D. I. *Re Population/Environment System of Barbados in the 1930s*. Cave Hill: Institute of Social and Economic Research Paper, 1978.

Marshall, T. 'Race, Class and Cricket in Barbadian Society, 1800–1970', *Manjak*, 11 November 1973.

Marshall, W. K. "Gary Sobers and the Brisbane Revolution." *New World Quarterly* 2 (1965): 35–42.

Nandy, A. *The Intimate Enemy: The Loss and Recovery of Self under Colonialism*. Delhi: Oxford University Press, 1983.

Parris, R. "Race, Inequality and Underdevelopment in Barbados, 1627–1973." Ph.D. Dissertation, Yale University, 1974.

Parry, S. J. "Hegemony and Sport." *Journal of the Philosophy of Sport* 10 (1984): 71–83.

Patterson, O. "The Ritual of Cricket." *Jamaica Journal* 3 (1969).

Reece, E. and Clark-Hunt, G. G., eds. *Barbados Diocesan History: In Commemoration of the First Centenary of the Diocese, 1825–1925*. London: West India Committee, 1925.

Report of the Commission on Poor Relief, 1875–1877. Bridgetown: Government of Barbados, 1878.

Report of the West India Royal Commission. London: HMSO, 1897.

Report of the West Indian Sugar Commission. London: HMSO, 1930.

"Report on a Housing Survey of Eight Slum Tenatries in Bridgetown". Bridgetown: *Advocate*, 1945.

"Report on a Preliminary Housing Survey of Two Blocks of Chapman's Lane Tenatry, Bridgetown". Bridgetown: *Advocate*, 1944.

Ross, A. *Through the Caribbean: England in the West Indies, 1960*, London: Pavillion, 1985 reprint.

Rules of the Pickwick Cricket Club. Bridgetown: *Advocate*, 1947.

Sandiford, K. and B. Stoddart. "Cricket and the Elite Schools in Barbados: A Case Study in Colonial Continuity." *International Journal of the History of Sport* 4 (1987).

Schomburgk, R. H. *The History of Barbados*. London: Longman, 1847.

Sobers, G. *Cricket Crusader*. London: Pelham, 1966.

Spencer, F. and G. King. *Lost Ball – Six Runs*. Bridgetown: Barbados Festival Choir, 1973.

St. Pierre, M. "West Indian Cricket." *Caribbean Quarterly* 19 (1973).

Starkey, O. P. *The Economic Geography of Barbados: A Study of the Relationships between Environmental Variations and Economic Development*. New York: Columbia University Press, 1939.

Stoddart, B. "Cricket and Colonialism in the English-Speaking Caribbean before 1914: Towards a Cultural Analysis." In *Pleasure, Profit and Proselytism: British Culture and Sport at Home and Abroad*, edited by J. A. Mangan. London: Cass, 1987.

Sturge, J. and T. Harvey. *The West Indies in 1837*. London: Cass, 1986.

Sugar Confidential: A Visit to Jamaica and Barbados. London: Cocoa, Chocolate and Confectionary Alliance, 1970.

Taylor, B. M. "Black Labor and White Power in Post-Emancipation Barbados: A Study of Changing Relationships." *Current Bibliography on African Affairs* 6 (1973): 183–97.

The Economic and Social Development of Barbados: Characteristics, Policies and Perspectives. Washington: OAS, 1976.

Thompson, L. O. B. "How Cricket is West Indian Cricket?: Class, Racial and Colour Conflict." *Caribbean Review* 12 (1983): 22–9.

Tiffen, Helen. "Cricket, Literature and the Politics of De-Colonisation: The Case of C.L.R. James." In *Sport: Money, Morality and the Media*, edited by R. Cashman and M. McKernan. Sydney: University of New South Wales Press, 1981.

Trollope, A. *The West Indies and the Spanish Main*. London: Chapman and Hall, 1860.

Wanders Cricket Club Centenary, 1877–1977. Bridgetown: WCC, 1977.

Warner, P. F. *Cricket in Many Climes*. London: Heinemann, 1900.

Wickham, C. "Colour Question – Some Reflections on Barbados." (no publishing details listed).

Wickham, J. "First Hundred Yews: A Salute to Wanderers Cricket Club." *Bajan*, July (1977).

Williams, R. *Problems in Materialism and Culture*. London: New Left Books, 1980.

Wilson, P. J. *Crab Antics: The Social Anthropology of English-Speaking Negrosocieties of the Caribbean*. New Haven: Yale University Press, 1973.

Caribbean Cricket: The Role of Sport in Emerging Small-nation Politics

Introduction

In 1988–89 I was Visiting Professor at the University of British Columbia in Vancouver, attached to the School of Human Kinetics replacing Rick Gruneau, who had shifted 'up the hill' to Simon Fraser University. Rick and I met, along with Alan Ingham, at a 1982 Brisbane Commonwealth Games conference. Rick and Alan were the two leading new critical sports sociologists, so the Brisbane days and subsequent ones elsewhere were highly stimulating. Rick now works mainly on media and, sadly, the hugely talented but troubledAlan is no longer with us – their work influenced me profoundly.

The UBC stint was wonderful: classes included painful discussions of the Ben Johnson 1988 Olympic win/loss, and dealing with the transfer of 'national icon' ice hockey genius Wayne Gretzky to the Los Angeles Kings. Then there were Vancouver Canucks matches – among the worst NHL teams, their fans were tested mightily and it was more fun watching them than the play. At UBC, too, I struck a great working relationship with Patricia Vertinsky who has remained a great friend ever since.

Things clearly were different in different places, but this experience produced another dimension. Late in 1988 I watched television as never before, the injured Kirk Gibson limping around the bases with his home run giving the Dodgers the win in Game 7 of that year's World Series. Symmetry was in this. One turning point for me going into sports studies came from two great friends. Robin Jeffrey introduced me to Roger Kahn's *The Boys Of Summer*, the story of the Dodgers 1952 World Series win with Jackie Robinson on board as part of the 'break the race ban' crusade. The book was marvellous. Shortly after, Peter Reeves arrived at my UWA office with a first edition found at a book sale.

Robin started his working life in Victoria, Canada as a sports journalist then saw India as a volunteer before becoming a PhD student of Kerala politics, and ultimately an eminent authority on Indian political and social history as well as contemporary Indian media. His departure from La Trobe for the Australian National University at the end of 2005 was well deserved, but his absence is felt keenly. When Peter came to UWA as Professor of History in 1974 I was in a deep slump – the thesis was going badly, I was about to give up. He read all my chapters and gave me a formal critique to put me back on track. Seminars at Peter's house were legendary: they started with Friday evening dinner and finished with Monday morning breakfast, concluding days and nights of discussion, food and wine. Robin and Peter encouraged me into sports history because they understood inherently what it meant both to me and culturally.

The other great friend, then and now, was Ken McPherson. We met in 1972 as he left for Heidelberg after finishing his theses on the Madras and Calcutta Muslims, and we taught together at UWA after his return, then again at Curtin University. Ken sharpened my quest for knowledge – he is still among the most widely read of people – but he also heightened my sense of the 'cultural' turn in art and antiques. My enthusiasm for *peranakans* porcelain is traceable to him (and in 2005 he was present at the purchase of the cabinet to house the collection), along with my mania for buying and selling art. He was best man at my second wedding: when I introduced Peter to Sandi, he raced off to his marks book register because he remembered her as a student and, so, paraded all the marks. Ken had tutored Sandi in the same course and at our wedding announced to Peter that he, Ken, had a strong hand in at least one of those papers.

When I reached Vancouver I had a south Indian background plus a Caribbean one, and was teaching into yet another different culture. That led directly to this essay. Watching Canada agonize over Johnson and Gretsky, it occurred to me that all modern cultures have sporting struggles that rehearse identity and meaning. We watched the Johnson 'win' with about twenty Canadians who had genuinely adopted the Jamaican as their own, and their despair was raw a few hours later as the revelations began. In retrospect, I had watched New Zealand rugby players disappear from teams to play South Africa, allegedly on form but clearly upon race. In Barbados, I heard my great Maple friend Maurice Taylor (who should have played for Barbados if not West Indies) rail against the 'white bastards' who barred his girlfriend from the Kensington Oval main grandstand – this was around midnight at our club after a one-day match final loss, many rums and much remorse. Having made the remark he realized my presence and said, 'Oh, Brian, you think like a black man even if you are white'. It was kind, but I wish it was correct.

That background helped me understand that for so-called entities like 'West Indies' (extant only in cricket and the University, not in politics), sport was often the only real international power and leverage they possessed. Playing power thus had a more important role than just winning – West Indies were ascendant in world cricket then so their views on South Africa held sway. As their playing power has subsided in recent years so, too, has their influence politically both inside and outside of the game itself.

* * * * *

On 29 June 1950 a team of cricketers playing as the 'West Indies' beat England in a test match for the first time since their accession to international status in 1928. The victory was all the more historic for being recorded at Lord's, the London ground dubbed the Cathedral of Cricket.[1] As the last English wicket fell to produce the win, those at the ground witnessed a 'rush of West Indian supporters, one armed with an instrument of the guitar family'.[2] That was Lord Kitchener, the famous calypsonian from Trinidad whose words and music led the celebrations in honour of a new cricket power, for West Indies went on to win two more tests and so the series that summer. For the cricket world, it was the moment when the name West Indies began to evoke images of rum, calypso and exciting play. But there was another dimension, too, missed by many outsiders: the rich political vein within Caribbean cricket which was both an inheritance of empire and a prophecy for independence.

This essay sketches some of the political richness inherent in Caribbean cricket, and it is important to note that it is really a discussion of the game's political culture. While in recent years there has been an increase in the number of works devoted to what is loosely described as 'sport and politics'; little of that material has proceeded from a base in political theory.[3] It has been overwhelmingly descriptive, seizing upon sport as an interesting political sidelight or political issue. That has been most noticeable in political coverage of the Olympic Games, for example – it is as if the 'politics' come around only every fourth year.[4] Much of the writing on sports politics, then, might fairly be described as incident-based, providing little in the way of continuing momentum or accumulating knowledge. There are exceptions, of course, but they generally serve to demonstrate the rule. This Caribbean case study suggests, however, that it is more fruitful to approach sport as a constant and complex political factor inextricably bound up with the cultural evolution of the society within which it is located. That is, it is not so much the facts of political history which determine the political nature of sport (development of constitutions, suffrage, parties, and so on) as the cultural history of which it is part.

The composition of that victorious West Indies team, to begin with, symbolized the Caribbean colonial inheritance. There were three players from Jamaica, now just over an hour's flying time from Miami and less from Havana (to highlight the regional political variety). One came from British Guiana, the only British possession on the South American continent and surrounded by Venezuela, Dutch Guiana (now Suriname) and Brazil. Jamaica and BG, as it was known, were well over 1,000 miles apart so that these 'West Indian' players very rarely saw each other except for a limited number of intercolonial encounters and the even more limited number of overseas tours. Another six players came from Barbados, a tiny 21-by-14-mile island out on the Atlantic side of the Caribbean island chain and the second oldest British possession in the world. The remaining six cricketers came from Trinidad, one of the truly multicultural countries in the world, which lies to the southwest of Barbados.

That distribution points immediately to the need to qualify the use of the term 'Caribbean cricket'. The game was clearly restricted to the English-speaking sections of the Caribbean and was dominated for a long time by its major population centres. And while the passion for cricket was prominent in all centres, it was more highly developed in some than in others. As a long-time British dependency it was (and remains) appropriate that Barbados constituted the great cricket centre with the game spread all over the island. In Jamaica, however, partly because of a more difficult geography and partly because of a more mixed historical evolution, the game was more centralized in Kingston.[5] 'Caribbean cricket' is a useful generic term, then, but should be used in the knowledge of the quite distinct patterns within the region.

Team photographs of 1950 reveal men of very different skin colours whose names reflected the diverse cultural backgrounds from whence they came and which were the products of colonialism: Gomez, Pierre, Christiani and Ramadhin (the first man of East Indian descent to play for West Indies), to name a few. The captain was John Goddard, a white Barbadian whose family rose from obscure origins to become one of the island's major trading houses. His vice-captain was Jeff Stollmeyer, another white man of German and English descent whose family became business and political leaders in Trinidad.[6] The great stars of the team were the 'three Ws': Worrell, Weekes and Walcott, darker coloured men from Barbados with the first two of humble origins and the last from a lower middle-class family.[7] These backgrounds are important because they indicate the only real common reference shared by all these men in cricket: the political economy of slavery and sugar and its post-colonial consequences. From the middle of the seventeenth century these British Caribbean territories produced sugar for the world's metropolitan markets aided by the labour of black slaves taken from Africa. By the early nineteenth century a minority of whites controlled commercial and political life while the majority black populations maintained the production.[8]

Relatively few alterations occurred in that economic relationship after the abolition of the slave trade in the British territories in 1807 and the final freeing of all slaves in 1838. There were some significant cultural shifts, however, in a region where British, French, Dutch, Spanish and Portuguese influences had all been felt at some stage. During the middle of the nineteenth century, for example, indentured labourers from India and China were engaged to replace the lost black slaves, especially in British Guiana and Trinidad, and this would serve in time to render even more complex the search for a Caribbean identity.[9] (One of Trinidad's best-loved cricketers of the 1940s and 1950s was Rupert Tang Choon of Chinese and black extraction.) The rise of cricket in the second half of the nineteenth century, then, coincided with the crucial post-emancipation period which was marked by significant social realignments within the individual colonies themselves and by a new awareness of the necessity for an elaborated regional outlook. Inevitably, a significant institution like cricket became a political consideration in and of itself within this shifting cultural environment.

By the turn of the twentieth century cricket had become an obsession throughout the British West Indies and has largely remained so.[10] Early English touring sides were astonished by the interest their visits aroused, intercolonial matches were occasions for public holidays, the game was a major topic of conversation and public discussion, cricketers were pre-eminent public figures, and when the 1950 side returned to the Caribbean it landed first in Barbados where yet another public holiday was declared. In 1954 the timing of the ceremony to grant ministerial government in Barbados would be altered so as not to interfere with a major match, and on the same island independence itself in 1966 was marked by a cricket match.[11] In the Caribbean today politicians of all persuasions have an interest in cricket with at least two of them, Wesley Hall in Barbados and Roy Fredericks in Guyana, being former prominent test players while Michael Manley, former prime minister of Jamaica, has now written a history of Caribbean cricket.[12] In Barbados it is said that if you want to see every politician and public servant at the one time, go to the members' stand at Kensington Oval during an international match.

The root of this passion was a conjunction of circumstances which guaranteed that cricket in the English-speaking islands would become more than a game. For one thing, cricket was synonymous throughout the British empire with the concept of fair play.[13] The English language itself reflected this: 'It's not cricket' described something unfair, 'caught out' meant to be discovered in a transgression, and 'playing by the rules' meant to observe social etiquette and rules of behaviour. Given that late nineteenth-century Caribbean society was preoccupied with community-building and social ordering (and what Norbert Elias would later term the 'civilizing process'), such a game was a powerful instrument in the hands of those directing such realignments.[14]

Conversely, of course, to excel at cricket became an objective for those people in the lower orders who sought an accommodation with the ruling elite. That led directly to the creation of clubs organized on the basis of social ranking rather than playing ability with colour, education and wealth being the intertwined determinants of member-ship.[15] Where Chinese and Indians were numerous, separate leagues were even established.[16] While in Barbados lower class blacks eventually had to establish a competition of their own – their class position excluded them from the regular cricket culture. Even the very construction of cricket teams and competitions, then, developed from the political conditions left by slavery and emancipation.

What gave the game commonality was its emergence from the British athletic revolution of the late nineteenth century, allied with the ease of its being played in the Caribbean.[17] Because cricket was considered such a benchmark of English culture and civilized behaviour, the Caribbean communities naturally turned to it in their search for cultural distinction. And it did not demand the use of sophisticated equipment to learn its basics. Many stars learned their skills with a rough piece of wood and either a breadfruit or rolled-up rags.[18]

From the first appearance of the game in the islands, its local devotees harboured the ambition of beating the mother country to demonstrate colonial progress. Of course, that attitude varied from group to group within the regional cricket hierarchy. The early bosses were whites from the plantation and commercial elite whose families had been among the founders and early developers of the West Indian colonies and whose objectives were to reproduce English society and culture in what were seen as the outposts of empire. These were anglophiles like Sir Harold Austin, considered the 'father' of West Indian cricket and a prominent political-commercial figure in Barbados until his death in 1943.[19] By contrast, among the early stars were men like Herman Griffith, the Barbadian and West Indian fast bowler of the inter-war years whose experience of whites (and blacks) in authority gave him a fierce desire to beat them overwhelmingly at cricket.[20] This pattern was strongly political, emanating as it did from a system of social ordering and the shaping of social relations in which cricket played a principal role. It was inevitable that the politicization of West Indian cricket should spill over into the realms of nationalism, ideology, party politics and international relations.

The first important manifestation of this process came with the rise to prominence of Learie (later Sir and finally Lord) Constantine who played for West Indies in the first official test match of 1928 and who continued to play with distinction until 1939.[21] His great-grandparents on both sides had been among the last African slaves shipped to Trinidad before abolition and his father, a cocoa plantation worker, toured England with the first West Indian team to go there in 1900. Constantine left school for a law office and became an outstanding cricketer, being selected in 1923 to tour England where some critics thought him already a great player, a reputation enhanced by a further tour five years later. His turning point came with an appointment as a professional cricketer with the Nelson club in the Lancashire League, one of the first of many West Indians who have joined sub-county competition in England. While Constantine's time in Nelson was largely happy, it was also there that he learned about illusion and reality in the social side of cricket. While he was accepted as a fine player, that did not mean he was immediately accepted as a social equal. To be blunt, he discovered that there was as much discrimination in English cricket as there was in Trinidad, and that colour was the common cause. The discovery heightened his political consciousness, and he began to campaign for social and political change in the West Indies. He was assisted in his work by C.L.R. James who joined Constantine in England during 1932.

James is a remarkable figure not only in the West Indian literature but also in that of sport and politics generally.[22] In his 1963 autobiography, *Beyond a Boundary,* he laid out a powerful analysis of the relationship between sport and political culture, an analysis moulded by his personal history as a Marxist. Since the 1920s his cricket writings have been shaped by political experience, and it has been to the detriment of many working in the field of sport and politics that they have discovered him so late or, even worse, have yet to do so.[23] Born in Trinidad in 1901 he was a lower middle-class, brown-skinned scholarship winner to the island's premier educational institution. A very fine player close to intercolonial standard, his love of English cricket was complicated by his desire for political independence from Britain. By the time he joined Constantine, James's position on the left had been fully delineated.

The importance of the activity undertaken by Constantine and James was that the late 1920s and early 1930s marked the beginnings of organized political movements in the English speaking Caribbean and of concomitant demands for political reform involving increased popular responsibility.[24] It was best symbolized, perhaps, in the work of Marcus Garvey whose United Negro Improvement Association had a major influence not only in the Caribbean but also in the United States. Additionally, though, more localized figures and movements started questioning the social order which had developed during the previous one hundred years. By the later 1930s the new sentiments were being expressed through labour union disturbances and political agitation in Barbados, Trinidad, St Lucia, Jamaica and other centres. While local power elites were reluctant to relinquish much of their authority, Labour party pressure in Britain helped prompt official and unofficial inquiries into West Indian affairs.[25] These reviews created a growing recognition that political dependence, a weakening economic position, and often quite appalling social conditions were a potential source of major disturbance.

Constantine, unlike his friend and collaborator James, never advocated radical or revolutionary activity and in that represented visibly in Britain the mainstream of what constituted nationalist sentiment within West Indian politics. A good example of such moderate opinion was Sir Grantley Adams in Barbados.[26] A lawyer, Adams played one intercolonial match as a wicket keeper and was a long-standing member of the Spartan club which served the cricket and social needs of the rising black middle class from the 1890s onwards. Throughout his career as chief minister in Barbados and then as prime minister of the ill-fated West Indian federation, Adams constantly followed a moderate line as the widening franchise gave political voice to a larger cross-section of the public. By the time John Goddard's men won that 1950 series, politicians such as Adams had begun taking the Caribbean colonies towards independence, but they were facing competition from increasingly radical politicians. While the moderates saw the victory as proof of increased standards and social progress, the more radical saw it as confirmation that the West Indian politics were ready for immediate change.

Against that dual background it is useful to review the claim that cricket has been a force for integration within the West Indian geopolitical region, the one social institution in which all classes and colours could meet to promote a common cause and identity.[27] At one level that is a valid view, but at another is quite misleading. From the beginning the very composition of representative teams was highly charged, with each colony claiming that its players were being discriminated against. For a long time the criteria for selection included not only ability but also colonial origin: there must never be too many Guyanese or Jamaicans or whomever else. And for a similarly long time the politics of colour were particularly delicate. There were a considerable number of hesitations and resentments at work within the successful Goddard team, for example, even though the popular vision was of a strongly united team. Goddard himself had a reputation for anti-black sentiments, and the Barbadian black stars had bitter memories of some of his actions as leader of the island team.[28] The whites constituted the authority bloc within the 1950 team, a condition resented by someone like Frank Worrell who was recognized around the world not only as a very fine player but as the possessor of a highly astute cricket mind. The West Indian team, then, had the capacity to be the most internally divided of any international team, and that to a large degree paralleled the status of West Indian political development by the early 1950s. While an extreme case in some respects, developments in British Guiana provide a good indication of the tensions.[29] The colony received its first elected parliamentary majority in 1943 and by 1952 had universal adult suffrage along with a constitution allowing for popular elections. It also had the People's Progressive Party

(PPP) which won the first elections in 1953 led by the two men who were to dominate political life in Guyana for the next thirty years: Dr Cheddi Jagan and Forbes Burnham. Within a few months the constitution had been suspended, British troops were in residence, and considerable political tension was evident which resulted in Jagan seceding from the PPP to form a party comprised largely of Indians, leaving Burnham with a predominantly black one. Similar battles were proceeding in Jamaica where Alexander Bustamante and his cousin, Norman Manley, ended up leading separate labour parties with Bustamante adopting a strong anti-communist stance.[30] Violence was not uncommon in these political contests, Bustamante openly admitting to carrying a gun. Given the state of the domestic political climate, the social significance of cricket and the importance attached to it by the public as well as these leaders and others, it was probably inevitable that the 1953–54 English tour of the Caribbean would become highly controversial.

Because West Indies had beaten England in 1950 and England had defeated Australia in 1953, cricket fans in the Caribbean and elsewhere pointed to the 1953–54 tour as the decider for an unofficial world championship.[31] That was given some credence by English authorities who chose the strongest possible team. Leonard Hutton became England's first ever professional captain (another dimension of sport in politics) so that he was particularly concerned to come away without losing, yet another source of tension as dour play was and remains unpopular with West Indian crowds. In cricket terms the result was two wins apiece and one draw (England staging a remarkable comeback from 2-nil down), but in public relations and political terms the tour was a disaster. Dubious umpiring decisions incensed some English players who showed open dissent, smashing the West Indian image of England as the home and arbiter of cricket and fair play. But two particular incidents revealed the depths of the all-pervading political sensitivity.

The first occurred during the third test match of the series played in Georgetown, Guyana, where an umpiring decision sparked off a major crowd disturbance. Late on the fourth day West Indies were fighting hard to save the match when a batsman (Clifford McWatt from Guyana itself, significantly) was given out, much to the chagrin of the crowd. As bottles, tins and boxes showered onto the field from several directions for at least ten minutes, the English team huddled in the middle of the field with the police apparently powerless to curb the disturbance. The game eventually proceeded, but under strained circumstances and a suspicion that the demonstration had been politically inspired. After all, this was at the end of February 1954, just a few weeks after the constitution had been suspended by Britain – an action highly criticized by Jagan and Burnham – and the deployment of British troops in the city had aggravated sensitivities. Then, word about the transgressions of the English team both on and off the field had preceded it to Georgetown so that whatever politically ambassadorial role the tour might have had in the Caribbean context was already well and truly undermined in such a highly charged environment.

A second and similarly damaging occurrence came during the fifth and final test in Kingston, Jamaica. The English captain was playing a long and crucial innings and, with his score on 205 after having batted for almost nine hours, Hutton returned to the pavilion for one of the meal breaks. On hand to congratulate him was Chief Minister Alexander Bustamante, a cricket enthusiast like his fellow leading West Indian politicians. Tired and not concentrating on who was in the crowd, Hutton walked past Bustamante's outstretched hand and was soon abused by a Jamaican official for having snubbed the politician. Although Bustamante himself was not upset, local officials were, several garbled newspaper stories appeared, and an official English apology was not published in full. Tempers ran high on both sides.

Underlying both incidents was the touchy issue of interracial relations fanned by local political aspirations and strongly nationalistic tendencies.[32] One of the most famous calypsos of the period, for example, was Attila's 'Britain, Why Don't You Give Up the West Indies'. Some of the English behaviour was the customary cultural aloofness, particularly on Hutton's part, but much of it was interpreted by blacks as condescension. Worse, many Caribbean white residents aggravated the situation by urging the English visitors to defeat West Indies in order to uphold British tradition, not to say political authority. Cricket had become a test of white supremacy at the very time political responsibility was being increasingly transferred to representatives of the black majority.

The racial division within the West Indies was underlined by one glaring practice in West Indian cricket, the habitual selection of a white as captain. With the political climate moving inexorably towards independence, it was clear that if non-whites were considered fit to run governments then they ought to be able to captain cricket teams, especially given the presence of such talented players as Frank Worrell. Because of cricket's symbolic power in the region, the captaincy issue became the subject of widespread and politically charged discussion. It was in many ways the forerunner of several battles over which social group would control which sections of the culture. The catalyst for change would be C.L.R. James whose return to Trinidad in 1958 after a lengthy spell in the United States coincided with the rise of Dr Eric Williams and the People's National Movement (PNM) on the island.

The connections between cricket, culture and politics in the West Indies are evident in any discussion of Williams and the PNM.[33] The Trinidadian-born Williams was a brilliant historian whose Oxford doctoral dissertation led to *Capitalism and Slavery*, the book which redirected the debate about the nature and consequences of Caribbean slave society. After teaching at the black Howard University in the United States, Williams joined the Caribbean Commission as its research leader and produced vital works on economics, culture and constitutional development. Given his background, his People's National Movement which won the 1956 elections was likely to give a good deal of attention to the role of culture in the creation of national identity. Williams firmly believed that cricket was important in that respect, as he demonstrated on two occasions. One was in 1964 when Gary Sobers was appointed to succeed Frank Worrell as captain of West Indies. Sobers was under contract to the South Australian Cricket Association at the time and Williams wrote to the Australian prime minister, Sir Robert Menzies, seeking assistance in obtaining a release.[34] Williams based his case entirely upon the importance of Sobers and cricket in the shaping of an emergent society. Sobers was released. But an even more important intervention had come during the events which brought Worrell the captaincy in the first place.

Quite simply, the cricket captaincy had been long regarded and preserved as the fief of the dominant white elite, a symbol of its control of matters West Indian. In 1928 the honour had fallen to Sir Harold Austin, the legislator-businessman from Barbados. He was followed by the brothers Grant, G.C. and R.S., who came from a Trinidadian trading family. For the 1930–31 tour of Australia, G.C. was chosen to lead West Indies even though he had been absent at Cambridge University for some time, and he first met many of his players when he joined the team in Australia.[35] Goddard was the next major figure and after relinquishing the leadership to Stollmeyer in 1953–54, he returned for a disastrous English tour in 1957 when West Indies lost the series 3–0. That loss rankled in the Caribbean, not the least for its coming on the eve of federation.

The concept of a federated West Indies had a long history in British colonial thought, but its modern elaboration began early in 1945 when the secretary of state for the colonies announced that West Indians themselves would decide the issue of closer regional relations. A series of conferences over the next ten years tested the way, culminating in the London conference of 1956 which resolved upon a federation of twelve islands with the headquarters in Trinidad. In 1958 the idea came to fruition, but by 1962 the federation was dead, an impossible dream which evaporated for many of the same reasons that made West Indian cricket such a politically fragile institution: a centralized and artificial authority attempting to meet the psychological doubts and economic jealousies of numerous territories feeling their way towards national identities.

During those difficult years, West Indies' fortunes as a cricket power had fluctuated: a series win at home over Pakistan (which began its international cricket programme with a series against India in 1952–53, just five years after the Hindu-Muslim butchery which accompanied the partition of the subcontinent), a win against India then a loss to Pakistan in away fixtures, losses in England then Australia, then wins at home over India and England. It was a disappointing record for a region which invested so much emotional capital in its international cricket showing, especially as federation was so clearly failing. And if the one highlight was Gary Sobers's 365 not out against Pakistan at Kingston in 1958 (which still stands as the highest score by an individual in a test match), then the low point was undoubtedly the Port of Spain riot during the 1959–60 series against England.[36] In response to a run out decision against a West Indies player, bottles poured onto the field followed by thousands of the people who had thrown them. The English players stayed on the field, hoping the crowd might disperse, but even appeals by Premier Eric Williams and Learie Constantine himself failed to take effect. Only after almost an hour of action involving the use of fire hoses, mounted troopers, and riot police did the disturbances subside. For many analysts it was just another demonstration against umpires (one of them a Chinese), but C.L.R. James saw it differently, placing the matter at the heart of West Indian political economy in the context of a federation whose capital was, of course, Port of Spain. It all emerged, he argued, from a fear amongst the people that anti-nationalist sentiments were gaining strength as independence grew nearer and that the symbol of this lay in the machinations of the power elite (mostly white) over the appointment of white cricket captains.[37]

By the late 1950s the black Barbadians, Worrell, Weekes and Walcott, were highly experienced, the white John Goddard was at the end of his career, and there was no obvious white successor. The selectors, however, opted for inexperienced leaders (if good players) such as Denis Atkinson and Gerry Alexander, much to the chagrin of the West Indian cricket public. Then, at the beginning of the English tour in 1959–60, James, as editor of the Nation newspaper in Trinidad, initiated a campaign to have Frank Worrell installed as captain. (The Nation was the official voice of the PNM.) His purpose was succinct: for the public which had no national tradition because of its tragically decultured past, black cricketers helped 'fill a huge gap in their consciousness and in their needs'.[38] Just after the riot James published an article calling for Worrell to replace Alexander, and the matter was supported by Eric Williams in his address to the PNM conference. Cricket and politics were clearly closely related, and Frank Worrell was eventually chosen to lead the tour to Australia in 1960.

James and others were right in ascribing deeper causes than cricket itself to what are, in fact, the remarkably few riots which have occurred at West Indian grounds. Although far better than they were, those grounds are still tiny, cramped, short on facilities, long on excitement, and fuelled by rum.[39] With the political strain added, these venues provide highly charged atmospheres at the best of times. In Kingston in 1978, for example, the Australian team experienced a serious demonstration set off by an umpiring decision but caused by a deeper political condition.[40] Police in riot gear and some armed with automatic rifles ringed the ground while the outbreak raged, even to the point where a fire was lit in one of the stands. Broken bricks thrown from the top decks of the stands suggested premeditation. The game had begun in a tense atmosphere following the exclusion from the West Indies team of those players who had signed with a breakaway international group known as World Series Cricket.[41] That exclusion was protested by trade union groups, and the Kingston chapter of the Pan-African Secretariat was refused permission to parade placards at the ground. Kingston was in a state of high political tension at this time.[42] The forthcoming 1980 elections were to end the eight year rule of Michael Manley's People's National party and put into office Edward Seaga's Jamaican Labour party. Manley was a brown-skinned democratic socialist, Seaga a white conservative pledged to support Reaganite policies in the Caribbean. And at the heart of this continuing ideological battle lay two particular issues: living standards, and the degree to which political intervention by outside agencies such as the government of the United States and the International Monetary Fund would be tolerated. During 1979 the struggle engendered widespread violence and hundreds of deaths, particularly in Kingston. Given the significance of cricket, it was clear that Sabina Park would become a natural venue for potential political demonstrations. As James had pointed out almost a decade earlier, the resentment was at outside interference. There was as much antipathy towards international cricket authorities for their hard line on World Series Cricket (and the consequent banning of Caribbean stars by the West Indies Cricket Board of Control) as there was towards the United States for its quite open hostility to Michael Manley.

All that lay ahead, of course, as Frank Worrell led the West Indies team to Australia late in 1960. He was in a delicate position, carrying the deeper-than-cricket hopes of the Caribbean people and symbolizing a new era even as federation was crumbling fast. That Australia was still dominated by a white Australian policy, which meant that few of his players would have qualified as immigrants had they wanted to do so, provided a further complication. Worrell was a marvellous success socially in Australia, and the sparkling play of his team makes it the most affectionately remembered of all sides to have visited the country.[43] Indeed, if it was not for cricket most Australians (and probably a number of other nations as well) would know little if anything of the West Indies. While it is true that West Indies achieved other sporting glory, most notably in the late 1940s and early 1950s through a quartet of magnificent Jamaican sprinters, Arthur Wint, George Rhoden, Leslie Laing and Herb McKenley,[44] the sustained advertising of the West Indies through sport concerned cricket. When Worrell relinquished the hard-won captaincy, he handed over to his successor, Gary Sobers, the makings of one of the world's great teams from which the West Indies drew great pride.

In many ways Sobers was the real break with the past.[45] Worrell won the captaincy only after having spent a long time in England, taken a university degree, and become acceptable within establishment circles in the Caribbean. Before his early death he went on to become an important figure within the University of the West Indies. Sobers was a brilliant player whose skills and charm took him well beyond his poor beginnings, but he remained essentially a people's man. He was far less concerned with the wider social issues than Worrell and that led to some awkward moments. During the fourth test against England in Port of Spain during the 1967–68 series, West Indies compiled a huge score, dismissed England for a reasonable total, and the match seemed headed for a draw. But Sobers, astonishingly, declared his team's second innings closed, left England a reachable target, and West Indies went one down in the series which they eventually lost. The crowd and the West Indian public was outraged at such a gift to the former colonial masters. In Port of Spain an effigy of Sobers was hung in a public square.[46]

A far more serious issue overtook Sobers towards the end of his test career when in 1970 he accepted an invitation to play in Rhodesia. At a time when the anti-apartheid movement in sport was gaining strength this was ill considered, at best. But when it is recalled that West Indian cricket authorities had for some time taken a consistently strong line against racism in South Africa, his action seemed inconceivable. South Africa, while in world cricket, never played West Indies for the very obvious reason that it would have meant black players appearing in that country or white South Africans having to meet blacks in the West Indies. For a region so keen to establish an independent identity and international respect as the West Indies, that South African attitude was anathema, especially when the background of Caribbean slavery was so easily equated with what was happening in South Africa. Rhodesia was considered in similar light. Sobers was criticized severely for losing sight of the political symbolism inherent in the Caribbean game.[47]

It is in this matter of cricket and racism that perhaps the most notable connection, between West Indian cricket and politics has been found in recent years. From the mid-1970s until the late 1980s West Indies has been the undisputed world cricket champions and as such has greatly influenced world cricket opinion, especially among non-white participants including India, Pakistan and Sri Lanka. Throughout that period, in order to meet an increasingly hard-line West Indian attitude towards South Africa, international cricket authorities have moved very cautiously in their relations with South Africa, no matter how willing they might have been to interact otherwise.[48] Even if the objective of the International Cricket Conference (the world ruling body) was to prevent a split between the white and non-white cricketing nations rather than simply to appease the West Indies, the fact remains that on this crucial issue the Caribbean has found its greatest influence and presence in the world political arena. That the West Indian authorities were prepared to move quickly and strongly was obvious. During 1982 several West Indian players (the so-called Rand rebels) played in South Africa, attracted by the lucrative financial offers from authorities (political and cricketing) anxious to revive flagging cricket and related political fortunes. West Indian authorities banned the rebels from international competition for life.[49]

This growing intransigence had been signalled the year before when England toured the Caribbean. A late replacement in the team was Robin Jackman who had prominent South African connections. The Burnham government in Guyana refused him entry, the test scheduled for Georgetown was cancelled following England's refusal to play, and the tour itself was very nearly called off. This revealed that Caribbean governments had begun to realize the political potency of cricket and the leverage it provided. A similar incident occurred during the next English visit of 1986. The English culprit this time was Graham Gooch who was quite unrepentant about his South African ties. Lester Bird, deputy prime minister of Antigua (and son of Prime Minister Vere Bird), was prominent among the politicians who called for action against the visitors, but the tour proceeded without undue incident amidst a good deal of careful manoeuvring.[50]

While the West Indian attitude towards South Africa has been radical, in some eyes at least, it would be misleading to imagine that the game in its contemporary phase has broken completely free of the colonial past in all of its social aspects. Indeed, the radical exceptions prove the rule. A leading radio commentator of cricket, Antigua's Tim Hector, is also leader of the Antigua Caribbean Liberation Movement which is really more social democratic than revolutionary. Throughout the 1980s Hector has been indicted by the Bird government for his political activities, but it is notable that his cricket affiliations have not won him much support in the wider political context.[51] That is particularly significant in that Antigua boasts the current West Indian captain (Vivian Richards) and a leading batsman (Richie Richardson).

The Jamesian view about the essential conservatism of cricket, dictated by its social roots, is most apt here.

The cricket establishment has also been suspicious of new social movements, such as Rastafarianism. With its mixture of Old Testament beliefs, mysticism and revivalism, along with its telling extension into reggae music and the associated drug culture, the movement has spread quickly and deeply throughout the Caribbean (and elsewhere – there are now Rasta cults amongst the New Zealand Maoris and among political activists in some Pacific island nations such as Fiji).[52] But cricket has treated it with great suspicion. There was wide concern expressed when Vivian Richards was observed wearing wristbands which bore the Rasta colours, and a number of regional cricket associations have banned Rastas from their competitions. The Rasta trade mark is long, ringleted hair. But when Everton Mattis walked out to face the English bowlers for the first time as a West Indies player in 1981, his dreadlocks had been cut. According to the English journalist, Frank Keating, 'there was a whiff of discrimination in the air'.[53]

In part, such action may be a rearguard attempt to maintain the dimensions of cricket as set in the colonial past but, if that is so, it seems likely to fall. Local politicians still turn up to watch a club match, an indication of the game's continuing electoral significance. Yet it is interesting to note that the smaller islands, such as Antigua and St Vincent, are now producing a greater number of international players. Some observers put that down to social change in the larger islands where cricket is beginning to lose its cachet. And some fear that the increase in 'tourist, cricket (playing host to lower grade cricketers, especially from England, out on tourist packages) is somehow devaluing the game. Still others fear that widespread emigration will eventually erode the cricket base. While all that is yet to be proved, Caribbean cricket is undergoing changes which have political significance both within and without the West Indies.[54]

The migration issue, for example, has introduced a new dimension to the politics of Caribbean sport in general and cricket in particular.[55] From the late 1940s onwards there was a substantial Caribbean migration to Great Britain, and by the 1970s the presence of those migrants had become a major political issue in classical terms: racism fanned by economic discontent. It is incontestable that most of the West Indian population in Britain was kept within the lower socio-economic ranks. As they sought a way out through participation in professional sports such as soccer, rugby league and boxing, racist sentiments became more apparent. It took them longer to penetrate county cricket ranks where middle and upper-class sentiments are still predominant, even though most of the teams had hired contract staff direct from the West Indies since the county clubs opened their doors to foreign players in the late 1960s. The situation became complex. It was ironic that one England player on the 1981 tour was Roland Butcher, a black born in Barbados but raised in England, while playing for West Indies was Gordon Greenidge, born in Barbados but resident in England.

As the racial situation in England became more difficult, Caribbean sentiment and sensitivity stiffened. This was borne out very clearly in 1984 when West Indies executed an historic massacre of England in England (5–0 in five matches, with the dose repeated at home in the Caribbean in 1986.) West Indian supporters were there in their thousands, just as Lord Kitchener and friends had been thirty-five years earlier. But this time it was an all-black team with a black captain, the incomparable Clive Lloyd, a leader in the cricketing and social style of Worrell.[56] The rout was labelled by these supporters as a 'blackwash' (as opposed to a whitewash), and it was very clear that they were celebrating not just a cricket victory but a far wider one in the wake of the Notting Hill and Brixton riots, inquiries into which revealed the full social and political plight of West Indian communities in Britain.

As West Indians look back now upon sixty years of international cricket competition and at least 120 years of regional play, it will be clear to them as it should be clear to others that the game is not just a sporting code but a political institution as well. That has come about because cricket was introduced by the imperial authorities for reasons other than recreation, because the colonial elites took it up for reasons other than exercise, and because the modern players have seen in cricket lessons other than purely sporting ones. And those of us attempting to understand the real wellsprings of the connection between politics and sport would do well to remember the words of C.L.R. James: 'What do they know of cricket who only cricket know?'[57]

Notes

[1] See National Library of Australia, Menzies Papers, 1950 correspondence between Sir Robert Menzies, Prime Minister of Australia, and Sir Pelham Warner, English cricket administrator.

[2] *The Times*, 30 June 1950, 4.

[3] See: Lowe, Kanin and Streak, eds, *Sport and International Relations*; Ilmarinen, ed, *Sport and International Understanding*; Allison, ed, *The Politics of Sport*. All these works are of interest, but produce little in the way of an integrated view on the sports politics phenomenon. Hoberman, *Sport and Political Ideology* attempts a pioneering view.

[4] Espy, *The Politics of the Olympic Games*; Kanin, *A Political History of the Olympic Games*; Tomlinson and Whannel, eds, *Five Ring Circus*. Again Hoberman attempts a different analysis – *The Olympic Crisis*.

[5] For Barbadian cricket, Stoddart, 'Cricket, Social Formation and Cultural Continuity in Barbados'. A quite different cricket is described in Manning, 'Celebrating Cricket' – it is about Bermuda, an island not generally considered part of the Caribbean cricket culture.

[6] Stollmeyer, *Everything under the Sun*.

[7] These three players figure prominently in any history of the game, be it about the West Indies or the world.

[8] There is a vast literature concerning Caribbean slavery, emancipation, and economic development. For some stimulating views in this area, Mintz, *Sweetness and Power*. A case study is in Parris, 'Race, Inequality and Underdevelopment in Barbados, 1627–1973'.

[9] See *Caribbean Quarterly* 22(March 1976), for a special edition on the Caribbean Indian community, and 32(Sept. and Dec. 1986) for a subsequent examination of the same community.

[10] For the history of West Indian cricket: Nicole, *West Indian Cricket*, 158; Cozier, *The West Indies*; Goodwin, *Caribbean Cricketers*, and *West Indians at the Wicket*.

[11] Sandiford and Stoddart, 'The Elite Schools and Cricket in Barbados'.

[12] Manley, *The History of West Indian Cricket*.

[13] For a description, Sandiford, 'Cricket and Victorian Society'.

[14] For the Eliasian approach to sport in society, Elias and Dunning, *Quest for Excitement*.

[15] The first real examination of this process came in James, *Beyond a Boundary*, Ch.4.

[16] The *Barbados Bulletin* of 2 December 1897 reported that some Chinese youths had begun playing cricket on land provided by the colonial government in British Guiana.

[17] For the British background, Mangan, *Athleticism in the Victorian and Edwardian Public School*.

[18] Hunte, *Playing to Win*.

[19] The Austin heritage is outlined in Burslem and Manning, 'An Old Colonial Family, 1685–1900'.

[20] Wickham, 'Herman'.

[21] See the excellent biography by Howat, *Learie Constantine*. Constantine's own writings are important. See, for example, *Colour Bar, Cricketers' Cricket*, and *Cricketers' Carnival*.

[22] For some of James's other works, see *Cricket* and *The Black Jacobins*.

[23] For one such late discovery and the thoughts so generated, Metcalfe, 'C.L.R. James' Contributions to the History of Sport'.

[24] A convenient background work is Lewis, *The Growth of the Modern West Indies*. Knight, *The Caribbean* provides a briefer history.

[25] See 'West India Royal Commission Report'; Macmillan, *Warning from the West Indies*; La Guerre, 'The Moyne Commission and the West Indian Intelligentsia, 1938–9'; Orde-Browne, *Labour Conditions in the West Indies*.

[26] Hoyos, *Grantley V. Adams and the Social Revolution*.

[27] The former West Indies captain, Clive Lloyd, is one who has promoted this view recently (*Advocate*, 11 April 1985), again revealing the generally close links between Caribbean cricket and politics. A fictional view is in Mittelholzer, *A Morning at the Office*, 128–9.

[28] Interview material. In 1939 the deputy mayor of Kingston called a protest meeting on the grounds that too few Jamaicans were chosen for the English tour that year: *Barbados Advocate*, 10 Feb. 1939, 1.

[29] For an account, Lewis, *The Growth of the Modern West Indies*, Ch.10.

[30] One outline is in Manley, *Jamaica*.

[31] For the 1953–54 events: Swanton, *West Indian Adventure: With Hutton's M.C.G. Team 1953–54* and Bannister, *Cricket Cauldron*. For Hutton's account of the Jamaica incident and the tour: *Fifty Years in Cricket*, Ch.6; also see Trueman, *Ball of Fire*, 45–9, and Compton, *End of an Innings*, Ch.9.

[32] For some important discussions in this area: Lowenthal and Comitas, eds, *Consequences of Class and Colour*; Smith, *The Plural Society in the West Indies*; Wilson, *Crab Antics*.

[33] See Lewis, *The Growth of the Modern West Indies*, Ch.8.

[34] Menzies Papers, Eric Williams to Sir Robert Menzies, 13 July 1964. Available in the Victorian State Library.

[35] Cozier, *West Indies*.

[36] An extensive account may be found in Robinson, *The Wildest Tests*, Ch.6.

[37] James, *Beyond a Boundary*, Ch.18, details the story and the campaign.

[38] Ibid., 225.

[39] Patterson, 'The Ritual of Cricket'; St. Pierre, 'West Indian Cricket'; Thompson, 'How Cricket is West Indian Cricket?'.

[40] Robinson, *The Wildest Tests*, Ch.20.

[41] The World Series Cricket story is outlined in Forsyth, *The Great Cricket Hijack*.

[42] For some explanations, Barry *et al.*, *The Other Side of Paradise*, 341–51. For the deeper background, Austin, *Urban Lift in Kingston, Jamaica*. For recent Caribbean political trends, Henry and Stone, eds, *The Newer Caribbean*.

[43] Moyes, *With the West Indies in Australia, 1960–61*. For Worrell himself, see Eytle, *Frank Worrell*. Tennant, *Frank Worrell, a Biography*, reveals a very thin grasp of the cultural complexity of Caribbean cricket.

[44] In the Helsinki Olympics of 1952 they won the 4 x 400-metre relay while Wint and McKenley finished 1–2 in the individual 400-metre event in both the 1948 and 1952 Olympics, and McKenley won silver in the 100 metres in 1952. See Wallechinsky, *The Complete Book of the Olympics*, 10–20 and 66.

[45] There is an excellent social analysis of Sobers in Marshall, 'Gary Sobers and the Brisbane Revolution'.

[46] Cozier, *West Indies*, 52.

[47] Interview material; daily issues of the *Barbados Advocate* for September and October 1970. For the South African situation, Archer and Bouillon, *The South African Game*.

[48] This was borne out very clearly in the 1987 International Cricket Conference compromise over a hard-line West Indian proposal relating to players with South African connections.

[49] Goodwin, *West Indians at the Wicket*, Ch.17.

[50] For the 1981 tour, Keating, *Another Bloody Day in Paradise!* For the 1986 tour, Edmonds, *Another Bloody Tour*. Also, Manley, *History Of West Indian Cricket*, 292–4.

[51] Interview material.

[52] *Caribbean Quarterly* 26 (Dec. 1980), special issue on Rastafari; Campbell, *Rasta and Resistance*; Barrett, *Rastafarians*.

[53] For the Richards case, see Macdonald, *Viv Richards, The Authorised Biography*. For one case arising from the banning of dreadlocks by the Leeward Islands Cricket Association, see *Barbados Advocate*, 21 Aug. 1985. Keating, *Another Bloody Day in Paradise!*, 37.

[54] Interview material. For 'festival cricket' see Goodwin, *West Indians at the Wicket*, Ch.14.

[55] Cashmore, *Black Sportsmen*. For some earlier general thoughts, Figueroa, 'British West Indian Immigration to Great Britain'.

[56] Lloyd, *Living for Cricket*.

[57] James preface to *Beyond a Boundary*. For some information on Caribbean sport in this respect, Martindale, 'The Role of Sport in Nation-Building'.

References

Allison, L., ed. *The Politics of Sport*. Manchester: Manchester University Press, 1986.

Archer, R. and A. Bouillon. *The South African Game: Sport and Racism*. London: Zed, 1982.

Austin, D. J. *Urban Lift in Kingston, Jamaica: The Culture and Class Ideology of Two Neighborhoods*. New York: Gordon and Breach, 1984.

Bannister, A. *Cricket Cauldron: With Hutton in the Caribbean*. London: Stanley Paul, 1954.

Barrett, L. E. *Rastafarians: The Dreadlocks of Jamaica*. London: Heinemann, 1977.

Barry, T., B. Wood and D. Preusch. *The Other Side of Paradise: Foreign Control in the Caribbeal*. New York: Grove, 1984.

Burslem, D. P. and A. D. Manning. *An Old Colonial Family*. Revised and updated by R. B. Austin and T. J. Smellie, 2002.

Campbell, H. *Rasta and Resistance: From Marcus Garvey to Waller Rodney*. London: Hansib, 1986.

Cashmore, E. *Black Sportsmen*. London: Routledge & Kegan Paul, 1982.

Compton, D. *End of an Innings*. London: SBC, 1959.

Constantine, L. *Cricketers' Carnival*. London: Stanley Paul, 1948.

Constantine, L. *Cricketers' Cricket*. London: Eyre & Spottiswoode, 1949.

Constantine, L. *Colour Bar*. London: Stanley Paul, 1954.

Cozier, T. *The West Indies: Fifty Years of Test Cricket*. London: Angus and Robertson, 1978.

Edmonds, F. *Another Bloody Tour: England in the West Indies, 1986*. London: Heinemann, 1986.

Elias, N. and E. Dunning. *Quest for Excietment: Sport and Leisure in the Civilizing Process*. Oxford: Blackwell, 1986.

Espy, R. T. *The Politics of the Olympic Games.* Berkeley, CA: University of California Press, 1979.

Eytle, E. *Frank Worrell.* London: SBC, 1966.

Figueroa, J. "British West Indian Immigration to Great Britain." *Caribbean Quarterly* 5 (1958).

Forsyth, C. *The Great Cricket Hijack.* Melbourne: Widescope, 1978.

Goodwin, C. *Caribbean Cricketers: From the Pioneers to Packer.* London: Harrap, 1980.

Goodwin, C. *West Indians at the Wicket.* London: Macmillan, 1986.

Henry, P. and Stone, C., eds. *The Newer Caribbean: Decolonization, Democracy and Development.* Philadelphia: India, 1983.

Hoberman, J. M. *Sport and Political Ideology.* Austin, TX: University of Texas Press, 1984.

Hoberman, J. M. *The Olympic Crisis: Sport, Politics and the Moral Order.* New York: Caratzas, 1986.

Howat, G. *Learie Constantine.* London: Allen and Unwin, 1975.

Hoyos, F. A. *Grantley V. Adams and the Social Revolution.* London: Macmillan, 1974.

Hunte, C. *Playing to Win.* London: Hodder and Stoughton, 1971.

Hutton, L. *Fifty Years in Cricket.* London: Stanley Paul, 1984.

Ilmarinen, M., ed. *Sport and International Understanding.* Berlin: Springer Verlag, 1984.

James, C. L. R. *Beyond a Boundary.* London: Hutchinson, 1963.

James, C. L. R. *The Black Jacobins: Toussaint L'ouverture and the San Domingo Revolution.* London: Allison & Busby, 1980.

James, C. L. R. *Cricket,* edited by Grimshaw Anne. London: Allison & Busby, 1986.

Kanin, D. B. *A Political History of the Olympic Games.* Boulder, CO: Westview, 1981.

Keating, F. *Another Bloody Day in Paradise!* London: Deutsch, 1981.

Knight, F. W. *The Caribbean: Genesis of a Fragmented Nationalism.* New York: Oxford University Press, 1978.

La Guerre, J. "The Moyne Commission and the West Indian Intelligensia, 1938–9." *Journal of Commonwealth Political Studies* 9 (1971).

Lewis, G. K. *The Growth of the Modern West Indies.* New York: Monthly Review Press, 1968.

Lloyd, C. *Living for Cricket.* London: Stanley Paul, 1980.

Lowe, B., Kanin, D. B., and A. Streak, eds. *Sport and International Relations.* Champaign, IL: Stipes, 1978.

Lowenthal, D. and L. Comitas, eds. *Consequences of Class and Colour: West Indian Perspectives.* New York: Anchor, 1973.

Macdonald, T. *Viv Richards, the Authorised Biography.* London: Sphere, 1985.

Macmillan, W. M. *Warning from the West Indies.* Harmondsworth: Penguin, 1938.

Mangan, J. A. *Athleticism in the Victorian and Edwardian Public School: The Emergence and Consolidation of an Educational Ideology.* Cambridge: Cambridge University Press, 1981.

Manley, M. *Jamaica: Struggle in the Periphery.* London: Third World Media, 1983.

Manley, M. *The History of West Indian Cricket.* London: Deutsch, 1988.

Manning, F. "Celebrating Cricket: The Symbolic Construction of Caribbean Politics." *American Ethnologist* 8 (1981).

Marshall, W. K. "Gary Sobers and the Brisbane Revolution." *New World Quarterly* 2 (1965).

Martindale, C. A. "The Role of Sport in Nation-Building: A Comparative Analysis of Four Newly Developing Nations in the Commonwealth Caribbean." Doctoral dissertation, City University of New York, 1980.

Metcalfe, A. "C.L.R. James' Contributions to the History of Sport." *Canadian Journal of the History of Sport* 18 (1987).

Mintz, S. W. *Sweetness and Power.* Harmondsworth: Penguin, 1986.

Mittelholzer, E. *A Morning at the Office.* London: Heinemann, 1974.

Moyes, A. G. *With the West Indies in Australia, 1960–61: A Critical Story of the Tour.* London: Heinemann, 1961.

Nicole, C. *West Indian Cricket.* London: Phoenix, 1957.

Orde-Browne, G. St. J. *Labour Conditions in the West Indies*. London: HMSO, 1939.

Parris, Ronald. "Race, Inequality and Underdevelopment in Barbados, 1627–1973." Doctoral Dissertation, Yale University, 1974.

Patterson, O. "The Ritual of Cricket." *Jamaica Journal* 3 (1969).

Robinson, R. *The Wildest Tests*. Sydney: Cassell, 1979.

Sandiford, K. A. P. "Cricket and Victorian Society." *Journal of Sport History* 17 (1983).

Sandiford, K. A. P. and B. Stoddart. "The Elite Schools and Cricket in Barbados: A Study in Colonial Continuity." *International Journal of the History of Sport* 4 (1987).

Smith, M. G. *The Plural Society in the West Indies*. Berkeley, CA: University of California Press, 1965.

St. Pierre, Maurice. "West Indian Cricket." *Caribbean Quarterly* 19 (1973).

Stoddart, B. "Cricket, Social Formation and Cultural Continuity in Barbados: A Preliminary Ethnohistory." *Journal of Sport History* 14 (1987).

Stollmeyer, J. *Everything under the Sun: My Life in West Indies Cricket*. London: Stanley Paul, 1983.

Swanton, E. M. *West Indian Adventure: With Hutton's M.C.G. Team 1953–54*. London: Museum Press, 1954.

Tennant, I. *Frank Worrell, a Biography*. London: Lutterworth, 1987.

Thompson, L. O. B. "How Cricket Is West Indian Cricket?: Class, Racial and Colour Conflict." *Caribbean Review* 12 (1983).

Tomlinson, A. and C. Whannel, eds. *Five Ring Circus: Money, Power and Politics at the Olympic Games*. London: Pluto, 1984.

Trueman, F. *Ball of Fire*. London: Granada, 1977.

Wallechinsky, D. *The Complete Book of the Olympics*. New York: Penguin, 1984.

'West India Royal Commission Report'. London: HMSO, 1945.

Wickham, J. "Herman." In *West Indies Cricket Annual*. Bridgetown: WICA, 1980.

Wilson, P. J. *Crab Antics: The Social Anthropology of English-Speaking Negro Societies of the Caribbean*. New Haven, CT: Yale University Press, 1973.

Sport, Cultural Imperialism and Colonial Response in the British Empire

Introduction

This might be my most important essay, because it set out deliberately to take sports culture into mainstream international academic thinking via a leading journal. Such work could not remain in the sports journal 'ghettos' if the field was to get wider recognition. I targeted *Comparitive Studies of Society and History* because it featured writings I admired, had the cross-disciplinary approach that (in my view) best stimulated insights into sport, had a high profile and reputation: the editorial board included Sylvia Thrupp, Albert Feuerwerker, Jack Goody, Eric Wolf, Bernard Bailyn, Barney Cohn, Clifford Geertz, Emmanuel Le Roy Ladurie and many others whom I had read and admired across a wide variety of fields. Who would not want a paper in such a journal? It took time and at least two versions before the essay was accepted, but when it happened I thought it a breakthrough.

That was especially so because *Saturday Afternoon Fever: Sport In The Australian Culture* had appeared in 1986 and while it brought sport as a deep social construct to a wide public audience (as Gordon Inglis had done with his 1912 *Sport & Pastime In Australia)*, some academic colleagues were dismayed by the absence of footnotes. There had been much discussion about this with the publisher, but the target audience was general not academic. I was content with that wider ambition. Early on in Canberra, responsible for the sports administration and sports journalism degrees and conscious of giving them credibility, I took every opportunity for media work, inserting sports analysis into general reporting wherever possible – along with match and injury reports listeners and readers got sports economics and politics. Similarly, when Steve Harris (later publisher and Editor-in-Chief of *The Age*, and even later CEO of the Melbourne Football Club) said he would publish everything I wrote for him as Sports Editor for *The Herald* in Melbourne, I responded.

The general reaction to *Saturday Afternoon Fever* was good: the anti-sports guru Keith Dunstan gave it a positive review, as did others. The academic reaction was more interesting. Some thought it lacked theory, others thought it too general, some that the thematic approach underplayed the general 'history' of Australian sport, and others again just did not 'get' it – one review constantly referred to the book as *Saturday Night Fever*! Mind you, not all caught the title's irony. Almost fifteen years later, a reviewer of another book thought *Saturday Afternoon Fever* captured the romanticism of an earlier era when, of course, the title was suggesting even then that sport on Saturday was already a relic.

The overall approach to the *CSSH* article was stimulated further by the 1986 appearance of the Geoff Lawrence and David Rowe collection, *Power Play: the Commercialisation of Australian Sport*, followed in 1990 by their collection, *Sport and Leisure: Trends in Australian Popular Culture*. I criticized some essayists for being formulaic and uninformed by data (as David criticized me for being atheoretical), and for simply laying over the Australian framework a theoretical position elaborated in the UK on the basis of social conditions that had evolved there. Put simply, I thought they took a UK-derived class/status/social Marxist position and tried to fit it on Australia (and by this time one *Quadrant* writer had declared me 'chillingly Marxist' in a piece I had written about music, so it was not that I was unsympathetic to the Lawrence and Rowe foundations). That said, though, Geoff and David influenced me considerably in two mains ways. First, they showed it was possible and important to take a critical sociological approach to Australian sport (remembering my affection for C. Wright Mills even if, apparently, he was not a nice man); and, second, the work strengthened my conviction that history, sociology and anthropology were necessary partners in unravelling the inner workings of sport (hence my admiration for people like Barney Cohn, Robert Darnton, George Lipsitz, Greg Dening and Marshall Sahlins).

Sociologists like Geoff and David brought to sport the rigour of their disciplinary practices, and the intersection with history is crucial. The sociological input to cultural studies confirms that, and for many in my generation the waves of analysis from Stuart Hall and the Birmingham School, Eric Dunning and Eliasians, the critical theorists and the cultural Marxists have been highly influential. The pioneering North American sports sociologists like my friend John Loy were important in raising the flag, but for many of us the real mind-shifting emanated from the European schools whence people like David Rowe emerged. That was why Rick Gruneau and Alan Ingham were important – they did not spring from the dominant structural-functionalist schools that overwhelmed American thinking. The flexibility within, and the historical turn of, the European thinking allowed far more insights into 'new' sites like Australia and the Asian settings, but only if nuanced fully by the historical contours that emerged there.

Since then, David Rowe has produced one of the best books ever on sport as popular culture (*Popular Cultures: Rock Music, Sport and the Politics of Pleasure);* the best book on sport media (*Sport, Culture and the Media*), and everything he writes is mandatory reading for anyone in sports culture. David republished a paper of mine on the impact upon sport of the internet, and the associated emergence of 'convergence' between electronic media and telephony, where I argued that sports consumers could now write their own views rather than consume those of the media moguls – needless to say, I am gratified now by the myriad of sports bloggers on-line. I was honoured that David thought it republishable, because I respect his work most highly.

Sports sociologists like David may have had it even tougher in Australian academic life than the historians – there are few of them and they have struggled for recognition. The early deaths of Geoff Watson and Kent Pearson hit hard, but Geoff Lawrence's elevation to the Academy of the Social Sciences in Australia underscores the general point: he was honoured for his rural sociology and not for that on sport. There is yet to be someone who is made an Australian academician on the basis of his or her work on sport, an oddity given the prevalence of sport in Australian life, but predictable given the difficulties establishing the field inside the universities.

Given that background, my deliberate focus on *CSSH* was even more significant in drawing upon deeper and wider influences than previously, and it was close to historical sociology. Perhaps for that reason some people (Pierre Lanfranchi among them, I am told), disliked the piece. So be it – making the new rather than reflecting the old has never been easy.

* * * * *

Throughout the vast literature on British and general imperialism, the emphasis is largely upon the winning, then subsequent loss, of political control by the imperial power in colonial settings. Consequently, debate about the accession to that power has revolved largely about the great triad of considerations: economic necessity, strategic calculation and civilizing zeal. Similarly, discussion of emergent nationalist movements has hinged upon remarkably similar lines: Was the leadership of those movements motivated solely by ideologically-inspired desires for independence, by the ambition to command the new sources of economic wealth developed under imperial rule, or by a simple thrust for political power to protect other interests? These are generalizations certainly, but, to take India as a case in point, much of the modern historiography has been concerned to demonstrate either how Britain 'lost' or how the Indian National Congress 'won' that power.[1] But among such generalizations upon the British imperial experience, one interesting question has gone begging.

That question concerns the means by which Britain was able to hold its vast imperial preserve for so long. It was certainly not through naked bureaucratic or military coercion. To take the Indian case again, at its numerical peak the elite Indian Civil Service cadre contained only about eleven hundred men, and for most of the 1858–1947 period the total was below one thousand.[2] There were large standing armies, certainly, but colonial recruits constituted a substantial section within them, and the armies might justifiably be seen more as symbolic deterrent than direct repressor. From the 1860s to the 1960s – from the first War of independence in India until the Mau Mau rebellion in Kenya – the imperial military and militia forces were called out in aid of the civil power in such diverse circumstances as the New Zealand wars of the 1860s, the 1876 constitutional riots in Barbados, the South African wars at the turn of the century, the Caribbean labour disturbances of the 1930s, the Malayan emergency of the 1950s, and many more besides.[3]

An important point to bear in mind, however, is not that such incidents occurred, but that in an empire of such vast scope they occurred relatively rarely and on a comparatively small scale. Indeed, the military story in what became known as the White Dominions suggests the development of a confidence on the part of imperial authorities that the military presence was rather a small part of imperial culture. As political responsibility devolved throughout the later nineteenth century upon Australia, New Zealand, Canada and South Africa, the imperial troops were withdrawn at such a rapid rate as to excite settler fears of vulnerability.[4] In part this was a drive to establish the principles of self-protection and self-reliance, but it also suggests that the perceived power of British imperialism lay outside simple bureaucratic and military force.

A more promising explanation for the continuance of British domination lies with what might be termed cultural power – the set of ideas, beliefs, rules and conventions concerning social behaviour that was carried throughout the empire by such British servants as administrators, military officers, industrialists, agriculturalists, traders, financiers, settlers, educators and advisors of various kinds. The significance of these ruling cultural characteristics is that they were consciously maintained within governing circles and were fostered within carefully selected sections of the colonial populations more through informal authority systems than through formal ones, such as the bureaucracy or the military. The success of this cultural power rested with the ability of the imperial system to have its main social tenets accepted as appropriate forms of behaviour and ordering by the bulk of the client population, or at least by those important sections of that population upon whom the British relied for the mediation of their ruling practices, objectives and ideology.

One obvious agent in such an informal authority process, for example, was the English language itself; not simply a conveyor of information between otherwise differing cultural groups, it was a medium for the exchange of moral codes and social attitudes. Attaining command of the 'proper' English language, accent as well as vocabulary and syntax, became the goal of innumerable colonial peoples in both the white and non-white sections of the empire. Thus the works of Alan Mulgan in New Zealand, Nirad Chaudhuri in India, and C.L.R. James in Trinidad might have differed in form and content, but they shared an awareness of and a respect for the force of literature as a sentimental bond between imperial power and colonial outpost.[5] The strength of these shared values is demonstrated by the widespread current interest in post-colonial 'Commonwealth literature' schools, and by the efforts of such scholars as Edward Kamau Braithwaite in Jamaica and Ngugi Wa Thiong'o in Kenya to create or revive nation languages which might undercut the inherited and pervasive cultural strength of English language and literature.[6]

But perhaps the most neglected agency in the process of cultural transfer from Britain to her colonial empire is that which involved sports and games.[7] Through sport were transferred dominant British beliefs as to social behaviour, standards, relations and conformity, all of which persisted beyond the end of the formal empire, and with considerable consequences for the post-colonial order. This wide-ranging influence of sport was consolidated through such avenues as organization and ceremony, patterns of participation and exclusion, competition against both the imperial power and other colonial states, and the strong centralization of authority in England, and especially in London, the capital of empire. Crucial to this effect was the fact that, despite considerable evidence to the contrary, sport gained a reputation as an egalitarian and apolitical agency which alone transcended the normal sectional divisions of the colonial social order. The present essay, drawing upon a wide selection of examples, will set a framework for an analysis of the elaboration of cultural power through sport, considering the origins of its introduction and strength, the patterns and significance of its spread, and some forms of colonial resistance to its influence. But, first, some theoretical considerations are necessary.

The concept of sport as an important part of cultural power may be set in the wider context of a strong theoretical literature that emanates largely from the work of Antonio Gramsci, whose analysis of hegemony has influenced a generation of social critics.[8] Gramsci switched the Marxist analytical emphasis from the economic base to the cultural superstructure, arguing from the Italian case that even severe deprivation in the base could not easily shake the belief of the masses in values shared with the ruling groups and conditioned by cultural attitudes formed in the superstructure. There are, Gramsci argues, beliefs and traditions in any society that may well transcend more divisive issues.

Gramsci's analysis has been supplemented by works from Pierre Bourdieu and from the Centre for Contemporary Cultural Studies in the University of Birmingham.[9] Bourdieu and his colleagues argue that cultural institutions such as art galleries, museums and sport play a central part in maintaining and promoting established class relations because of socially shared beliefs, and that those institutions, while largely the preserve of a cultural elite, are also considered valuable by the mass even though individuals from the mass might not attend or participate in them. Work from Birmingham in popular culture confirms Bourdieu's findings. Moreover, the Birmingham work draws heavily upon that of the Frankfurt School to substantiate the significance of culture, high and low, in the processes of social formation, processes that forge strong interrelationships between base and superstructure.[10]

From this conceptual basis, sport may be envisaged as a powerful but largely informal social institution that can create shared beliefs and attitudes between rulers and ruled while at the same time enhancing the social distance between them. This is particularly the case in the British imperial setting, where sport became a strong determinant of social relations, beginning with the British environment itself, from which the games code was exported.

It is significant that the growth of the 'new' British Empire in the second half of the nineteenth century coincided with what constituted a games revolution at home.[11] The first Football Association Cup final was played in 1853, the football league organized soon afterwards, and the county cricket championship was inaugurated in 1873. Modern tennis was patented during the 1870s, with the first Wimbledon titles staged in 1877, the year of what is now recognized as the first official cricket test match, played in Melbourne between England and Australia. Rugby union was codified and the Home Nations championship inaugurated, with the rival rugby game setting up in the industrialized north of England during 1890s. Golf spread southwards from its Scottish homeland with the first of the Open championships staged during the 1870s. Horse racing, although institutionalized through the 1809 formation of the Jockey Club, developed into a major activity during the later nineteenth century. All of this activity was boosted by the popular press and the telegraph, both of which carried voluminous amounts of sporting information.

It was amateurs drawn from the middle classes that this sports activity was either played by or directed at, with the assistance of a professional sports caste drawn generally from the lower orders.[12] Quite distinct social relationships were thus elaborated in most sports, with the process of codification the remaining preserve of the privileged even though the leading practitioners in games such as football, cricket and golf were usually professionals. The key source of the division lay with the emergence of sport as a central feature in the British public-school system, which stressed in particular the social values of team sport.[13]

By playing team sports, participants were thought to learn teamwork, the value of obeying constituted authority, courage in the face of adversity, loyalty to fellow players, and respect for the rules. To *play cricket* or *play the game* meant being honest and upright, and accepting conformity within the conventions as much as it meant actually taking part in a simple game. Beyond that, informal social networks developed outside of professional or occupational spheres of interaction, arenas in which people of like minds politically and economically might mix while theoretically at leisure. These people from the public schools and the old universities went into the City as bankers or lawyers, the civil service as diplomats or policy formulators, the world of politics as masters of power, and the military as officers; or they returned to education as teachers and perpetuators of the system (as Bourdieu suggests) or went into the established church, where many of them became 'muscular Christians' with a belief in the good of games.[14] Many of them, too, went as servants of empire to Africa, Asia, the Pacific or the Caribbean, taking with them their ingrained acceptance of the social power and importance of games.

Initiated and encouraged by these administrators, missionaries, educators, bankers, lawyers, industrialists, traders and settlers, the enthusiasm for sports and games had become widespread throughout the empire by the turn of the century. Horse racing was universal; by the 1870s most of the principal clubs were already established in the African colonies, India, Hong Kong, Australia, New Zealand and Trinidad, to name just a few.[15] Cricket took firm root in Australia principally, but was also important in South Africa, India, New Zealand and the British West Indies.[16] Golf and tennis spread but not with the same degree of social popularity; rifle shooting (with its defence connotations) became especially popular, with the annual Queen's Prize shoot at Bisley one of the great imperial pilgrimages.[17] Football codes, however, were generally slower to take off and produced far more varied patterns.[18] Genteel games like croquet were to be found in most outposts of empire, along with indoor activities such as billiards, board games, and different forms of card playing. By the end of the nineteenth century all these activities were served by a substantial magazine and book literature that carried information not only about how to play but also how to dress, behave and conform to imperial models of social performance.[19] All over the empire, race meetings of both humble and grand status, major cricket matches, annual championships, and especially competitions against the imperial power became occasions for the reaffirmation of belief in the imperial ideology, not to mention for the continuance of colonial social ordering by such means as establishing, confirming and ratifying marriage contracts within appropriate circles.[20] In all this, the imperial order was served by two agencies in particular.

The first was education. Just as the elite English schools embraced the games ethic, so did similar institutions throughout the empire, schools which were invariably staffed by products of the English system. Prince Ranjitsinjhi, who became one of the greatest cricketeers in England before the First World War and consequently the popular model for what was 'possible' more widely in India, was educated at Rajkumar College, set up in Rajkot State to educate sons of the Indian princes.[21] Ranji spent hours every day under the tutelage of an English cricket coach, becoming the living proof, it was thought, of the adage that practice makes perfect. Games, especially cricket and rugby union, were prominent in the curricula of the 'great' schools such as Sydney and Melbourne Grammar in Australia; Auckland Grammar and Christ's College in Christchurch, New Zealand; Queen's Royal College in Trinidad (recalled vividly as an English institution by C.L.R. James); and Harrison's College in Barbados.[22] As late as the 1930s and the 1940s Harrison's still took pride in the tradition that its staff was drawn entirely from Home, that its curriculum was still heavily classical, and that games like cricket were sacrosanct.[23] The games code and its system of values took firm root in these schools, so that generations of students were influenced by it.

The church was the second major agency through which the cultural power and shared values of games were spread throughout the British Empire. Given the close connection between church and education in England during the late nineteenth century, it is not surprising that muscular Christianity emerged. These young men took holy orders after having been imbued with the games spirit, and they naturally saw a connection between 'healthy' sport and the civilizing properties of Christianity. Consequently, in many parts of the empire clerics were either keen players or supporters or both of the mainstream games; for example, the Reverend the Honourable A.V. Lyttleton, 1890s president of the Wodehouse Cricket Club in the Kimberley region of southern Africa. C.T. Studd, of a famous late-nineteenth-century cricketing brotherhood, gave up a promising playing career to undertake missionary work; Bishop Tyndale-Briscoe was a notable imperial muscular Christian, and Archie Liddell, the 1924 Olympic sprint champion, was another famous example, though his field of service was in China rather than the empire.[24] The practice was taken up within the empire itself, so that G.C. Grant, from the famous Trinidadian trading family, went to missionary service in Africa after his Cambridge education and a stint as captain of the West Indies cricket team.[25] Around the empire, from the later nineteenth century onwards, these people stressed the importance of games as a training ground for life. There was a direct link, then, between the Reverend Greville John Chester, who during the 1860s argued the need for poor West Indian black youths to learn cricket, and the 1930s missionaries in the Trobriand Islands who introduced the game there to break down tribal warfare.[26]

Given the social significance and responsibility placed upon games, then, it follows that their introduction into the colonial system was a natural development. But it was not an uncontrolled development, because it also follows that the types of sports to be introduced would be monitored closely so that desirable rather than undesirable social characteristics would be engendered amongst the subject populations.

Racing provides an excellent example of this careful control because of its inevitable connection with gambling. The sport of kings, as it was known widely, was inevitably among the first of sporting activities to be introduced to new colonial situations, partly because of the availability of horses, partly because of its traditional association with the English landed gentry, and partly because of its established gambling tradition. Whatever else, considerable numbers of colonial subjects took to racing (mostly as spectators) in locations as different as Durban, Bombay, Hong Kong, Port of Spain, Melbourne and Christchurch, and despite the vociferous opposition from established churches and their clerics, who attacked the profligate economic waste committed by those who gambled away their hard-earned money with bookmakers and on colonial inventions like the totalisator.[27] The colonial elites resorted to two basic defences in order to counter or, at least, control the spreading popularity of racing. First, official membership in the prestigious racing clubs became so severely restricted that, by the 1890s, institutions such as the Australian Jockey Club in Sydney were said to be more difficult to enter than the colonial parliaments.[28] As late as 1961 the Jockey Club of South Africa still had only 480 members.[29] These associations of the socially powerful were given symbolic support all over the empire by colonial governors who turned race days into glittering celebratory occasions. Then, second, the reports of numerous official inquiries into the state of colonial racing displayed an explicit class base.[30] It was argued consistently that the colonial elites alone had the means and the self-control to indulge in gambling. The lower orders were to be excluded wherever possible to prevent them from neglecting such social duties as paying their debts. It becomes evident from this case, then, that for the ruling colonial culture sport had a major role to play both in determining and in exhibiting the ranking of social groups. Moreover, specific groups within that ranking were often trained into, or prepared for, their social tasks by way of sports and games, as demonstrated in the evolution of polo.

At its mid-nineteenth-century discovery in the Himalayan hill states, polo emphasized the display of personal skill in handling horse, stick and ball. There were no goals, no teams, no restrictions on the number of players and no physical boundaries. Within twenty years it had been transformed by the British military establishment in India. There was a prescribed field of play, rules, a set number of players with designated roles and positions on the field (an emphasis on specialization), recognized tactics increasingly written up in manuals, a regulated competition, and an emphasis upon the importance of good equipment and horses.[31] This last point caused financial embarrassment to so many individual military officers that regiments set up financial pools for the purchase of ponies.[32] The polo cult was so strong in India that around the turn of the century it occasioned little surprise when one military commander replaced all non-playing officers with players, underlining the essential lessons thought to be inherent in the game. In its transformed condition polo was considered to provide practical experience in giving and taking orders, holding position, devising and executing tactics, assessing enemy strengths and weaknesses, and maintaining a state of readiness by looking to material preparation. It also provided training in logistics, with teams moving by railway to and from interregimental tournaments all over north India. Because of this background, polo remained largely a military-station preoccupation, played by officers and watched by the other ranks along with attendant families and support personnel.

Tennis was different in social purpose and directed towards a different social clientele. It was deemed a 'social' game, meaning that it was designed to bring people of like mind and social rank together in a leisure setting rather than to stimulate competition, stress development of sporting skills, or strive for excellence. Consequently, tennis 'parties' (the term itself suggesting a nonserious purpose) were invariably staged at courts in the grounds of private homes, with participants drawn from upper social echelons. One visitor to Melbourne late in the nineteenth century characterized these as vicious gossip sessions more than anything else. He was right in one sense but missed the significance of such gatherings in providing opportunities to gain information that might not have been circulating in more formal channels.[33] This was particularly the case with the mixing of the sexes. There was a strict formality and social distance in many British colonial settings, a condition which mitigated against indiscriminate mixing. Tennis parties and similar events frequently had the explicit purpose of allowing one person to meet another of the opposite sex but same social stratum.

But of all the games so carefully introduced to the empire by colonial rulers, cricket received primary emphasis. This was no accident. Cricket was considered the main vehicle for transferring the appropriate British moral code from the messengers of empire to the local populations. Colonial governors were especially important in emphasizing cricket as a ritual demonstration of British behaviour, standards and moral codes both public and private. Lord Harris, first of the modern English cricket bosses and a late nineteenth-century governor of Bombay, believed that selected groups of Indians would be ready for some political responsibility when they had assimilated the playing and behavioural codes of cricket.[34] Lord Willingdon, a former English county player who became a later governor of both Bombay and Madras before becoming governor-general of Canada and then viceroy of India, took a similarly strong interest in cricket as a moral guide. So, too, did Sir Stanley Jackson, one of England's finest players and captains around the turn of the century, who became a 1930s governor of Bengal.[35] In the West Indies, the emphasis came from men like Sir Augustus Hemming, governor first in British Guiana and then in Jamaica between 1897 and 1904, and Sir James Hay (like Willingdon an imperial handyman), who governed Barbados at the turn of the century after periods in Gambia and Sierra Leone.[36] In Australia and New Zealand, the trophies for state and provincial competitions were donated by two administrator-sportsmen, Lords Sheffield and Plunkett. In southern Africa of the 1880s and 1890s, governors such as Sir Henry Loch (whose service had included India, the Crimea, China and Victoria) had taken charge of local associations.[37]

By the end of the nineteenth century, then, all these and other sports were solidly established throughout the British Empire, with their social purposes widely accepted and understood. Furthermore, their administrations were set and centralized in a hierarchy commanded from London with, if anything, a control even tighter than that exercised from Whitehall itself. The Marylebone Cricket Club (M.C.C.) was the supreme lawmaker and settler of behavioural standards in that game, just as similar bodies were in the football codes, tennis, hockey, netball, golf, racing and athletics. These hierarchies were a most important part of imperial rule because culturally they emphasized the all-pervading British influence.[38] Disputes over rules were referred to these bodies, and as imperial sporting tours became increasingly numerous, they, too, were orchestrated from Britain. British writers wrote the manuals determining techniques and styles while British sports results, emerging from what was considered the world's premier sporting site, were eagerly awaited in the colonies.

As a result of the constant cultural reinforcement, the standards of behaviour to be lived up to by players, administrators and spectators were very high. Because of that, just as there was care in the evaluation of sports chosen to become colonial transplants, so also was care exercised in the selection of the social groups which might be admitted to those sports. The development of polo is again an excellent indication of this process.

The Indian princes were the main client group encouraged to take up the game. At the formalization of British rule in 1858, the princes retained at least semi-autonomous control over their territories but were, at the same time, subject to British attempts to 'improve' their administrations. Education was important, as in the Ranji case, and in sport polo became a major shared value. Anxious for an accord with the imperial power and to identify with British cultural standards, the princes found in polo two principal symbolic qualities. First, it showed an identity with the British military presence while simultaneously establishing a symbolic military equality. By the later nineteenth century numerous princes were scrambling to 'buy' a polo championship by recruiting superior players. Many of them hired British officer coaches for their princely armies, promoting those Indians who displayed polo prowess. The maharajahs of Jodhpur provided a string of such examples, and the maharajah of Patiala produced one of the greatest ever teams in the 1890s by promoting players like Heera Singh from non-commissioned to officer rank.[39] Second, polo allowed the princes scope for an activity which served both their new and traditional cultural roles – conspicuous consumption. Polo was, and remains, an extremely expensive business. Indian princes were expected by their subjects to demonstrate lavish wealth. Many princes themselves believed that the British would better appreciate the economic viability of their states if shown the princely capacity to spend widely. Consequently, the princes spent vast sums on polo players, advisers, ponies, equipment and transport.[40]

Although the princes represented the supreme example of the exclusive circles into which polo was introduced, they were by no means unique in the empire. By the late nineteenth century polo had begun its career as an elitist sport in South Africa, Kenya, Australia and New Zealand, where, although the military impetus was important, wealthy pastoralists and graziers had taken it up mainly as a means of continuing cultural identity with Britain. This was, perhaps, even more the case in areas of the informal empire, such as Argentina.[41] Matters of cost helped keep the sport exclusive, certainly, but social narrowness was also important. In both South Africa and Australia, for example, particular landholding families such as the Barlows and Ashtons became prominent, and they used polo as a proof of their successful incorporation of British social standards.

An important point needs to be stressed here, and that concerns the processes by which the promotion, acceptance, and incorporation of games occurred. There were occasions when it was clearly part of a conscious and formal decision-making condition, as exemplified by the officer who so respected the moral powers of polo that he eliminated non-players from his corps. Fiji produced a similar case in which the power of sport as a social and cultural agency was indicated and understood at a quite conscious level. During 1933, colonial authorities there sought financial support from their London masters in order to construct a golf course, citing Hong Kong and Ceylon as areas where similar action had boosted tourism. The Colonial Office agreed but, pointing to golf's reputation for being socially exclusive (they were clearly surveying the English rather than Scottish scene), only on the clear understanding that the Fijian club should not become just another way to discriminate against the Indian population there.[42] In some environments, then, sport was regarded quite openly as providing opportunity for conscious social ordering as well as mere recreation.

For the most part, however, the real power of sport did not come from being laid out formally by colonial masters to be studied by colonial subjects. Instead, it perhaps belonged more in the realm of what the Annales school of historiography has identified as *mentalités*, a set of beliefs acquired subconsciously. To continue the polo case as an example, the British arrived in India with a set of cultural beliefs and attitudes learned during their early socialization, considered them to be the proper bench marks of civilization, and so were likely to look favourably upon subordinate groups that appeared anxious to share those qualities. The sport similarly attracted the princes, who could maintain at least some of their own cultural continuities by way of polo, but at the same time help position themselves within the new political order by demonstrating to the imperial power that they shared some of its ideals. It was largely this subconscious element, outside the bounds of formal policy making, which rendered sport so powerful a factor in the maintenance of, and reaction to, British control throughout the empire. It was this subtle indoctrination that allowed the persistence of the view that the 'invaluable trait of give and take' in sport 'enabled the progress of civilisation'.[43] That civilization, of course, was culturally defined in very careful ways to support the dominant imperial view of social relations.

Again, this process of social and cultural formation and ranking through sport as an informal social agency was most pronounced in cricket, the game through which many colonial societies measured their progress against the bench mark of British achievement.[44] In Australia and New Zealand, although player participation began to broaden in social scale by the advent of the First World War, control of the game still rested with local social, economic and political elites who subscribed fully to British philosophies of sport.[45] This was particularly pronounced in the composition of the cricket associations in the Australian states and in the overarching Australian Cricket Board of Control, and reached its perfect symbolism during the 1950s and 1960s reign of Sir Robert Menzies as prime minister, when official meetings in London inevitably coincided with test matches.[46]

Similar and even tighter lines of social demarcation and hierarchy within cricket, lines which extended into the wider milieu, were found around the colonial globe. Until well into the 1930s in the Caribbean, playing – let alone administrative participation – was restricted largely to local white planters and their supporting administrative elites dedicated to the British model.[47] Leading clubs in Jamaica, Trinidad, British Guiana and Barbados (Kingston, Queen's Park, Georgetown and Wanderers, respectively) were white, with a small leavening of very high mulatto in some cases, and socially prestigious.[48] From these clubs came people like Sir Harold Austin. A member of Wanderers, he was also the father of West Indian cricket, captaining touring teams to England and being instrumental in setting up the West Indies Cricket Board of Control in 1927. He came from a merchant family of long West Indian heritage, became a member of the Barbados legislature at a young age and ended his public life as speaker of the house. His love of things English was renowned, one satirist dubbing him Baron Enmore (after his Bridgetown residence) because of his affected English accent and personal style.[49]

It is important to recognize here that admission to the playing ranks in many sports was guarded jealously, not for reasons of ability but because of concerns about status, social respectability and group relations. This was particularly marked in white minority settings such as South Africa, India and the West Indies, where social distances were considered an important and integral part of maintaining order. Following the creation of the Union of South Africa, for example, rugby union was regarded as an important part of the process in bonding 'the two white sections' (in defence, as it were, against the non-white sections). Given that concern with reconciling Boer and Briton, black and coloured communities had few if any opportunities to play rugby union. In Fiji during the 1930s, there were 'six European and seven Fijian teams' in the local rugby union competition with 'special portions of the recreation grounds' allotted to the Fijians.[50] Sport was clearly not an integrating force in those situations, nor in others like them. In India, minority communities and government service personnel provided the founding groups in cricket, and the game grew little beyond them, remaining a largely urban and upper middle-class phenomenon. For example, the Parsis as a cultural minority were able to accommodate themselves with the British rulers in part, at least, by taking up British cultural pursuits like cricket.[51] In the West Indies, too, non-white groups were admitted very slowly to cricket, as in the Barbadian example.[52] Spartan became in the 1890s the first non-white club and was made up of medical practitioners, lawyers and civil servants, many of whom were mulattoes. The next black club gained entry to the competition only in 1915, when Empire was created as a lower-status break-away from Spartan composed of minor civil servants and small businessmen. Whatever else, this paucity of black clubs in Barbados was not the result of an insufficient following for cricket amongst the population at large, because public holidays and weekends saw innumerable pickup games being played. The lack stemmed directly from the colonial elite's views as to who might and might not play (which depended upon their degree of commitment to cricket's imperial ideology) and from their local supporters' obedience to the cultural norm of the ruling society.

In fact, much of the potency of cricket as cultural imperialism came from the sport's voluntary imposition by its new converts rather than from an arbitrary imposition by the imperial masters (an important point confirmed in the theories of Gramsci and Bourdieu). In cricket, some of the strongest upholders of the faith were Indian and West Indian players or administrators newly won over. In Barbados, for example, Fitzherbert Adams was a late nineteenth-century schoolteacher of modest means, a member of the tiny middle-class black community that saw its future in developing a taste for things English so that it might create in part, at least, a sense of identity in the eyes of the white elite. Among those cultural emphases was cricket, which Adams instilled in his children as a code of conduct for life. One of his children went on to become Sir Grantley Adams: English-trained barrister, Spartan captain, Oxford and Barbados player, first chief minister under self-government in Barbados, prime minister of the ill-fated West Indian Federation, lifelong believer in the moral power of cricket. Sir Grantley's son, J.M.G.M. 'Tom' Adams, also trained in England, became prime minister of Barbados and, although not as accomplished a player as his father, a serious historian of cricket who respected the game as a training for life.[53]

The local conversion process was enhanced from the late nineteenth century onwards by the mobilization of tours from Britain to the colonies, and vice versa, in a wide variety of sports: cricket, tennis, rugby union, lawn bowls and many others. Again, the emphasis was not simply upon the improvement of playing skills – social education was a major objective. On a 1900 West Indian cricket tour of England, for example, a black fast bowler sought permission to play without footwear for greater comfort and grip. '"Certainly not, my good man"', retorted his white captain. '"This is England and a first-class county to boot, sir."'[54] Cricket was as much about social instruction, decorum, and respectability as about physical exercise.

And, as Tony Cozier writes of the West Indies' first official English tour in 1928, 'the Marylebone Cricket Club, in the manner of a discerning schoolmaster, deemed the student had developed sufficiently and was ready for graduation to the highest class'. One cartoon for that tour had a West Indian cricketer saying, 'We have come to learn,

Sah'. But even after a second tour in 1933, the West Indians believed there was still much learning to do. One West Indian editorial lamented that native sons still 'showed a mercurial disposition that precluded any show of fighting qualities when faced with difficult situations'. It was that very mercurial disposition that the imperial masters constantly tried to eliminate from their subject populations by way of sport, along with such other cultural institutions as education. A later extension was the tour between the greater and lesser 'developed' areas of the empire. Rugby union was established in Fiji under the influence of British officials, and in 1939 a team managed by whites (an important point) toured New Zealand, losing just one match. Both Fijian colonial officials and New Zealand rugby authorities derived considerable satisfaction, not just from the results but also from the great behaviour of the Fijians and their 'true rugby spirit'.[55]

An important contributing factor here was the role of the sports hero in raising both expectations and aspirations as well as in providing a colonial role model. It is well understood now how figures such as Dr W.G. Grace were heroes in Britain, but not so well recognized is that they were also imperial heroes who symbolized the shared collective values of the empire.[56] As an element of the tours, particularly, but also in the more everyday arenas, these heroes served a ritual purpose by constantly reminding colonial subjects of the British order of things, and for that were warmly regarded. General Sir Douglas Haig, for example, set his mark by scoring the winning goal in an interregimental polo final shortly after his arrival in India as a young subaltern.[57] Much the same could be said of the young Winston Churchill, and of other, less well-known figures.[58] Brigadier-General R.M. Poore learned his cricket from textbooks while on the staff of Lord Harris in Government House, Bombay. When transferred to South Africa, Poore developed into a fine batsman and even played for South Africa against England in 1895–96. But it was upon his subsequent entry to English county cricket that the soldier became the centre of national and imperial attention. During 1899 he scored more than 1,500 runs for Hampshire, including seven centuries, one of the best performances ever to that point. But Poore was not just a cricketer. During a two week period in June of 1899 he scored three successive centuries, was a member of the winning team in the interregimental polo tournament (he was one of the world's leading polo players), and won the best man-at-arms fencing title at the Royal Naval and Military Tournament.[59] When he returned to South Africa on service, he was the imperial epitome of the sportsman as moral exemplar.

The consensus of colonial officialdom and its supporters as to the power of these imperial bonds through sport was especially well demonstrated in the concern exhibited at activities that were regarded as threats to the established order of social behaviour in sport. During the 1890s, W.W. Read, the Surrey cricketer, undertook an 'amateur' tour in South Africa but created considerable resentment through what many colonists considered an excessive and 'professional' concern with money.[60] In 1905, a serious amount of ill-feeling arose during the very first New Zealand rugby union tour of Great Britain: The visitors lost a test match against Wales because of a disputed try – New Zealanders claimed that Bob Deans scored but was pulled back from the tryline by Welsh players before the arrival of the referee, while Welshmen claimed Deans had been tackled short of the line. The controversy raged for years.[61] In 1931, a period of intense political agitation in India, the M.C.C. selected a team of just average players to tour the subcontinent. Lord Willingdon as viceroy fielded substantial criticism from the Indian princes who controlled the Indian cricket administration. Since he was attempting to retain their political loyalty, Willingdon feared that the M.C.C.'s lack of finesse might damage further the delicate situation.[62] A few years later, at the height of the Hindu-Muslim butchery that accompanied partition in the subcontinent, there was apprehension within the India Office that the troubles might prevent a good 'Indian' presence showing empire strength and solidarity at the 1948 Olympic Games in London.[63] But the most celebrated threat to imperial sporting ties came in the Australian summer of 1932–33 and involved *the imperial game*, cricket.[64] England won the test series four matches to one, but her tactics so enraged the Australians that the affair became part of official diplomatic and political action, the tour was nearly cancelled at midpoint, and many Australians considered that the M.C.C. had destroyed the basic fabric of imperial unity, harmony and cooperation. It was a threat to Anglo-Australian relations as serious as many disputes in economic or political fields, such as the rescheduling of Australian loans by the British Treasury or the deployment of Australian troops by British generals during the war. In all these sporting cases, the concern amongst participants was of a possible breakdown in the cultural code trusted and agreed upon by a wide range of social groups within the British imperial setting.

At the height of empire, then, sport as a cultural bond had considerable force, conveying through its many forms a moral and behavioural code that bonded the imperial power with many if not most of the influential colonial quarters. Perhaps the most symbolic expression of this cultural unity came in the formation and development of what are now known as the Commonwealth Games. The idea of an imperial sports festival emerged in the early 1890s, proposed by the Australian John Astley Cooper, again showing the powerful and empire-wide sense of shared cultural values.[65] In 1911 the first and only such festival was held, to be followed in 1930 by the first British Empire Games, which were staged in Canada. The emphasis was solidly upon imperial unity and identity, significant, coming as it did at a time when the seeds for the breakup of empire had been well and truly laid, demonstrated most substantially in 1911 and 1930 by the mass agitation on behalf of demands for increased political autonomy in India. In 1938 the games were held in Sydney to mark the 150th anniversary of the founding of Australia as a British possession, the convict origins of the first settlers (those of the lower orders whom Britain did not want to keep) conveniently forgotten. And at a very early point in the development of the games system, an elaborate set of rituals emerged to celebrate the centrality of the monarchy, the homage of athletes as citizens towards that monarchy, the unity of empire, and the persistence of cultural ties despite political change. And again, as a symbolic reminder of the imperial hierarchy and of the connections between sport and general life, it is interesting that the Commonwealth Games have been staged in a less-developed, non-white majority centre only once – Kingston in Jamaica in 1966 just after the island's celebration of political independence. Sport was simply yet another arena in which non-white colonial peoples had to aspire to the standards of rulers from (and local supporters of) the developed imperial world.

However, in the very success of this socially segmented and skewed imperial ideology that paralleled life and sport lay the origins of some major complications for the empire and what became of its post-colonial commonwealth. These complications emerged from an enormous contradiction that existed within the imperial construction of sport: On the one hand it showcased sport as an influential agency that would 'improve' colonial peoples socially and politically, but on the other it attempted to maintain the fiction that sport was a discrete, apolitical institution. Sport was promoted as an instrument of apparent transcultural unity (ignoring considerable evidence to the contrary), but within it were several strands of potential conflict. Not the least of these was the fact that from the First World War onwards, the increasing international politicization of sport caught Britain in a situation where alterations to its fundamental ideology of sport became substantial. But even before those changes occurred in the 1920s and 1930s, challenges to the model had arisen in the colonies.

One immediate problem for the imperial power was that, having encouraged the measurement of social progress by comparing colonial against British achievements in sport, there would always come the day of a colonial victory that might be interpreted as symbolic of general parity. As W.F. Mandle points out, Australians certainly began to think themselves the equal of Englishmen as their tally of test cricket victories mounted.[66] The same might be said of rugby union in both South Africa and New Zealand, and rugby league in Australia. In some senses the impact of those achievements was lessened because of the favoured political and economic positions occupied by these White Dominions, but in areas of greater subjugation the impact was more far-reaching.

Early in the twentieth century the British divided the Indian province of Bengal into East and West, exacerbating existing tensions and occasioning a series of nationalist demonstrations. By 1911 the move was deemed a failure, Bengal reunited and the capital of British India removed from Calcutta to New Delhi. The period saw the first of the mass-activity campaigns that were to make the Indian independence movement.[67] Against this background, in 1911, occurred one of the most famous victories in Indian football. Organized football began in Calcutta during the 1880s and for some time consisted only of British, mostly regimental teams.[68] Gradually Indian teams were introduced. One of the first was the Mohan Bagan district side which, in 1911, defeated the East Yorks regiment two goals to one to record an Indian team's first premiership. Coming as it did at a time of intense political unrest, the victory was widely regarded as a sign of Indian development, equality and even superiority. As one Bengali-language newspaper put it, 'It fills every Indian with pride and joy to know that rice-eating, malaria-ridden, bare-footed Bengalis have got the better of beef-eating, Herculean, booted John Bull in that peculiarly English sport.'[69]

That sentiment was widespread. The eighty thousand people at the match, and many more not there, became caught up in a new sense of Bengali strength. It was an especially important turning point, as John Rosselli's work confirms.[70] He points out that during the second half of the nineteenth century, some sections of Bengali society sought to improve their standing with the British by way of physical education. The argument promoted by these groups was that the British set high store on manly physical culture, thought it lacking in Bengalis, and so despised them as a race. The Mohan Bagan victory did much to overcome the Bengali sense of physical and, therefore, cultural inferiority.

Satisfaction with sporting victories as symbolic of national achievement was particularly pronounced in cricket, naturally. It took New Zealand until the 1977–78 southern-hemisphere summer to achieve a test match victory over England, and when it arrived there was almost a sense of relief at reaching the cultural milestone. In 1950 the West Indies not only won its first test match on English soil but also went on to win the series, the end of which was marked by celebrating West Indians (the earliest of the post-war migration groups) being led onto the ground by the great calypsonian Lord Kitchener, whose songs about black cricket heroes became best sellers. India was delighted when its players beat England in a test just four years after independence, but the real triumph came in 1971 when Ajit Wadekar's team won a series in England – upon its return, the team was showered with gifts and praise. And in 1954, just seven years after their nation's creation, Pakistanis were thrilled that their team won a test during its very first tour to England, the only team in cricket history to have done so.

At a less spectacular level came the colonial modifications whereby the styles of play did not match the expectations or meet with the approval of imperial sporting authorities. Rugby union was by definition a physical game, but in much of its British heritage there was scope for risk taking, an emphasis on individuality within the conformity of team play (especially amongst backline players), and a minimum of stress on simple physical strength and vigour.[71] Welsh rugby began to alter some of that (for many of the reasons prevalent in settings more normally recognized as colonial), but the big alterations came from New Zealand and South Africa.[72] While both produced outstanding backline players such as George Nepia and Dame Craven, respectively, the hallmark of their play became rugged, unified, driving work from big, strong forwards. Violent play became relatively common, exceeding the bounds laid down in the largely unwritten moral code of sport elaborated in later nineteenth-century Britain. British commentators began to argue that rather than being a means to an end (training for life) the game had become an end (life) in itself through being taken far too seriously.

The concern for the serious turn taken by sport became especially pronounced in imperial attitudes towards Australia. Touring English cricketers from the later nineteenth century onwards complained about the tough, no-compromise approach adopted by their Australian counterparts, who performed as if the outcome of a match was life or death itself.[73] In tennis, the rise of Norman Brookes (later Sir Norman) brought a new age of intensity to the game, taking it far beyond its original party atmosphere into one of power, skill and intense competition.[74] From Brookes's time onwards, Britain ceased to be a tennis power, with Fred Perry and Bunny Austin the two exceptions to establish the rule. In billiards and snooker, the Lindrum family, Walter especially, developed their skills to new heights such that basic rules had to be altered to restrict their success. The dilemma for imperial authorities in these games, of course, was that the original intentions were fast disappearing and, along with them, some of the basics of the social code that had underlain their very creation.

In some areas, the colonial reformulation of the model was striking but was tolerated by imperial observers as a transitional phase. By the turn of the century Samoan cricket had adopted 'quaint and liberal interpretations' of the rules, but the elimination of protective gear was considered a laudable extension of the desire for manliness.[75] In Tonga, the Europeans found it difficult to counter the skills of locally produced devotees of *kilikiti,* as it was there known, but again took heart from the sportsmanship and love of the game displayed along with the irreverence for rules and the unorthodoxy of style.[76] But at its most extreme, these modifications of the imperial model could almost constitute a rejection of it, as spectacularly demonstrated in the case of Trobriand cricket.

In traditional fashion, British missionaries who went to the Trobriand Islands in the 1930s, following in the Melanesian steps of Bronislaw Malinowski, hit upon cricket as a means by which the local people might be brought to civilization and so eschew their tribal warfare practices.[77] The Trobrianders took to the game enthusiastically, but rejected the English style as being too slow. Far from forsaking tribal practices, the Trobrianders incorporated them into their version of cricket. Instead of bowling overarm, players delivering the ball used their spear-throwing actions. They were so accurate that the imperially codified width of the stumps had to be reduced. Any number of players might participate, so long as team numbers were even. Playing in restricted spaces kept tactics to a minimum. Tribal markings and war dances were made part of the rituals of play. Games became the focal point for village political activity, with the days before and after the match devoted to gift exchange and discussion. As for the match itself, the home side always won, but not by so many runs as to cause offence to the visitors. Cricket in the Trobriands, then, passed rapidly from missionary control and imperial model to a complete reshaping by the local population.

From the 1920s onwards this process of colonial reformulation of, and challenge to, the model (of which the Trobriand Islands example was the most dramatic) became further complicated for the imperial power because its own belief in the ideology came under siege. Although sport was supposedly above worldly matters, the British government in 1929 banned an English trades-union soccer team from touring Russia, arguing that the team contained known communists.[78] Its concern was bolstered by the growth in Europe of left-wing, politically inspired sports competitions in which many English teams sought to participate.[79] England's premier international football team played several politically controversial matches against teams from Italy and Germany during the 1930s, including one in Berlin during 1938 in which the

English team performed the Nazi salute.[80] British riding and shooting teams were prevented from competing in Europe on political grounds, while the 1936 Olympic Games in Nazi Berlin confirmed that sport was in a different age. Within the empire, however, sport continued to be measured against its late nineteenth-century characteristics. In both 1919 and 1946, games were the means by which pre-war normality was sought to be resurrected.[81] The inter-allied games and the hastily organized Anglo-Australian cricket tours were not greatly successful, in part at least because in both situations the wartime experience had considerably shaken the faith in empire.

The wartime fate of some imperially popular games confirmed the new pessimism. Throughout the empire many recruiting campaigns had been directed at sportsmen, who were called upon now to do the duty for which, essentially, their sports had prepared them.[82] Colonial newspapers proudly recorded the names of sports stars who volunteered for service in the First World War, and enthusiasm was high until the casualty figures for Ypres, Paschendale, Vimy Ridge and Gallipoli began to pour in, the names of men such as Tony Wilding, New Zealand and Australasian Davis Cup tennis hero, among them. All those officers trained through polo went off to be mown down by new-era machine guns, and the decline of polo as a military service industry was set with the first appearance of tanks. After the First World War, certainly, and after the Second, to a degree, the symbolic value of sport was at low ebb in the empire, coinciding with the institution's increasing complication by political consideration.

As the decolonization process gathered speed following India's independence in 1947, the contradiction of sport representing the ideals of a vanishing empire on the one hand, and becoming a no-longer apolitical ideal on the other, proved to be an important post-colonial problem. In field hockey, for example, India and Pakistan fought out in miniature many of the grievances that were to flare into military action during the 1950s and on into the 1970s. In Pakistan itself, the control of sport became an increasingly political occupation, as demonstrated by Air Vice Marshal Nur Khan, who from the 1950s while a member of government was also prominent on the national boards of several major sports. But there were more subtle problems as post-colonial states came to realize that, while the formal and institutional trappings of power could be readily taken over, the principles of cultural power, especially sport, were not so easily shifted, particularly as a number of states sought to use that cultural power themselves for nation-building purposes.[83]

By the early 1950s in the West Indies, for example, the bulk of political power had been shifted to black responsibility in a prelude to full independence, with men such as Norman Manly, Sir Grantley Adams, Forbes Burnham and Eric Williams proving to be formidable and talented architects of their people's futures. (Most, if not all of them, were also keen cricket supporters and saw in the game and in West Indian success at it a chance for self-respect.)[84] Yet, until 1960 no black player captained the West Indies on a regular basis; the captain frequently was the only white player on the team, a symbol of continuing white cultural domination during a period in which non-whites were becoming increasingly influential in other areas of political and economic life.

During the 1950s the continued white domination in cricket induced ill feeling, even bitterness, particularly during the disastrous 1954 M.C.C. tour of the Caribbean. Many of the tourists and their local white supporters alienated black leaders by their assumption of social superiority, indicated by such remarks as those of England's captain Len Hutton, who in his autobiography lamented the disappearance of white West Indian cricket officials – he imagined, presumably, that the black replacements were incapable of doing the job properly.[85]

The struggle for black parity was best shown in the matter of captaincy, however. When Frank Worrell was chosen in 1960, it was not simply because he was the best black candidate. He had also been 'civilized' in the best English games tradition by playing in England, living there for a long time, and taking an economics degree from Manchester University. That is to say, he was a black man who fitted the mould of a successful white captain. It was only with the appointment of Garfield Sobers as Worrell's successor that the West Indies had a genuinely home-grown captain.[86] More so than in many other areas, in sport the colonial baggage was difficult to dislodge.

This fact has been most dramatically borne out in all the discussion as to the place to be occupied by South Africa in Commonwealth and world sport.[87] As early as the 1930s, Johannesburg was rejected as a site for the Commonwealth Games on the grounds of inappropriate racial provisions. With the coming of the National Government in 1948 and the subsequent imposition of hard-line apartheid conditions, the contradictory attitudes in imperial sport – that is, the old ideology versus the new reality – began to be divided along lines whereby the old, white-client nations followed imperial sporting theories and the new black nations sought to use one of their few sources of bargaining power to influence Pretoria. For the new nations, sporting prowess became a bargaining resource in the way that oil or military power did for some others. As late as 1985 New Zealand rugby authorities proposed to send a team to South Africa on the grounds that they were interested in 'sport', not 'politics'. This echoed the 1984 sentiments of the England Rugby Football Union authorities whose team, unlike that of New Zealand, actually played in South Africa. In cricket for much of the 1970s and 1980s, West Indian authorities adopted a very hard line on contacts with South Africa and, because of West Indian strength in world cricket, their view has commanded considerable attention. Elsewhere, demonstrations against South African golfers, tennis players, netball teams and the like have all revealed the post-colonial power of an imperial sporting ideology born in the later nineteenth century. Sport was a preparation for life but not an integral part of it.

Sport, then, must be reckoned a most pervasive and enduring theme in the history of British imperialism. The central feature of its power is the subconscious influence it has exerted in both colonial and post-colonial conditions, frequently softening the strength of social and political change experienced in other areas of its specific cultural context. Its capacity to masquerade as an apolitical agency enhanced its ability to influence, because it appeared as one area of the social arena in which otherwise differing peoples might meet. For that reason, perhaps its most enduring monument remains the Commonwealth Games, a festival that reflects apparent unity among widely divergent nations that have little in common apart from the fleeting heritage of a now defunct imperial master. For that reason, the role of sport in the empire was strikingly similar to the power of the English nobility as sketched by T.F. Dale in 1901, 'This influence is entirely unsupported by force; it is all so intangible and made up of so many threads that it is almost impossible to define.'[88]

Notes

[1] Compare Low, ed., *Congress and the Raj*; Gallagher *et al.*, *Locality, Province, and Nation*. Alternative views are now being promoted in the *Subaltern Studies* series of essays edited by Guha.

[2] For the Indian Civil Service, O'Malley, *The Indian Civil Service, 1601–1930*; Blunt, *The ICS*; Spangenberg, *British Bureaucracy in India*.

[3] There is an enormous literature on imperialism in general and British imperialism in particular. One especially provocative work so far as this essay is concerned, however, is Maunier, *The Sociology of Colonies*.

[4] For examples of colonial planning, Preston, *Defence of the Undefended Border*; Preston and Wards, 'Military and Defence Development in Canada, Australia, and New Zealand'.

[5] Mulgan, *Home*; Chaudhuri, *The Autobiography of an Unknown Indian*; James, *Beyond a Boundary*.

[6] For the origins of the nation language theme, Braithwaite, 'The African Presence in Caribbean Literature' and *History of the Voice*; and Thiong'o, *Decolonising the Mind*.

[7] The role of sport is invariably overlooked in general studies on British imperialism, but one small exception is in Hyam, *Britain's Imperial Century, 1815–1914*. A limited set of essays is Mangan, *The Games Ethic and Imperialism*.

[8] See, for example, Gramsci, *The Modern Prince and Other Writings*; Femia, *Gramsci's Political Thought*; Hoffman, *The Gramscian Challenge*; Lears, 'The Concept of Cultural Hegemony'. For some cautionary remarks, see the interview with Eric Hobsbawm in Hobsbawm, Abelove *et al.*, *Visions of History*. For some applications to sport, see Parry, 'Sport and Hegemony'.

[9] For examples, Bourdieu, 'Sport and Social Class' and *Distinction*; Hall and Jefferson, eds., *Resistance through Rituals*.

[10] See discussion of works by Theodore Adorno and Walter Benjamin in Held, *Introduction to Critical Theory*. A good example of the influence of this general work on sports analysis is Hargreaves, *Sport, Power, and Culture*.

[11] For a review, Sandiford, 'The Victorians at Play'. For a case study of cause and effect, Mandle, 'Games People Played'.

[12] For an indication, Bailey, *Leisure and Class in Victorian England*; also Meller, *Leisure and the Changing City*.

[13] The main work in this area is Mangan, *Athleticism in the Victorian and Edwardian Public School*.

[14] For example, Scott, 'Cricket and the Religious World in the Victorian Period'.

[15] Longrigg, *The History of Horse Racing*, outlines this spread; for the British origins, Vamplew, *The Turf*.

[16] Swanton, ed., *Barclay's World of Cricket*, is a convenient guide.

[17] Johnstone, *A Brief Historical Survey of the British West Indies at Bisley, 1902–1950*.

[18] Mason, *Football!*, sketches the story. For a major example, Chester and McMillan, *Centenary*.

[19] For example, the Badminton Library series of instructional works on sport, edited by the Eighth Duke of Beaufort and A.E.T. Watson.

[20] For example, Buckland, *Sketches of Social Life in India*; Troup, *Sporting Memories*; Inglis, *Tent Life in Tigerland*.

[21] See Mangan, 'Eton in India'; Wild, *Ranji*; Nandy, 'Ranji'.

[22] For example, *The Harrisonian 25th Anniversary Issue* (Bridgetown: Harrison's, 1983); also Sandiford and Stoddart, 'The Elite Schools and Cricket in Barbados'.

[23] *Harrisonian* (December 1932).

[24] *South African Cricketers' Annual* (1891–92), 21; Grubb, *C.T. Studd*; Mangan, 'Christ and the Imperial Games Fields'; Liddell was portrayed in the film *Chariots of Fire*.

[25] See *West Indies Cricket Annual* (1979), 82.

[26] Chester, *Transatlantic Sketches*; the Trobriand case is outlined later in this article.

[27] See Pollard, *The Pictorial History of Australian Horse Racing*, 164, for the background; also O'Hara, *A Mug's Game*.

[28] *Referee* (22 Jan. 1890), 1.

[29] *The Rules of the Jockey Club of South Africa*. For an indication of racing's longstanding popularity, *Johannesburg*, 29.

[30] For example, 'Report of the Select Committee of the Legislative Assembly'.

[31] See Dale, *Polo Past and Present*. For an account of the original form of the game, Dufferin, *Our Viceregal Life in India*, 402.

[32] deLisle, *Polo in India*, iii.

[33] Finch-Hatton, *Advance Australia*, 363.

[34] Harris, *A Few Short Runs*.

[35] Willingdon took a keen interest in the game in all its colonial settings, and Jackson became a Marylebone Cricket Club Committee member.

[36] For these two, Hawke, *Recollections and Reminiscences*, 165; Williams, *How I Became a Governor*, 229.

[37] *South African Cricketer's Annual* (1891–92), 1

[38] For example, the Imperial Cricket Council was not transformed into the international Cricket Council until the 1960s, well into the phase of political devolution.

[39] Williams, 'Polo in Jodphur'.

[40] The maharajahs of Jaipur were especially prominent in this regard.

[41] Board, *Polo*. For a national example, Little, *Polo in New Zealand*.

[42] Colonial Office, (hereafter cited CO), 83/203/4, Public Records Office, London (hereafter cited PRO).

[43] *Sports and Sportsmen: South Africa*, 1, v.

[44] For the Indian case, Cashman, *Patrons, Players, and the Crowd*; for Australia, Mandle, 'Cricket and Australian Nationalism in the Nineteenth Century'.

[45] For Australian regional examples, see Stoddart, 'Sport and Society, 1890–1940'; Vamplew, 'Sport: More than Fun and Games'.

[46] See the many references to cricket in the Menzies Papers, National Library of Australia, Canberra.

[47] For this story, Stoddart, 'Cricket and Colonialism in the English-Speaking Caribbean to 1914'.

[48] For an example, James, *Beyond a Boundary*, 55–7.

[49] See Wickham, *Pen and Ink Sketches*.

[50] *Who's Who in the Sporting World*, 23; *Fiji: Handbook of the Colony*, 138.

[51] Cashman, *Patrons, Players, and the Crowd*; also Pavri, *Parsi Cricket*.

[52] See Stoddart, 'Cricket, Social Formation, and Cultural Continuity in Barbados'. A good fictional description of the Trinidadian situation is Mittelholzer, *A Morning at the Office*.

[53] The Adams story may be followed in Hoyos, *Grantley Adams and the Social Revolution*.

[54] This section is from Cozier, *The West Indies*. The 1900 story is retold in Keating, *Another Bloody Day in Paradise!*, 31.

[55] CO 831233/11, PRO. For a detailed example of touring impacts, Brown, 'Canadian Imperialism and Sport Exchanges'.
[56] For Grace, see James, *Beyond a Boundary*; and Mandle, 'W.G. Grace as a Victorian Hero'.
[57] *Polo Monthly* 1, 2 (April 1909), 92.
[58] For Churchill on polo, see his *My Early Life*, 132–4.
[59] See *Wisden Cricketers' Almanac*, 914–15.
[60] *South African Cricketers' Annual* (1891–92), 67.
[61] There is a lengthy account in Smith and Williams, *Fields of Praise*, 154–68; see also Phillips, *A Man's Country?*, Ch.3.
[62] For one version, Hammond, *Cricket My World*, 101.
[63] See L/1/1/259-58, L/1/11251-58-1, India Office Library, London.
[64] The specific discussion of the imperial dimension to this story is in Sissons and Stoddart, *Cricket and Empire*.
[65] The general picture from Stoddart, 'Sport, Culture, and Postcolonial Relations'; for the detailed origins, Moore, 'The Concept of British Empire Games'.
[66] Mandle, 'Cricket and Australian Nationalism'.
[67] Sarkar, *Swadeshi Movement in Bengal*.
[68] See *The Englishman* (13 Feb. 1895).
[69] *Nayak* (30 July 1911) in *Native Newspaper Reports: Bengal* (5 Aug. 1911).
[70] Rosselli, 'The Self-Image of Effeteness'.
[71] For the British story, Dunning and Sheard, *Barbarians, Gentlemen, and Players*.
[72] For some indications, Wakelam, *The Game Goes On*.
[73] For example, Hobbs, *Recovering the Ashes*.
[74] For the rise of Australian sport, see Stoddart, *Saturday Afternoon Fever*.
[75] Christian and Fischer, 'Cricket as She is Played in Samoa'.
[76] Christian and Fischer, 'Cricket in the South Seas'. For Fiji, see also Des Voeux, *My Colonial Service*, 11, 88–9.
[77] This story is best portrayed in the ethnographic film, *Trobriand Cricket*, made by Jerry Leach; for a similar view concerning Ocean Island, see Grimble, *A Pattern of Islands*, 48–52.
[78] Foreign Office, 371/12606/3771/38, 11 Aug. 1927, PRO. See also Juries, 'State Intervention in Sport and Leisure in Britain between the Wars'.
[79] Jones, 'Sport and Politics'.
[80] Stoddart, 'Sport, Cultural Politics, and International Relations'; Beck, 'England v. Germany, 1938'.
[81] For example, *The Inter-Allied Games*, 1919.
[82] See McKernan, 'Sport, War, and Society'; and Veitch, 'Play up! Play up!'.
[83] For example, McHenry, Jr., 'The Use of Sports in Policy Implementation'.
[84] For the general story, Lewis, *The Growth of the Modern West Indies*.
[85] See Swanton, *Sort of a Cricket Person*, 180–3.
[86] Marshall, 'Gary Sobers and the Brisbane Revolution'.
[87] There is a considerable literature on this subject, but see Archer and Bouillon, *The South African Game*.
[88] Dale, *The Eighth Duke of Beaufort and the Badminton Hunt*, 137.

References

Archer, R. and A. Bouillon. *The South African Game: Sport and Racism*. London: Zed, 1982.
Bailey, P. *Leisure and Class in Victorian England: Rational Recreation and the Contest for Control, 1830–1885*. London: RKP, 1978.

Beck, P. "England V. Germany, 1938." *History Today* 32 (1982).

Blunt, Sir Edward. *The ICS: The Indian Civil Service*. London: Faber, 1937.

Board, J. *Polo*. London: Faber, 1956.

Bourdieu, P. "Sport and Social Class." *Social Science Information* 17, no. 6 (1978).

Bourdieu, P. *Distinction: A Social Critique of the Judgment of Taste*. Cambridge, MA: Harvard University Press, 1984.

Braithwaite, E. "The African Presence in Caribbean Literature." *Daedalus* 103 (1974).

Braithwaite, E. *History of the Voice: Development of Nation Language in Anglophone Caribbean Poetry*. London: New Beacon, 1984.

Brown, D. "Canadian Imperialism and Sport Exchanges: The Nineteenth-Century Cultural Experience of Cricket and Lacrosse." *Canadian Journal of the History of Sport* 18, no. 1 (1987).

Buckland, C. T. *Sketches of Social Life in India*. London: Allen, 1884.

Cashman, R. *Patrons, Players, and the Crowd: The Phenomenon of Indian Cricket*. Bombay: Orient Longman, 1980.

Chaudhuri, N. *The Autobiography of an Unknown Indian*. Berkeley, CA: University of California Press, 1968.

Chester, G. J. *Transatlantic Sketches in the West Indies, South America, Canada and the United States*. London: Smith Elder, 1869.

Chester, R. H. and N. A. C. McMillan. *Centenary: 100 Years of All Black Rugby*. Auckland: Moa, 1984.

Christian, F. W. and E. H. Fischer. "Cricket as She Is Played in Samoa." *Badminton Magazine* ((July–Dec. 1907): 78–84.

Christian, F. W. and E. H. Fischer. "Cricket in the South Seas." *Badminton Magazine* (July–Dec. 1907): 553–62.

Churchill, W. *My Early Life*. London: Macmillan, 1943.

Cozier, T. *The West Indies: Fifty Years of Test Cricket*. Brighton: Angus and Robertson, 1978.

Dale, T. F. *The Eighth Duke of Beaufort and the Badminton Hunt*. London: Constable, 1901.

Dale, T. F. *Polo Past and Present*. London: Country Life, 1905.

deLisle, H. deB. *Polo in India*. Bombay: Thacker, 1907.

Des Voeux, Sir G. W. *My Colonial Service*. London: Murray, 1901.

Dufferin and Lady. *Our Viceregal Life in India*. London: Murray, 1893.

Dunning, E. and K. Sheard. *Barbarians, Gentlemen, and Players: A Sociological Study of the Development of Rugby Football*. Canberra: Australian National University Press, 1979.

Femia, J. V. *Gramsci's Political Thought: Hegemony, Consciousness, and the Revolutionary Process*. Oxford: Oxford University Press, 1981.

Fiji: Handbook of the Colony. Suva: Government of Fiji, 1936.

Finch-Hatton and The Hon. *Advance Australia*. London: Allen, 1885.

Gallagher, J. *et al. Locality, Province, and Nation: Essays on Indian Politics, 1870–1940*. Cambridge: Cambridge University Press, 1973.

Gramsci, A. *The Modern Prince and Other Writings*. New York: International, 1975.

Grimble, A. *A Pattern of Islands*. London: Murray, 1952.

Grubb, N. P. *C.T. Studd: Cricketer and Pioneer*. London: Butterworth, 1933.

Guha, R., ed. *Subaltern Studies*. Delhi: Oxford University Press, 1984.

Hall, S. and T. Jefferson. eds. *Resistance through Rituals*. London: Hutchinson, 1976.

Hammond, W. *Cricket My World*. London: Paul, n.d.

Hargreaves, J. *Sport, Power, and Culture: A Social and Historical Analysis of Popular Sports in Britain*. New York: St. Martin's Press, 1986.

Harris, Lord. *A Few Short Runs*. London: Murray, 1921.

Hawke, Lord. *Recollections and Reminiscences*. London: Williams and Norgate, 1924.

Held, D. *Introduction to Critical Theory: From Horkheimer to Habermas*. London: Hutchinson, 1980.

Hobbs, J. B. *Recovering the Ashes. An Account of the Cricket Tour in Australia, 1911–12.* London: Pitman, 1912.

Hobsbawm, E., H. Abelove *et al. Visions of History.* Manchester: Manchester University Press, 1983.

Hoffman, J. *The Gramscian Challenge: Coercion and Consent in Marxist Political Theory.* Oxford: Blackwell, 1984.

Hoyos, F. A. *Grantley Adams and the Social Revolution.* London: Heinemann, 1974.

Hyam, R. *Britain's Imperial Century, 1815–1914: A Study of Empire and Expansion.* New York: Harper and Row, 1976.

Inglis, J. *Tent Life in Tigerland and Sport Work in the Nepaul Frontier.* Sydney: Hutchinson, 1888.

Johannesburg: A Sunshine City Built on Gold. Johannesburg: JPA, 1931.

Johnstone and Captain R. *A Brief Historical Survey of the British West Indies at Bisley, 1902–1950.* Port of Spain: Government Printing Office, 1951.

Jones, S. "Sport and Politics: The Community Sports Movement in Britain, 1928–1935." *Eighth International Economic History Congress.* Budapest: 1982.

Juries, S. G. "State Intervention in Sport and Leisure in Britain between the Wars." *Journal of Contemporary History* 22 (1987).

Keating, F. *Another Bloody Day in Paradise.* London: Deutsch, 1981.

Lears, T. J. J. "The Concept of Cultural Hegemony: Problems and Possibilities." *American Historical Review* 90, no. 3 (1985).

Lewis, G. K. *The Growth of the Modern West Indies.* New York: Modern, 1968.

Little, K. M. *Polo in New Zealand.* Wellington: Whitcombe and Tombs, 1956.

Longrigg, R. *The History of Horse Racing.* New York: Stein and Day, 1972.

Low, E. D., ed. *Congress and the Raj: Facets of Indian Struggle, 1917–47.* London: Heinemann, 1977.

McHenry, D. E. Jr. "The Use of Sports in Policy Implementation: The Case of Tanzania." *Journal of Modern African Studies* 18, no. 2 (1980).

McKernan, M. "Sport, War, and Society: Australia, 1914–1918." In *Sport in History*, edited by R. Cashman and M. McKernan. University of Queensland Press, 1979.

Mandle, W. F. "Cricket and Australian Nationalism in the Nineteenth Century." *Journal of the Royal Australian Historical Society* 59, no. 4 (1973).

Mandle, W. F. "Games People Played: Cricket and Football in England and Victoria in the Late Nineteenth Century." *Historical Studies* 15, no. 60 (1973).

Mandle, W. F. "W.G. Grace as a Victorian Hero." *Historical Studies* 19 (1981).

Mangan, J. A. "Eton in India: The Imperial Diffusion of a Victorian Educational Ethic." *History of Education* 7, no. 2 (1978).

Mangan, J. A. *Athleticism in the Victorian and Edwardian Public School: The Emergence and Consolidation of an Educational Ideology.* Cambridge: Cambridge University Press, 1981.

Mangan, J. A. "Christ and the Imperial Games Fields: Evangelical Athletes of the Empire." Edmonton: University of Alberta paper, 1983.

Mangan, J. A. *The Games Ethic and Imperialism.* Londin: Viking, 1986.

Marshall, W. K. "Gary Sobers and the Brisbane Revolution." *New World Quarterly* 2, no. 1 (1965).

Mason, N. *Football!* London: Temple Smith, 1974.

Maunier, R. *The Sociology of Colonies: An Introduction to the Study of Race Contact.* 2 vols. London: RKP, 1949.

Meller, H. E. *Leisure and the Changing City, 1870–1914.* London: RKP, 1976.

Mittelholzer, E. *A Morning at the Office.* London: Heinemann, 1974.

Moore, K. "The Concept of British Empire Games: An Analysis of its Origin and Evolution from 1891 to 1930." PhD thesis, University of Queensland, 1987.

Mulgan, A. *Home: A New Zealander's Adventure.* London: Longmans, 1927.

Nandy, A. "Ranji: Cricket, Nationalism, Politics, Person." *Frontline* 3, no. 9 (1986): 108–18.

O'Hara, J. *A Mug's Game: A History of Gaming and Betting in Australia*. Sydney: University of New South Wales Press, 1988.

O'Malley, L. S. S. *The Indian Civil Service, 1601–1930*. London: Cass, 1965.

Parry, J. "Sport and Hegemony." *Journal of Sport Philosophy* 10 (1984).

Pavri, M. E. *Parsi Cricket*. Bombay: Thacker, 1901.

Phillips, J. *A Man's Country? The Image of the Pakeha Male: A History*. Auckland: Penguin, 1987.

Pollard, J. *The Pictorial History of Australian Horse Racing*. Sydney: Landsdowne, 1981.

Preston, R. A. *Defence of the Undefended Border: Planning for War in North America, 1867–1939*. Toronto: McGill University Press, 1978.

Preston, R. A. and I. Wards. "Military and Defence Development in Canada, Australia, and New Zealand: A Three-Way Comparison." *War and Society* 5, no. 1 (1987).

'Report of the Select Committee of the Legislative Assembly Appointed to Inquire into the Alleged Surfeit of Horse Racing'. In *Parliamentary Papers of Western Australia*, 1905.

Rosselli, J. "The Self-Image of Effeteness: Physical Education and Nationalism in Nineteenth-Century Bengal." *Past and Present* 86 (1980).

Sandiford, K. A. P. "The Victorians at Play: Problems in Historiographical Methodology." *Journal of Social History* 15, no. 2 (1981).

Sandiford, K. A. P. and Brian Stoddart. "The Elite Schools and Cricket in Barbados: A Study in Colonial Continuity." *International Journal of the History of Sport* 4, no. 3 (1987).

Sarkar, S. *Swadeshi Movement in Bengal, 1903–1908*. New Delhi: People's, 1973.

Scott, P. "Cricket and the Religious World in the Victorian Period." *Church Quarterly* 3, no. 1 (1970).

Sissons, R. and B. Stoddart. *Cricket and Empire: The 1932–33 Bodyline Tour of Australia*. Sydney: Allen and Unwin, 1984.

Smith, D. and G. Williams. *Fields of Praise*. Cardiff: University of Wales Press, 1980.

Spangenberg, B. *British Bureaucracy in India: Status, Policy, and the I.C.S. In the Late Nineteenth Century*. Delhi: South Asia, 1974.

Sports and Sportsmen: South Africa. Cape Town: Atkinson, n.d. [1929].

Stoddart, B. "Sport and Society, 1890–1940: A Foray." In *A New History of Western Australia*, edited by C. T. Stannage. Perth: University of Western Australia, 1981.

Stoddart, B. "Sport, Cultural Politics, and International Relations: England Versus Germany, 1935." In *Sport History*, edited by N. Muller and J. K. Ruhl. Neidernhausen: Schors-Verlag, 1985.

Stoddart, B. *Saturday Afternoon Fever: Sport in the Australian Culture*. Sydney: Angus and Robertson, 1986.

Stoddart, B. "Sport, Culture, and Postcolonial Relations: The Commonwealth Games." In *Sport and Politics*, edited by G. S. Redmond. Champaign, IL: Human Kinetics, 1986.

Stoddart, B. "Cricket, Social Formation, and Cultural Continuity in Barbados: A Preliminary Ethnohistory." *Journal of Sport History* 14, no. 3 (1987).

Stoddart, B. "Cricket and Colonialism in the English-Speaking Caribbean to 1914: Towards a Cultural Analysis." In *Pleasure, Profit and Proselytism: British Culture and Sport, at Home and Abroad, 1750–1914*, edited by J. A. Mangan. London: Cass, 1988.

Swanton, E. W., ed. *Sort of a Cricket Person*. London: Fontana, 1972.

Swanton, E. W., ed. *Barclay's World of Cricket*. London: Collins, 1980.

The Inter-Allied Games. Paris: Games Committee, 1919.

Thiong'o, N. W. *Decolonising the Mind: The Politics of Language in African Literature*. London: Curry, 1986.

Troup, Major W. *Sporting Memories: My Life as Gloucestershire County Cricketer, Rugby, and Hockey Player, and Member of the Indian Police Service*. London: Hutchinson, 1924.

Vamplew, W. *The Turf: A Social and Economic History*. London: Allen Lane, 1976.

Vamplew, W. "Sport: More Than Fun and Games." In *The Flinders History of South Australia*, edited by E. Richards. Adelaide: Wakefield, 1986.

Veitch, C. "Play Up! Play Up! And Win the War! Football, the Nation, and the First World War, 1914–1915." *Journal of Contemporary History* 20, no. 3 (1985).

Wakelam, H.B.T. *The Game Goes On.* London: Barker, 1936.

Who's Who in The Sporting World: Witwatersrand and Victoria Rugby. Johannesburg: Sporting Who's Who, 1933.

Wickham, C. *Pen and Ink Sketches.* Bridgetown: Herald, 1921.

Wild, R. *Ranji.* London: Rich and Cowan, 1934.

Williams, A. H. "Polo in Jodphur." *Polo and Hunting Journal* 1, no. 1 (1925).

Williams, Sir R. *How I Became a Governor.* London: Murray, 1913.

Wisden Cricketers' Almanack. London: John Wisden, 1939.

Wide World of Golf: A Research Note on the Interdependence of Sport, Culture and Economy

Introduction

How and why sports historians choose their subjects has always fascinated me. In the United Kingdom, sports historians pay more attention to football (soccer) than to rugby league, rugby union, netball or even cricket. In North America, baseball is preferred to either football (gridiron) or basketball. In New Zealand, rugby union predominates. Patterns elsewhere are less distinct but discernible: football (soccer) in Latin and South America over rugby union or polo (in which sports individual nations from the region are world competitive); cricket over squash racquets and (field) hockey in India and Pakistan.

At one level the reasons are obvious. UK football, New Zealand rugby and South Asian cricket are major consumer sports (via newspapers, radio, television and the internet in that accumulating order), and at some time were *the* participant sports as well. They naturally attract an analyst trying to make sense of cultural patterns surrounding sport – sports grounds like Wembley, Lancaster Park and Brabourne Stadium were physical indicators that specific sports were important: why would they exist otherwise?

At another level, the reasons are not so clear. There is always something about the historian's 'origins and evolution' in the subject choice, and that reaches the heart of the field's ideological and theoretical debates discussed in the prolegomena. There is a line of analysis that links the sport chosen for study to the historian's social origins and professional training. A superficial scan of my long-time friends and colleagues suggests that in the UK few of them played cricket, few played football or basketball in the United States, few rugby union in Australia, and few hockey in South Asia. They grew up where football, baseball and cricket dominated sports access and choice. They 'knew' those sports, and having done their professional training in Tudor and Stuart diplomatic history, say, or nineteenth-century English economic history they returned to those sports when the time came for sports history. There were and remain 'cross-overs', clearly: Richard Cashman's passion for Australian cricket helped spark his curiosity about the Indian game; Chuck Korr's time in England studying Tudor and

Stuart foreign policy exposed him to West Ham United Football Club; Patricia Vertinsky's training in English physical education led to her North American investigations into body culture; Bill Murray's football heritage matched his training in European history.

Which leads to this piece. Having played a marvellous club cricket season in Barbados, further playing experiences could only be disappointing so I not so much 'retired' as 'slipped away from playing'. But I had played sport all my life, and learned from the 'inside' much about the cultural patterns and social relationships that I saw in the histories. That was really an excuse to find another sport, and that was golf.

In my first Ashburton High School year, the local golf club approached the Principal seeking students interested in learning the game. Several of us took it up: Doug Bruce (New Zealand level junior tennis player, gifted cricketer and long-serving 1970s All Black); Peter Wall (elegant batsman and later bank manager in Fiji); Doug Papps (field athlete, Canterbury rugby player, health economist and now North Island wilderness guide) among them, cycling 3–4 miles to the course early on Saturday mornings in the Canterbury Plains frost. Doug, Peter and others were naturals but I was not and remain a 'manufactured' player reliant on practice, graft and hours now unavailable on the practice range: some of my best golf has been played on the range. I played junior tournaments in Christchurch, saw the private clubs there and rejoiced when fellow Kiwi lefthander Bob Charles won The Open Championship (British Open) in 1963, but I did not register the social contours. In my memory (à la M.N. Srinivas' *The Village Remembered)* the Ashburton Golf Club was open socially, even if office-holders came from business and the professions.

My re-entry was to the Federal Golf Club in Canberra. Returned from the Caribbean I was back on radio, received invitations to do public talks, and one was to Federal. They offered a fee, agreeing the sum would be reduced from the nomination fee if I joined. This was a very different golf world from that of Ashburton. Canberra was small but there were five major golf clubs, all with a social 'rank', waiting lists and fees to match. Royal Canberra was pre-eminent, and one city joke was about avoiding Wednesday illness because the specialists were all playing at Royal, along with the diplomats and senior civil servants. That had evolved, though – my friend Rob Chalmers, Royal Canberra historian, was a self-employed journalist who joined early point and watched the social profile 'rise'. Then came Federal with mainly middle level public servants, self-employed business people and similar, including odd academics.

The social historian's gaze focussed quickly. There were the individual stories. A successful businessman who joined in my cohort really caught the golf 'disease'. He went through several businesses in twelve months, and bought one of the first mobile phones to run his affairs from the course. He took six calls in the first two holes on one occasion I played with him. There was then a popular telephone ad on TV with a punchline, 'Get On The Phone!' Every time this man collected a prize, up would go that cry. Professionally he was a mess, and his wife eventually had him banned from the club – but in that first twelve months his handicap reduced from 19 to 5.

Question: what drives people to that? The sobering point was that while I did not reach that level, I was certainly fixated about reducing my own handicap.

Then there was the sheer scale of golf, especially in Australia's private club versus public access structures. The average golf course covers a minimum of 50 hectares, and many older clubs now occupy prime space in inner suburban locations. Water – on one trip to Arizona I discovered that almost 50 per cent of industrial water use there was golf-related. The link to the environment was obvious. The economic scale was enormous. At that time the average Australian private club golfer had a minimum equipment investment of about $2,500 – that meant at Federal, on Saturdays, about $500,000 worth of equipment was lying around that club alone. It was a significant industry, but most manufacturing had gone offshore. Then I began playing in America and in Scotland, particularly (watching Greg Norman win the Open in 1986 at Turnberry then effectively throw it away at Troon in 1989), and began seeing patterns again. Later still I witnessed the golf boom in Asia and the associated environmental degradation.

Yet there were virtually no references to golf in the academic literature, so I started researching and writing. That led to the official history of The Royal Sydney Golf Club with Colin Tatz. Royal Sydney had a great archive along with residential accommodation, so for a year I flew to Sydney from Canberra every second Friday, booked into my Royal Sydney room, played a few holes before dark, had dinner, went into the archives and worked late, got up early to hit balls before getting back into the archives and, eventually, flew back to Canberra Sunday night clutching two bottles of the club's own-label whisky, one to share with my Canberra neighbour and fellow Federal member, Eric Hanfield – Eric was a New South Wales junior level soccer player before the Second World War, joined Shell in Burma, then went to South Africa to train as a pilot and became an instructor. After the war he joined Foreign Affairs and immediately spent five years in Moscow.

One of my first golf pieces referenced the looming environmental question. That prompted an invitation to address a GAGM (Global Anti-Golf Movement) meeting in Japan, but I declined – I could not visit Japan without experiencing the frenetic golf culture there, but could hardly turn up at Narita with my golf clubs and explain that to GAGM. (Ironically, GAGM headquarters were in Penang but I never ventured in while living there, even though I was observing across Malaysia, Indonesia and Thailand the developments that validated the organization's very existence). It was not for me a question of banning golf but of finding ways to resolve problems, and progress has been made there. Instead of joining GAGM, I signed into the World Scientific Congress of Golf series as its sociology convenor, and that included playing the Old Course at St Andrews on a winning 'Rest Of The World' team led by that wonderful teaching professional Ross Herbert who fixed my putting woes (but who, sadly, later died of cancer). Was it Trevelyan who said the social historian needed muddy boots?

* * * * *

This research note argues that while golf is perhaps the most socially pervasive of games on a global scale, its social contours have been ignored by academic analysts. The essay isolates three themes as being likely avenues for further investigation: environmental issues, the internationalization of golf and its economy, and social access to participation. By virtue of its heavy demands on natural resources of land and water, golf is rapidly becoming an environmental issue. International economic patterns are altering traditional golf participation patterns, course ownership and equipment production. Then, the predicted 1990s golf boom may occur among social groups previously untouched by the game, again with implications for its social contexting. In each of these three themes there are clear overlaps and social interlocking that render golf an excellent research site for many of the issues in sport sociology.

Although the unofficial title of the 'world game' is generally accorded to soccer on the grounds of its international spread and massive spectator appeal, the title arguably belongs to golf. Since the beginning of its modern rise in 1860 when Willie Park Sr. won the first of the Open Championships in Britain, the dimensions taken on by golf have been enormous. Golf courses and players are found everywhere in the world, with the Soviet Union and the People's Republic of China making beginnings recently while the game has long been established in North America, Australasia, Asia, Africa, Latin America and Europe.

There are now over 25,000 courses in diverse settings around the world,[1] and well over twenty-five million registered players in the US alone, while similarly high proportions of golfers are found in Scotland (which has over 425 courses) and Australia. Moreover, the enthusiasm for golf is growing rapidly. American golfers in 1989 brought over 33,000 sets of golf clubs every day. It is calculated that by the year 2000 the US will have over forty million registered players. The value of the professional circuits around the world is escalating exponentially with the US Tour, for example, rising from less than $1 million in 1968 to over $40 million by 1988 (PGA Tour, 1989). The European tour in 1979 was worth around $3 million but by 1989 had grown to almost $30 million.[2] In Australia today, a population of 17,000,000 is supporting a professional tour worth close to $10 million.

Unlike soccer and probably all other sports, the economic complex of golf is far-reaching and takes on vast proportions. It is closely interlocked with television. There is now almost a tournament a week in the US, and the major ones are televised. The story is similar in Japan, Europe, Asia generally, and Australasia. The golf boom is inextricably linked with real estate developments worth billions of dollars internationally. Golf course architecture is now highly lucrative as an insatiable demand for development sweeps the world. Some thirty-three new golf courses are needed every month in the US to meet the needs of the 1.5 million new players each year.[3] As the number of courses grows, so too do the associated costs. One 1985 survey calculated that courses in the US cost over $3.5 billion annually to maintain.[4] The equipment industry is similarly gargantuan, and so too is the clothing trade that accompanies it.[5] Notwithstanding the popularity of soccer, golf is clearly the major sport in terms of its socioeconomic impact.

Yet only rarely is that impact commented upon in academic literature concerning the social and economic parameters of sport, while in the golf-specific literature which dates back to the late nineteenth century there is scarce comment upon the wider implications of the game. This essay will not cover all aspects concerning the evolution and social morphology of golf, though it should now be clear that the game offers vast scope for research. Rather, the essay sets out to posit, directly and indirectly, a research agenda based on three major planks of specific importance to golf itself and to sports more widely.

Environmental issues will become increasingly important in golf as course expansion in the international context takes up more and more natural resources with greater ramifications for flora and fauna. The internationalization of golf in the ownership of courses, production outlets and distributional patterns is having a substantial effect in altering traditional golf practices specific to national cultures. Also, the question of social access to golf (a long-time issue in the sport) is now particularly important as changes are wrought in equipment patterns, course designs and membership structures. Within these three issues lie many subthemes, of which it is possible to consider just a few.

The research methodology for the essay is based upon these principal components: the scant academic literature, the undifferentiated golf industry literature, national statistical data, newspaper and periodical material and observational and interview information gathered in Canada, the US, Australia, New Zealand and Great Britain. The interpretations forwarded are tentative but point to a growing and complex interdependence between the game of golf, its supporting industry, its social context and its natural environment. The way toward more substantial interpretations, by association, lies with a strong cross-disciplinary approach to this sprawling area of social research based in sport.

Environmental Issues

The environmental impact of golf courses and golf course development has always been a consideration within the sport. As early as 1936, for example, the Australasian Ornithologists Union requested the New South Wales Golf Council to have courses declared as bird sanctuaries wherever possible, and the Council agreed.[6] But with the growing strength of green movements and the emergence of green parties during the 1980s in several parts of the world which have coincided with the golf boom, the issue has become increasingly significant.[7] Long-established courses occupy what are now prime real estate sites, as with the famous sandbelt clubs in Melbourne, Australia, and the similar strips within major cities like London and New York.

Conservation issues have become significant, as the Royal Canberra Golf Club in the Australian federal capital discovered. At its creation in the 1920s, the course was filled with exotic trees. When it was proposed to remove a stand of a rare species in preparation for a 1988 professional tournament, conservationists took up the fight to the point of damaging sections of the course. Although mainstream conservationists hitherto have overlooked the golf question, that situation is changing rapidly. Alarmed by the threat posed to flora and fauna by new course developments, the Nature Conservancy Council in Great Britain has issued a guide to conservation aspects involved in golf.[8]

The central problem, of course, is that golf is resource-hungry in demanding large spaces and substantial water supplies. On both counts it places heavy demands wherever it seeks to expand, especially in fragile ecological environments or where it simulates 'foreign' landscape patterns and where the demand for new courses is voracious. Additionally, given the sprawling nature of golf courses and their heavy emphasis on grooming, the use of fertilizers and insecticides has gone without question. Now, as the impact of such chemicals upon the natural environment is better known, golf courses are under greater scrutiny. Early in 1990 the New South Wales government in Australia pointed out that under new legislation club directors could face fines of up to $1 million and possible jail terms for using pollutant insecticides.[9] The accumulated impact of all these trends stands revealed in a Canadian example:

Vancouver is the country's major golf centre because its climate allows almost total year-round play, but because of major population growth the city is now very short of courses.[10] The topography of the city dictates that a 50,000-hectare region of wetlands and forest to the southeast is the only logical golf course development area, and by mid-1989 the local council had proposals for nineteen new courses to consider. However, the area is also one of North America's main bird habitats and conservationists are concerned that golf courses would destroy the avian food chain and so destroy the birdlife. One case study concerned Townsend's vole, a cousin to the field mouse. Experts argue that fairways and greens would destroy the vole's natural home; the animal would disappear, taking with it the hawks and owls for which it is a major food source.[11]

Similar environmental issues are arising in the mountain resort of Whistler Valley to the north of Vancouver. Whistler has been developed as a spectacular ski centre but, influenced by two considerations, planners and developers have already opened one international class golf course and others are planned. First, the greying of the North American population is thought to contain within it a downturn in the volume of demand for skiing. Second, the need to develop Whistler as a summer as well as winter resort, in order to maximize cash flow and profit margin, has meant a natural turning to golf. Some critics have pointed to a third consideration: There is some evidence of decreasing snowfall in the area, thus another industry might be a necessity rather than a simple addition. Whatever the combination of factors, environmental critics are concerned that golf course development added to ski resort growth, with attendant increases in pollution, constitutes a major threat to a fragile ecology that could well suffer irreversible damage.

Such controversies are now widespread. The golf industry in Arizona is worth up to $800 million annually for state revenue, but it uses 10 per cent of municipal water consumption and 40 per cent of industrial and commercial water usage.[12] With over 100 courses in existence and numerous others planned around Tucson and Phoenix, the matter is becoming crucial as the desert is pushed back at resorts such as Desert Mountain. Governmental regulation and industrial research is occurring, but the results are open to interpretation. For example, developers are required to preserve all saguaro cactus on their courses, but critics label the result as 'Disney Desert'. Course designers are beginning to respond, as with Tom Fazio's tough Ventana Canyon layout, which has achieved minimal environmental interruption.

Ventana Canyon points to a crucial debate that requires much more research: Can golf courses have a positive environmental impact? Some research suggests that at centres such as Palm Springs, extensive fairways and trees can reverse the greenhouse effect,[13] helping counteract conservationist criticism during drought when water must be transported in to maintain courses. Other claims have it that animals and birds are attracted to and encouraged by courses, as at Ventana Canyon and at Federal Golf Club in Canberra, where native parrots abound. This is a complex issue but one that needs attention as magazines such as *Golf West* continue to stress golf-related expansion into virgin country.[14]

An important consideration here concerns the pace and scope of impact, as demonstrated by some international examples. Spain now has well over 100 courses catering to the new boom.[15] The South Carolina resort of Myrtle Beach now offers about fifty golf courses and almost twice that number of accommodation outlets.[16] In each respect the numbers are increasing substantially each year. West Palm Beach County in Florida now has well over 100 courses, with more opening each year. And the Gold Coast to the south of Brisbane, Australia, has sixteen courses with another forty in the design stage. The area is now being called the Golf Coast.[17] In all these cases, given that the average course covers at least 50 hectares, the environmental impact possibilities are clear: encroachment upon natural resources, pollution and pressure upon flora and fauna.

Internationalization and Economics

What becomes important at this point is the realization that environmental issues, important though they are in their own right, are considerably interlocked with the social morphology of golf. In Japan for example, golf has become a national obsession. But in a country with a high population density, little available land, and a very healthy economy, the result is inevitable: golf is exceptionally expensive.[18] Two companies listed on the Tokyo Stock Exchange trade solely as brokers in golf club memberships, a lucrative business as institutions such as the Koganei Country Club near Tokyo now cost approximately $3 million to join and there is a waiting list.

Golf lore worldwide is now rich in consequential stories such as the Japanese executive whose company bought him a corporate membership at Royal Melbourne Golf Club in Australia. He flies from Tokyo to Melbourne for two weekends per month, and it is still cheaper than playing at home where daily fees as high as $300 are quite common and even the massive and numerous driving ranges are expensive by international standards. These conditions have led to the development of schemes such as that proposed by Canada's Fairway Capital Partners. For the purchase of an $18,000 unit, tradable on specified stock exchanges, investors gain access (that is, 'membership') to 160 golf clubs around the world and proposed developments in Canada.[19]

Little wonder, then, that a major phenomenon has been the Japanese buying of foreign courses.[20] Japanese interests now own some famous name golf courses such as Turnberry in Scotland, and La Costa and the Riviera Country Club in California.[21] Virtually all the resort courses on Oahu in Hawaii and on the Gold Coast in Australia are Japanese owned. In other cases, Japanese money has bought major shares in significant clubs. Wentworth in England, for example, was bought by an English property company for $60 million in 1988. The company then offered forty Japanese investors life membership in return for a total of $64 million. Regular members were unimpressed, particularly when it appeared that, for obvious reasons, they would have to find another name for the 'Burma Road' course.[22]

In Australia the ultimate irony is that Riverside Oaks, the headquarters course of the Australian Professional Golfers Association just outside Sydney, is now owned by a Japanese company. Given appropriate governmental standards on foreign ownership, that shift is not in itself a bad thing, although in Australia, Canada and the US at least, it seems there is no systematic record of such ownership changes. In Western Australia, for example, a Japanese company has developed a resort and residential golf complex called The Vines, rated the second most difficult course in the country. Of the fifty-six luxury condominiums and 349 residential lots in Stage 1 of the project, at least half went to overseas buyers with no apparent difficulties raised by the federal Foreign Investment Review Board.[23]

This pattern of internationalization may be discerned, with variations, in numerous parts of the world. The Spanish boom is being matched in France with American money and design to the fore, a principal target market being British golfing holiday makers.[24] On the Caribbean island of Jamaica, where all economic indicators are very low, a substantial strip on the northern coast is now given over to luxurious golf resorts aimed at North American and European customers. Again, the investment capital is foreign. In Barbados, where land is extremely scarce, the Sandy Lane course is attached to a luxurious hotel and both are owned by offshore companies and aimed primarily at foreign visitors.

The hidden text is that these trends help to alter the cultural patterns of golf specific to countries and localities. Green, for example, reports that the Valencia complex in southern California was transformed from a $37 per round facility into a private concern costing $27,000 for individual membership and $54,000 for companies.[25] A considerable number of public links players are now looking for somewhere else to play in an already crowded situation. In Hawaii the state government had to decree a reduced rate of green fees to allow Hawaiian citizens the opportunity to play courses in their own state.

In Australia, similarly, the foreign-owned resorts charge foreign rates for tourists, with a twofold result. At a time when Australian participation rates are increasing, the expansion in the number of courses by itself has done relatively little to accommodate the growth. Also, traditionally low fees for golf in Australia are now under pressure because of foreign examples. And there are the long-term possibilities. Gold Coast courses have been aimed at the Japanese market as part of a tourism drive. But Australia was paralysed by a domestic pilots' strike for the second half of 1989 and tourism declined dramatically; the future health of golf in that circumstance is unclear.

But it is not only the club or public links player being affected by these economic alterations; the professional arena is also now seeing some consequences. During 1988 there emerged within the Australian PGA a major factional power struggle. On the one side were several prominent players with major Japanese connections established by way of their playing success on the Japanese tour. On the other side were players connected with the American tour and with a former Australian media tycoon. Adding complexity to the debate were the presence of a Japanese sports management company, DSE (Dunlop Sports Enterprises), confronting the most famous group of all, IMG (International Management Group), owned by Mark McCormack. DSE won the rights to promote several Australian tour events, put them into Japanese-owned resorts, included Japanese television interests in the telecasting deals, and demanded the presence of numerous Japanese players to satisfy Japanese viewers. [26]

Some Australian professionals mounted a strong protest at being excluded from events staged in their own country, yet their own organization adopted as its logo the frill-necked lizard, an Australian identity much loved by Japanese tourists. To capitalize on the divisions and tensions, IMG interests are now developing several course projects. Either way, Australian professional golf is yielding its sovereignty to foreign interests. The long-term implications here are unclear, given the absence of detailed research, but several points are worth investigating, such as the potential effects of any downturn in the Japanese economy.

Social Access to Golf

One of the most important considerations in countries enjoying a boom in playing numbers concerns whether the courses being built serve the needs of all those new participants. Analysts such as Andrews interpret National Golf Foundation data as suggesting that baby boomers constitute the real growth area, and this line of thinking has determined the overdevelopment of private, upscale courses. Near Toronto, Canada, for example, the Curtis Strange-endorsed King Valley Golf and Country Club has been set up to serve 450 memberships at $65,000 each.[27] While over half of new Canadian courses are planned for the Toronto region, ventures such as these are doing relatively little to alleviate the general pressure. And even then there are doubts about the discretionary income of those targeted high-salary families; it must be noted that projections of high income course developments have not always worked.[28]

In recent years, for example, the USPGA has sponsored its own courses in association with developers, proceeding from the principle that average players will be keen to challenge courses associated with professional golfers. By and large the TPC

(Tournament Professionals' Championship) courses have succeeded, but not always. The Star Pass TPC in Tucson, Arizona, was originally planned as a membership course but failed because of recession in key areas of the city's narrow-based economy. By early 1989 the course had reverted to a daily fee at the supposedly bargain price of $45. Even in one of America's winter golf capitals, at that price the Star Pass future was unclear because most of the public courses were priced at $25 or less. Thus, because of its ill-defined audience the Star Pass project was struggling financially in the midst of a supposed golf boom. Not surprisingly, a group within the PGA is now keen to develop lower cost courses aimed more toward the public links players (who gain access to a course by payment of a fee per round), identified by other analysts as being at the heart of the growth.[29]

This confusing pattern of disjuncture between supply and demand is not exclusive to North America. In France, Spain and Italy for example, the game is still geared largely toward the needs of the upper socioeconomic levels, while in Australia relatively few new municipal courses are being constructed to serve the needs of golf's newcomers. In the US, the National Golf Foundation calculates that almost 80 per cent of golfers pay some sort of daily fee, yet as little as 15 per cent of new courses may be aimed toward that group.[30] The situation may well be worse in the United Kingdom, where private clubs constitute up to 80 per cent of available courses in some areas. Yet by the year 2000 Great Britain will need almost 700 new courses to keep pace with the projected boom, and most will need to be in the public category.[31]

One key difficulty here is that while groups such as the National Golf Foundation and the Royal and Ancient are accumulating data concerning the current and potential golf market, it seems the data are nationally generalized rather than regionally specified. And even then, much of the social impact of a new course rests with the developers and the brief given to their architects.[32] The architects in fact again demonstrate the intertwining effect of course, environment, social impact and internationalization. While many players and former players have now joined the ranks of the professionally trained course architects, the trade is dominated by just a few names, most notably that of Robert Trent Jones Jr.

During the last twenty years Jones has built well over 100 courses (his fee is around $1 million per course design) in America, Europe, Asia, Australia, and now China and the Soviet Union.[33] While he is noted as an architect who does not shift a lot of dirt and considers himself an environmentalist, there is a distinctive feel about many of his courses regardless of their location. In that sense the game itself becomes internationalized. More important, though, outside of the US courses are now being styled at costs of up to $300 million. Even a resort course with high player turnover at that cost is forced to charge very high fees, thereby restricting the possible clientele.

Moreover, such pressure creates potential conflict with developers moving in on established sites where the social practice of popular access is well set. During 1989 for example, a consortium headed by Australian superstar player Greg Norman and including wealthy businessmen sought to take over a club in Sydney, Australia. Close to the city and located on spectacular coastline, the course and adjoining land was a perfect resort site. However, the course was also a popular public links as well, whose members did not want their playing traditions altered. The developers exerted considerable economic pressure and waged a high-profile media campaign in an attempt to win the site, but they failed to shift the resolve of the membership. The conflict here was clear: local tradition versus development that had an eye to a foreign market. Local interests have not always won such victories.

Equipment Issues

During the 1980s in particular, an interconnected concentration of equipment production outlets and the internationalization of production ownership has also helped reshape playing practice in many settings. Since the mid-1970s Australia has had no production of golf equipment but rather the assembly of components. The overwhelming percentage of Australian equipment now comes from Taiwan and Japan.[34] That Australian condition resulted from tariff structures and a sales tax that rendered the local product uncompetitive.[35] In turn, that created a loss of jobs and a loss of skills – a good golf club maker is now an Australian rarity.

What has begun to happen in Australia as a result is that the club professional faces a declining revenue from equipment sales, losing out to the mass discount houses, and the consumer has a narrowing range of product choice. The average Australian player, for example, can read the American edition of *Golf Digest* but find precious few of the products advertised therein available locally. And because many of the excise problems still prevail in Australia, superior equipment in particular is still very expensive.

Similar situations have arisen in the US, where famous companies such as MacGregor and Wilson have finally passed to foreign companies such as the Amer group of Finland. It seems that the combined impact of foreign competition, mostly from Japan, and high domestic overheads created severe economic difficulties for previously successful companies. As a result there is market domination: Four companies dominate golf ball manufacturing, and similar domination is beginning to mark the manufacture of clubs. While it is clear that companies like Spalding have always been dominant whereas companies like Hogan have occupied a small but notable niche, it is also clear that these patterns are shifting. Hogan is now part of a non-American conglomerate, while Spalding's market share is weak. They are being displaced by major overseas groups like Mizuno and Daiwa and by an apparent range of brand names which, in reality, emanate from the same source. Although experts like Ralph Maltby can point to a substantial list of boutique club manufacturers (he lists sixty, some of which have since been taken over), such as Cleveland Classics and Cobra, legendary club makers like Tony Penna are now absorbed into conglomerates while bulk componentry becomes increasingly significant.[36]

Consequently, the possibilities of market manipulation are on the increase, there are already concerns about the quality control of manufacturing, and it may be that traditional standards are declining. Nostalgia alone surely does not dictate the high prices that top players are prepared to pay for 'classic' clubs. These are the clubs of renowned quality that players no longer consider to be available, hence the escalating prices. And in the case of wooden headed clubs there is a related conservation issue. Traditionally, the best drivers and fairway woods were turned from blocks of persimmon, a tree now in short supply in the US, its main source. In turn this has helped create another problem where conservation, commercialism and internationalism interact with modern technology.

A major trend in recent years has been the use of non-traditional materials in the manufacture of golf clubs. This originated in Japan and has been taken up in other manufacturing centres so that graphite, carbon, titanium, ceramics, plastic and metal mixes are now common in both heads and shafts. Given research programmes, development costs, exchange rates, and taxes, such equipment is becoming prohibitively expensive. During 1990 for example, Japanese star 'Jumbo' Ozaki introduced his American professional colleagues to a new graphite driver that was allowing him to out-hit them by at least 50 metres from the tee. The driver will retail in the US for around $600, confirming the possibility that equipment costs may become even more an issue in the question of social access than it has in the past.

Between them, the trends in golf course construction, equipment manufacture, and internationalism have gone to the heart of golf philosophy: Should the game be made easier for the masses now taking it up? Historians remember, for example, that Chick Evans won the 1916 US Open with a marvellous score of 286 at the Minikhada Country Club course in Minneapolis using just seven wooden shafted clubs.[37] The question concerning many in the golf fraternity is whether playing skills like these will be subverted by technological assistance. This tension between tradition and modernity is perhaps more obvious in golf than in any other sport, and the game's governing bodies have been tested severely in recent years. Two examples will suffice:

Karsten Solheim's Ping Company of Phoenix, Arizona, produced a line of clubs with unconventional grooves in the irons. They were squared rather than tapered into the clubs and produced much greater backspin on the ball so that making shots from sand and difficult lies was infinitely more easy. The US Golf Association and the Royal and Ancient Golf Society of St Andrews, Scotland (the two major golf governing bodies), banned the clubs on the grounds that they were technically illegal. In reality they were arguing a contravention of tradition. Solheim initiated a multi-million-dollar lawsuit to have the ban lifted; a compromise was reached during 1990 but all parties were reluctant to claim victory. The second example concerned the long-shafted putter. Putting has always been a notoriously difficult part of golf. One discovery was that by lengthening the putter shaft and placing one hand at the top and another halfway down while resting the chin on top of the shaft, a pendulum effect was created to eliminate the twitches associated with conventional putting. Again, this has come under suspicion for flouting the traditions of golf.

Although this sort of controversy is not new to golf, it is arguably becoming more frequent and more problematic. The governing bodies have long been active in banning or challenging innovation, such as when steel shafts were first introduced and when radical design shifts have been involved, and in restricting technological alteration that would shift playing conditions, such as golf balls that might fly 350 metres. Now, however, the question might be even more urgent. Unfettered technological advance in equipment, for example, would render extant golf architecture obsolescent, new courses would require even greater reserves of natural resources, playing costs would rise accordingly, and the question of social access would be necessarily aggravated.

Conclusion

What even this brief essay should demonstrate, then, is that golf represents perhaps the quintessential case study of the inherent relationship between sport, economy, society and environment present in many contemporary national and transnational settings. Yet the ramifications of that relationship remain unexamined by academic analysts and unremarked upon by the golf industry itself. Not only does the golfing subculture itself offer rich ground for sociological investigation but so also does its intricate relationship with the wider social framework that supports it. As the predicted 1990s golf boom unfolds, so too should the deeper investigation of its inner workings.

Notes

[1] Green, *Golf*.
[2] PGA Tour, *Official PGA Tour Book*.
[3] D. Purgavie, 'Dermot Purgavie's America'. *Daily Mail*, 17 July 1990, 10.
[4] Bailey, 'Over the Mounds and into the Rough'.
[5] Cody, 'Golf's Biggest Show'.
[6] Innes, *The Story of Golf in New South Wales*.
[7] Anderson, L. 'Course Builders Face Environmental Odds'; McCleery, 'Golf Breaks into the 1990s'.
[8] Nature Conservancy Council, *On Course Conservation*.
[9] 'Club Directors Face Million Dollar Fines'. *Golf News* 1990, 9.
[10] 'Golfers Starved for Places to Play'. *Vancouver Sun*, 16 July 1988, H 1–2.
[11] 'Golf's 18 Holes Threaten Lowly Voles, Delta Warned'. *Vancouver Sun*, 25 April 1989, 1–2.
[12] Colie, 'Is Golf Killing the Desert?'.
[13] 'Report on Golf's "Greenhouse" Effect', 14.
[14] *Golf West*, March–April 1989.
[15] Spanish Golf Federation, *Guide to Golf in Spain*.
[16] Myrtle Beach Tourist Association, *Myrtle Beach Golf Holiday*.
[17] Tourism and Real Estate Monitor, *Japanese Tee up Long Term Profits*.
[18] 'Report on Japanese Gold Costs', 14.
[19] *Australian*, 'Report on Fairway Capital Partners', 15.
[20] J. Huxley, 'A Yen for Golf: Keepers of the Greed'. *Good Weekend*, 29 Nov. 1989, 44–50.
[21] Green, 'Japanese Investors Move on U.S. Golf Properties', 44
[22] Many British troops died fighting the Japanese during the Second World War, and many more died as prisoners during the construction of the 'Burma Road'. 'Members Grumble at Japanese Investors'. *Weekend Australian*, 7–8 Oct. 1989, 24.

[23] 'Investor to Spend $30 Million on Upgrade', *Weekend Australian*, 21–22 Oct. 1989, 17.

[24] Cambio, 'Reglas De Oro Para Jugar Al Gold' [Rules for Playing Golf]; Green, *Golf*.

[25] Green, 'Japanese Investors Move on U.S. Golf Properties'.

[26] J. Ramsay, 'Japanese Firm Tray Snap up Top Events', *Sydney Morning Herald*, 7 July 1989, 7. At the launch of the Vines Classic, for example, the opening address was given in Japanese.

[27] Andrews, 'The Explosive Future of Golf'; National Golf Foundation, *Golf Projections 2000*; King Valley Golf and Country Club, Prospectus.

[28] During preparation of this study two further social issues developed. The first concerns the racial, ethnic and religious composition of club memberships at championship courses. The second concerns native rights, treaty issues, land ownership and golf course development, as manifested by the barricades at Oka, near Montreal. Maclean's, 'The Hottest Game'.

[29] Burbaum, 'America's Favorites: Baseball, Apple Pie ... And Golf!'

[30] Ibid.

[31] Royal and Ancient Golf Club of St. Andrews, *The Demand for Golf*.

[32] Cornish and Whitten, *The Golf Course*.

[33] E. Kiersh, 'Leonardo of the Links: The Art and Bombast of Golf-Course Designer Robert Trent Jones Jr', *New York Times Magazine* 13 Nov. 1988, 49–50, 84–5, 91–2.

[34] 'Foreign Trade, Australia: Imports, 1985–86.' edited by Australian Bureau of Statistics, 1987.

[35] Industries Assistance Commission Report, 'Sporting and Recreational Equipment'.

[36] Maltby, *Golf Club Design, Fitting, Alteration, and Repair*.

[37] Sommers, *The U.S. Open*.

References

'89, Pro-Golf. *The Official Pga European Tour Book*. Wentworth, UK: European PGA Tour, 1989.

Anderson, L. "Course Builders Face Environmental Odds." *Golf Digest* (1989): 75–6.

Andrews, P. "The Explosive Future of Golf." *Golf Digest* (1989): 103–16.

Bailey, R. "Over the Mounds and into the Rough: The Ideal Golf Course." *Parks and Recreation* (May 1989): 38–40.

Burbaum, B. "America's Favorites: Baseball, Apple Pie ... And Golf!." *Parks and Recreation* (1989): 26–31.

Cambio. "Reglas De Oro Para Jugar Al Gold." [Rules for Playing Golf] *No. 967* 1990.

Cody, D. "Golf's Biggest Show." *Sky* (Nov. 1988): 66–76.

Colie, N. "Is Golf Killing the Desert?" *City Magazine* (1989): 26–33.

Cornish, G.S. and R.E. Whitten. *The Golf Course*. New York: Routledge, 1981.

'Foreign Trade, Australia: Imports, 1985–86'. Edited by Australian Bureau of Statistics, 1987.

Green, R. *Golf: An Illustrated History of the Game*. London: Collins, 1987.

Green, R. "Japanese Investors Move on U.S. Golf Properties." *Golf Digest* (1988): 44.

Industries Assistance Commission Report. *Sporting and Recreational Equipment*. Canberra: AGPS, 1979.

Innes, D.J. *The Story of Golf in New South Wales*. Sydney: NSWGA, 1988.

King Valley Golf and Country Club. Prospectus 1988.

McCleery, P. "Golf Breaks into the 1990s." *Golf Digest* (Feb. 1990): 50–5.

Maclean's. "The Hottest Game." 102 15 1989.

Maltby, R. *Golf Club Design, Fitting, Alteration, and Repair: The Principles and Procedures*. Newark, OH: Maltby, 1982.

Myrtle Beach Tourist Association. *Myrtle Beach Golf Holiday*. Myrtle Beach: Tourist Association, 1988.

National Golf Foundation. *Golf Projections 2000 (Vol. 11)*. Jupiter, FL, 1988

Nature Conservancy Council. *On Course Conservation: Managinng Golf's Natural Heritage*. London: 1990.

PGA Tour. *Official PGA Tour Book*. Ponte Vedra, FL, 1989.

'Report on Fairway Capital Partners'. *Australian* (29 May 1990): 15.

'Report on Golf's "Greenhouse" Effect'. *Golf Digest*, 1989.

'Report on Japanese Gold Costs'. *Golf Digest*, 1989.

Royal and Ancient Golf Club of St. Andrews. *The Demand for Golf*, St. Andrews, UK, 1989.

Sommers, R. *The U.S. Open: Golf's Ultimate Challenge*. London: Hutchinson, 1987.

Spanish Golf Federation. *Guide to Golf in Spain*. Madrid: Spanish Golf Federation, 1989.

Tourism and Real Estate Monitor. *Japanese Tee up Long Term Profits*, 1989.

Cricket, Literature and Culture: Windows on the World

Introduction

This essay was delivered as the Barry Andrews Memorial Lecture at the Australian Defence Forces Academy, University of New South Wales in Canberra, probably the most emotional presentation I have faced.

Barry was among the *Sporting Traditions* originals, a gifted cricketer and great academic who died far too young at 44. He was one of those great advisors, confidantes and friends whom you might not see for a while but when you did things took up immediately from where they had left off last. Our 1977 meeting was in the classic Australian sense: he arrived as literary analyst, critic, sports fan and, above all, *bon vivant.* Like most of us there Barry loved a drink, and the morning after a dinner to mark Day 1 of *Sporting Traditions* 1 [1], Barry turned up saying 'Fellas, do you know where I left my car?' I loved him for that, and for his marvellous insight. He was notoriously badly organized, even by the normal academic standards, and his other great line was 'Sorry I'm late, fellas'.

He was short, red-headed and leprecaunish. On one celebrated occasion the ANU cricket side, of which Barry was coach, played a visiting English side and Barry went to bat with his side in deep trouble. One of the opponents opined that they would rid themselves quickly of this little 'red-headed c . . . t'. Barry scored a marvelous century, all the while reminding the English 'voice' of his comments.

Barry was most famous for his joint editorship of the *Oxford Companion To Australian Literature*, a signifier that he had been through the credibility mill long before he got to sports studies, because Australian literature in some realms of the older Australian universities then was an oxymoron. His other great work was on the Australian comic strip character, Ginger Meggs, whom Barry saw as a litmus test for the Australian character, and in whom many observers saw the perfect litmus test for Barry.

In the sports world he is legendary for two marvellous pieces. Aggrieved by the *Australian Dictionary of Biography*'s disdain for sport, at one conference Barry delivered an imaginary *ADB* entry for one *Lap, Phar* – the legendary horse Phar Lap, iconic in Australian folklore. Barry had 'Lap' born in New Zealand where he was 'educated' (trained) privately, accompanied always by colourfully dressed people (jockeys), idolized by 'modest speculators' (punters), supported by 'publishers' (bookmakers) like the renowned Jack Waterhouse, occasionally addressed as 'you mongrel' (on the occasions when the horse did not win); and buried in Wellington, Canberra and Melbourne. It was pure Barry to conclude the piece by noting that 'owing to an unfortunate accident in his youth [Phar Lap]left no children' – the horse had been gelded. The speech was a triumph, and appeared later in print. It changed *ADB* practice, because sports people began to appear and now when I write entries (such as on Joe Kirkwood and Bill Williamson) I pause to thank Barry for making it possible.

His 'Tugging Four Bits Off The Deck At The WACA', found in the second *ST* conference papers collection (*Sport: Money, Morality and the Media,* edited by Richard Cashman and Michael McKernan), was a triumphal insight into sports language. I loved it because in our many conversations Barry emerged as an ethnographer like me, only better. The piece analyzed cricket and other sports language, taking readers inside a playing subculture with its own codes. It opened with Barry's recollection of a match during which a fellow player told him that you could 'safely tug four bits off the deck at the WACA without fear of getting rissoled for a gozzer by a guzunder' (that is, at the Western Australian Cricket Association ground you could confidently hit across the line of the delivery without worrying you might be bowled for no score by a ball coming through low!). Whenever I heard golfers talking about 'hitting it pure' and cricketers getting a 'jaffa', again I remember Barry. He would have been fascinated by the current reference to 'playing good cricket' and all the meaning buried inside those words.

Barry died in 1987 and I was with him shortly before the end, wondering why it was happening and thinking there was more to life than sport. But there was to remember the Barry Andrews who created a philosophical debate out of his local babysitting group. He turned up to babysit one night, but the neighbour argued it should be Robin Andrews not Barry who undertook the task. That led to a full scale group debate with Barry, rightly, arguing that it was a curious feminist position where men were denied babysitting tasks. It was the same Barry whose house was just a suburb away but it took me an hour to reach when first in the unfamiliar 'planned' Canberra environment.

On the night I last saw Barry we had a visitor, Shane Withington, then the star of 'Country Practice' whom we had met in the Solomon Islands while travelling there. The next morning came the call to say that Barry had died, and I was feeling very low. Shane emerged and when I asked him how he had slept he replied, 'I died'. He was embarrassed when told the context but I started to laugh, because that was the humour Barry adored.

When asked to do the Memorial I was deeply honoured, and wanted to do a cricket piece Barry would have liked. It started with the comics in which my mother had indulged me, moved via a novel for juveniles, and evoked the great Ginger Meggs. The piece went on into postmodernism but mixed the game with the theory, because Barry was supremely good at that. The piece crossed many boundaries because Barry, too, believed sport to be more complex than it appeared on the surface. Many times yearly I regret Barry's absence, because he was a major reason many of us can do the work in which we believe.

* * * * *

We begin with an encapsulation of a novel entitled *Malleson at Melbourne* written by William Godfrey.[2] Henry 'Abdul' Malleson is a 40-year-old English amateur cricketer who is vice-captain of both his English and county teams, being the deputy and friend to a more dashing contemporary, a fellow amateur. Born in India, Malleson is supported financially in his devotion to cricket by a small business founded by his parents on their return from the Empire. The business also supports the public school education of Malleson's son, Clive, whose mother died during childbirth. Malleson is contemplating a life after cricket but, when his friend and captain undergoes serious cancer surgery, the loyal servant is persuaded by MCC to lead its inexperienced team to Australia without any great expectations of success.

There are two other significant figures on this, cricket's equivalent of the Children's Crusade. The first is a young, raw and self-doubting fast bowler in whom Malleson has enormous faith, and who is on the tour only because of the honourable veteran's persuasive influence on the selection panel. Then there is the vice-captain, a former professional, now reinstated amateur, the darling of the popular press, and the reason for the MCC's pleading with Malleson to take the team.

Malleson's side sweeps all before it in Australia until the middle of the tour, winning the first two tests comprehensively and largely because of the young fast bowler's efforts but abetted by Malleson's leadership skills. Then Malleson, troubled by rheumatism, steps down for four matches. The vice-captain undermines the confidence of the young fast bowler, the team loses the next two tests and Malleson comes under extreme pressure both publicly and privately.

Malleson selects the fast bowler for the final test against the wishes of all quarters and everything goes wrong. Halfway through the match Clive is injured in a laboratory explosion at his school and Malleson's life is in tatters. In the denouement, the unscrupulous vice-captain engineers the broken fast bowler and the ravaged captain to be the last wicket pair for England facing a hopeless task. Realizing at last the perfidy of his deputy Malleson takes charge, scores a century, brings the young bowler through a maturing experience, defeats the scheming vice-captain, wins the series for England and flies home in triumph to devote his time to Clive who survives his own crisis.

Devotees of Roland Barthes, of course, will recognize all this as being a morality play, a struggle between good/evil, right/wrong, honour/dishonour as played out in the French analyst's essay on wrestling.[3] Such a recognition of the deep structure of sport in its cultural setting (the invocation here being Clifford Geertz and Pierre Bourdieu) is the starting point for this essay on cricket, literature and culture.[4] Of all the world's games very few come close to cricket in its symbolic representation of a culture's moral values – baseball and sumo wrestling are among the few to reach the same significance. For that reason, it is time to test some of the links because cricket historians have rarely ventured into the world of literature even though the references are plentiful. The Pickwick Cricket Club in Barbados, for example, takes its name from Dickens' Pickwick Papers in which a key figure refers to having played cricket in the West Indies. C.P. Snow's hero in the 'Strangers and Brothers' sequence begins his story with a reminiscence of the pre-World War One county cricket ground. Several other writers of academic novels refer to cricket somewhere in their texts. A.A. Milne, Ben Travers, Harold Pinter and Tom Stoppard are just some among the diverse range of British writers who have referred to, or derived inspiration from, cricket. George Lamming, Austin Clark and Edward Kamau Braithwaite are just three African-Caribbean writers whose work features the game; Alan Mulgan from New Zealand and Dal Stivens of Australia are others.[5] That is before moving to juvenile literature in which cricket constitutes a major bloc.

This is borne out by E.W. Padwick in his cricket bibliography.[6] He lists over thirty fictional works containing cricket themes, over 130 more with cricket references, almost fifty short stories, over 160 poems, well over 100 humorous or satirical pieces, a dozen plays, and in excess of 250 works of children's fiction. Among the latter may be noted Mary Grant Bruce's *Mates at Billabong*, Anthony Buckeridge's Jennings series, John Finnemore's Teddy Lester series; G.A. Henty's *With Kitchener in the Sudan* and Howard Spring's *Darkie and Co.*

The flavour of these juvenile works may be gauged from some of their titles: *The Making of Jerry Dickson; One for a Win; Not Cricket – A School Story; Won for the School; A Born School Captain; The Demon Cricketer; The Schoolboy Test Cricketer; Playing the Game; Winning His Laurels; Pals at Allingham; Tufty's Cricket Triumph.* It is unnecessary, perhaps, to point out that all the schools referred to here are, by definition, public ones. As Tony Mangan has demonstrated, sport, and most particularly cricket (being prized for inculcating honour, loyalty, honesty, determination, courage and team values), lay at the heart of the Victorian and Edwardian school spirit.[7] The obvious connection here is to C.L.R. James's increasingly influential *Beyond a Boundary* which demonstrates successfully the power of cricket and literature as colonising agencies and, in so doing, provides an early if implicit example of Gramsci's concepts of hegemony through culture.[8]

Interestingly enough, though, James speaks to English literature in its canonical sense rather than to the specific cases of cricket in literary, that is, fictional, form. What James does best, then, is to provide the most telling case of cricket as a cultural force by tracing its playing story in a particular environment. What he does not do is to examine the conveying of the moral messages through the ancillary force of cricket literature itself. In order to make the point more solidly, then, we need to return to *Malleson at Melbourne* to explore some of its meanings as a text in my personal historical construction.

Good structuralist analysis, that is, demands an explanation of how this morality play comes to constitute the key to this essay, and there are two obvious starting points: the author, and the context in which the book appeared.[9] William Godfrey, the author of *Malleson at Melbourne*, turns out to be a pseudonym for Samuel Youd, a prolific English writer with a professed fascination for studying humans under stress.[10] Under other pseudonyms such as John Christopher, Peter Graaf, Peter Nichols and Hilary Ford, Youd has explored this fascination via science fiction, detective novels and psychodrama. His very selection of cricket as a vehicle for further exploration is in itself recognition of the important place occupied by the game both in English social place and English collective mentality.

Youd, or Godfrey, was born in 1922 near Liverpool in a village between Huyton and Knowlsey, two famous cricket centres in Lancashire. At the age of 10, and in the year of Bodyline, his family shifted to Hampshire and he was educated at Peter Symond's School in Winchester (Douglas Jardine's school town) where, as in other public schools at that time, cricket was de rigueur.[11] After war service Youd became a professional writer whose output sustained his family, and its lifestyle on Guernsey, rather than making a great literary impact.

I knew none of this when, at the age of 11, my parents gave me *Malleson at Melbourne* for my birthday in 1957, the year before New Zealand went off to England to be defeated 4–0 in the test series, my father and I listening to the radio in vain through the long winter nights for a crumb of success, particularly from my left-handed role model, Bert Sutcliffe. At that point I was a player and enthusiast rather than an analyst, but I know now that *Malleson* appeared in 1956 at an auspicious juncture in cricket. That year England defeated Australia 2–1 with 2 drawn in which England was well on top. In the fourth test English offspinner Jim Laker took nineteen wickets in the match, still a record. English cricket was on a high, and led by P.B.H. May (of Charterhouse, Cambridge and Surrey), the archetypal amateur hero of schoolboy fiction. That was important, in that May followed Len Hutton (of Pudsey School and Yorkshire) who was one of England's most daring post-war social experiments, a professional player who became captain, the first in modern English cricket.[12]

I knew of the Empire through cricket or, more precisely, through the literature of cricket. South Africa was peopled by villains like Neil Adcock, the fast bowler who bit Bert Sutcliffe on the head during the second test of the 1953–54 tour. The Kiwi returned to the field in Johannesburg to score eighty, partnered at the end by Bob Blair who batted despite the death of his fiancée in New Zealand's biggest railway disaster. This was life predating the art of *Malleson*. The West Indies I knew because of Everton Weekes' magnificent batting in 1956 while on tour in New Zealand. India and Pakistan I knew because of Ranjitsinjhi who was also one of the reasons I 'knew' English cricket. Most of all, I knew England through books and comics, mostly about cricket.

Youd (aka Godfrey) encoded in *Malleson at Melbourne* the values which, for me, constituted the right behaviour in cricket, the right protocols and, subconsciously, the most significant approach to life. Malleson himself, of course, embodied the right approach: he did not play cricket for a living, he was loyal, never questioned an umpire's decision, was self-effacing and quietly confident, and played cricket as a game even against the Australians who, in this book, bear no resemblance at all to the so-called 'ugly Australians' led in reality by Ian Chappell just fifteen years after the book's appearance.[13] Contrarily, the vice-captain displayed all the wrong traits: cricket was a search-and-destroy mission in which the other team were enemy, teammates were expendable, individual success paramount and sharp practice a necessity. In this, Youd clearly sets up a vision of the established cricket traditions triumphing over the nouveau (a Leavisite versus a postmodernist position, if you like), but at the end of the book the inescapable conclusion is that the victory of good over evil might not necessarily be permanent.

An inescapable feature of cricket fiction, then, is its insistent emphasis upon the game as a moral force and a bulwark against change either in the game itself or in the society which has constructed the game. Lewis Eliot, of the 'Strangers and Brothers' sequence, was a great Leicestershire partisan from whose marvellous hitters like Jessop and Tyldesley he chose to elevate C.J.B. Wood on the grounds that he was 'sounder', that is, more reliable.[14] Soundness looms large in the literature, as do all the other virtues displayed by Abdul Malleson (note, by the way, the general confirmation of Said's orientalist argument contained in the nickname). Said, in fact, provides an important inscription by which the argument may be taken forward here:

> in the transmission and persistence of a culture there is a continual process of reinforcement, by which the hegemonic culture will add to itself the prerogatives given it by its sense of national identity . . . its power as an implement, ally or branch of the state, its rightness, its exterior forms and assertions of itself and most important, by its vindicated power as a victor over everything not itself.[15]

This, of course, is purely Gramscian and is especially apposite here even if Gramsci never wrote about cricket.[16] It is a truism, now, that wherever cricket went it took with it a culture which went far deeper than the simple form of play contained within the rules and conduct of the game. As Orlando Patterson observed, for example, cricket in the Caribbean was (and remains) a white man's game played by black men dressed in white clothes.[17]

Perhaps the most startling example of this came in the form of Prince Ranjitsinjhi who became the first Indian to play for England, followed by Duleepsinghi and Raman Subba Row. Ranjitsinjhi displayed the full cultural power of cricket, most notably in the final chapter of his *The Jubilee Book of Cricket* published in 1898. He notes, for example, the association of ideas contained within the game:

> No doubt when people play the game on a rough jumble of veldt-grass and mine-tailings in the outskirts of Johannesburg, half the pleasure they find is the result of association of ideas. The feel of a bat and its sound against the ball bring back memories of the green turf and cool breezes of England.[18]

A recurrent theme in cricket literature, the environment of the cricket field becomes an arm of cultural power linking colonial outpost with the heart of imperial authority.

It is for that reason that the ultimate form of accommodation is to become good at cricket. As Lord Harris put it, Indians would never be ready for self-government until they mastered cricket.[19] Well, Ranji did master the game, becoming perhaps its greatest star at the turn of the century. Importantly, his mastery was derived from the perfect moral standpoint: by way of hard work, practice and commitment rather than by indolent, flashy natural ability. In real life, that is, Ranji lived out the dictates of the juvenile public school literature, then went on to prove (to the public if not the British government) that cricket was, indeed, the perfect training for a life of responsibility and command.[20]

The locations of cricket fiction are invariably set in rural England, with the players caught in a momentary cross-class alliance. Squire might be organizer and leader but he is first amongst equals along with blacksmith (inevitably a fast bowler), baker, teacher, postman, publican *et al.* It is a collective to represent the community against another community: Dingley-Dell versus All-Muggleton, Herecombe versus Therecombe, Tillingfold versus Wilminghurst. In John Parker's *The Village Cricket Match*, for example, there is expressed the view that the cooperation involved in making the village cricket pitch embodied the same spirit that won the wars for Britain. Moreover, 'the cricket field had been a source of pride, argument and occasionally furious divisions in Tillingfold for longer than anyone could remember'.[21] It is as if the heart of rural England lies protected under its innumerable strips of green in the middle of the village ovals.

In that respect, Malleson's crusade is unusual in being for and on behalf of England. Cricket's fiction is more interested in re-imposing cultural purity and authority at the wellsprings of Britain's moral power, the village and countryside amongst the common but decent folk. They might well be laughable figures as in A.G. Macdonnell's representation, but they are never pathetic.[22] As in all elements of their lives, they give cricket their best. The representations of cricket, in this instance, are about cultural cohesion and the maximizing of talents no matter how limited they might be in their natural state.

One overwhelming memory from my 1950s reading of Tiger comics comes from the series in which a father takes his young son to an island, chains a cricket bat to his wrist and sets out to make the boy England's best-ever batsman. At the time, that did not strike me as an odd thing to do in the pursuit of batting perfection – after all, the chain was removed for fielding practice! Interestingly enough, even though the son displayed some impatience with the practice there was little if any criticism aimed at the parent throughout the text. Importantly, the boy did go on to represent England – that is, the practice worked which constituted justification.

It is interesting to note in passing here that cricket fiction on the whole refers to pre-1967 England, that being the year in which county cricket was opened to overseas players who have dominated the top ten in bowling and batting lists every year, despite increasing attempts to restrict their participation. Similarly, the subject of English cricket fiction is rarely to be found in the leagues, those semi-professional competitions inside counties which from the 1920s onwards were manned quite considerably by players from the Empire. The convention, then, is for white, amateur county players or salt-of-the-earth rural artisans to carry the cultural messages of cricket.

Women, of course, feature in quite standard roles: housewife, mother, fiancée, housekeeper or kindly aunt. Their places in the action are divided between making lunch, standing near the tea-urn, or sitting in a deckchair trying to catch the eye of the team's leading chap who is, of course, devoted to the game but an awfully nice man. While relatively few schoolgirls play cricket in the literature, a larger number of boys who do are created by women writers: Margaret Biggs, Dorita Bruce, Rita Coatts, Penelope Leslie and Isabella Plunkett, just a few of those who wrote about public school life with an emphasis upon the important role of cricket as moral moulder.

In total, then, much if not most of this cricket fiction has been reaffirmative, nostalgic and hegemonic. Within the English civic and literary canon the game became not only a familiar social landmark but also a symbol of ruling class culture with its tenets accepted across all social segments. Lewis Eliot's father stands out as being distinctly odd at the county match, the one person at the ground who seems not to understand the nuances, customs, conventions and symbolism of cricket. He is, in effect, the exception to prove the rule.

Is there no room for resistance in all this? Gramsci, Said and the rest, after all, derive much of their inspiration from Hegel's postulations about the lines of tension drawn between domination and subordination, the struggle between those in authority and those under command.[23] Perhaps predictably, the possibilities and actualities of resistance through cricket come from those parts of the Empire where the political struggle was most pronounced. The inscription here comes from Ashis Nandy:

> Cricket does not yield any ultimate truth; like everyday Hinduism, it only yields diverse instructions of truth, allows them to co-survive, and gives a ritual structure to that diversity and co-survival.[24]

At the risk of a gross generalization, this is a most 'Indian' of approaches to the game which goes on to explain why the sub-continental style is so different – resistance, that is, through style rather than through the very rejection of the activity itself.

In George Lamming's autobiographical novel, for example, the game has a much more socially convoluted contour than that presented in the literature discussed to this point.[25] Its setting is in what was known as Carrington's Village, one of the most notorious 'estates' (for which read 'slums') in Barbados up until the 1960s. The cricket played there/in the novel, was quite different from that played in the island's formal competition. For one thing, matches involved money stakes, a form of economic exchange within a world of limited resources. For another, it was quite openly recognized that the island's cricket was socially stratified, unlike that of the fictional England where the suspension of knowledge becomes a leitmotif.

There is something of an extension to this in James Berry's nation language poem on cricket which transforms the crowd to an active, participant part of the match rather than the Lords-like lethargic group which watches the game in England.[26] In Bruce Hamilton's *Pro*, the hero (a rare professional) discovers, to his surprise, an unusual crowd in Barbados: 'eager, vociferous, following every ball with the keenest interest, the tattered negroes round the wing constituted a crowd ludicrously different from any to be seen on an English county ground. It was not only their extreme vivacity. The main difference was the somewhat surprising one that they knew the game.'[27] Again, the emphasis is upon resistance through style in an attempt to escape the hegemonic sway as delineated by Gramsci. In reality the debate is about whether this form of resistance is substantial enough – in the fiction the other side of the debate is much underdeveloped.

It is appropriate to return to *Malleson* here because 'the tour' from England to anywhere in the cricketing Empire is most significant in the relations of cultural power. It is in these tours that the dominant seeks to reassert moral force over the subordinate and, vice versa, the subordinate attempts to exercise at least a momentary superiority over the dominant. In *Malleson*, the struggle is a close one and the dominant comes out only just ahead with the important feature not being so much the narrowness of the victory itself as the uncertainty of moral superiority always winning out no matter which protagonist prevails (unlike the case in Barthes' wrestling or Geertz' Balinese cockfight where evil can prevail).

Those tours, too, highlight the clash between the oppositional views of the moral code along with the attendant cultural styles. That is particularly so when England or Australia plays India, Pakistan or the West Indies. One easy way to judge that lies in the different fictional accounts of crowd behaviour patterns in foreign climes allowing, however, for the depth of knowledge the accounts of Australian crowds in *Malleson at Melbourne* suggest that Youd had not too much first hand or detailed knowledge.

Perhaps the most important point to concentrate upon in the Nandy inscription is that of ritual as in rites of passage. The bulk of the cricket fiction in any setting deals with an individual becoming either a better player or person or both by virtue of an experience in the game itself. In Youd's book it is both Malleson (who proves his playing and leadership qualities to himself for once and for all after a career of uncertainty) and the fast bowler (who overcomes his self-doubt through his own efforts and through leadership-by-example from Malleson). While cricket might be viewed as a simple vehicle of convenience and agency for this type of metamorphosis, again it is necessary to remember the sheer bulk of it in the juvenile literary categories to recognize its inherent symbolic strengths. Throughout these texts there is a constant emphasis upon social learning, interaction and performance. The learning of roles in a cultural environment is at the centre of the process. While these learning processes are highly stylized they are necessarily significant as the links between the physical attributes of a game and the mental/cultural traits seemingly prized by the host community.

That is the point at which Ashis Nandy makes what is probably his most important contribution to an analysis of this connection between cricket, literature and culture, a contribution which draws us more into the world of Bhaktin and the investigators of carnival:

> Cricket as a dreamland includes the conventional values of social life but it offsets these values against the utopian aspects of social life to provide a playful but serious critique of everyday life.[28]

While cricket undoubtedly can be an exciting game in which nerve and moral code are both tested severely, the literature is inevitably an overdrawn depiction of what passes for constructed reality: a hopeless pair does not win a test series in a gallant last wicket stand, schoolboys do not play for England, Australians are not humble losers, women do not wait by the tea-urn, and selection panels do not support their captains. If all that is valid observation then cricket, in the literature, is indeed a dream world as Nandy suggests.

The life of cricket in the novels is an evocation of a past and idealized world. It is an idyllic representation. David Lamb recently spent a year travelling America's minor league baseball sites where he found a world different to that of the major leagues: players were people not stars, crowds still loved the game uncritically, owners were prepared to lose money for the sake of the game.[29] There is a similar concern with presenting an ordered, acceptable world in the cricket literature. It is about nostalgia more than reality.

Unfortunately, life is not like that which is where the link between literature and culture can be seen most clearly in its connections with the game. The spirit of cricket is the spirit of a past England and a faded Empire which is one of the central reasons why the game has vainly tried to stay as what it sees as 'above' politics in the case of South Africa, the case of rights for players as in World Series Cricket, and in effectively maintaining the divide between the white and the non-white worlds. What it really stays above, of course, is an imperial context in which 'colonial' has become 'post-colonial' so that each cultural component has constructed its own practices which often vary greatly from the original model. (Outbursts against West Indian fast bowling tactics over the past fifteen years by the former imperial cricket rulers is probably the easiest and most apposite example of this point.) In the fiction, for that very reason, England's contests are with Australia and not India or Pakistan. The implications are obvious: Australia as the extension or, albeit distorted re-creation of British moral culture (New Zealand provides an infinitely better model in the moral code stakes, but the suspension of disbelief on the playing side could be pushed only so far – incredibly, it wasn't until 1978 that New Zealand won its first test match against England. Even the fictional schoolboy test cricketers could find little sport in beating such weak opponents who were, nonetheless, a credit to the game and fine ambassadors for their country!)

While the worlds of cricket, culture, politics and education have moved on, the game in its literary setting has been left increasingly in the role of the ingénue. In that sense, it would be wrong to see cricket in the light of opera, even in its soap version. As Peter Conrad points out, the characters of opera are amoral, gluttonous, lustful, devious and unconventional.[30] Cricket characters are quite the reverse, and in that seem increasingly unrealistic: they rarely exploit the opportunities for dramatic excess.

Now, of course, cricket is a pre-industrial game caught in a post-industrial, even postmodern age. Its strength is its sense of history, which is why its inner meanings defy the analyses of the postmodernists. Cricket's literary vehicles all have a sense of history whether in the comparison of present performances with the past, golden moments of triumph and dark ones of defeat, remembered heroes and villains, all of which encompasses two central features: the triumph of progress located in the preservation of traditional values. That is precisely why in *Malleson at Melbourne* the MCC selectors call on the aging, creaking workhorse to lead their crusade rather than go to the bestial version of their particular postmodern nemesis, the professional manqué/reinstated amateur who probably belongs more properly in Wagner than in St John's Wood. There is, then, a great civic certainty buried in the rural and amateur heartland of English cricket as cast in the literature.

Which is probably why the genre is a dwindling one. The writers of this fiction have been unrelievedly upper middle class, public school oriented and amateur in outlook. One curious indication of this lies in the cricketer-writers. One of the first was Sir Jack Hobbs, and his children's novel is a perfect indication of what he and batting partner Herbert Sutcliffe aspired to, professionals who could be easily mistaken for amateurs.[31] Walter Hammond wrote one, too – if he had not lost out in the psychological stakes while on tour in Australia in 1946 he could have been the model for Abdul Malleson's vice-captain, a reinstated amateur.[32]

One of the clearest expressions comes in 'Lord' Ted Dexter's *Testkill* whose protagonist declares:

> My background was comfortable and conventional and at forty-five I am now considered by many to be yet another representative of a dying class. I was a public schoolboy and learned my cricket by a combination of good coaching, good wickets and strong competition. I was a cricket blue, a Rugby blue, a fair sprinter and a top amateur golfer.[33]

Unfortunately, England ran out of amateurs to the point where the Gentlemen versus Players matches were abandoned after 1962.

The point here, then, is that the genre is not in decline because of itself but because its producers went into decline along with the role models. As well as the surfeit of play came an excess of reportage about the game and its players. Cricketers became celebrities as much as players so that interest in them spread from the sports to the gossip pages and, importantly, television talk shows. All this restricted the possibilities for social instruction so inherent in the earlier literature. Ian 'Tonking' Botham of 1981 is one thing but Ian 'Bonking' Botham of 1986 West Indies fame is quite another, just as Mike 'Barmaid' Gatting is not exactly hero material for juvenile fiction. Then, Malleson was born in India (as were Douglas Jardine and Colin Cowdrey) but he was an expatriate, that is, white. The current England team, better known as the United Nations XI (former South Africans, Zimbabweans, Dominicans, Barbadians and the like), can scarcely be linked to the village green so beloved by de Selincourt, MacDonnell, Parker and the rest, or to the public schools of Jennings and his pals.

For one thing, after Packer it became increasingly difficult to believe that the game itself was the reason for playing. Cricketers of all nations became drawn into a dizzying programme in which all matches tended to blur into one another. English cricket attempted to retrieve lost ground by creating the national village competition but it, too, descended to postmodern pastiche when it was revealed that several villages had bought players in an attempt to buy the title. The game was most definitely not the thing.

Perhaps, then, we have seen the end of a unique literary form precisely because its *raison d'être* has gone along with its innocent amateurs. Symbolically, the madcap works of William Rushton and David Rayvern Allen now best represent the face of modern cricket.[34] For me, though, the images of Bert Sutcliffe in Johannesburg and Malleson in Melbourne will continue to provide the link between life and art, reality and dreams, and the forever expectation/memories of great moments to come because, in the end, this literature was about the dreaming of human ambition and triumph.

Notes

[1] *Sporting Traditions* 1 [*ST*] was the first *ST* conference.

[2] Godfrey, *Malleson at Melbourne*.

[3] Barthes, *Mythologies*.

[4] Geertz, *Local Knowledge* and Bourdieu, *Language and Symbolic Power*. See, too, Kramer, 'Literature, Criticism and Historical Imagination'.

[5] Examples: Milne, *The Day's Play*, Mulgan, *Flame*. Collections may be seen in Arlott (ed.), *My Favourite Cricket Stories* and Frewin (ed.), *The Rest of Cricket's Fiction*. The range may be said to run from Blunden, *Cricket Country* to Woolf, *Mrs Dalloway* – in the latter, one protagonist sees cricket as 'no mere game. Cricket was important.' (I owe the reference to Maureen Bettle.) For a sociological account of English cricket, see Brookes, *English Cricket*.

[6] Padwick, *A Bibliography of Cricket*.

[7] Mangan, *Athleticism in the Victorian and Edwardian Public Schools*.

[8] James, *Beyond A Boundary*.

[9] No great theoretical point is being claimed here, simply an acknowledgment of the complex issues involved.

[10] For description of Youd: Wakeman, *World Authors, 1970–1975*.

[11] On Bodyline, see Sissons and Stoddart, *Cricket and Empire*. For an interesting if too one-dimensional study of cricket's influence on Jardine, see Douglas, *Douglas Jardine*.

[12] Hutton (with Alex Bannister) *Fifty Years in Cricket*. On May, Rodrigo, *Peter May*.

[13] Chappell, *Tigers Among the Lions*.

[14] Snow, *Time of Hope*, ch.2.

[15] Said, *The World, The Text and the Critic*, 14.

[16] For example, Hoare (ed.), *Selections from Political Writings*.

[17] Patterson, 'The Ritual of Cricket'.

[18] Prince Ranjitsinjhi, *The Jubilee Book of Cricket*, 449.

[19] Lord Harris, *A Few Short Runs*, Ch.IX.

[20] Perhaps the most interesting analysis of Ranji is that by Nandy, *The Tao of Cricket*, Ch.2.

[21] Parker, *The Village Cricket Match*, 23.

[22] MacDonnell, *England, Their England*, Ch.7.

[23] For some ideas on and about resistance, Spivak, *In Other Worlds*, esp. Ch.12.

[24] Nandy, *The Tao of Cricket*, 51. For similar, more literary views, see Nandan, 'The Mahabharata and Modern Fiction'.

[25] Lamming, *In the Castle of My Skin*.

[26] Berr, '"Cricket Sing-Song"'. The genre draws much from Edward Kamau Braithwaite, of course.

[27] Hamilton, *Pro*, 152. The novel was published originally in 1946.
[28] Nandy, *The Tao of Cricket*, 115.
[29] Lamb, *Stolen Season*.
[30] Conrad, *A Song of Love and Death*.
[31] Hobbs, *Between the Wickets*.
[32] On Hammond, Howat, *Walter Hammond*.
[33] Dexter and Makins, *Testkill*, 10.
[34] Rushton, *W.G. Grace's Last Case*; Allen, *Tales from the Far Pavilion*. For an intellectual indication of trends, see Harriss, 'Packer, Cricket and Postmodernism'. For a literary view, Matthews, *Oval Dreams*, esp. 'Channel Nine Cricket: the Death of a Thousand Cuts'.

References

Allen, D. R. *Tales from the Far Pavilion*. London: Collins, 1985.

Arlott, J., ed. *My Favorite Cricket Stories*. London: Lutterworth, 1974.

Barthes,.R. *Mythologies*. London: Paladin, 1974.

Berr, J. "Cricket Sing-Song". *Bim* 17, no. 68 (1984): 76–7.

Blunden, E. *Cricket Country*. London, 1945. Reprinted, London: Pavilion Books, 1985.

Bourdieu, P. *Language and Symbolic Power*. Cambridge: Polity/Blackwell, 1991.

Brookes, C. *English Cricket: The Game and Its Players through the Ages*. London: Weidenfeld and Nicolson, 1978.

Chappell, I. M. *Tigers Among the Lions*. Adelaide: Investigator, 1992.

Conrad, P. *A Song of Love and Death: The Meaning of Opera*. London: Hogarth, 1989.

Dexter, T. and C. Makins. *Testkill*. London: Allen and Unwin, 1976.

Douglas, C. *Douglas Jardine: Spartan Cricketer*. London: Allen and Unwin, 1984.

Frewin, L., ed. *The Rest of Cricket's Fiction*. London: Macdonald, 1966.

Geertz, C. *Local Knowledge: Further Essays in Interpretive Anthropology*. New York: Basic, 1983.

Godfrey, W. *Malleson at Melbourne*. London: Museum Press, 1956.

Hamilton, B. *Pro*. London: Baker, 1970.

Harris, Lord. *A Few Short Runs*. London: Murray, 1921.

Harriss, I. "Packer, Cricket and Postmodernism." In *Sport and Leisure: Trends in Australian Popular Culture*, edited by D. Rowe and G. Lawrence. Sydney: Harcourt, Brace, Jovanovich, 1990.

Hoare, Quintin, ed. *Selections from Political Writings (1921–26)*. London: Lawrence and Wishart, 1975.

Hobbs, L. B. *Between the Wickets*. London: Black, 1924.

Howat, G. *Walter Hammond*. London: Allen and Unwin, 1984.

Hutton, L. (with A. Bannister). *Fifty Years in Cricket*. London: Paul, 1984.

James, C. L. R. *Beyond a Boundary*. London: Hutchinson, 1963.

Kramer, L. S. "Literature, Criticism, and Historical Imagination: The Literary Challenge of Hayden White and Dominick Lacapra." In *The Cultural History*, edited by L. Hunt. Berkeley, CA: University of California Press, 1989.

Lamb, D. *Stolen Season: A Journey through America and Baseball's Minor Leagues*. New York: Warner, 1992.

Lamming, G. *In the Castle of My Skin*. London: Joseph, 1953.

MacDonnell, A. G. *England, Their England*. London: World, 1941.

Mangan, J. A. *Athleticism in the Victorian and Edwardian Public Schools*. Oxford: Oxford University Press, 1981.

Matthews, B. *Oval Dreams*. Ringwood: McPhee Gribble, 1991.

Milne, A. A. *The Day's Play*. London: Methuen, 1919.

Mulgan, A. *Flame: A New Zealander's Adventure*. London: Longman's, 1927.

Nandan, S. *The Mahabharata and Modern Fiction. Bruce Bennett and Dennis Haskell's Myths, Heroes and Antiheroes*. Perth: University of Western Australia, 1993.

Nandy, A. *The Tao of Cricket*. New Delhi: Penguin, 1989.

Padwick, E. W. *A Bibliography of Cricket*. London: Library Association/McKenzie, 1984.

Parker, J. *The Village Cricket Match*. Harmondsworth: Penguin, 1978.

Patterson, O. "The Ritual of Cricket." *Jamaica Journal* 3 (1969).

Ranjitsinjhi, Prince. *The Jubilee Book of Cricket*. London: Blackwood, 1898.

Rodrigo, R. *Perter May*. London: Phoenix, 1960.

Rushton, W. *W.G. Grace's Last Case*. London: Methuen, 1984.

Said, E. W. *The World, the Text, and the Critic*. London: Faber, 1983.

Sissons, R. and B. Stoddart. *Cricket and Empire: The 1932–33 Bodyline Tour of Australia*. Sydney: Allen and Unwin, 1984.

Snow, C. P. *Time of Hope*. New York: Scribner's, 1949.

Spivak, G. C. *In Other Worlds: Essays in Cultural Politics*. London: Routledge, 1988.

Wakeman, J. *World Authors, 1970–1975*. New York: Wilson, 1980.

Woolf, V. *Mrs. Dalloway*. London, 1925.

Sport, Television, Interpretation and Practice Reconsidered: Televised Golf and Analytical Orthodoxies

Introduction

My analytical media work began similarly to that on golf. My first newspaper piece was on the Indian elections held after the 'Emergency' declared by Indira Gandhi around the time I first went there, then I wrote later for cricket magazines. When I joined Curtin, the University was opening a community radio station and that provided good opportunity to talk to more people. It was fascinating learning to communicate with different audiences in different ways, and the work set me up for transition into the media course in Canberra. At Curtin I did programmes on current affairs and politics, Asian studies, ran a series on the social history of music, and did a lot on sport.

There were great moments, especially one getting the great historian of France and other things, George Rude, on air. In the Battye Library (the Western Australian Archives), I spied someone consulting convict records (Western Australia was a late-stage convict colony following complaints to Britain about labour shortages). Some checking revealed it was Rude. Generously, he visited the then distant and desolate Western Australian Institute of Technology campus to spend a couple of hours recording an interview. Having long admired his French revolutionary crowds and early nineteenth-century English agrarian riots writings, his reminiscences fascinated me, especially a story of being locked not out of but inside the Bibliotechque Nationale with Richard Cobb! Cobb was another of my favourite writers: the longtime French resident wrote not only great history but marvelous memoirs, including an essay on the Tour De France. Years later, Paul Strickland at the European Commission Delegation in Canberra remembered being a student of Cobb's. The great man lectured always with a large Guinness at hand, most of which finished on the floor because Cobb never stopped talking long enough to get it in his mouth!

One year at 6NR, as the Curtin station was known, we must have had the world's most over-qualified breakfast lineup because four of the five daily presenters had PhDs. One was singer-songwriter Graham Turner, now President of the Academy of the Humanities Australia and Australian cultural studies leader. I had the privilege of putting on air for the first time now radio icon Geraldine Doogue – she was then Perth correspondent for *The Australian* newspaper, and we had her talk politics. (Through

Geraldine I met Sandi, so the Perth mafia has always been alive and well!) Another memorable interview was in Adelaide during an Australian and New Zealand Association For the Advancement of Science (ANZAAS) conference, a long session with electronic composer Tristram Carey, son of novelist Joyce Carey so famous for the academic novel *Lucky Jim*.

This sort of work took me wider afield. I did a little ABC radio work that gave an insight into how 'real' radio worked, including one spectacular night when a monumentally stoned newsreader actually read the news, articulately, in the allotted time. Because I talking analytically about sport, that led to further possibilities. One was an interview on the Perth version of the *This Day Tonight* current affairs programme. The Subiaco Football Club was in financial difficulty stemming from some massive changes in football organization that helped create the West Coast Eagles (for which I was a minor consultant), one of football's first private franchises. *TDT* wanted to discuss it. The interviewer said he knew nothing about the story so would ask just one question. If I gave him a three word answer he was, I quote, 'stuffed'! He asked the question, got a long answer that he duly cut and edited so I became a television as well as radio regular.

That and Bodyline led to several appearances on the Peter Luck/David Salter series, *This Fabulous Century*, one of the greatest Australian TV social history series. *TFC* haunted me for years. When the series was shot I had long hair and a Zapata moustache, but when I met Sandi that had become a beard and, at one point, an Afro perm. One night she heard my voice and went in to see someone on television she did not recognize: it was a *TFT* episode. In the late 1990s in Alor Setar, Malaysia (home of longtime Prime Minister Dr Mahathir Mohammad) visiting a partner university, late one night in my hotel I watched yet another *TFT* re-run with a person on screen from another age.

The media work included *Bodyline*, the television series created by Kennedy-Miller before their huge success with the *Mad Max* films. As historical advisor I worked mainly with scriptwriters and directors, but saw up close the early work of actors like Hugo Weaving and Gary Sweet (Jardine and Bradman, respectively). The key directors were Denny Lawrence (whom my daughters were later delighted to meet when he had worked on *The Bill* and *Monarch of the Glen*) and Lex Marinos (cricket fanatic, co-editor of a book of rugby league essays, and most recently on-camera presenter of ballroom dancing shows). Denny and David Salter were enormously helpful during establishment of the sports journalism programme – as Executive Producer for Sport at Channel Seven later, David hired Kerryn Pratt from a tape we did for a non-existent position. Kerryn was among the first programme graduates and is now a regular Wimbledon commentator.

The radio work continued in Canberra. I joined the Australian National University Cricket Club because Barry Andrews was there, and in the first match squared up against a competitive opponent. There was much sledging, he and I at the centre. When play finished we had a drink, he discovered I had done radio. He was morning host on Canberra's leading commercial radio station. That led to on-air work with him and a slot as Sports Director. For two years that meant going early into the station to broadcast live sports reports, then record stories for later before going off to University tasks. The competitive cricketer/broadcaster turned friend was the marvelous Dean Banks who shifted later to Melbourne as perennial anchor for 3AW's breakfast programme *Lawyers Guns and Money*, named after the Warren Zevon song.

Given that long media association, Canberra teaching responsibilities and the new golf curiosity, the three coincided intellectually. There was much golf on television but little real 'inside' analysis of televised sport. Most critical commentary seemed to be read 'off the screen', rather than come from an informed view about its creation. With help from people like David Salter and some University funding, I spent two years examining the making of Australian outside golf telecasts. It was a great project because besides seeing how television 'worked' I saw many great players at close range, providing further insights into sports subcultures.

* * * * *

There are few points of agreement in the widening international literature concerning the relationship between sport and television,[1] but there is a dominant analytical theme: that television has corroded the quality and character of sport. According to Lasch,[2] the American television industry has turned athletic prowess into show business. Rader argues that television 'has diminished the capacity of sports to furnish heroes, to bind communities, and to enact the rituals that contain, and exalt, society's traditional values'.[3] Clarke and Clarke contend that televised sport is a re-presentation of the original which 'becomes merely a novelty'.[4] Lawrence considers Australian cricket 'manipulated by commercial television for the benefits of advertisers', an analytical line developed by Jhally.[5]

Goldlust declared all sports undermined by a television industry lacking 'any consideration of the organic significance of these games, as collective social and cultural resources'.[6] Superficial evidence supports this pessimistic view. Various sports have had their rules, practices, scheduling, locations and financial viability restructured following an intersection with television. No major modern sports event is complete without pre-game and half-time entertainment more for the benefit of television viewers than spectators at the venue.[7] Then there is the assertion that television has put too much money into sport and so created superstars, destroyed traditional loyalties, alienated traditional publics, and created a concern for finance rather than for art.

There are, however, substantial weaknesses within the dominant analytical mode concerning the sport/ television nexus. First, as Grossberg points out, one major block is that popular culture (and sport, of course, is clearly part of that) is treated as if it were either high art – amenable to the same kinds of critical concerns and practices as the more institutionally sanctioned forms of culture – or documentary evidence – as if its status as popular were insignificant to its active insertion into the lives of people.[8]

Lipsitz makes a similar point about rock music, when he argues that the dominant analysis has reified social complexities into abstract structures given meaningless labels.[9] These points are apposite here, where, so far, there has been a dominatingly dualistic approach to the analysis of televised sport. Either there is a one-dimensional and socially decontexted reading [10] or a deep symbolic role that conveys agreed-on and shared social meanings from producers to consumers.[11] As both Lipsitz and Grossberg would point out, the problem is that both approaches analyze televised sport not within its own framework and terms but by grafting to it labels and hypotheses elaborated elsewhere.

The second major weakness is an important corollary to the first. The sports examples on which these conclusions have been drawn are very narrow and frequently ignore sports with as great or even greater an impact on television audiences. In the United States, football and baseball have provided the most analytical examples, leaving aside professional wrestling and automobile racing. In Britain, the emphasis has been on soccer (and cricket to a lesser degree) to the exclusion of darts and snooker. In Australia, the focus has been on cricket rather than on the different football codes. The significance of this observation is central – there is a little challenged assumption that the social impact of televised sport is spread universally and to be read unilaterally no matter which sport is selected, thereby ignoring the condition whereby sports themselves are inevitably marked by considerations of class and status, let alone cultural specificity.[12]

The third major weakness relates to similar concerns about dominant views concerning television itself. If the contours of sport are flattened out, so too are those within the technological form that conveys the images of sport. Put simply, much analysis is read 'off the screen' with little reference to the complexities of the delivery system. There is an assumption that throughout the system there is a shared, consensual view about what the images represent symbolically, what they are meant to say to the viewer, and that there is no change in the coded contents of those images. The implication is that this consensual view crosses all barriers between telecasting systems, personnel, and international boundaries. Just as sport becomes homogenized in the dominant analysis, so too does the television system itself.

The Proposition and the Sport

Given this situation, the dimensions of the revisionist task were clear: conduct a detailed ethnography of television coverage surrounding a major viewer/participant/-spectator sport, which had as yet seen little formal analysis. In so doing, test the assumptions and weaknesses outlined above, thereby opening new lines of reconsideration about televised sport. The choice was surprisingly simple. From the early 1960s onward, homes around the world have witnessed thousands of hours of televised golf. In many respects golf is now the world game,[13] yet its television construction has attracted little attention.

As the Dunlop Sports Enterprise roster reveals,[14] several major professional golf tournaments are played each week throughout the world. The American tour has an event almost every week; the Japanese tour, too, has a tournament most weeks.

A two-month winter break in the lucrative European tournament roster allows many players to join either the African or the Australasian circuit. The boom has spread into Seniors golf (for those 50 years of age and older), with the Japanese and American tours showing few free weeks. The women's professional circuits are similarly extensive. Virtually all tournaments are covered by television, some on a localized level, with others telecast internationally, carried live or on tape delay via the complex of satellites that now make global viewing possible. As the proliferation of cable outlets spreads to Europe, Asia and Australasia from America, the outlets for golf increase and so does the coverage. In fact, during 1993, announcements were made in the United States concerning an all-golf channel to be funded by a group of businessmen including the legendary player Arnold Palmer, the first modern sports millionaire whose career was driven by television.

The importance of such golf coverage for critical analysis was clear. Few sports create so many technical demands for network personnel in production terms, so many opportunities for constructed image making (given the number of players and the amount of time involved), so many avenues for 'framing' given the physical environments over which the play is conducted, and such a multitude of opportunities for crass commercialism.

Methodology

Over the course of two summers, I gained full access to the detailed workings of golf coverage conducted by three major networks in Australia, one a state-funded organization (the Australian Broadcasting Corporation), the other two run by commercial interests. My principal questions were the following:

1. In these vast undertakings, how tight was the central control, where was the locus of that control, and what was the directing philosophy concerning imagery?
2. To what extent was the creation of imagery driven by craft pride or ideological direction?
3. To what extent did readings 'off the screen' match the details of construction witnessed through observation?

In each case, I spent a week with the television crews from setup phase through testing and then into live telecasting. I observed all levels of operation at close quarters for long periods. All observations were then compared with tapes of the coverage that went to air. My overall goal was to test the findings of this detailed observation against the prevailing views in the analytical literature.

The Case Study

The 1990 Coca Cola® Classic played over the Royal Melbourne Golf Club's composite course provides an excellent study. It was a full-scale coverage by the ABC, with six hours of live action shown on each of the final two days following seven hours of transmission in total over the first two days. The coverage was of all eighteen holes on the course. The ABC feed was taken on-course by the Tokyo Broadcasting Service and, with supplementary material, beamed live into Japan (the tournament was part of an international tour arranged by Japanese promoters and sold as a television package). The Coca Cola® Classic, then, was a perfect example of modern television golf coverage in its technical scope and complexity, its international dimensions, and its inextricable connections with management and promotional agencies.

The telecast seemed simple enough. Cameras fed pictures into one of four outside broadcast (OB) vans, each responsible for covering particular 'patches' around the course. Each OB van selected a picture, by choice or under central direction, to be sent up the line to the main production control (MPC) van. The MPC production staff then chose from available pictures and sent one to air. To the picture feed were added preproduced aerial views of each hole, still diagrams of those holes, player and course statistics, interviews, player profiles and library footage. The resultant mixture combined with the on-air commentary constituted the telecast golf package.

Even at that simple level, however, there are questions about the wisdom of the monolithic, dominant degradation analysis. Not all golf tournaments are covered the same way in Australia, let alone anywhere else. The first major distinction is between the state-funded ABC approach and that of Australia's commercial networks. In the latter case, camera coverage is fed straight back to a studio where composition direction is determined, returned to the course for commentary, and then fed to the reception grid. There is, therefore, a reduced amount of composition at the OB van level compared to the ABC system. Then, commercial composition is calibrated by the advertising that underwrites the cost of production, an element largely absent from the ABC form. That leads to the question of purpose and, ultimately, formulation. The two networks' approaches to the one sport are distinctively different.

That question is particularly significant in the ABC case. Why should a state-funded broadcaster invest so much capital in telecasting golf? After all, the organization deployed 135 personnel on-site (remembering that others were involved off-site), concentrated over $10 million worth of equipment at Royal Melbourne for a full week, and spent at least $500,000 putting the programme to air. Some costs were offset by fees received from the Tokyo Broadcasting Service, but the outlay was still substantial.

When asked to justify this expenditure and logistic effort, the executive producer (EP) replied candidly that he could not, and his elaboration cast doubt on the dominant views of the interrelationship between sport and television. Far from social engineering, ABC golf's appearance on television was a historical accident. One of his predecessors as controller of sport had been a keen golfer who orchestrated ABC involvement and established long-term contract relationships with tournament organizers. In economics and technological production, golf had become exponentially more complex over the years, but ABC involvement had remained.

Golf became an event in which a section of the ABC developed great skills of coverage (many of its techniques adopted by other telecasters around the world) in which they took pride. The coverage, that is, was not determined by a set view of shared consensual values nor by a specified view of symbolic construction. Rather, it was underwritten by craft pride, a point little in evidence in the extant literature. That is not to say that consensus and symbolism are absent at subconscious levels or that they play no part in the assemblage of coverage. Rather, it is to suggest that the standard intellectual analyses of televised sport are based on narrow understandings of how the viewed pictures are created in individual circumstances and, therefore, the analyses themselves become inadequate, even misleading. It is at this point, then, that the production process for this event should be considered in detail.

Cameras

A convenient starting point lies with the camera crews. For the Classic, twenty-four cameras were positioned for maximum flexibility, covering several action sites. Some were in fixed positions to cover one green and the next tee, some were vehicle mounted so that they could position themselves for the best shot, others were tower-fixed to pick up the ball in flight, and still others were mounted on cherry pickers to cover blind spots from a height or provide elevated views. Each camera crew was assigned to a specific OB van.

The camera crews exercised considerable creativity at their own discretion. Although there was a brief concerning the top players on whom they had to concentrate, they could suggest camera shots of those players. Truck-mounted cameras roamed freely in search of better angles. Cameramen took cameras off tripods to produce new ways of looking at players. Although the van producer (VP) refined shots by demanding tighter or wider views, the determination of the shot still lay with the camera crew.

Contrary to the extant literature, then, camera shots are not all produced to order, in this setting at least. That initiates two thoughts. First, if all sports telecasting is symbolically determined, then this case study is very different. Second, there is a clear need to distinguish the context of the specific sports telecast before discerning blanket assumptions. Not all telecasting of all sports is the same; it cannot be.

Vans

This principle of autonomous creativity flows into the VP role. Like the camera crews, the VPs share a framework within which to work that was articulated at each day's production team meeting attended by on-air staff, floor managers, producers and assistants, and executive production staff. Within that framework, VPs had considerable room to move. How they handled coverage of 'key' players moving through their respective patches was left to them. VPs and assistants watched the procession of players through their patch, calculating arrival times at particular points given the speed of play. The important decision was which action to throw up 'live' for the SP and which to videotape for possible replay.

It is interesting to reflect on the VPs themselves here: One had risen through the ranks from cameraman, another with a long ABC career had spent years trying to break into the sports division, and a younger one had come from a drama background. All had been groomed into the golf telecast, but all retained professional characterizing traits, as the EP pointed out. When asked to nominate his perfect VR, he chose characteristics from each of his personnel, emphasizing their individuality. Individual creativity was valued here more than conforming to any tightly prescribed central philosophy.

Production 'Control'

The MPC van is the heart of the ABC golf production. Its main compartment houses three tiered rows of seats with space for six people who face an individual set of controls and a bank of thirty television monitors on the facing wall. Those monitors carry the line-in feed from the OB vans, from two roving cameras mounted on golf carts, from the videotape machines, and from the on-air commentary team in addition to still diagrams, aerial shots, player statistics, the leader board, all the character-generated titles and information, and the special effects machines (which create those split screens and boxes within pictures), fast camera machines, and the transmission monitor that carries the selected pictures seen by the audience.

All this is commanded by the production assistant, audio mixer, vision mixer, technical director, supervising producer and executive producer. Each has a marked area of responsibility and works on it autonomously, with the exception of the vision mixer who executes shot calls from the supervising producer. Each contributes ideas to the shape of the telecast within the general framework. Although the executive producer nominally commands the operation, the supervising producer runs the minute-by-minute process. As several crew members mentioned, the rule here was democratic, but all could name autocratic executive producers both overseas and within Australian commercial television networks.

That is an important point because it reveals the significance of national televised sporting genres within specific cultural factors that go unmentioned in the literature. This is doubly significant in Australia, where 'models' of construction have long been sought overseas. First it was the BBC, then American networks and, only recently, Australian adaptations. When the Australian pioneers of television golf looked first to Britain they did not much like what they saw. They later turned to the American coverage and then began to elaborate their own style. That was connected inextricably with the specific golf cultures of the three countries based on social status, economic disposition and access practice.[15]

The morning production meetings were run but not dominated by the VP and SP. They commented on the previous days images, listed the present day's priorities, and set the telecast parameters. OB van directors had substantial influence by delineating the possibilities and limitations of their respective patches. For example, they would eliminate particular shots or coverage because cameras were out of commission or particular angles were impossible or because playing timetables did not suit a particular progression. The EP and SP then factored these considerations into their telecast strategy.

Of all the omissions in the dominant degradation thesis, perhaps the most glaring is the lack of attention accorded the pressure of the television sport workplace.[16] Although pressure applies to all levels of the telecasting, it is at its most obvious with the EP and SP. The EP controlled the entire operation, liaising with the Japanese connection as well as with tournament authorities in addition to linking network requirements. The SP concentrated solely on the pictures on Saturday and Sunday for the full six hours of the telecast, making up to ten decisions a minute. It is the most demanding position in ABC television production, according to insiders. For both producers, on-air time was tense and draining, which, they argued, mitigated against their being sources of inspiration for the construction of symbolism or philosophy. The EP cited two main restraints on his exercising such influence: history and context. He had overall control, but given the varied inputs of his team and the sheer scope of the telecast, his capacity for tight and dictatorial direction was reduced. Moreover, he had inherited the prevailing practice in a television culture where dictatorial control was not favoured.

Commentators

That uncertainty flows into the most obvious of the televised sport components: the on-air commentary team, which has been a favoured site for academic analysis.[17] The two major figures here were a former great Australian international professional golfer and a veteran teaching professional with long-standing television experience. These two were supported by a network commentator, who coordinated the technical requirements of the telecast (studio crosses, affiliate connections) and provided the statistical base (player performance, leader board), and the host, who conducted opener and closer segments and also did interviews.

None had any control over the pictures on which they worked, although they volunteered their preferred picture types to the ER There is little evidence that their requests were acted upon. Although the on-air team itself had some domestic discussions about its approach, it received minimal direction from the MPC or anywhere else. Such direction as there was mainly concerned which player might be a guest commentator. In essence, the on-air team constituted yet another cell of localized decision making, as did, for example, each of the OB van units.

It is worth dwelling on this self-contained principle. The production meetings did not involve all personnel but only the key operators, who, in principle, relayed information, instructions and, importantly, impressions back to those in their immediate working environment. Consequently, many people working on the project did so within their own little world rather than part of the overall team. They were not tightly structured into a prevailing blueprint.

Discussion

What we have to this point is a complex system of picture creation, selection and rejection that contradicts many if not most tenets on which the dominant degradation position is based. Rather than there being a clear source of ideological and/or symbolic influence, the assemblage of pictures can be traced to several levels of input in a non-autocratic environment, which produces a sense of shared creation. This output over extended periods is assembled under great pressure, which allows little, if any, time for reflective or philosophical direction.

The significant analytical point here is that in the extant literature the review of televised sport and its symbolic contents has proceeded from what the viewer actually consumes. Although that is a legitimate exercise, it should be clear that it is a limited one. To test the power and consistency of what goes to air, there is a need to test, in this case, the production output of a specific van and the filtration process applied to it so as to determine the principles by which the to-air pictures are selected. This would then locate more precisely any creativity in the production process and, by definition, any trends in symbolic production. This does not mean that production philosophy is entirely absent, but it heightens doubts about the unquestioned validity of established interpretations by striking at the foundations of thought about the construction of social symbolism.

Making Pictures

As Rick Gruneau confirms, the most commonly voiced production crew response to questions about its work/formulation practices was 'instinct'.[18] What the crew meant was that they were guided by a learned response system that informed the craft framework of the total team. This was most evident within the induction process for new producers, whose first task was to produce the daily highlights package shown nightly after the end of play. The job involved monitoring the transmission feed during the live telecast and then selecting segments that covered the days 'story': leaders, good shots, unusual incidents and 'name' players.

This induction process serves important purposes. It eases trainees into the production processes inherent in the golf telecast and also exposes them to senior staff practices so that the training or 'shaping' is indirect rather than direct. Then it exposes trainees to golf itself, an important function because many new crew members know little of the game.

What About the Game?

Again, this raises a point at variance with the bulk of the literature where there is an assumption that television people care little for the aesthetics and/or principles of the game(s) with which they are dealing. That was not the case here, where, as a result of the induction process, the protocols of golf along with its playing practices were to the fore. The degree of difficulty of any stroke was well understood from the cameraman level up, the 'bad boy' players were well known, and never appeared in shot unless they happened to be high on the leader board, and the traditions of golf were well respected. There was an air, almost, of the telecast being an important part in the preservation of 'traditional' golf, despite the ever-present and unavoidable commercial intrusions. This has a direct link to the production process itself.

Principles

Although the absence of production guidance is frequently explained (especially by senior staff) as the result of a long-established team working by instinct, it really results from a surprisingly simplistic approach to telecasting, as revealed in the few basic written notes that circulate among the team. The main guide, ABC Spores Golf Coverage, concentrates heavily on logistic details and on a very few organizational factors, such as camera locations and formats for information to be superimposed on pictures. Even where 'shooting' directions are given, they are mostly for practical purposes. When players putt out, for example, the picture is to be held for 3–4 seconds to allow information on scores to be superimposed. And where philosophy is approached, it is basic: 'Each highlights package must tell the story of the day's round!' Symbolism, shared social values, commercialization, drama and personalities get no mention.

More presentational issues appear in a less formal document, 'Notes on ABC Golf Production', circulated by one SP to his VPs. There is again a historical element, with coverage to be 'a refinement of the techniques and experience evolved and gained over the last few years'. But there is more shaping here, too: Atmosphere should be built up with players on the tee, capture player reactions to a stroke by 'boxing' them in a corner of the main picture that follows the ball flight, and 'bleed' putts for as much atmosphere as possible. Comments such as 'this type of shot can be very dramatic' (when putter, ball, and hole can be framed in one shot) are rare because, overall, 'our aim is to tell the story of an event'.

When pressed, the EP and SP became more expansive, conceding points that approach a philosophy of golf telecasting, all the while declaring that no such philosophy exists. Both see golf as an analogy for life, a series of highs, lows, successes, failures and dramas dictated by the score – hence the importance of camera crews 'chasing the ball into the hole', as stressed at one production meeting. What happens to the ball determines player fate. Much of the telecast works off this point. One favoured technique, for example, was a tight close-up shot on hands holding a putter, which highlights not so much a player as the physical means by which the score was determined and that the lowest score wins the tournament.

But that is far from 'seeing' a highly structured set of symbolic presentations that portrays shared cultural values, consciously and elaborately organized as a means for preserving the social status quo in the interests of capitalism and the corporate world. This is not the malevolent, destructive force of television that Kidd and MacFarlane portrayed in North American hockey.[19]

Concluding Remarks

What emerges here should not be read as simple apology for television's intersection with high-level sport or as a denial of any texted meanings in the televised representation of sport. Full consideration of all the ethnographic material was not possible here, but what was presented reinforces Real, albeit with a slightly different bent, when he noted that televised texts do not show us the whole of a culture but only a particular face of it at a particular time. The different bent is that the same point applies to televising itself.[20]

This ethnography produces a more complex picture of the relations of power inside the production process than that traced in orthodox analyses of televised sport. At each point there existed some source of influence over the final product even though, theoretically, the executive producer and supervising producer held final sway. Cameramen and the van producers, for example, had space within which to benchmark their particular contributions. For this production at least, consensual and negotiated images appeared for the viewing public rather than the dictated and dictatorial ones expected from a reading of the mainstream literature.

The implications for the mainstream view are substantial. Every separate piece of televised sports production should be subjected to close cultural analysis before any generalized interpretation of its meaning can be made. Such analysis might reveal major possibilities for resistance to the dominant capitalist and commercialized productions assumed so quickly in the literature. A cultural approach then adds a further layer of subtlety in that the same sport televised in different national settings may well produce quite different imagery with quite different deep meanings. Further, the structure of ownership and purpose for the television agencies will vary and therefore take different approaches to the texting of events. Ultimately, however, such a culturalist approach to televised sport helps break the barrier that any social scientist will find in the literature to date. That is the pervasive sense in which the technology ('television') is seen to have driven the process rather than human agency itself. This is an obvious point, but a rereading of the literature confirms the low level of attribution to human agency apart from cursory and, usually, isolated references to obvious individuals like Roone Arledge.

In order to capitalize on this beginning, then, the goal should be a close investigation of all aspects in the production process for televised sport, and in different cultural settings. By so doing, not only will we bring finer senses of meaning to this modern phenomenon but we will open other means of assessing the social impact of all that imagery.

Notes

[1] Barnett, *Games and Sets*; Blain, Boyle and O'Donnell, *Sport and National Identity in the European Media*; Buscombe, *Football on Television*; Lawrence and Rowe, eds. *Power Play*; Rader, *Its Own Image*; Wenner, ed. *Media, Sports and Society*; Whannel, *Fields of Vision*.

[2] Lasch, *The Culture of Narcissism*.
[3] Rader, *Its Own Image*, 6.
[4] Clarke and Clarke, 'Highlights and Action Replays', 76.
[5] Lawrence, 'Its Just Not Cricket!'; Jhally, 'The Spectacle of Accumulation'.
[6] Goldlust, *Playing for Keeps*.
[7] Wenner, ed. *Media, Sports and Society*.
[8] Grossberg, 'Putting the Pop Back into Postmodernism'.
[9] Lipsitz, *Time Passages*.
[10] Bryant, Brown, Comisky and Zillman, 'Sports and Spectators'.
[11] MacAloon, 'Missing Stories'.
[12] Gruneau, *Class, Sports and Social Development*; Stoddart, *Saturday Afternoon Fever*.
[13] Stoddart, 'Wide World of Golf'.
[14] *1990*. Edited by Dunlop Sports Enterprises.
[15] Green, *Golf*.
[16] O'Neil, *The Game Behind the Game*.
[17] Bryant *et al.*, 'Sports and Spectators'; Comisky, Bryant and Zillman, 'Commentary as a Substitute for Action'; Rainville and McCormick, 'Extent of Covert Racial Prejudice in Pro Football Announcers' Speech.'
[18] Gruneau, 'Making Spectacle'.
[19] Kidd and MacFarlane, *The Death of Hockey*.
[20] Real, *Super Media*.

References

1990. Edited by Dunlop Sports Enterprises, 1990.

Barnett, S. *Games and Sets: The Changing Face of Sport on Television*. London: BFI, 1990.

Blain, N., R. Boyle, and H. O'Donnell. *Sport and National Identity in the European Media*. Leicester: Leicester University Press, 1993.

Bryant, J., D. Brown, E. Comisky, and D. Zillman. "Sports and Spectators: Commentary and Appreciation." *Journal of Communication* 32 (1982): 109–10.

Buscombe, E. *Football on Television*. London: BFI, 1975.

Clarke, A. and J. Clarke. "Highlights and Action Replays: Ideology, Sport, and the Media." In *Sport, Culture, and Ideology*, edited by J. Hargreaves. London: RKP, 1982.

Comisky, P., J. Bryant, and D. Zillman. "Commentary as a Substitute for Action." *Journal of Communication* 27 (1977): 150–3.

Goldlust, J. *Playing for Keeps: Sport, the Media and Society*. Melbourne: Longman Cheshire, 1987.

Green, R. *Golf: An Illustrated History of the Game*. London: Collins, 1987.

Grossberg, L. "Putting the Pop Back into Postmodernism." In *Universal Abandon? The Politics of Postmodernism*, edited by A. Ross. Minnesota: University of Minnesota Press, 1989.

Gruneau, R. *Class, Sports and Social Development*. Amherst, MA: University of Massachusetts Press, 1983.

Gruneau, R. "Making Spectacle: A Case Study in Televised Sports Production." In *Media, Sports, and Society*, edited by L. A. Wenner. Newbury Park, CA: Sage, 1989.

Jhally, S. "The Spectacle of Accumulation: Material and Cultural Factors in the Evolution of the Sports/Media Complex." *Insurgent Sociologist* 12, no. 3 (1984): 41–57.

Kidd, B. and I. MacFarlane. *The Death of Hockey*. Toronto: New Press, 1972.

Lasch, C. *The Culture of Narcissism: American Life in an Age of Diminishing Expectations*. New York: Norton, 1978.

Lawrence, G. "Its Just Not Cricket!" In *Power Play: The Commercialisation of Australian Sport*, edited by G. Lawrence and D. Rowe. Sydney: Hale & Iremonger, 1986.

Lawrence, G. and Rowe, D., eds. *Power Play: The Commercialisation of Australian Sport*. Sydney: Hale & Iremonger, 1986.

Lipsitz, G. *Time Passages: Collective Memory and American Popular Culture*. Minneapolis: University of Minnesota Press, 1990.

MacAloon, J. "Missing Stories: American Politics and Olympic Discourse." *Gannett Center Journal* 1, 2 (1987): 111–42.

O'Neil, T. *The Game Behind the Game: High Pressure, High Stakes in Televised Sports*. New York: Harper and Row, 1989.

Rader, B. *Its Own Image: How Television Has Transformed Sports*. Newport: Free Press, 1984.

Rainville, R. and E. McCormick. "Extent of Covert Racial Prejudice in Pro Football Announcers' Speech." *Journalism Quarterly* 54 (1977): 20–6.

Real, M. *Super Media: A Cultural Studies Approach*. Newbury Park, CA: Sage, 1989.

Stoddart, B. *Saturday Afternoon Fever: Sport in Australian Culture*. Sydney: Angus Robertson, 1986.

Stoddart, B. "Wide World of Golf: A Research Note on the Interdependence of Sport, Culture and Economy." *Sociology of Sport Journal* 7 (1990): 378–88.

Wenner, L. A., ed. *Media, Sports and Society*. Newbury Park, CA: Sage, 1989.

Whannel, G. *Fields of Vision: Television, Sport and Cultural Transformation*. London: Routledge, 1992.

A Transnational View

Introduction

Between 1995 and 1998 I was posted as on-site Academic Director for an RMIT University campus development in Penang, Malaysia – RMIT partnered a local businessman to provide tertiary-level engineering and business education for Malaysian students. A far-sighted, difficult project that deserves an academic novel à la Malcolm Bradbury and David Lodge, it would succumb to the late-1990s Asian 'financial crisis'.

When the opportunity arose I grabbed it quickly. Having done the Dean's job for almost five years I sought a change, and believed that Australian university managers needed Asian on-ground experience. I had visited Penang first in 1971 *en route* to India. The *SS Rajula* left Singapore for Madras via Port Klang near Kuala Lumpur, Penang, across the Bay of Bengal to Negapatinam (hit by the 2004 Boxing Day *tsunami)* and on into Madras. The ship carried indentured labourers between India and Singapore/Malaysia with only about 100 cabin passengers but something like 1,200 held below deck where they stayed for the entire five days across the Bay. Negapatinam was like a scene from the *Barbary Pirates,* if that is not too 'Orientalist' a term. The port there was shallow so a fleet of lighters came out to the *Rajula* whose crew threw ropes over the side. Lighter crew climbed the ropes, raced into the holds, opened the small loading doors and threw trunks and belongings into the lighters many feet below while passengers jumped down. For a small-town New Zealand boy, this was a long way from home.

The ship had a few days in Penang, showing me 'Pearl of the Orient' as it is still called now but with less justification. It was a free port with a bewildering mix of Indians, Chinese and Malays with all the attendant food and cultural differences, magnificent heritage architecture, and a fabulous beach at Batu Ferringhi ('Foreigners' Beach'). After my first long fieldwork stint I returned to the beach for two weeks writing.

Penang was vastly different by 1995, but amidst the complex management issues I was still observing the sport/culture mix in yet another different setting. Cricket was dominated by Indians, springing from railway development up and down the Peninsula – imported Tamil labour, mostly from Ceylon/Sri Lanka, brought cricket across the Bay to augment the tiny English tradition centred on clubs like the Royal Selangor in Kuala Lumpur. Dr 'Ratna' Ratnalingam, a great colleague on the project, was a Rhodes Scholar who led Malaysia at the mini-World Cup in 1979. He introduced me to the Penang Sports Club (PSC) that had begun as a European enclave then gradually expanded. On the other side of town, the Chinese Recreation Club (CRC)also had a century-old tradition following the Chinese having been excluded from PSC membership. In a fenced off corner of the CRC there is a statue of Queen Victoria, erected by founding members to underline the fact that they were still colonially loyal to the Crown. That was a direct replication of Herman Griffith's deliberate act in Barbados of calling his new club 'Empire', an indication of continuing themes.

Those patterns and more abounded in Malaysia. There was a *sepaktakraw* court near my house where the locals practiced that skilled combination of badminton, volleyball and soccer in which teams keep a rattan-woven ball moving over a high net. My daughter became involved in *Budokan* karate, a martial arts variant dominated by Chinese in contrast to the Southeast Asian *silat* dominated by the Malay-speaking population. Golf was elitist both socially and economically, with entry to clubs highly expensive. The original Penang Golf Club is still located within the Penang Turf Club complex, a perfect combination of elite pursuits. The newer golf courses were all resort-type ones with more attention paid to developing the clubhouse than the course. One course was a major retreat for the Japanese expatriate community in Malaysia – their economic presence was tolerated, but local memories of wartime atrocities made them unpopular so the golf course became an escape.

All this was a rich additional bonus; my twin interests in Asia and sport deepened considerably and ranged across history, sociology, economics and politics. An International Cricket Council mini-World Cup tournament, for example, was staged in Kuala Lumpur and, very quietly, an Israeli team was admitted to Malaysia, a leading member of the Organization of the Islamic Conference (OIC). This displeased sections of the less secular Muslim community, and demonstrations ensued. Front page newspaper reports subtly connected demonstrators to an outlawed Islamic sect by reporting specific prayer rituals enacted at a mosque near the demonstrations just prior to the incidents. This was fascinating stuff for any social analyst.

The opportunity to participate in the IOC's 'Sport and Culture' seminar allowed me to be in Lausanne as an unofficial representative of both the Australian and Malaysian Olympic authorities. It was an extraordinary experience for someone never an enthusiast for the modern Olympic system, especially after the Jennings/Simpson *Lords Of The Rings* revelations and after the machinations that gave Sydney the 2000 Games. Delegates stayed in the *Lausanne Palace Hotel*, then the permanent residence of Juan Antonio Samaranch and the most expensive place I had ever stayed in: 'happy hour' in the bar, discovered by Indian writer and critic Patwant Singh, offered Heideseck, Krug or Kristal champagne! There was much talk of 'reforms' in wake of the revelations. On my last morning I took breakfast with a delegate who waxed eloquent about the Olympics spreading peace and friendship, then took on his mobile phone an update on aerial bombings of rebels back in his home country. In the sessions I was reminded of university politics: 'dear colleagues' was frequently the opening of an attack on a rival person/country/federation/sport. Much later, in Calcutta during 2005, I would gain greater insights from John Macaloon, a reform insider.

* * * * *

While, arguably, it was already replacing religion as the opiate of masses and elites alike around the very time Marx wrote his famous line, sport is now certainly a major benchmark of the modern age, as some simple examples demonstrate. When satellite television is introduced into a new environment, a key selling point invariably is that Star-TV or ESPN or another sport provider is part of the programme suite.[1] In similar vein, sports programming has been a staple in so-called free-to-air terrestrial television for at least thirty years, throughout the world.[2] Another example lies with the serious policy and financial commitments made by both western and non-western governments wanting their countries to become successful in international sports.[3] Then there is the enormous industrial base of sport ranging from manufacturing to service industries; where once we spoke of the military-industrial complex, now we might quite justifiably refer to the sports-industrial complex.[4] Rising fast, too, is the overwhelming presence of sports on the Internet which has the capacity to alter considerably the mediation of sport and its consumption patterns by fans and which, of course, raises all over again the issue about equality of access in a world where economic and social status have long patterned the contours of sport.[5]

Concomitantly, over the past thirty years or so an increasing amount of academic work (in addition to journalistic and more impressionistic writings) has analysed the role of sport in society either in specific histories of countries or sports, economics, sociologies, biographies, psychologies and other disciplines, quite apart from the applied and functionalist works of sport science. A predictable range of radical and conservative interpretations may be noted and, as with other fields of intellectual inquiry, new approaches such as postmodernism and/or cultural studies have intervened to create rich debate and invective, sometimes in equal share.[6] There is a further continuity with the wider fields of inquiry, too. Much of the work has centred upon the developed (or metropolitan) world, even though the most powerful examples of the sport/culture nexus have often come from the 'Other' worlds, as they are now referred to in some intellectual circles.[7] Underlying this comment, of course, is the important argument about modes and minds sparked off by writers such as Edward Said. In so rich a field of inquiry as the investigation into the culture of sport, however, much analysis remains to be done if the phenomenon is to be regarded as a major means of understanding modern life rather than merely as an object of simple antiquarian or novelty value.[8]

The issue, then is not the fact or the artefact of sport, but what Michel Foucault might have called the archaeology of sport, the full unlayering of its myriad meanings in a myriad of cultures and microcultures.[9] The intellectual search, in other words, is for meaning rather more than narrative (although, of course, the best narratives usually invoke meaning). This essay sets out to identify some key areas for review and agenda – setting in that search for meaning, so that the study of sport may deepen to become even more recognized as an intellectual activity which enhances an understanding of modern life in all its contradictions, complexities and simplicities.[10] It begins with a conceptualization.

Disjunction and Continuity

The issue of globalisation has been a major discussion point with the social scientists of sport recently.[11] It is not so much the debate as one of its consequences which is important in the context of this essay. That consequence is the idea of disjunction and continuity in sports practice in its various settings. If sport is truly both a product and a shaper of a culture, then by definition it is subject to social change wrought by the wider social forces constantly at work – historians will see here an implied criticism of some works which celebrate sport as a once honourable institution now ravaged by virtue of its surrender to commercialism, while sociologists will see an even deeper invocation to understand the evolution of sport before attempting to decode its modern contours.[12]

In understanding the social role of sport (or sports) in any given context, the concept of continuity and disjunction becomes useful – which sports practices endure, and which ones either wither or die? Put another way, the point is about which sports continue to give social meaning, which ones do not and, in interesting cases, which ones are created or borrowed to fill a gap in meaning.[13]

Japan provides two sports – sumo and baseball – which serve as helpful case studies. With its strong and extensive history and rituals which both draw upon and feed Japanese cultural traditions, sumo for many citizens provides continuity in a modern world much changed. Baseball, on the other hand, has become a major means by which Japan has engaged culturally with the world's so-called 'leading' power and with modern transnational culture.[14] In both cases, then, alteration causes great interest and either anxiety or satisfaction. In the sumo case, allegations of match-rigging caused enormous concern, not simply because of the possible corruption but more because of the perceived undermining of a central social tradition.[15] In the case of baseball, the great success of Hideo Nomo as a pitcher for the Los Angeles Dodgers has, in some ways, been seen as a 'coming of age'. There is a strong case to be made, then, for seeing these sports as a major means by which to analyse both the Japanese tradition and its modernised dealings with the rest of the world.

To continue the Japanese case for a moment, golf there provides an interesting example which combines cultural tradition and international engagement. The Asian golf boom began there and set many of the patterns.[16] While most Japanese courses reflect something of traditional landscape patterns, social practice in the golf environment reinforces in substantial way patterns of social distance – club membership is the preserve of a wealthy elite, and playing patterns (for example, the concept of time) differ remarkably from those in the Occidental world. Yet the 'golf course as business venue' concept pioneered in the west has been taken to art form status in Japan (as well as in other parts of Asia). As in the fields of trade and commence more widely, penetration of the Japanese golf market has been achieved only with great difficulty by outside agencies, while at the same time the force of Japanese economics saw golf resorts all over the world become Japanese-owned.[17]

The point here is that the Japanese case demonstrates perfectly the complex intertwining of sports and social practice, tradition and modernity, and levels of meaning which underlie the concept of continuity and disjunction. The importance of vested meaning in sports becomes apparent, too, in the debate about adding new sports to old programmes. Two excellent examples in recent years involve the addition of beach volleyball and mountain bike riding to the Olympic programme. Disquiet about such change is not so much about the forms of the activity themselves, but about how to 'read' their significance – arguments about 'tradition' in such a context are really arguments about meaning, about the social significance of the activity to be invested by viewers and/or spectators. Much the same can be said of the debate engendered by attempts to alter, for example, aspects of traditional equestrian events.

If that is a reasonable analysis, then one direction for a fuller analysis of sport involves ritual. One reason for Caribbean cricket having produced such a rich literature, quite apart from the spectacular settings for, and the rich physical action of, the game itself, is that early analysis identified symbolic meaning as an important avenue and set a trend.[18] English cricket sets the reverse example, because there are surprisingly few analytical works which really explain the significance of the game in English culture, despite its obvious importance both domestically and in the export of British values and mores.[19] Interestingly, one of the most interesting recent works on English cricket came from a transplanted American with, it might be argued, something of an but even that does not satisfy any reader looking for the anthropological approach to the subject evolution of the game there.[20]

Already, a principal line of argument is apparent here – that separate strands of analysis in history, sociology and anthropology now, more than ever, need to be drawn much closer together in cultural analysis mode if the full flavour and meaning of sports in the various settings are to be revealed. In turn, such an integrated analytical mode will help explain more adequately the fierce controversies which erupt within and between sports practices. Significantly, the approach will also help provide a more insightful approach to discussions about the impact of globalized and globalizing sports upon autochthonous forms.

Levels of Action

While, naturally, much intellectual analysis of sport (especially at the global level) has concentrated on elite activity now inevitably 'commercialized', it is fair to point out that much of the real social meaning of sport lies at planes way below that level. While international and elite representational sport creates great passion and interest, it is questionable that the heights of such passion and interest are diminished at the more obscure levels of activity. Community-based sport is also a global phenomenon, and from their organized beginnings many modern sports forms had their organizational structures rooted in community spirits.

The real point here, of course, is precisely how that 'community' was formed, defined and then interpreted, from the viewpoints of both the community members and outsiders regarding the group. Tottenham Hotspurs Football Club in London, for example, has always enjoyed and been reputed to enjoy a good following from the Jewish communities in the immediate localities. Because of that, there is a curious link between the recent Mark Bosnich 'Nazi salute' incident and the England-Germany match staged at the club's ground in 1935. In the latter case supporters of the club, with allies in the anti-Fascist leagues and the trades unions, attempted to have the match banned by British government authorities, on the grounds that it would otherwise seem to condone actions taken by Nazi gangs against persecuted groups in Germany. Just as it was seen as an affront to White Hart Lane locals if German players were allowed to appear there in 1935 so, too, was Bosnich's unfortunate gesture seen to invoke memories of an unhappy past for members of the Jewish community.[21]

Other 'communities' may be constituted by ethnicity, especially in 'new' sites where community identity might seem to be threatened. In Australia, for example, football (or soccer, as it is known locally) became a major participation and spectator sport from the 1950s onwards, with most clubs being made up from specific ethnic and intra-ethnic groups including Greek, Italian, Croatian, Maltese, Portuguese, Spanish, Dutch and German communities in all major cities in the country. In the earlier phase, soccer had grown on the coalfields where British workers made up the bulk of the workforce.[22] In the Union of South Africa era (from 1907 onwards) rugby union, having been introduced by British settlers, became 'colonized' by the Afrikaaner community as a means of demonstrating its superiority over the English-speakers. Inevitably, the game became entwined with Afrikaaner political movements like the Broederbond and the National Party.[23] In California between the two world wars, sport was also an important component in the establishment and presentation of community by Japanese Americans.[24]

In other cases, 'community' might be established by wealth and/or status, establishing the point that community groups are often formed by a wish to be separated from others as much as to be with like-minded people. Country clubs in the United States, Asia and elsewhere in the world are all calibrated by access (or perceived access) to wealth, along with conformity to group norms.[25] In a similar way, the exclusiveness of some clubs is marked by elite social standing which does not give way to 'new' wealth. Leading golf clubs in the former British empire are good examples here, as is the Marylebone Cricket Club (MCC) and the All-England Lawn Tennis and Croquet Club.[26] The variations on this theme are endless as, for example, in places like the Royal Selangor Club in Kuala Lumpur, Malaysia, and the Secunderabad Club in Hyderabad, India. In both locations, the practices of the pre-independence colonial elite have continued under the control of the post-colonial elite. That is, the traditions of the dubs established under one social regime have continued into another even though the political contexts and the social regimes have altered remarkably.[27]

There are endless numbers of clubs around the world which each contain a community's story, and the increased understanding of those stories helps make much more sense of particular incidents. In the highly commercialized upper levels of Australian Rules football, for example, it was thought that proposals to abolish the Footscray Football Club in Melbourne would create no great concern because of an assumption that community pride in dub's was a thing of the past. Quite the reverse happened, with Footscray residents, many with no deep interest in or love for football, turned out in defence of what they considered to be a crucial 'badge' of the community. This community-based action thwarted the desires of the football tsars.[28]

Much invaluable research, then, is still to be done in discerning the lines of 'community' affiliations because they reveal the inner strengths and fears of these social collectivities. Worker sport is a very good example, as some recent work reveals.[29] That case is particularly important because in the lexicon of the old left, such 'extraneous' action as sport was seen to he diversionary. What we now see is that such action was at the core of group strategies. That must be the overall research aim, to reveal the centrality of sport in the social arena. Importantly, the significant levels of action are not exclusively at the upper levels of competition, because for real social drama it is often hard to go past the local community sports club.[30]

Levels of Politics

It is but a short step from the concept of community to that of politics, because in any social organism the distribution of power, goods, resources and services comes through the elaboration of a political system. Sport is not exempt and, again, there is still a great deal of work to be done on the levels of sporting politics which range from community activism through to the politics of the international order. What was surprising, for example, about some Turkish reactions to Istanbul being eliminated from contention to stage the 2004 Olympic Games was not the linking of the rejection to a perceived global political order (the world of Islam being rejected by the West and the rest), but the fact that some observers found the linking to be extreme and offbeat. In his popular if debatable recent thesis, Samuel E. Huntington argues that the choice of Sydney for the 2000 Summer Games followed what he calls 'civilizational' lines, with cultural groupings lining up alongside likeminded groups.[31] In an extended sense, of course, he is right to argue the connection between politics and sports decision-making, but many of the analyses so far have not penetrated the inner core of the sports/politics nexus. An important point to note is that any discussion which seeks a separation of sport and politics is essentially fruitless, because if sport is truly a cultural form (which it is being accepted as such here) then politics is an inevitable accompaniment.[32] In that sense, Malaysian Deputy Prime Minister Datuk Seri Anwar Ibrahim's disapproval of one Islamic political party's protest at the presence in Kuala Lumpur of Israel for the 1997 International Cricket Council's World Cup qualifying tournament was disingenuous, at best.[33] (It also had little effect upon followers of the party who subsequently caused the abandonment of a match not involving Israel – the venue for Israel's game that day had been changed).[34]

What becomes significant, then, is an identification of the levels of political action, the issues at stake, the tactics employed to achieve the desired ends, and the elaboration of the goals of the action. These will vary from site to site, but each will be revealing about the local condition and cultural penetration. In Malaysia, for example, in each of the states which make up the country the Chief Minister by constitutional right becomes President of his (there have as yet been no women Chief Ministers) local Football Association. Quite apart from anything else, that makes a nonsense of the oft repeated desire to separate sport and politics. On the contrary, it demonstrates an understanding and an acceptance of the relationship between sport and state which has frequently been a matter of unease in the West (and, of course, makes the Deputy Prime Minister's comment even more incongruous).[35] The imminent National Sports Act in Malaysia would give the state even further powers of intervention in the affairs of sports bodies in a way which would be fought vigorously in other politics. In Malaysia, with its particular form of democratic government, the argument is straightforward – sport is now regarded as an important state function for both domestic and international purposes, therefore the government must have some power over the system of development which involves amounts of taxpayers money.[36] This is particularly so with Malaysia hosting the 1998 Commonwealth Games, becoming a participant in Formula One motor racing, staging the 1999 World Cup of golf, and seeking other major events – all this is seen quite openly as a test of the nation's growth towards becoming a 'developed' country.

That is quite different from Australia, for example, where federal government dealings with sport have largely been delegated to a statutory authority, the Australian Sports Commission, which handles all policy and funding matters. In many ways, that reflects a history of sports policy being elaborated independently of government, and the relationship between the two bodies is still relatively uneasy with many sports organizations welcoming federal funds but resenting the bureaucratic accountability which goes with those funds. New Zealand has gone one step further, in line with its wholesale divestment of state control, by setting up the Hillary Commission and its essentially privatized arms of sport and recreation.

The point here is that in Malaysia, Australia and New Zealand, there is a complex interplay between the historical growth of both sport and political system to produce the current forms of delivery and cultural contour. Joseph Arbena makes much the same point in dealing with the history and contemporary use of sport as a means of promoting social development in Latin America.[37] The same may easily be said of the United States (where there is very little in the way of a state control) and Great Britain (where the drive to government funding of elite sport has been quite slow, as befits the home of the ideals of 'amateurism' and sport as a means to an end rather than an end in itself). More spectacular examples of such a complex arrangement were to be found, of course, in the former Soviet Union and East Germany, and remain in China and Cuba, for two. The linking of state policy and sport were quite straightforward there.[38]

Those latter cases point again to the importance of ritual and symbol in sport. (This one finds a curious parallel in the rise of both the Christian athlete and the Islamic one – in both cases, their God becomes both the source and the object of their athletic endeavours. Some would see a further parallel between that and the older adage that every army in history had God on its side). In the old clashes between the United States and the Soviet Union the symbolism was obvious, but similar 'clashes' (again to invoke Huntington) occur around the world of sport in various ways: China versus Taiwan, Croatia versus neighbouring states, Turkey versus Greece, India versus Pakistan to name a few. In those cases, sport becomes the symbol of, and the ritual for, wider sets of political issues, and in some cases provides a rare form of contact through which the passions may become revealed. The annual meeting between Scotland and England in rugby union, for example, often is a sporting re-enactment of a centuries-old political struggle, and in the same code the fixtures between New Zealand and South Africa could be read at one level as the struggle for primacy in the colonial stakes at one level, and a meeting of the southern settler minds at another.[39]

It is a short step from there to that of sport as part of the international diplomatic scene, with sport often providing an opening gambit. At a major Australian representational effort in India late in 1996, for example, it was remarkable how many speakers noted the indissoluble link forged between the two countries by way of cricket.[40] The irony was that India was long treated by Australia as a playing minnow beyond worth as a fishing expedition, and even now few Australian players relish the thought of going to such a 'foreign' (for which read Other) place. Despite the long history of cricket in India, it was well after the Second World War when formal cricket relations began to develop.[41]

It is interesting that in the field of international relations, despite the richness and the significance of the examples available, sport figures at a very low level. (After all, in a very long book Huntington mentions only the Olympics, and only twice in any real sense.) Yet sport clearly provides much of the cultural underpinning for international relations, and for showcasing a number of the struggles which occur – the rights of women from Islamic countries, and from other states where women's rights are subjugated to those of males, to compete in sport is a very good case in point. Arguably, many more people get to know about those cultural struggles than would have done so otherwise. A Pakistani women's cricket tour of New Zealand early in 1997 was more interesting for the struggle to make it happen than for the playing rights.[42] Despite the primacy of Pakistani male cricket in world terms, the women received little or no help from most of the male stars placed in an Islamic context.

A major issue is in how to read this richness. It is clear enough that a traditional analysis will not reveal fully the contours of such politicized sport or spotted politics because it would miss the passion which frames and directs sport. The politics of nationalism comes close in some respects, in that the element of emotional commitment is similar, but even that is not fully satisfactory – in sport, ultimately, a nation loses nothing save pride. What is required, then, is a special reading of sport politics which is about the personal politics of attachments.[43]

In many senses, that is the thrust of this essay which proceeds from a position that, despite the amount of work completed on sport in recent years, the elusive analytical goal is still about why people in many cultures attach so much importance to sport, why they invest so much emotional capital in the activity; and why it occupies so much space in modern culture.[44] Moreover, how do people learn these cultural practices, and for what purposes?

When I was growing up in New Zealand in the 1950s and 1960s, there were two major sports for males, rugby union and cricket, two of the main sports taken around the world by British imperialists. The games served two quite different cultural purposes.[45] It was every boys dream to play for the All Blacks (the misnamed national rugby union team which then contained few Maoris, especially in fixtures against South Africa). The game was based around strength and masculinity, and national success in rugby was seen as a cultural success, a representation of the country's economic and political growth. It was the stuff of myth – how the original All Blacks were 'robbed' of victory against Wales in 1905, how Kevin Skinner 'tanned' the Springboks in 1956, how Maoris like George Nepia could become great if they 'Persevered'. Above all, rugby was about conformity so that 'rebels' like Bob Burgess (who refused to go to South Africa) and Chris Laidlaw (who did but spoke out on his return) were viewed with great cultural suspicion. All this was taken very seriously – when I played one of my last games in a small country town of 5,000, I became the first player from my team in almost thirty years to visit the clubrooms of our great rivals. For years a long forgotten controversy had divided the teams and the town during the winter months.

Cricket was different with the struggle being (and remaining) a search for respectability in the international playing arena. But it was also a search for moral respectability, because the New Zealand traditions of the game were very much of the English public school, cricket as a learning ground for life. The umpire's decision was to be respected, whereas in rugby what you did out of sight of the referee was all part of the game. In cricket we were honest, 'walking' from the pitch if we knew we had given a catch not detected by the umpire – in rugby we did not honour the same code. In cricket we respected the English (or the British) whereas in rugby we hated them, with rare exceptions like the 1959 British Lions; in rugby we respected the South Africans who played the same physical, sharp practice game that we did. The point about all this is the recognition that in youth and sport we learn cultural attitude and practice, so if we are to effect social change through sport then we must start in youth.

Indeed, it might safely be argued that in the youth sport of any culture may be read much of the social make-up of that culture. That is certainly so in contemporary Malaysia where a much vaunted youth sport programme is deemed to have failed, and many commentators see a link between that and the apparent rise of social problems among youth – the programme is now being revamped, so that belief in sport as an agent of social harmony still prevails. On the other hand, in western countries there has raged a debate for years about whether or not competitive sport for young children is a healthy matter. In Australia, the rise of modified rules (so that children might learn the basic skills more readily) ignited a major controversy which had its roots in sociopolitical standings – 'freemarket' advocates tended to support a neo-Darwinian view that the full sport versions helped weed out the non-competitive, while 'socialists' were deemed to support the modified rules as an arm of the egalitarian welfare state.[46] In the United States, similar discussions have been waged about the social merits of junior baseball and other sports forms.

Looked at in this way, of course, the issue is not about kids learning sport but about kids learning how to negotiate their own cultures and to interpret others. For that reason alone, the origin of the gender debate in sport starts very much in youth. My daughter attends an international school in Penang and is horrified that boys always captain the mixed soccer team (in which few girls are selected) because the coach, a Malaysian Chinese, believes that soccer is a 'boys' game. The girls, he says, can be captains when a 'girls' game is played, but the problem is that few such girls' games (like netball) are ever played. In Malaysia, predictably, women have a very difficult time of it in many mainstream sports, even though they figure prominently at world level in activities like bowling. The gender patterns are set in youth and may be changed in youth – the fact that my daughter is horrified by the soccer situation shows that her social patterning is quite different from that of preceding Australian generations. It has long been my contention that sport has been a major moulder of gender attitudes and roles for both men and women, but that it can be changed.[47] While that change is too slow for many observers it is change, nonetheless, which is an integral part of a much wider social shift.

It is through sport, too, that much of the argument about world youth being globalized and, by definition, decultured (in the nationalist sense) is run. Because kids in Asia, Africa and elsewhere 'know' Michael Jordan to the point of wearing basketball clothes, including the de rigueur cap backwards, it is believed that they somehow are abandoning national sports and, therefore, national traditions. It is, of course, not as simple as that. Near my house is a small outdoor court on which is played sepaktakraw, the traditional southeast Asian game (sometimes described as volleyball for the feet played on a badminton court with a rattan ball).[48] Many of the local players of this traditional game are urbanized and modernized Malaysians who adopt in leisure the trappings of basketball. By the very playing of the game they demonstrate the power of cultural resistance which lies in sporting activity.

A more spectacular example concerns the transformation of cricket in many Pacific islands such as the Trobriands, Samoa and, to a lesser degree, Fiji. The game was introduced by the English, especially the missionaries, as a so-called 'civilizing' force. Local populations, however, reconverted the sport in line with local practice, to the point that in some locations it became a major political tool in the struggle against colonialism. The English rules were thrown out, along with English cultural practice.[49] In Samoa, the German authorities between 1900 and 1914 waged a campaign to eliminate cricket because they believed it to be socially subversive.[50]

Again, the message is clear – this was not just about sport as a physical activity on the fringes of mainstream life. It was an integral part of cultural form, adaptation and preservation of long held beliefs in which people posited great inner meaning.

Communicating Sport

It is in the communication, or the representation, of sport that much of its cultural power lies. In contemporary society there is an overwhelming concentration on the appearance of sport on television in the analysis of that communication, but much of the approach misses the historical significance across cultures of the means by which the messages of sport were conveyed and how those messages were interpreted. Through juvenile literature, for example, many of the moral messages of sport were carried.[51] English comics, like Tiger (along with their 'annuals'), for boys in the 1950s routinely carried sports fiction in which young heroes saved the day for their country while upholding the best traditions of sportsmanship.[52] While there are now societies for the study of sports literature, and while the representation of sport in art is being increasingly pursued, there is still much for social analysts to uncover.

There is a thriving market, for example, in golf art which analysts of power and landscape might find revealing about social attitudes prevalent in the game.[53] In the presentation of golf courses, for example, the scenes are usually uncrowded, the players are inevitably male and well (traditionally) dressed and accompanied by caddies, and the air is one of privilege and social exclusion.[54] For many golf outsiders, of course, that is the image of the game and one which drives their interpretations of the players and the sites. While there is much in golf that differs from such an image, the communication of the game through art and literature emphasizes such an exclusivist image.[55] The point here, of course, is upon the image. To continue the golf story; the image of women's professional golf has always been uncertain or, more precisely, undefined. On the one hand, players like Jan Stephenson who played upon their sexual attractiveness were thought to bring the game into disrepute, while on the other the tour has always had to fight insinuations of lesbianism.[56] On a wider scale, the communicated image of women's sport has been one of the major obstacles in its drive towards equality – it has had to overcome generations of depictions of 'slower, lower, weaker', to adapt a very well known expression. In the search for cultural change, one of the starting points must be with the adaptation of image, a theme with applications right through the areas of race and ethnicity as well as west and non-west: the power of the dominant really comes from the power of the image, the representation.[57]

The structures and the organizations of representation have an enormous impact on the ways in which sport 'appears' in modern culture. One obvious example concerns the 'shape' of the 1936 Olympics as portrayed in the Leni Riefenstal film. A very different one is the deliberately stylized 'sport' depicted in the for-television World Wrestling Federation series as contrasted with, say, Roland Barthes' celebrated essay on wrestling as a struggle between 'good and evil' (which puts it immediately in the same company as Clifford Geertz's equally celebrated article on Balinese cockfighting).[58]

Yet another is the depiction of karate and the martial arts generally in films such as 'The Karate Kid' and those starring Jackie Chan, Bruce Lee, Steven Seagal, Chuck Norris and Jean Claude van Damme. They are not 'the real thing' or are, at least, a variation on that condition, yet for the unknowing consumers the images portrayed are a depiction of reality.

Perhaps that is why there are spectacularly so few sports-based novels and films which are culturally satisfying – the search for the essential character of the main players always seems to be so elusive. Historical accuracy aside, 'Chariots of Fire' worked because the sport came out of the characters rather than vice-versa, the inner struggle of the athletic ideal and endeavour was so well portrayed. That immediately sets the film well apart from films such as 'The Tin Cup' which is not so much about sport as about finding yet another vehicle for Kevin Costner – the film is unsatisfying because it is not about the athletic struggle. The same goes for the Rocky series in which boxing becomes a simplistic allegory for the last years of Cold War politics. Similarly, most surfing films become caught in either endless seascape scenes or representations of an alleged lifestyle.

The very rise of organized sport around the world from the middle of the nineteenth century onwards has been accompanied, at least, and in many senses formed, by these communicated images. At first the images were created by the writers of sport in the daily press and in the specialist sports publications which appeared in many cultures. Looked at this way, the centrality of sport in modern culture owes much to these writers, yet we still know very little about them. Alfred E.T. Watson, for example, played a major role in the appearance of the Badminton Library series of books in Britain either side of 1900, in the magazine series of the same name which ran for almost thirty years from the 1890s, in several other sports-related publications, and wrote an autobiography – yet we still know remarkably little about him and his circle. If we are to understand the images then we need to know the creators.

From the 1920s onwards in a large number of cultures the radio commentators then arose to challenge the writers, with the medium itself having an impact upon sports forms themselves – sumo bouts, for example, began to fit in with radio broadcasts from the 1920s onwards. In the United States the images created by and for many baseball teams had as much to do with their radio commentators as with the players themselves. By definition, the play-by-play commentator told an interpretation as much as a narrative, with many nationalist versions of sport being spun – in New Zealand, for example, rugby union commentators like Winston McCarthy created images of the nation being involved in some kind of cultural crusade against the 'Other' by way of the sports medium. In Australia in the 1930s cricket commentators took it one step further, recreating play with sound effects but based on telegrams despatched from England where the games were actually being played.

Then came television which undoubtedly had a major impact upon the playing patterns of sport, upon the opportunities created for further commercial expansion, upon the internationalizing of certain sports forms, and upon the amount of sport potentially to be consumed by populations around the world.[59] Significantly, however, television had an enormous impact upon creating or recreating cultural images. Most Australian cricket audiences 'knew' West Indies cricket either from touring teams, writers or radio broadcasters until the early 1990s when the technical difficulties of telecasting from the Caribbean were overcome. At that point, the real passion of the Caribbean game became evident to Australians, because they saw the game in its own setting (that leaves aside all the debates about the ways in which television 'frames' sport, but those debates are important, clearly, in any discussion about the formation of cultural attitudes concerning sport).[60]

While all that was going on, writing about sport continued to evolve so that in several cultures the sportswriter became as much social commentator as sports narrator, again emphasizing how sport had become a core cultural value. That in itself raised several problems about the image and the standing of sport as a social institution, in that many citizens (and not a few sports authorities) resented any work which challenged the myth of sport as a 'good' cultural commodity. It is not that such work was necessarily new, as in England writers like Frederick Gale had written 'critical' works during the later nineteenth century. But it was that such works increased during the last twenty-five years or so of the twentieth century, were supported by much of the work in the social analysis of sport conducted in universities around the world, and stood in stark contrast to some of the productions by television conglomerates.[61] It may be argued that in contemporary sport the media writers have been to the fore in exploring the wider range of sports issues than the academicians, but that is a debate for another occasion.[62]

The message again, however, is that there is still a great deal of work to be done before we really understand the full dynamics which underlay the creation of sport as a central social feature of postmodern society. For all the discourse on the various facets of sport, it may be argued that our genuine 'understanding' is still highly undeveloped.

On Reflection

What, then, is the agenda now? Essentially, it is not to argue that sport is a major cultural form, because that is now, surely, beyond doubt (although the point might not have been made so easily twenty years ago and more). It is more to develop our understanding of how and why sport came to be that way, of the myriad of meanings now invested in sport, of the reactionary as well as the progressive aspects of sport, of sport as a genuine business as well as a recreation form, and many other dimensions. The challenge is to analyze the cultural phenomenon in all its settings, levels and forms, and not to treat it as a monolithic or one-dimensional feature. If wisdom comes from knowledge, understanding and experience, then wisdom about sport will come from the joining of the experiential, intellectual and expressional communities to further elucidate the growth of sport as perhaps the great transnational cultural form of the twentieth century and beyond.[63]

Notes

[1] This is happening currently in Malaysia with the introduction of ASTRO.

[2] The best and pioneering example here is that of ABC in the United States led by programming guru Roone Arledge who was cloned around the globe as by, for example, Australian David Hill who introduced 'Wide World of Sport' for Kerry Packer's Channel 9 and then, later, went to FOX to reshape American football coverage for Rupert Murdoch.

[3] For example, see the grant of almost US$1 million (along with a naval promotion) given by the government of Thailand to 1996 Olympic gold medallist featherweight boxer Somluk Kamsing, and the formulation of a National Sports Act by the Government of Malaysia, as well as the serious efforts made by the Government of South Africa to have sport become a major vehicle for that country's 're-entry' to the world in the post-apartheid era.

[4] The rise of university-based programmes in sports management around the globe, and the associated rise of publications like the *Cyber-Journal of Sports Management* (an Internet-based publication) underline this point.

[5] On this general point, see Stoddart, 'Convergence: Sport upon the Information Superhighway'. For a print-based but rapidly dating guide to sport on the Net, see Maloni, Greenman and Miller, *Netsports*.

[6] As examples of the debates, see: Bourdieu, 'Program for a Sociology of Sport'; Gruneau, 'The Critique of Sport in Modernity'; and, in particular, the exchange between Douglas Booth and William J. Morgan over the latter's *Leftist Theories of Sport*-see *Sporting Traditions* 12, 2 (May 1996).

[7] One longstanding exception here has been Janet Lever's work on Brazilian football, *Soccer Madness*.

[8] Perhaps his most important works here are, first, *Orientalism*, and, second, *Culture and Imperialism*.

[9] Foucault, *Order of Things*.

[10] Some scholars of sport now argue that the study of sport is more widely recognized in scholarly fields, but a brief review of undergraduate texts in history, sociology and anthropology would suggest otherwise.

[11] See, for example, the special issue of the *Journal of Sport and Social Issues* 20, 3 (Aug. 1996).

[12] This has been the subject of much argument in some quarters – see Rowe and Lawrence, 'Beyond National Sport' which continues a spat between sociologists and historians which does lead to further understanding of the sport phenomenon.

[13] Anthropologists, of course, will see here the importance of ritual. For present purposes, Hobsbawm and Ranger (eds), *The Invention of Tradition*.

[14] For the baseball story, Whiting, *You Gotta Have Wa*; Cromartie (with Robert Whiting), *Slugging It out in Japan*.

[15] 'Sumo Wrestling In Grip Of Corruption', *Daily Telegraph* 22 May 1996.

[16] Norman Sklarewitz, 'Is This The Next Nomo?', *Asiaweek* 30 May 1996.

[17] Some background is set out in Stoddart, 'Wide World of Golf'.

[18] An interesting response to all this comes in the form of the Global Anti-Golf Movement (GAGM). For some of its approach, see *GAGM Update*, 1 (1996).

[19] The beginning point is James, *Beyond a Boundary*; an important milestone was Patterson's 'The Ritual of Cricket'; and a convenient collection of the range is Beckles and Stoddart (eds), *Liberation Cricket*.

[20] For an overview of this point, see Stoddart, 'Sport, Cultural Imperialism and Colonial Response in the British Empire'. The most often-cited work is Brookes, *English Cricket*.

[21] For the 1935 story, see Stoddart, 'Sport, Culture and International Relations'. For a literary reference to the Spurs image, King, *The Football Factory*, 55.

[22] Marqusee, *Anyone but England*. The advantage of being a cultural 'outsider' in such circumstances is a reminder of the point made by C. Wright Mills about the amount of 'cultural baggage' taken for granted when analysing one's own culture – see the chapter on 'history' in his *The Sociological Imagination*.

[23] Mosley has done the most work on these issues: 'Ethnic Involvement in Australian Soccer'.

[24] A good guide to this is Grundlingh, 'Playing For Power'.

[25] Regalado, 'Sport and Community in California's Japanese American Yamato Colony'.

[26] In one such club in Australia, for example, part of the entry procedure requires provision of twelve referees who will attest to the applicant's good standing. As one applicant pointed out, it is easier to get into the national parliament than into that club. Interview material.

[27] For example, Tatz and Stoddart, *The Royal Sydney Golf Club*.

[28] Fieldwork observations.

[29] This story and its context may be followed conveniently in Linnell, *Football Lid*.

[30] Kruger and Riordan (eds), *The Story of Worker Sport*.

[31] This is demonstrated in literary form in such works as David Williamson's play, *The Club*, about the Collingwood Football Club in Melbourne first screened in 1980.

[32] Huntington, *The Clash of Civilizations*, 197.

[33] For some approaches to sports politics, see Allison (ed), *The Changing Politics of Sport*; Hill, *Olympic Politics*; Houlihan, *Sport and International Politics*.

[34] *Star*, 26 March 1997.

[35] This whole story became most interesting – the general view was that the Malaysian government had allowed the Israeli team to participate in an attempt to soften relations and stimulate trade and so show a 'soft' face of Islam. Immediately after the conclusion of the tournament, however, Malaysia joined other nations at the Non-Aligned Movement meeting in New Delhi to freeze relations with Israel in protest at activities on the West Bank – *New Straits Times* 5 April 1997, 11 April 1997.

[36] It was a matter of some moment when the Chief Minister of Johore (a former federal Sports Minister) announced that he would not take the post on the grounds that such a position was not in the best interests of either football or the Chief Minister.

[37] This thinking underlay the construction of the 1997 National Sports Act which occasioned a vigorous debate between the Olympic Committee of Malaysia, the National Sports Council and the Minister for Sport.

[38] Arbena, 'International Aspects of Sport in Latin America'.

[39] Riordan (ed.), *Sport Under Communism*. A more specific case study may he found in Gilbert, *The Miracle Machine*, which analyzed the situation in the-then German Democratic Republic.

[40] The nature of the New Zealand-South Africa connection is demonstrated in Pearson, 'Heads In The Sand', and Roger, *Old Heroes*.

[41] The occasion was the 'New Horizons' series of conferences designed to enhance trade, commerce and cultural contact between the two countries.

[42] For an entertaining account of Indian cricket culture, see Levine, *Into The Passionate Soul of Subcontinental Cricket*, and for a far more elaborate cultural reading, Nandy, *The Tao of Cricket*. An excellent insider account is Mukherjee, *Autobiography of an Unknown Cricketer*.

[43] Personal observation.

[44] The politics of Gaelic sport provide some useful examples here. Mandle, *The Gaelic Athletic Association and Irish Nationalist Politics*.

[45] One excellent ethnography which reveals the extent to which sport can rule a life is Hornby, *Fever Pitch*, the story of an Arsenal Football Club supporter.

[46] For some interesting background, see Phillips, *A Man's Country*.

[47] There is an interesting parallel here in the current Australian controversy about 'capitalist' and 'community' views of sport in the marketplace. The debate was ignited by Quick, 'Paying To

Win', and quickly taken up by a variety of writers in issue 10 of the *Bulletin of Sport and Culture*. (March 1997).

[48] Stoddart, *Saturday Afternoon Fever*, Ch.6. For some other views, see Vertinsky, 'Gender Relations, Women's History and Sport History'.

[49] For a description, Arlott (ed.), *The Oxford Companion To Sports And Games*, 810–11.

[50] See the film 'Trobriand Cricket' for an excellent account.

[51] I have written about this in my chapter 'Other Cultures' in Stoddart and Sandiford (eds), *The Imperial Game*.

[52] As an example, see Stoddart, 'Cricket, Literature and Culture' [the text version of The Barry Andrews Memorial Lecture 1992, Australian Defence Force Academy, Canberra].

[53] One such story which I remember from Tiger at that time concerned a father who chained a cricket bat to his son's wrist so that the boy might never go without practice, the bat being removed only so that fielding practice could be carried out. Nowadays that would be tantamount to child abuse, another reminder of how the social context for sport alters.

[54] The insights from landscape analysis come from writers such as Mitchell, (ed.), *Landscape and Power* and Daniels, *Fields Of Vision*. For a rather bland view of the golf landscape, Adams, 'Golf'.

[55] Some random examples here include: Finn (1861–1901), 'The First Tee at St George's, Sandwich, 1896'; Campbell (contemporary), 'The 14th Green, Kings Course, Gleneagles', Shearer (1925),'Royal Dornoch, 1982'.

[56] For an indication of the vast coverage of golf in communicable form, see the Rhod McEwan series of catalogues produced from his base in Ballater, Scotland. For further details see www.rhodmcewan.com.

[57] For some works here: Crosset, *Outsiders in the Clubhouse*; Kahn, *The LPGA*; Bamberger, 'Living with a Lie'.

[58] Some excellent work in this area has been that done by Margaret Carlisle Duncan, as in 'The Politics of Women's Body Images and Practices'. See, too, Vertinsky, *The Eternally Wounded Woman*.

[59] Barthes in his *Mythologies* and Geertz, 'Deep Play'.

[60] For some background, see Whannel, *Fields of Vision*; Wenner (ed.), *Media Sport and Society*; Barnett, *Games and Sets*.

[61] See, for example: Trevelyan and Jackson, 'Clash of the Codes'.

[62] A sample of such works: Brohm, *Sport*; Hoberman, *Sport and Ideology*; Gruneau, *Sports, Class, and Social Development*; Hargreaves, *Sport, Power and Culture*.

[63] I argued this in a paper delivered in 1993 to a joint North American Association for Sport History/Australian Society for Sports History meeting in Hawaii.

References

Adams, R. L. A. "Golf." In *The Theater of Sport*, edited by Karl B. Raitz. Baltimore: Johns Hopkins, 1995.

Allison, L., ed. *The Changing Politics of Sport*. Manchester: Manchester University Press, 1993.

Arbena, J. L. "International Aspects of Sport in Latin America: Perceptions, Prospects and Proposal?" In *The Sports Process: A Comparative and Developmental Approach*, edited by E. Dunning, J. McGuire and R. Pearton. Champaign, IL: Human Kinetics, 1993.

Arlott, J., ed. *The Oxford Companion to Sports and Games*. London: Paladin, 1977.

Bamberger, M. "Living with a Lie (from Sports Illustrated)." In *The Best American Sports Writing 1996*, edited by J. Feinstein. Boston, MA: Houghton Mifflin, 1996.

Barnett, S. *Games and Sets: The Changing Face of Sport on Television*. London: BFI, 1991.

Barthes, R. *Mythologies*. London: Paladin, 1973.

Beckles, H. and B. Stoddart, eds. *Liberation Cricket: West Indies Cricket Culture*. Manchester: Manchester University Press, 1995.

Bourdieu, P. "Program for a Sociology of Sport." *Sociology of Sport Journal* 5 (1988).

Brohm, J-M. *Sport: A Prison of Measured Time*. London: Ink Links, 1978.

Brookes, C. *English Cricket: The Game and the Players through the Ages*. London: Weidenfeld and Nicolson, 1978.

Bulletin of Sport and Culture. 10 1997

Cromartie, W. (with R. Whiting). *Slugging It out in Japan: An American Major Leaguer in the Tokyo Outfield*. New York: Signet, 1992.

Crosset, T. W. *Outsiders in the Clubhouse: The World of Women's Professional Golf*. Buffalo: SUNY Press, 1995.

Daniels, S. *Fields of Vision: Landscape Imagery & National Identity in England and the United States*. Cambridge: Polity, 1993.

Duncan, M. C. "The Politics of Women's Body Images and Practices: Foucault, the Panopticon and Shape Magazine." *Journal of Sport and Social Issues* 18, no. 1 (1994).

Foucault, M. *Order of Things: Archaeology of the Human Sciences*. New York: Vintage, 1994.

Geertz, C. "Deep Play: Notes on the Balinese Cockfight." *Daedalus* 101 (1972).

Gilbert, D. *The Miracle Machine*. New York: McCann and Geoghan, 1980.

Grundlingh, A. "Playing for Power? Rugby, Afrikaaner Nationalism and Masculinity in South Africa, c. 1900–70." *International Journal of the History of Sport* 11, no. 3 (1994).

Gruneau, R. S. *Sports, Class, and Social Development*. Amherst, MA: University of Massachusetts Press, 1983.

Gruneau, R. "The Critique of Sport in Modernity." In *The Sports Process: A Comparative and Developmental Approach*, edited by E. Dunning *et al.* Champaign, IL: HKP, 1993.

Hargreaves, J. *Sport, Power, and Culture*. New York: St. Martins Press, 1986.

Hill, C. R. *Olympic Politics*. Manchester: Manchester University Press, 1992.

Hoberman, J. *Sport and Ideology*. Austin, TX: University of Texas Press, 1984.

Hobsbawm, E. J. and Terence Ranger, eds. *The Invention of Tradition*. Cambridge: Cambridge University Press, 1983.

Hornby, N. *Fever Pitch*. London: Penguin, 1993.

Houlihan, B. *Sport and International Politics*. London: Harvester Wheatsheaf, 1994.

Huntington, S. P. *The Clash of Civilizations and the Remaking of World Order*. New York: Simon and Shuster, 1996.

James, C. L. R. *Beyond a Boundary*. London: Hutchinson, 1963.

Journal of Sport and Social Issues. 20, no. 3 (Aug. 1996).

Kahn, L. *The LPGA: The Unauthorized Version of the History of the Ladies Professional Golf Association*. GFP: Menlo Park, CA, 1996.

King, J. *The Football Factory*. London: Vintage, 1997.

Kruger, A. and J. Riordan, eds. *The Story of Worker Sport*. Champaign, IL: HKP, 1996.

Lawrence, G. "Beyond National Sport: Sociology, History and Postmodernity." *Sporting Traditions* 12, no. 2 (1996).

Lever, J. *Soccer Madness*. Chicago, IL: University of Chicago Press, 1983.

Levine, E. *Into the Passionate Soul of Subcontinental Cricket*. New Delhi: Penguin, 1996.

Linnell, G. *Football Lid: The inside Story of the AFL*. Sydney: Macmillan, 1995.

Maloni, K., B. Greenman, and K. Miller. *Netsports*. New York: Random-Woolf, 1995.

Mandle, W. F. *The Gaelic Athletic Association and Irish Nationalist Politics*. London: IUP, 1987.

Marqusee, M. *Anyone but England: Cricket and the National Malaise*. London: Verso, 1994.

Mills, C. W. *The Sociological Imagination*. Harmondsworth: Penguin, 1970.

Mitchell, W. J. T., ed. *Landscape and Power*. Chicago, IL: University of Chicago Press, 1994.

Morgan, W. J. *Leftist Theories of Sport: A Critique and Reconstruction.* Champaign, IL: VIP, 1994.

Mosley, P. *Ethnic Involvement in Australian Soccer: A History, 1950–1990.* Canberra: National Sports Research Centre Report, 1995.

Mukherjee, S. *Autobiography of an Unknown Cricketer.* Delhi: Ravi Dayal, 1996.

Nandy, A. *The Tao of Cricket: On Games of Destiny and the Destiny of Games.* New Delhi: Penguin, 1989.

Patterson, O. "The Ritual of Cricket." *Jamaica Journal* 3 (1969).

Pearson, M. N. "Heads in the Sand: The 1956 Springbok Tour to New Zealand in Perspective." In *Sport in History,* edited by R. Cashman and M. McKernan. Brisbane: University of Queensland Press, 1979.

Phillips, J. *A Man's Country: The Image of the Pakeha Male – a History.* Auckland: Penguin, 1987.

Quick, S. E. "Paying to Win: The Business of the AFL." *Bulletin of Sport and Culture* 9 (1996).

Regalado, S. O. "Sport and Community in California's Japanese American Yamato Colony, 1930–1945." *Journal of Sport History* 19, no. 2 (1992).

Riordan, J., ed. *Sport under Communism.* Canberra: ANU Press, 1978.

Roger, W. *Old Heroes: The 1956 Springbok Tour and the Lives Beyond.* Auckland: Hodder and Stoughton, 1991.

Rowe, D. and G. Lawrence. "Beyond national sport: sociology, history and postmodernity." *Sporting Traditions* 12, no. 2 (1996).

Said, E. *Orientalism.* Harmondsworth: Penguin, 1979.

Said, E. *Culture and Imperialism.* New York: Vintage, 1993.

Sporting Traditions. 12, no. 2 (May 1996).

Stoddart, B. "Sport, Culture and International Relations: England Versus Germany, 1935." In *Sport History,* edited by N. Muller and J. Ruhl. Niederhausen: Schors Verlag, 1985.

Stoddart, B. *Saturday Afternoon Fever: Sport in the Australian Culture.* Sydney: Angus & Robertson, 1986.

Stoddart, B. "Sport, Cultural Imperialism and Colonial Response in the British Empire: A Framework for Analysis." *Comparative Studies in Society and History* 30, no. 4 (1988).

Stoddart, B. "Wide World of Golf: A Research Note on the Interdependence of Sport, Culture and Economy." *Sociology of Sport Journal* 7, no. 4 (1990).

Stoddart, B. "Cricket, Literature and Culture: Windows on the World." *Notes and Furphies* 30 (1993).

Stoddart, B. "Convergence: Sport Upon the Information Superhighway." *Journal of Sport and Social Issues* 21, no. 1 (1997).

Stoddart, B. "Other Cultures." In *The Imperial Game,* edited by Brian Stoddart and Keith Sandiford. Manchester: Manchester Univesity Press, 1998.

Tatz, C. and B. Stoddart. *The Royal Sydney Golf Club: The First Hundred Years.* Sydney: Allen and Unwin, 1993.

Trevelyan, M. J. and S. J. Jackson. "Clash of the Codes: A Comparative Analysis of Media Representations of Violence in Rugby Union and Rugby League." In *Sport, Power and Society in New Zealand: Historical and Contemporary Perspectives,* edited by J. Nauright. Sydney: ASSH Studies in Sports History no.11, 1995.

Vertinsky, P. A. *The Eternally Wounded Woman.* Champaign, IL: University of Illinois Press, 1994.

Vertinsky, P. A. "Gender Relations, Women's History and Sport History." *Journal of Sport History* 10, no. 1 (1994).

Wenner, L. A., ed. *Media, Sport, and Society.* Newbury Park: Sage, 1989.

Whannel, G. *Fields of Vision: Television Sport and Cultural Transformation.* London: Routledge, 1992.

Whiting, R. *You Gotta Have Wa.* New York: Vintage, 1990.

Orientalism, Golf and the Modern Age: Joe Kirkwood in Asia[1]

Introduction

Joe Kirkwood is a wonderful Australian story combining many elements: a character, golf, globalization, Asia and more.

Kirkwood, in some ways, started my return to Asia intellectually. India made me as an intellectual, and as a person – if I have any patience, I learned it there. As with anyone doing a thesis, there were moments I was convinced that I had discovered *the* magic piece of information. One such was the moment I discovered that an 1890s file from the old Madras Agriculture Department had never been transferred to the Archives. Immediately I leaped to the conclusion that this *had* to be significant, otherwise why would it have been retained? So off I went to the Department, complete with book to fill in waiting time. Three days later I received the file and there was absolutely nothing in it, literally: there was a cover and no contents. Back I went to the Archives to continue the quest. There were people, insights, alternatives, ideas, curiosity and more, along with the gut-wrenching poverty and stark contrasts of life. Long after I went off to 'discover' sport, those memories and experiences remained with me because they contained the real significance of inquiry – somehow, it connected to the otherwise unimaginable and indescribable passion for cricket found in India along with the passion for law, debate and complexity.

The characters I discovered in India, both live and in the archival materials, led me back to Kirkwood indirectly. There was, for example, A.M.A.C. Galletti, the Indian Civil Service officer who joined in Madras in 1900, retired in 1935 and who, in between, gave the Raj some unpleasant moments – with an Italian father and English mother, he inherited a spirit for nationalism, and for average English taste showed too much sympathy for independence-seeking Indians. The trail led to his daughter, another character who revealed a family full of characters. This experience led me to think more about sport characters in sport and, sequentially, biography.

While never a great devotee of biography, it began to occur to me that (a) sports biographies might unlock major insights, and (b) I could recall few good sports biographies. Most have been more like hagiographies, at worst, and one-dimensional shallow reflections of interesting people at best. Christopher Douglas, for example, wasted an opportunity with his Douglas Jardine biography. All but a couple of chapters featured Bodyline, as if that was all there was to the man. Bodyline brought Jardine to notoriety, but having reached there he could well have been the touchstone to the paradoxes and twists of early twentieth-century England. Douglas had little, really, to say of Jardine's father, a man of India and Empire and cricket and confidant of that great Scots figure, Andrew Lang who was really Jardine's stand-in father. Lang, anthropologist, folklorist, collector of fairy tales and member of the literary establishment led Jardine the younger in many directions. Jardine himself knew people in the psychic movement including astral traveller Joan Grant, herself of the Aleister 'The Beast' Crowley circle. Jardine became deeply interested in Eastern philosophy and spiritualism – this was no ordinary man who had become England captain, yet his biographers have either known little of the deeper story or thought it insignificant.

That lay in the background when I returned to golf and its history and I found Kirkwood, a talented but flawed player close to genius. If Australia had a class clash, he reflected it through his lifelong rivalry with Jim Ferrier, another great Australian player from a 'better' section of Sydney society. Kirkwood became part of Australia's First World War conscription debate, his travel to England raising questions about his patriotism. He nearly made it as a tournament player, but lacked the mental toughness to reach the top. He turned himself into the world's greatest trick shot player, joining forces with one of golf's toughest ever mentalities, Walter Hagen, with whom he toured the world endlessly. Kirkwood was among the first Australian sports people to fashion a lucrative career from something so socially unproductive as an ability to hit a ball. He was controversial, colourful, troubled, self-promoting and entertaining.

More importantly, he spent a lot of time in Asia, including places I had been. The idea that a golfer had been there first made me think about the parallel lives people often have: I knew professional golfers who made a living out of playing and teaching in Asia, and they were following Kirkwood whether or not they realized that. As academics we investigated Asia in all its political and social dimensions yet knew almost nothing of people like Kirkwood who attracted vast crowds, influenced important people, and were debarred from what academics normally considered historically important.

One curious influence was Richard Bosworth, Italianist Professor of History at the University of Western Australia. We met at an early-1990s Melbourne conference convened by Greg Dening, discovered a mutual interest in golf as well as history and stayed in touch. Richard produced a marvelous book on the historiography of the combat nations in the Second World War, *Understanding Auschwitz and Hiroshima,* reminding me just how great history could be, then produced one of the great Mussolini biographies, revealing a truly multi-dimensioned person. This was technically distant from sport and Kirkwood, but Richard knew the role played by sport in Mussolini's state. Richard also has a great and infectious passion for his subject – he asked great questions of my material, and propelled me towards a preliminary biographical analysis of Kirkwood.

It was extension rather than shift, though, because I was always curious about individuals and what motivated them: I still have records on thousands of individuals listed as jailed, members of committees, part of crowds, or otherwise involved in south India's 1920s–1930s nationalist movement. That crowd approach emanated from Rude, of course, and still interests me. Ordinary people like Kirkwood do just as extraordinary things as Mussolini. The trick is to find those people in sport. There are great biographies of people like Muhammad Ali because he was obviouly more than a sports person, but there is still no great biography of Bradman or Ranjitsinjhi or Suzanne Lenglen or Danie Craven Babe Diderickson or George Nepia or....

* * * * *

If remembered at all Joe Kirkwood is recalled as golf's greatest trick shot artist, long-time exhibition and touring partner for the wonderful Walter Hagen, a snappy dresser, and a player who never fulfilled his playing potential.[2] Commanding little presence in golf histories despite his early admission to the Hall of Fame in the United States, even in his native Australia standard references frame Kirkwood as an oddity valued most as the source of colourful stories.[3] His 'autobiography' adds weight to that view: a mixture of extraordinary anecdote, factual misrepresentation and fantastic interpretative stretch.[4]

A more modern, perhaps postmodernist interpretation casts Kirkwood in different light.[5] The argument here is that Kirkwood played an important but ambivalent role in the globalization of golf, particularly in its spread to Asia which has become the heartland of the game's later twentieth-century growth. Kirkwood was a pioneer in Asia, but characterized the ambiguities and contradictions of the game's development there and which continue now in an interesting version of the debate about 'Otherness'. He also typified the understanding/misunderstanding dilemma, which runs through contemporary East/West golf relations as much as it does in wider economic, political or cultural spheres.[6] In short, Kirkwood's experiences in Asia foreshadowed many of the current debates about the impact of the global on the local, and about supposedly transnational practices (like golf) intersecting with local cultural conditions.[7] This is the context of the reference to 'Orientalism'.

As delineated by Edward Said, 'Orientalism' suggests that western analyses of 'the Orient' (which, of course, does not exist other than as a concept or, more accurately, a masking short-hand) justified western intervention in various Asian cultures, and western adaptations of those cultures, as much as they tried to understand the 'East'.[8] Northern or metropolitan hemisphere constructs like 'the Far East' and 'the wily Oriental' created typologies of Asian behaviour and attitudes, which combined to produce a superiority complex in the west and an inferiority one in the east. Ashis Nandy is prominent among those to have elaborated on this theme for specific areas of Asia, demonstrating the thorough-going nature of the process along with its consequences for colonial-going-into-post-colonial nations.[9]

This is no simple academic treatise because the debate informs modern East/West-North/South relations, as typified in some of Said's other work, most notably on Palestine and on the wider question of cultural imperialism.[10] While it may appear that foreign values were imposed upon colonial society, Said contends that many cultures self-imposed such values so alienating their central sense of being and identity. Here, of course, he echoes Gramsci whose works underpin much modern cultural and post-colonial theory, and C.L.R. James whose work on Caribbean cricket has inspired rich analysis.[11] The struggle for equal recognition which goes on in the United Nations, as a consequence of this dichotomy, is repeated in the struggle for power in cultural structures such as the Olympic movement – it is the struggle between the metropolitan and the provincial, a reminder of the powerful cultural/religious imperative which runs from the Crusades (itself an Orientalist notion) through to the demonizing of Iran and Afghanistan more recently.[12]

This is not so far away from Joe Kirkwood as might be imagined. The Orientalist sway, the persuasion of non-Western cultures to Western practices took many forms. Sporting ones were not only noticeable but also long-lasting and deep-seated. Indian subcontinental cricket springs to mind immediately as an example of an alien cultural practice that becomes a major social feature. Even though it has developed its own forms in India, Pakistan, Sri Lanka and Bangladesh cricket, nonetheless, is a vivid reminder of a colonial and colonized past.[13]

Among many Asian power elites golf became a pre-eminent cultural form and forum, in most if not all sites simply replacing the cast rather than the script – that is, post-colonial powers replaced imperial ones.[14] The beginnings of the introduced practice resonate now and, so, figures like Kirkwood assume dimensions well beyond their immediate sporting ones. To demonstrate that, three particular episodes from his 'adventure' (for as such were they written) are decoded to reveal much about golf, life, cultural spread and cross-cultural complexity, and to relate those episodes to some modern trends in Asian golf and its analysis by the west. The unifying theme is that as a key cultural icon in modern life, golf and its spread both bridge and divide East and West, but within an assumed globality based upon Orientalist assumptions.

Johore Joe

In a section entitled 'Sultana' (an evocative term in the Orientalist lexicon), Kirkwood claims that during the 1920s he was summoned to the Malayan palace of the Sultan of Johore who was married to an Australian. He was to teach the family golf.[15] The travelling golfer's description of the palace matches that of any 'Oriental' site rendered by other western travellers: gold chandeliers, gem-studded hallways, satins, silks, art, Persian rugs. But the Sultan also had a private nine-hole course, beautifully kept. Young elephants were used to carry the bags, at each tee there was a refreshment hut, and the tee markers were blue for men and pink for women. Needless to say, the Sultan's swing improved under Kirkwood's tutelage, in return for which the coach was allowed to escort the Sultan's daughter.

For Kirkwood, the highlight was a dinner party at which all women present were given swimming suits as gifts by the Sultan, and invited to use the Olympic-sized pool. Consulting his watch after a time, the Sultan then beckoned the men to the balcony at just the moment the swimming suits began to disintegrate as part of an elaborate practical joke. The golfer summed it up thus:

> It was quite an adventure, a memorable interlude in my life. But I am convinced that there exists the world over a universal basic brotherhood common to all. For golfers seldom go their way alone. There are no barriers of breeding, colour or creed. A golfer is judged by his character, conduct and deeds, and the sultan further proved to me that golfers are brothers.[16]

The point, of course, was that Kirkwood was mistaken entirely. He had access to the privilege of social position rather than the brotherhood (let alone sisterhood) of golf. The states in Malaya were run under a complex system of British intervention combined with the continuity of autochthonous power in the form of the sultans, members of traditional ruling families who had great sway among their subjects.[17] As in other settings, such as India, the sultans heightened their conspicuous consumption in an attempt to display parity with the parvenu authorities.

Golf became one of those displays, recognized as a benchmark of exclusivity. The Sultan's private course was an excellent example. In the Saidian view, the behaviour expected by the foreign power became encultured in the group from whom it was expected. What Kirkwood really experienced was the aristocracy rather than the democracy of golf – at best, it was an Orwellian democracy in which some players were more equal than others. And that included Kirkwood, beguiled by the Orientalist spectacle but misled about his position in the display, that of hired entertainer in the way that many colonial administrators might well have been regarded over the long periods of foreign rule.[18]

The full import of this was demonstrated, almost thirty years later, by another wandering player, this time an Englishman. When Peter Alliss played in Singapore and Malaya, he spent considerable time with the colonial rulers who were at the end of their days, enjoyed it very much, and began to reflect on golf as the Australian had. The golf club, in distinction to the course, Alliss mused, played a central part in the lives of the British overseas, offering 'rich delights and warm fellowship ... to mankind'.[19]

During that tour, Alliss shot a record 69 on the racecourse layout on the island of Penang, a long-time British possession and free port. The course was later upgraded to an eighteen-hole course thanks to the generosity of Tunku Abdul Rahman, first Prime Minister of Malaysia and scion of the ruling house of Kedah, a counterpart to the Sultan of Johore who had entertained Kirkwood. 'The Tunku', as he is still known, was a great golf enthusiast, and typified the behaviour admired by the British in those colonial elites whom they regarded as having become 'civilized' – a variation, clearly, on the Orientalist vision, local 'natural rulers' who retained 'Oriental' form but who had taken on British substance. The reverse was represented by those locals who could not or would not adapt.[20]

What Alliss saw, but did not necessarily recognize, was the protection of social space or, at least, a transition in the ownership of that space. That is, golf in its Malayan setting was still a domain of privilege, and while regimes changed the practices in the club did not, simply the nature of the personnel. In the colonial sports world, the golf one specifically here, that was the triumph of Orientalism – the local conviction about the value of a metropolitan ideal, with continued metropolitan reinforcement, through admiration and approbation, underpinning the social process.[21]

A more complex later view emerges from the book written by journalist Desmond Zwar with the great Australian player, Peter Thomson.[22] Zwar was a straightline journalistic interpreter but Thomson was much deeper and more perceptive, as revealed in his comments on the evolution of the golf clubs and on some of their practices.[23] Thomson spent considerable time in Asia during the 1950s and 1960s and did much to popularize the game there. Later, he became a very successful designer there (some of his work was handled by his son Andrew – a former Minister for Sport in the Australian Government – who was based in Japan for many years).

Zwar reflected Kirkwood, in many respects – he claimed, for example, that golfers remembered two things about Thailand: the noise of the traffic, and the girls:

> They are perhaps the gentlest, softest, most feminine females in the world. They bow their heads, hands in the self-effacing prayer position when they are told they are lovely, and they bring a lump even to the most lecherous golfer's throat.[24]

This is pure Orientalism, the ascribing of idealized characteristics to 'Other' people, especially women. The attitude has continued in interesting ways. Thai women caddies, for example, were employed at a particular golf club in the Malaysian state of Kedah during the mid-1990s. Kedah is among the more socially conservative of Malaysian states (that is, more avowedly Islamic so that men golfers, for example, may not wear shorts there), and the wives of golf club members had the caddies removed for fear that other services might be offered to interested players.[25]

Shanghai Show

In 1938, Kirkwood and Hagen arrived in the internationalized Chinese city of Shanghai to play the Hung Jao course (as Kirkwood termed it) at the height of the Sino-Japanese conflict which would spill over into the Pacific war.[26] Japanese authorities had acquired the country club as a command post but, according to Kirkwood, golf continued amidst bombing and fighting. He claims that to honour him and his partner, Chinese and Japanese authorities called a day's truce, with the match staged only after all corpses were removed from the course. At tea, cheongsam-clad Chinese women mixed with kimono-clad Japanese ones, and both groups contrasted with chic westerners attached to trading houses and embassies still plying their business in the midst of both the shooting war and the civil conflict heralding, eventually, the creation of the People's Republic of China.[27] At one point, Japanese officers dressed some of their own men in Chinese uniforms, had them charge Kirkwood with bayonets and rifles, only to be driven back ostensibly by the accuracy of the golf balls he struck towards them. According to Kirkwood, the scenes were used later in a Japanese propaganda film to illustrate Chinese cowardice – how could they face guns if they capitulated to golf balls? The bunkers on the course, he claimed, were actually burial sites where, in wet seasons, bones protruded from the sand so deterring the player. Of all this, he noted:

> we couldn't become embroiled in the politics and economics of the various countries we visited to entertain. Our goals were to bring laughter, sport, and comradeship to people, and these objectives seemed to be universally appreciated.[28]

A (possibly) unfair interpretation is that Kirkwood assumed laughter, sport and comradeship were otherwise absent in those countries, so adopting the imperious position of 'civilizing' the colonies, that most strong of strands in the Orientalist spread of British games.[29] Sports such as golf and cricket were seen as excellent ways of teaching local peoples the proper attitudes, behaviours and beliefs necessary in modern, civilized polities. Games were as much about moral training as they were about physical exercise and prowess. In Said's view, of course, this is a major dimension in Orientalism – while there was a great deal of reference to the mysteries, beauty and wisdom of the 'East', there was a parallel move to reform what were seen as its less attractive characteristics.

Of modern interest here is the idea of golf being a transnational, transcultural force, and the inevitability of its arrival and acceptance in those parts of Asia still left to be 'conquered'. In recent years, of course, the 'opening' of China has been a major business and commercial objective, the lure being a potentially huge consumer market.[30] Golf has been no exception and, along with Macdonald's and Coke, may be reckoned as a visible sign of ideological change there.[31] The mushrooming of golf courses in places like Shanghai has matched that seen elsewhere regionally, and so does the practice of exclusivity – most courses are private membership ones with clientele drawn from among the relatively instant millionaires created by the new economic circumstances. All of this has made the region a target for outside agencies. The Queensland Chamber of Commerce and Industry in Australia reckoned that it developed A\$3.5 million in export revenues for the state from its activities at Golf Asia '97 in Singapore, the region's leading golf industry showcase. Similarly, Scottish Trade International, another development agency, specifically includes golf in its plans for entering the Asia-Pacific.[32]

The point, of course, is an underlying theme that the arrival of golf in 'Communist' China demonstrates the inevitable power of western ideology. It is simply a later modern version of the earlier Orientalist mission outlined by Said. Golf, in this sense, is an industrial commodity rather than a cultural artefact. But it is still in the Orientalist paradigm, with metropolitan agencies working upon the drawing power of an implanted ideal.

Nowhere is this seen more powerfully, perhaps, than in the debate about the environmental impact of golf course development in Asia. Until relatively recently, the apolitical view espoused by Kirkwood was applied by a good many developers in Asia, the result being that precious natural resources were taken over for golf developments enjoyed by a very small number of people. Not only were land and water sources jeopardized, in some cases the accustomed holders of those resources were dispossessed. So serious did this development become that a major social uprising against golf development was formed.[33] There is a direct link, then, between the notions of Orientalism. formed around golf in Asia during Kirkwood's time, and later practices which ignored or overrode local needs and inclinations.

Bali High

The most evocative story, though, concerns Kirkwood's visit to Bali, the quintessential site for Orientalism.[34] He went to the Indonesian island with the Hinduised culture to visit a man he called Le Mare, actually Adrien-Jean Le Mayeur de Merpres (1880–1958), a Belgian artist (sometimes described as the Gauguin of southeast Asia) who settled in Bali in 1932 and married Ni Polok, a local dancer who was also his main model.[35] Le Mayeur's house in the now tourist area of Sanur has become a museum.[36] Presumably Kirkwood met Le Mayeur on the continent or in Britain, referring to him as an old Belgian friend, a once unknown amateur painter who later exhibited 'in the Orient and Paris'. Whatever the reason for the visit, Kirkwood was bitten by 'Bali Fever': 'for it was here that I decided I had found the paradise that we all long for, but somehow find illusive [sic] in the busy commercial world'.[37]

His depiction of Bali was classic Orientalism, matching the exoticism seen in his friend's paintings of people and surroundings. According to Kirkwood, Balinese people were 'without problems or complexes', innocents without shame. He was then instructed, by his own account, to teach golf to the daughter of yet another well-born and wealthy Asian, and the pupil turned up topless. In the classic style, she became a conquest while showing him some of the most beautiful natural surroundings in the world.

Meanwhile, Kirkwood laid out a small golf course so that he might practice and that attracted much local attention. In doing so, he was an architect forerunner of Peter Thomson (who designed Bali Handara), the Nelson-Wright-Haworth team (Bali Golf and Country Club), and Greg Norman (Meridien) – the last follows Kirkwood along a beach, the previous incorporates local culture into course artefacts, while the first lies in a particularly lush, 'Orientalised' setting.[38] Kirkwood's extended from a beach into (in his eyes) an abandoned rice field. The Orientalist continuities are there, and so was the nature of his leaving. The temple dancers:

> were dressed in their traditional, fabulous costumes, made entirely of woven eighteen-carat gold studded with semi-precious stones. The girls had come from all over the island, and their dance in the firelight made a special dream of the night. The strangely beautiful fleeting music played by gongs and tiny bells still lingers in my memory and always will. That evening – in that moment of time – and the soft smile of Bali would be with me forever.[39]

The girl, of course, was not.

Mode Moderne

Because of their continuing symbolic importance, there are three main recurring themes of interest in these Kirkwood stories: power, gender and culture.

Power

An obvious point in Asian golf is that the power of position has been supplemented, possibly even replaced by the power of wealth. The two were not dissociated in earlier times – Thomson and Zwar, for example, noted that Tun Abdul Razak, then Deputy Prime Minister but to become Prime Minister of Malaysia, sported the upmarket Kenneth Smith of Kansas City handmade clubs – but in the modern location the accumulation and display of wealth is a paramount feature of Asian golf.[40] An advertisement for membership in a fifty-four hole complex in Johore (the site of Kirkwood's Malaysian endeavours), with one of the courses each designed by Jack Nicklaus, Gary Player and Arnold Palmer, declared 'Don't worship the ground they walk on, buy it!'[41] Most courses built in the region are private membership ones, with prohibitive prices. Those memberships are tradeable commodities, a sure sign that golf is folded into the commercial environment. As elsewhere, business has long been done on the golf course, but now the golf course is the business. Membership of these establishments goes with ownership of a luxury car, an expensive (usually genuine Rolex) watch, brand name clothes (Zegna, Boss and the upper-market golf brands) and the postmodern versions of Kenneth Smith-type display (Callaway is ubiquitous). The social display factor is pronounced. In 1997, for example, a member of Royal Perak Golf Club in Ipoh, Malaysia was suspended after an alleged incident in the bar. He took the club to court to seek reversal of the decision because, he claimed, he had been 'shunned by various club members and friends', and that he had been evicted from his business offices which were owned by a club vice-president.[42] The intersection of business, position and golf was clear: association with the game is still about social networking, but money rather than status is the main commodity.

The Shanghai story underlines the importance of the military and the political cadres as a social power in many Asian sites. In Thailand, for example, the armed forces have several on-base golf courses which almost certainly have hosted discussion of many political developments there. Golf frequently serves as a location for Asian political activity – the prime photograph for a story about the 1997 succession of power in the Philippines showed President Fidel Ramos at golf with Singaporean Prime Minister Goh Chok Tong. Neither golf nor Goh appeared in the story.[43] A former Malaysian High Commissioner to Australia noted that it was mandatory for his country's foreign service officers to play golf or tennis, with the smart ones choosing golf.[44]

In Orientalist vein, the point is clear: the social and power relations of modern Asian golf proceed from a view transferred during colonial times, that the conspicuous consumption of leisure is a symbol of authority and standing.

Gender

As Kenneth Ballhatchet pointed out, gender relations (for which read sexual attitudes) were a recurring theme in colonial contexts but overlooked or avoided by earlier analysts and critics.[45] Kirkwood exemplified many of the attitudes held, and still held in some quarters, by males about the 'Orient': that it was a prime place for sexual pleasure. Some evidence, for example, supports the fears held by the Kedah club wives – in Thailand there have been alleged cases of female caddies also being involved in prostitution.[46] It can be argued that such predatory attitudes within golf are not unique to Asia – one 1930s official of The Royal Sydney Golf Club was said to have lost his position for propositioning the wife of a member at a social function; and an Australian professional of more recent times was said to have found himself banished to Asia (an ironic fate in this context) following his seduction of a lady member of his club.[47]

Barbara Fey, compiler of the Kirkwood biography, identified her subject as 'a man's man', which immediately points to the other dimension in this gender issue, the construction of male identity and the male role.[48] In several photographs in Kirkwood's book, Balinese women invariably appear topless but, more interestingly, they are all in subservient roles: housemaid, pupil, admirer, demonstration assistant. This theme is constant. Two European women appear in other photographs – one lying on her back with a tee in her mouth and Kirkwood astride her ready to hit the ball balanced thereon; the other in which the woman is prostrate at his feet, one of her feet in the air and on it a ball about to be struck by Kirkwood. Elsewhere, both Hagen and Kirkwood appear with topless African women. And in a photograph from Japan four women, elegant in traditional dress, wait upon Hagen and Kirkwood with umbrellas and are ready to carry the bags. The prime social role in all this is male, the marginal exception being a photograph in which the exiled Duke and Duchess of Windsor are seated immediately behind Kirkwood as he gives an exhibition in the Bahamas – the woman there is exalted by association with the (slightly tarnished) royal male.

Much of this pattern remains in Asian golf, a subset of general male social dominance. At most golf venues women appear as servants in one form or another: caddies, waitresses, attendants, clerks, sales, ground staff. At one club in Bangkok, four male players were observed being attended by twelve female caddies – four carrying bags, four carrying umbrellas and portable stools, four fetching drinks.[49] Female membership of clubs is extremely low. Where such membership exists, it is almost exclusively as an offshoot of association with a man who has membership. That is, few women have independent membership of golf clubs with the reason immediately obvious. Women have only recently begun to assert commercial and financial independence in the region, so few have the financial capacity to buy private club membership.

There is distinct continuity between the Kirkwood and the modern Asian golf eras here. The consequences of a colonial imperative may be observed in the post-colonial setting: the local elites taking on those aspects of social behaviour considered appropriate by their rulers.

Culture

Le Mayeur takes us to another realm of Orientalism, that of representation where his paintings convey a sense of place and which, in turn, create a mindset of that place. Kirkwood's reaction to his Asian settings falls in with wider contemporary views of those places: the seductive beauty of Bali, the wealth and taste of the world's titled irrespective of location, the chaos and human harshness of China.[50] Above all, he conveys views on 'civilization'.[51]

Two particular dimensions have a bearing upon current practice: the depiction of Asian golf, and the very creation of the golf site itself.[52]

In tourist literature, especially, Asian golf is represented as an idealized space where wider locational difficulties do not appear. The massive Bangkok traffic problems are never mentioned in advertisements for golf courses there, while the heat and humidity of many locations are similarly overlooked. Rather, the emphasis is upon beauty and mystery – one agency, for example, emphasizes the 'charming helpful [female] caddies' and 'unique culture' found in Thailand.[53] Kirkwood would have recognized that. This emphasis is most evident in modern photography because, unlike in Europe or the United States, there is as yet in Asia little 'artistic' representation of golf. Some strong continuities from the word pictures of Kirkwood are revealed in the work of Brian Morgan, most spectacularly in a photograph from Kathmandu of an elephant watching on as a golfer tees off. Similarly, one from Calcutta reminds us of social distance as a golfer, supported by caddies, drives off while more humble people wash themselves and their clothes in a stream.[54]

Such representation stems from the golf courses and the ways in which they are framed.[55] The sense and power of the golf landscape is extremely significant as in, for example, attempts to recreate specific settings in 'alien' contexts – 'New St Andrews' in Japan has an 'Old Course' complete with a recreation of the Swilcan bridge.[56] Ronald Fream, an active course architect in Asia, announced that the Silang Golf & Country Cub near Manila would have a 'Scottish Highlands philosophy',[57] while Desmond Muirhead's Subic Bay course incorporates themes from Philippine history. While such re-creation attempts are not unique to Asia, they are particularly pronounced there, and raise interesting questions about identity in a post-colonial, post-Orientalist world. Kristal Golf Resort in Penang, Malaysia, for example, is owned and operated by Japanese interests, and the course itself is Japanese designed (by Hideyo Sugimoto). The use of water and stonework is reminiscent of Japan, as is the clubhouse with its traditional Japanese-style baths.[58] This is a deliberate attempt to create a specific environment in an 'Other' setting. Asian design itself is much under-researched in this sense, as shown in the standard reference work on golf architecture (Cornish and Whitten) with Shunsuke Kato and his 'distinctly American style of architecture' among the few mentioned.[59]

It is complicated further because many Asian courses are designed by 'outsiders', so that where they refer to local sentiment they often do so through their own social and cultural prism, as did Kirkwood. The work of J. Michael Poellot in Japan is very interesting in this respect. Where there is no reference to locality the golf course becomes a homogenized, rootless tract of land. If not the 'carpark with flags' decried by touring pros, it has no cultural sense or symbolism. Many resort courses in Asia carry this mark, such as the Penang Golf Resort in Malaysia and the much more upmarket Banyan Tree in Phuket, Thailand. Where the cultural context is there, the results can be spectacular (as in the Thomson-Wolveridge-Fearn effort at the Awana resort in Malaysia).

Kirkwood's rudimentary layout on Bali, then, inspires much thought and analysis about the creation of the golf environment in Asia and, while he was not the first designer to work there, his reminiscences reveal the interrelationship between player, setting and culture, as well as the way in which the interrelationship is marked by Orientalist interpretation.

At the 19th

Joe Kirkwood was many things to many people in many parts of the world. An objective of this essay has been to explore some deeper meanings and significance in his Asian life and activities, in order to show that while golf is, indeed, a global game it is not a borderless one. Like all other aspects of globalized and globalizing cultures, it can be at once invasive and protecting, developing and exploitative, recreation and business, deep and superficial. Kirkwood demonstrated all of that, and Edward Said might see in this life much that was reflected in other aspects of the East-West confrontation.

Notes

[1] This is a much-expanded version of a paper delivered at the Third World Scientific Congress of Golf, St Andrews, Scotland, 20–24 July 1998, and which appears in Martin Farrally, ed., *Science and Golf Ill: Proceedings of the Third World Scientific Congress of Golf*.
[2] Stoddart, 'Joseph Henry Kirkwood'.
[3] Pollard, *Australian Golf*.
[4] Kirkwood with Fey, *Links Of Life*.
[5] There are several important, if eclectic theoretical and empirical influences here, among them: Harvey, *The Condition of Postmodernity*; Hobsbawm and Ranger, eds, *The Invention of Tradition*; Geertz, *Local Knowledge*; Darnton, *The Great Cat Massacre*; Mitchell, ed., *Landscape and Power*.
[6] There is a vast underlying theoretical strand here, but for some indications see, variously, Bhabha, *The Location Of Culture*; Guha and Chakravorty Spivak, eds, *Selected Subaltern Studies*; Easthope, *British Post-Structuralism since 1968*; Thomas, *Colonialism's Culture*.
[7] An exemplary and marvellous example of the more general discussion is to be found in Lipsitz, 'Cruising Around the Historical Bloc', and reprinted in his *Time Passages*.
[8] Said, *Orientalism*.
[9] Nandy, *The Intimate Enemy*.
[10] Said, *Peace and its Discontents*, and *Culture and Imperialism*.
[11] Gramsci, *Selections From Cultural Writings*, and James, *Beyond a Boundary*. See, too, Cudjoe and Cain, eds, *C.L.R. James*, as an example of the re-thinking of James. Beckles and Stoddart, eds, *Liberation Cricket*.
[12] Simson and Jennings, *The Lords of the Rings*; Said, *Covering Islam*.
[13] For South Asian cricket, see Nandy, *The Tao of Cricket*. In this marvellous book, Nandy spells out fully his view of Prince Ranjitsinjhi, the first Indian to play for England and a quintessential Orientalist figure; see esp. pp.55–75. See also, Levine, *Into the Passionate Soul of Subcontinental*

Cricket; Cashman, *Patrons, Players and the Crowd*, and Mukherjee, *Autobiography of an Unknown Cricketer*.

[14] An amusing but most insightful account appears in Houghton, *Golf Addict Goes East*.

[15] Kirkwood, *Links of Life*, 60–6.

[16] Ibid., 66.

[17] Milner, *The Invention of Politics in Colonial Malaya*. For some of the later developments, Crouch, 'Malaysia' and his later *Government and Society in Malaysia*.

[18] Frykenberg, *Guntur District, 1788–1848*, was a very early and very interesting work on this possibility.

[19] Alliss (with Bob Ferrier), *Alliss Through The Looking Glass*, 14.

[20] This is an area for considerable further investigation.

[21] It is interesting here to read Clougher, ed., *Golf Clubs of the Empire*. All the 'foreign' clubs were listed simply as if they were as easily reached as those in Great Britain.

[22] Thomson with Zwar, *The Wonderful World of Golf*.

[23] Ibid., 92–3, 125–6.

[24] Ibid.

[25] Interview material.

[26] Kirkwood, 'Halting a War.'

[27] It is interesting to think that Hagen and Kirkwood were in China at the same time as the great American correspondent Edgar Snow, who reported the rise of Mao to the west – Snow's personal papers are now housed in Kansas City, home also to Tom Watson.

[28] Kirkwood, 'Halting a War', 93–4.

[29] Stoddart, 'Sport, Cultural Imperialism and Colonial Response in the British Empire'.

[30] For an indication of this, Blackman, *Negotiating China*.

[31] 'Lighting Up China's Golf Boom', [special supplement of *Asian Golfer*], Nov. 1995.

[32] Newsletter 3, vol. 4, *Queensland Tradelinks*, Apr. 1997, http:llwww.qci.com.aulib/tr/i/vol4/vol4new3.htm, 'Scotland in Asia', Scottish Trade International, http:// scotexport.org.uk/stiasia.html.

[33] This is a large and fascinating story, the detail of which is beyond the scope of this essay. For an indication, Stoddart, 'Golf, Development and the Human Sciences'.

[34] Geertz, *Negara*; Boon, *Affinities and Extremes* – surely one of the most awkwardly expressed titles of all time – Vickers, *Travelling to Bali*.

[35] Sprult, *Artists on Bali*.

[36] For a disillusioned contemporary view of Bali, see Keith Loveard, 'The Paradise Paradox', *Asiaweek*, 3 Oct. 1997.

[37] Kirkwood, *Links of Life*, 83.

[38] Clarke and French-Blake, eds, *South East Asia Golf Guide*.

[39] Kirkwood, *Links of Life*, 89.

[40] My copy of Kirkwood's biography was apparently once part of a collection held by Smith, for it contains his stamp.

[41] *New Sunday Times*, 24 Nov. 1996.

[42] 'Golfer Sues Club for "Unlawful" Suspension of His Membership', *New Straits Times*, 20 Sept. 1997.

[43] Jose Manuel Tesoro and Antonio Lopez, 'Un-Candidate', *Asiaweek*, 4 July 1997.

[44] Interview material.

[45] Ballhatchet, *Race, Sex and Class under the Raj*.

[46] Tanida Sirorattanakul, 'Clubs, Sweat and Tears', *Bangkok Post*, 23 June 1995, reprinted in GAG'M Update, 4, 1, 1996 - the Global Anti-Golf Movement is a coalition of social forces opposed to golf course development.

[47] Interview material.

[48] Barbara Fey in Kirkwood, *Links of Life*, xiv.
[49] Fieldwork observation.
[50] For some ideas here, Daniels, *Fields of Vision*; Wrede and Adams, eds, *Denatured Visions*; Smith, *European Vision and the South Pacific*. In the golf realm, Doak, *The Anatomy of a Golf Course*.
[51] While there is a very long way between Kirkwood, the golfer, and Sam Huntington, the political scientist, it is interesting to note that both believe somewhat in the power and significance of transcultural elites –see Huntington, *The Clash of Civilizations*.
[52] This point leads on to one about resistance to globalization, the ways in which local cultures sustain themselves in the face of intervention, but space precludes an analysis here. For an indication of some general literature, 'Cultural Resistance to Globalisation Bibliography', http://www.stile.lut.ac.ukl ~ gyobs/GLOBAL/t0000064.html
[53] 'Golf in Thailand', Golf Orient, http:llwww.goiforient.com.
[54] Morgan, *A World Portrait of Golf*, 87, 90–1.
[55] While beyond the immediate bounds of this essay, there is a great deal of very interesting work to be done on the representation of golf courses around the world – Adams, 'Golf' does little to move into the arena of landscape and power.
[56] Morgan, *A World Portrait of Golf*, 151.
[57] September Newsletter, 1997, Ronald Fream Group, http:llwww.golfpian.com/ newslett.html.
[58] Fieldwork observations.
[59] Cornish and Whitten, *The Architects of Golf*. As a good guide, though, see the 'Architects' section in *Asian Golf Review* at http://www.asia/com.sg/golf/designer/designt.html.

References

Adams, R. L. A. "Golf." In *The Theater of Sport*, edited by Karl B. Raitz. Baltimore, MD: Johns Hopkins, 1995.

Alliss, P. (with B. Ferrier). *Alliss Through the Looking Glass*. London: Pelham, 1963.

Ballhatchet, K. *Race, Sex and Class Under the Raj: Imperial Attitudes and Policies and Their Critics*. New York: St. Martin's Press, 1980.

Beckles, H. McD and Stoddart, B., eds. *Liberation Cricket: West Indies Cricket Culture*. Manchester: Manchester University Press, 1995.

Bhabha, H. K. *The Location of Culture*. London: Routledge, 1994.

Blackman, C. *Negotiating China: Case Studies and Stratagies: The Hows and Whys of Successfully Negotiating Business with the Chinese*. Sydney: Allen & Unwin, 1997.

Boon, J. A. *Affinities and Extremes: Criss-Crossing the Bitter-Sweet Ethnology of East Indies History, Hindu-Balinese Culture, and Indo-European Allure*. Chicago, IL: University of Chicago Press, 1990.

Cashman, R. *Patrons, Players and the Crowd: The Phenomenon of Indian Cricket*. Delhi: Orient Longman, 1980.

Clarke, A. and N. French-Blake, eds. *South East Asia Golf Guide*. Syresham: Priory, 1995.

Clougher, T.R., ed. *Golf Clubs of the Empire: British Golf Clubs by Road and Rail*. London: Clougher, 1928.

Cornish, G.S. and R.E. Whitten. *The Architects of Golf*. New York: Harper Collins, 1993.

Crouch, H. "Malaysia: Neither Democratic nor Authoritarian." In *Southeast Asia in the 1990s: Authoritarianism, Democracy and Capitalism*, edited by K. Hewison, R. Robison, and G. Rodan. Sydney: Allen & Unwin, 1993.

Crouch, H. *Government and Society in Malaysia*. Sydney: Allen & Unwin, 1996.

Cudjoe, S.R. and Cain, W.E., eds. *C.L.R. James: His Intellectual Legacies*. Amherst, MA: University of Massachusetts Press, 1995.

Daniels, S. *Fields of Vision: Landscape Imagery and National Identity in England and the United States.* Oxford: Polity, 1993.

Darnton, R. *The Great Cat Massacre: And Other Episodes in French Cultural History.* New York: Vintage, 1985.

Doak, T. *The Anatomy of a Golf Course: The Art of Golf Architecture.* New York: Lyons & Burford, 1992.

Easthope, A. *British Post-Structuralism Since 1968.* London: Routledge, 1988.

Farrally, M., ed. *Science and Golf III: Proceedings of the Third World Scientific Congress of Golf.* Champaign-Urbana: Human Kinetics Press, 1998.

Frykenberg, R. E. *Guntur District, 1788–1848: A History of Local Influence and Central Authority in South India.* Oxford: Clarendon, 1965.

Geertz, C. *Negara: The Theater State in the Nineteenth Century Ball.* Princeton, NJ: Princeton University Press, 1980.

Geertz, C. *Local Knowledge: Further Essays in Interpretive Anthropology.* New York: Basic Books, 1983.

Gramsci, A. *Selections from Cultural Writings.* Cambridge, MA: Harvard University Press, 1991.

Guha, R. and G. Chakravorty Spivak, eds. *Selected Subaltern Studies.* Oxford: Oxford University Press, 1988.

Harvey, D. *The Condition of Postmodernity: An Enquiry into the Origins of Cultural Change.* Oxford: Blackwell, 1989.

Hobsbawm, E. and T. Ranger, eds. *The Invention of Tradition.* Cambridge: Cambridge University Press, 1983.

Houghton, G. *Golf Addict Goes East.* London: Country Life, 1967.

Huntington, S. *The Clash of Civilizations and the Remaking of World Order.* New York: Simon & Schuster, 1996.

James, C. L. R. *Beyond a Boundary.* London: Hutchinson, 1963.

Kirkwood, J. with B. Fey. *Links of Life.* Oklahoma City: Kirkwood, 1973.

Levine, E. *Into the Passionate Soul of Subcontinental Cricket.* Delhi: Penguin, 1996.

Lipsitz, G. "Cruising around the Historical Bloc: Postmodern and Popular Music in East Los Angeles." *Cultural Critique* 5 (1986).

Lipsitz, G. *Time Passages: Collective Memory and American Popular Music.* Minneapolis, MN: University of Minnesota Press, 1990.

Milner, A. C. *The Invention of Politics in Colonial Malaya: Contesting Nationalism and the Expansion of the Public Sphere.* Cambridge: Cambridge University Press, 1994.

Mitchell, W. J. T., ed. *Landscape and Power.* Chicago, IL: University of Chicago Press, 1994.

Morgan, B. *A World Portrait of Golf.* New York: Gallery, 1988.

Mukherjee, S. *Autobiography of an Unknown Cricketer.* Delhi: Dayal, 1996.

Nandy, A. *The Intimate Enemy: Loss and Recovery of Self under Colonialism.* Delhi: Oxford University Press, 1989.

Nandy, A. *The Tao of Cricket: On Games of Destiny and the Destiny of Games.* Delhi: Penguin, 1992.

Pollard, J. *Australian Golf, the Game and the Players.* Sydney: Angus & Robertson, 1990.

Said, E. *Orientalism.* Harmondsworth: Penguin, 1978.

Said, E. *Culture and Imperialism.* New York: Vintage, 1993.

Said, E. *Peace and Its Discontents: Essays on Palestine in the Middle East Process.* New York: Vintage, 1996.

Said, E. *Covering Islam: How the Media and Experts Determine How We See the Rest of the World.* New York: Vintage, 1997.

Simson, V. and A. Jennings. *The Lords of the Rings: Power, Money and Drugs in the Modern Olympics.* London: Simon and Schuster, 1992.

Smith, B. *European Vision and the South Pacific.* Oxford: Cambridge University Press, 1989.

Sprult, R. *Artists on Bali, Nieuenkamp, Bonnet, Spires, Holka, Le Mayeur, Arie Smit*. New York: Tuttle, 1997.

Stoddart, B. "Sport Cultural Imperialism and Colonial Response in the British Empire: A Framework for Analysis." *Comparative Studies in Society and History* 30 (1988).

Stoddart, B. "Golf Development and the Human Sciences: The Swing Is Not the Only Thing." In *Science and Golf II: Proceedings of the World Scientiic Congress of Golf*, edited by A.J. Cochran and M.R. Farrally. London: Spon, 1994.

Stoddart, B. "Joseph Henry Kirkwood." *Australian Dictionary of Biography*, edited by J. Ritchie. Melbourne: Melbourne University Press, 2006.

Thomas, N. *Colonialism's Culture: Anthropology, Travel and Government*. Cambridge: Polity, 1994.

Thomson, P. and D. Zwar. *The Wonderful World of Golf*. London: Cassell, 1969.

Vickers, A. *Travelling to Bali: Four Hundred Years of Journeys*. Oxford: Oxford University Press, 1995.

Wrede, S. and W. H. Adams, eds. *Denatured Visions: Landscape and Culture in The Twentieth Century*. New York: Museum of Modern Art, 1991.

Sport, Colonialism and Struggle: C.L.R. James and Cricket

Introduction

I finish with James, inevitably, because that is where I came in. The piece happened because Richard Giulianotti, the wonderfully-named and gifted Scots sports sociologist, was at the University of New England on exchange while I was there as the Pro Vice-Chancellor (Research and International). He talked about his projects, including one to consider leading sociologists' work and its application to sports culture, and asked if I would write on James. Strictly speaking, I suggested, neither James nor I were sociologists but Richard's response was that everyone thought we were and was reason enough to carry on. I had written a remembrance at James's death but this required a clinical reassessment, and it came at a time good for me (while the article appeared in 2004 it was completed some time earlier).

Academic work means that as we age we take on new approaches and theories, but framed against the canons with which we began. The *subaltern* movement, for example, created new insights then ran into assertions that many of its texts were either not new or missed the essential *subaltern* tone. Such reflection helped create strong works like Sumit Sarkar's *Writing Social History*, he reassessed not only the work of others but his own, including commentary on the work of E.P. Thompson and his father, Edward Garrett Thompson was a gadfly on the Raj establishment.

Sports culture, however, escaped much of the insightful struggle over postmodernism and cultural studies, among other movements. Some sports works attempted such approaches, but in largely limited and superficial ways. One *Sporting Traditions* conference invoked Francis Fukuyama and pronounced the end of sports history, but in unconvincing fashion. Sports history has remained preoccupied more with historiography than with new ways of seeing, and that has been restricting. It has also become belligerently so, with protagonists like Douglas Booth arguing that there is just one acceptable way to 'do' sports history. That is ahistorical, clearly, and ignores the great historical debates where arguments between exponents of different traditions produce greater meaning: Lawrence Stone and H.R. Trevor-Roper spring to mind, as do the great arguments over the course and meaning of the French Revolution, as do the works of the insightful English social Marxists such as Christopher Hill and Rodney Hilton, let alone all the works of the *Annales* school.

James is a case in point. For a very long time his influence on sports analysis was restricted to cricket followers – writers from Orlando Patterson onwards through to my friend and colleague Hilary Beckles all drew upon James as a starting point. James connected cricket to cultural and political change, and we all followed suit. Patterson saw cricket as a form of slavery and moved from there to write his influential works on that subject. Hilary moved from a Marxist analysis of slavery learned at Hull to an investigation of Caribbean cricket that concentrated upon liberation (hence the title of our joint book of writings). It was taken for granted that James was the starting point, and for a very long time the only dissenting voice was that of Helen Tiffen in *Sport History*. It took James's death for the revision to begin.

By then, ironically, his appeal had broadened. Alan Metcalfe, an insightful early social historian of sport, discovered James and began to apply his findings to areas of both British and North American sport with some effect but also some awkwardness. Other less gifted analysts fell upon James as some sort of theoretical prop, reminiscent of the way in which some theories had been applied to the Australian condition. As those applications frayed in conviction so, too, did James in a way. His book had always been timeless, but now it was starting to age as frameworks such as feminism and studies of ethnicity tuned writers and readers to ask different questions and seek different answers. While much of the reassessment that followed his death was reverential, some thoughts began to approach the canon more quizzically.

That was accompanied and probably influenced by a spectacular West Indies fall from grace on the playing fields at home and away. I had seen West Indies first on losing sides in Australia, then watched the rise to dominance through the 1980s when their brutal efficiency thrust all others aside. Their unbeatability at that time had actually supported the essential rules laid out in James: through cricket the Caribbean way would come cultural liberation and social reconstruction. What did it mean, though, when they began to lose during the 1990s and reached almost deadbeat status early in the twenty-first century? The multitude of explanations that involved alternative sports, a 'soft' society, lack of professionalism, decultured societies, rampant island parochialism, decaying economies, fragile states and moral decline, naming but a few, all toyed with the connection between sport and culture laid out by James. Like James, however, they all missed an essential fact: any sports condition changes, just like the culture that supports the condition.

James never prepared anyone for that, and that seems to me now to be one of the major reasons for two particular characteristics in much writing about sport. The first is that, despite all contrary protestations, there lurks persistently a view that, somehow, it was all just that much better 'back then' when sport was about a moral rather than a dollar, glory rather than a career, and honour rather than deification. Much sports writing is analytical, let me add quickly, but much is not and sees sport as a corrupted ideal rather than an iterating social construct. The second is that the Jamesian 'fixed' view in some ways obliterated the need for alternative theories or frameworks, the answer was already there so the wider reading was not really necessary and certainly not embedded in most courses of sports history, allowing always for the notable exceptions. The wider clamours about particular historical or social theories did pass by much of sports analysis, then, and mainly for the reasons that we 'had' the answers when, in fact, we were really not asking the right questions.

That all said, though, James certainly started me along the journey, and at this point of re-questioning him he still shows me that there is much yet to be done.

* * * * *

C.L.R. James was born in Trinidad in 1901 (the same year as Chairman Mao) and died in London in 1989. During an intellectually rich life he witnessed a myriad of events that interacted to produce in him a unique standpoint on life, art, sport and politics.[1] He

- was influenced by the birth and demise of the Soviet Empire.
- was marked by the revelations about Stalinism.
- observed the zenith and the disintegration of the British Empire.
- experienced the rise of Cold War America and suffered the excesses of McCarthy.
- was close to the centre of Pan Africanism.
- was in the vanguard of post-colonialism.
- posited culture and cricket at the heart of politics.

Throughout that same life James watched the West Indies enter world cricket as students and become undisputed world champions. More significantly, he identified that cricket rose as an inherent part of the Caribbean post-colonial struggle through both race and politics. Consequently, he had a strong influence over the social analysis of sport but, ironically (given the title of his best known work), within some specific cultural boundaries.

Three aspects of James work should be noted here, and not only because they are reflected in the approach taken to writing this piece. First, and unlike most other subjects in this collection, James's approach to cricket/sport was principally autobiographical so that his 'theoretical' approach was a 'lived' one, essentially. His views on the intersection of cultural practice, race, rank and caste were formed by his own experiences or observations. In some senses it was ethnographic work, but he would not have described it as such. The second aspect flows from this. Again unlike most subjects here, James 'theory' cannot easily be lifted from its cultural *milieu*. His view of the Caribbean is not one he would have seen as automatically transferable to any other setting. He was a 'theory arising from practice' observer, rather than a 'theory being applied to a situation' one. Then, thirdly, there is the deep paradox that James himself recognized as embedded in his work on both cricket and Marxism. He saw his deep love for cricket (and literature) at odds with his desire for social and political change in that cricket was an 'establishment' game seeking to preserve into the industrial and post-industrial ages a set of social relations more appropriate to a pre-industrial time.[2] In that, he recognized the power of cricket (and sport in general) as a reifying agency, but one whose charms he could not resist. His cricket writing, then, attempted to justify his acceptance of the game and to find a 'revolutionary' strain within it. That paradox and/or challenge has been an ongoing problem for many Caribbean intellectuals. Understanding these three aspects alone helps explain most of James's strengths and shortcomings in any attempt to apply his principles to the wider sports world.

That Book

When it appeared in 1963, *Beyond a Boundary* was starred immediately as the greatest cricket book ever written. The first edition dust jacket signalled the book's difference and, cautiously, suggested its significance:

> A great nuggetty goldmine of a book ... a grandly exciting cricket book, but something much more ... it was through English cricket and English literature that he and his people have made their most fruitful and most enduring contact with the essence of English life.

To a 17-year-old New Zealand schoolboy and cricket fanatic, the book seemed misplaced in the sports shelves of the Ashburton library. Every other cricket book he knew recalled a tour, deified a player, celebrated a great moment or rejoiced in the grandeur of English cricket along with the style and standards it had exported to its empire.[3] In New Zealand, cricket was conducted to English standards and the icons (buried in a pitiful international playing records) were people like Martin Donnelly, a graceful strokemaker who went to Oxford, had a career and treated the game as a pastime.

The problem with the book at that time for that reader was that it drew on many issues and experiences other than cricket. While there was a dim general awareness that cricket was located in cultural practice after all – English comics like Lion and Tiger carried uplifting stories about cricket as a social training ground this book revealed much more.

For a start, the book was about the 'West Indies' in which James grew up, which he left, to which he returned to and then left again physically but never spiritually.[4] With the limited exception of England, because of the post-war wave of Caribbean migration,[5] 'West Indies' as a cultural and political construct was then little, if at all, known around the cricket world. West Indies was known for its playing style, but the culture within which that style was shaped constituted unknown territory. The book's wider references to Caribbean affairs, then, made it a bewildering read for anyone unschooled in the region's rich history. Family, education, politics and learning ran through the book in a breathtaking display of intellectual power.

Then, there were indications that in the Caribbean some aspects of cricket's 'shape' were socially questionable – other cricket literature portrayed the game as a bastion of fair play and honourable thought. Here, people were regarded as much if not more for who and what they were (or were not) than for their cricket field achievements. From there, James argued that cricket was as powerful a force in moulding Caribbean society as any political movement, economic force, religious entity or educational system. Cricket was a system around which society played itself out.

There should be a suspicion, then, that references to the 'greatest cricket book' came from reviewers seeing 'different' as 'great' or even as 'so complex it must be great' but, appearing when it did, the book opened several analytical lines in cricket and in sports more widely. Significantly, intellectual weaknesses in the book took a long time to appear and some, at least, did so only when political and ideological tastes changed. The best example is that of women. Very few appear in the book because it was a man's world that was being deconstructed. Those women who did appear, however, were extremely powerful and, in many regards, their influence underpins much of the world portrayed. At one non-sports conference, an eminent historian commented that my analysis of some Caribbean cricket aspects was 'very gendered' overlooking, it seemed to me, the central point about exclusion/inclusion and discrimination as a whole.[6]

The Other

For many in the imperial and post-imperial world by 1963, West Indies was still unknown as a social entity, as distinct from a cricketing one. England had lost the 1950 test series to them at home, but the overwhelming images were of Caribbean migrants celebrating in carnivalesque fashion, dashing batsmen and energetic bowlers, all with flashing smiles. These were cricket's happy jesters, in the common view.[7] In places like New Zealand, a tour by West Indies just a little later seemed to confirm those images. At that point, a decade or so before the book's appearance, West Indies cricket success was explained, where it was explained at all, largely by reference to greatly talented individuals whose sheer skills overcame a lack of a team approach, as understood in the purely Anglo world. In New Zealand, as in the rest of the Anglo world, the quiet team player had emerged from the English style canon as the most valued player. For West Indies, that appeared not to be the case.

James exposed that imagery as superficial, and revealed a world where cricket was marked by the past in a way that would never leave that specific cultural game form. The theme may be seen clearly in James's other writings that are, by and large, ignored by analysts of sports culture. *The Black Jacobins*, for example, is an exquisite re-examination of the Haitian slave revolt that he transmutes from a sporadic, instinctive uprising to a cool political plan.[8] Slaves think for themselves and fix upon a determination, in James's view, as opposed to the 'instinctive uprising in the face of tyranny' argument that had prevailed before. There are interesting parallels in changes to our understanding of the French Revolution, of course. It is interesting to note, too, that the 'sub-altern School' of South Asian studies that appeared during the 1980s went to great lengths to prove the same point, yet never referred to James.[9] That might be something of a motif: James as an unknown, sometimes unrecognized force.

In the literature, 'The Other' refers largely to cultures other than those located in the so-called 'metropolitan' world and James fits that. However, his work also referenced a different Other in the cricket world, the unknown players. Most previous cricket literature dealt with international and first class levels with rare, and idealized, excursions into the English village cricket world.[10] James showed us very different people. In Telemaque, for example, he found the exemplar for his views on colour, class and cricket. Telemaque played for Stingo in Trinidad, a team for 'plebeians' as James put it, a black club with no social status.

A waterfront worker and trade unionist, Telemaque was a good all-round player never selected in the island team but who should have been. Through him, James pondered the politics of selection based on other than playing skills. Did cricket's Trinidadian ruling elite overlook Telemaque because of his labour activism? Who knows, but the impression was there, and in James we find some of the greatest insights into the power of representation.

Over twenty years after having read *Beyond a Boundary* for the first time (but having read it many times since), I was reminded of Telemaque and representation. My team in Barbados, a black team akin to Stingo, played a final at the island's cricket headquarters. For some obscure reason, the girlfriend of one player was refused entry to the main grandstand. At a wake following the loss of the match, the player-boyfriend attributed her exclusion to the 'white bastards' who ran the cricket association. Many thought the boyfriend, a powerful batsman, should have played for Barbados just as Telemaque should have played for Trinidad fifty years earlier. The representation of power and classification was as strong as it had been when James was playing and observing.

James creates many such reflections. For example, just one black man has played for Australia in over a century of international cricket, and he was not an indigenous Australian (what work has been done on cricket in that community owes much to James because the politics of race have been as powerful there as in the Caribbean). Sam Morris played one test for Australia in the late nineteenth century before retiring, becoming a groundsman and going blind. He is as unknown as Telemaque, and all references identify him as the son of Barbadian 'immigrants'.[11] It seems highly unlikely that his parents were 'immigrants' within ten or twenty years of emancipation. More likely, they arrived in Australia in another form of bondage: that of transported convicts. Fittingly, Morris lived long enough to witness West Indies's first tour of Australia in 1930–31 when the Barbadian fast men, George Francis and Herman Griffith, led the bowling and their fellow islanders, Derek Sealy and Lawson Bartlett, were leading batsmen.[12] All descended from slaves. My interest in Sam Morris comes directly from James's demonstration of the power that lies within individual stories.

In some ways the James pointers remain unheeded in the West. Sports sociology and history are fixated on metropolitan practice, and forays into the Other are rare, certainly when compared with other fields of inquiry.[13] That is natural, in some ways – we need to understand our own cultural forms, after all. However, James would have suggested that the inner workings of those forms are often best explained by reference to something very different: come to know thyself by looking at others. Even in cricket, though, his advice has been ignored because West Indies, India,

Pakistan and the rest are regarded mainly by Western rather than local terms.[14] Most sports historians and sociologists are not as widely read or experienced as James and their work reveals that.

The History

James pointed out, through people like Telemaque, that West Indian cricket was marked irrevocably by the history of the society within which it took root. The passage from slavery and beyond, from subjugation to self-respect was not only spelled out in cricket. Implicit in the book was the idea that cricket, as a social system, was responsible for carrying the memories and patterns of slavery long past the days of its official bonds, and of the political reconstructions that marked Caribbean societies through the first half of the twentieth century. He echoed Gramsci's 'cultural' Marxism in that view, but the Italian was far from seeing the reifying social effects of sport recognized by James (even though sport was a powerful tool in Fascist Italy).[15]

All Caribbean cricket work emanates from James and through it runs one important, central condition: while slavery was abolished in the first third of the nineteenth century, cricket helped carry the pattern of social relations established during slavery well into the twentieth and, even, the twenty-first century. That was most evident in James famous account of the campaign to have a black man appointed West Indies captain. The good news was that it occurred in 1957, the bad news that it might have been for the wrong reasons or, at least, on the basis of the wrong criteria (not that James alludes to the point).

Even when West Indies first toured England in 1900, black players predominated but whites held firm control over authority positions. That situation continued into the 1930s and 1940s when very few white players were good enough to be selected. In the years preceding 1957, the captain was frequently the only white team member. Non-white West Indians 'read' in that circumstance the abiding presence of a mentality descended from plantation slavery when 'Massa' controlled all aspects of life. At a time of growing political independence, how could that continue? By 1957 the West Indian Cricket Board of Control was still dominated by whites even though white players were scarcely in evidence. The Board's solution, urged by James (a direct activist in the debate) was to appoint Frank Worrell as captain. He was black, but atypical. Born in Barbados, he was never comfortable there and transferred to Jamaica but played much of his cricket in England where he gained a university degree. In that, then, he was West Indies captain but based largely in England so that the representation, obviously, was of the Board selecting someone who was non-white but projected 'white' qualities (whatever they might have been). What could not be argued were his playing and leadership qualities, and his success was palpable. Nonetheless, James avoided much of what his own analysis might have told him: was the election of Worrell a black 'victory' or, more controversially, another control set piece constructed by the minority elite descended from earlier dominant days? This question must not be seen as a criticism of Worrell, whose record speaks loudly, but as a question of James for not following his own logic.

Beyond the captaincy lay the broader issue of access to cricket for all social groups, and the history that was much more powerful. From the outset, access in all Caribbean sites had two major dimensions. First, there was the question about whether or not a player could join a club at all then, and secondly, which club could it be? The reason was simple: each club was coded by a matrix of class, status, colour, occupation and even religion. James's explanation of the differences between Queens Park, Shamrock, Constabulary, Shannon, Maple and Stingo in Trinidad is probably the most famous section in *Beyond a Boundary*. What these clubs preserved were the social patterns that had evolved during and after slavery. That was inevitable, sociologically, as we know now, but it was not the real thrust of the James message. He showed that sport would always be associated with class, economy, politics and identity. The importance of that message was that it ran completely counter to the dominant views, in 1963 and well beyond, of sport being a classless, apolitical and harmonious state within which players and spectators alike shrugged off their everyday baggage.

Incidentally, James underlined a significant analytical point here, through his demonstration that he knew to which club he belonged. That is, it was not just that other people told him where to go, he understood clearly his structural place and that, of course, was little different from slavery days. One Barbadian black batsman, who went to a school where whites were among his teammates, told me that the day he left school he knew exactly which club he must join. He and his white friend and opening partner walked out the school gates, went in different directions and never again played together. This too evokes Gramsci in that self-ascription has been a major force within the social structuring of sport but is still little understood or recognized, even.

The principle spreads well beyond Caribbean cricket fields, and an understanding of James is invaluable in sports ethnography. Playing in Australia, I was struck frequently by how opposition teams characterized my university teammates socially and culturally. Those teammates responded in kind. Memorably, there was one serious standoff between my university's 'privileged, upper class snobs' (as characterized by the opposition using stronger language) and a team of 'ethnic, working class yobbos' (as depicted by my teammates just as colourfully). Without James it would have been difficult to explain this fracas arising from an insignificant cricket match. Given Jamesian insight, it was a case of identity and ascription, clearly! At more elevated levels, James helps find a way into the different social typologies constructed about each other by cricket-playing nations, especially in playing or administrative crises – cultural differences abound at those moments, as in Australia/India interaction, for example.[16]

The significance of James's breakthrough in this general area has been immense in the West Indies, as the Garry Sobers and Everton Weekes stories confirm. Both were immensely successful internationally, and became West Indies icons. Yet they reached those heights by chance. Both were born into poor families on plantation lands and, as such, had insufficient social standing to enter the Barbados Cricket Association that supplied the island team and enabled West Indies selection. Thousands of poor black players like them were excluded in that system, so an alternative competition arose in the 1930s. Sobers and Weekes played first for teams in this sub-class league. Powerful white figures then engineered places in the 'senior' competition for them, Weekes joining the Army and Sobers the Police (he was placed in the band even though he did not play an instrument). Both succeeded. The point was that their success still depended upon white orchestration and navigation of the social system (revisiting the Worrell point). That dependency caused trouble throughout their careers and years after his retirement Weekes told me, with bitterness, that he had to 'pay his dues' to get where he had.

James drew far less attention to other excluded groups such as the Indians and the Chinese. These groups were introduced to Trinidad and what was then British Guiana (now Guyana) during the later nineteenth century to fill the labour vacuum resulting from the abolition of slavery. What emerged was just as exclusionary a structure as that with emancipated blacks, and the cricket contours were reproduced. Indians and Chinese had their own leagues and found it difficult to gain West Indies selection.[17]

In part, this gap in James's analysis proceeds from a more socially monolithic projection of the West Indies than might have been anticipated. He hints at differences, as in the politics of regional selection, but never really explores how those differences proceeded from cultural variety. Michael Manly, a later prime minister of Jamaica, repeated the weakness in his Caribbean test cricket history that was really a book about Jamaica.[18] The important lesson for sports cultural theorists is that theories based upon one cultural construct cannot easily be transferred to another. This is a major weakness in some cultural studies works taken from their English context and transferred elsewhere on the assumption that the underpinning frameworks must be the same.[19]

The final irony of all this in the post-independence period was that West Indian white players experienced similar selection difficulties as others had earlier. In fact, one white Barbadian who probably should have played for West Indies, but never did, was the son of the man who engineered for Everton Weekes his Army place. James would have understood the poignancy of that situation and, for that reason alone, must be seen as a pioneer in identifying sport as influential in forming social stratification.

The Politics

James went first to England in the company of Learie Constantine who was there to play professional cricket but who ended up in the House of Lords. That is clear proof in itself of the link between Caribbean cricket and politics. What the pair found in England was a gap between what cricket and literature 'told' them about English culture, and what English cultural practice actually did. Put simply, the cricket canon was about unity and cooperation while they experienced division, derision and discrimination. The solution to, as well as the source of, that contradiction lay in politics.[20]

The principal legacy of the link lies in the sporting campaign against South African apartheid. In cricket, but for West Indies' unshakeable stand, the ban on South Africa would not have lasted so long and, perhaps, not even begun. The focus here is not that campaign against South Africa, but the source of and support for West Indies' stand, because it may be attributed directly to James. What South Africa represented to Caribbean activists was the continuation of a racially dominant regime reflecting the power that had permeated Caribbean slavery.

Particularly, activists recognized sport as central to the South African power structure in a way that activists elsewhere did not. In Australia and New Zealand, where the Anglo code prevailed, the idea of separating sport from politics was strong. In West Indies, observers knew the connection between sports form and social structure more intimately. That was the point of James's work.

From there it is an easy step to the politics of sports organizations. Given that cricket was a significant cultural force, control of the game was an important site for struggle, of which the captaincy issue was just one aspect. In Barbados, the difficult circumstances for Sobers and Weekes sprang from a white, dominant class control of the Barbados Cricket Association long after the group had declined as a playing and/or political force.

James gave us an excellent starting point for an analysis of why sports politics have been so important at two levels: the domestic, and the global. Domestically, it reveals why people work so hard to maintain sports organizations as conservative social forms. Young people have often found themselves at odds with sports organizations over dress, general appearance, behavioural forms and even training approaches. James would have understood why a West Indies player made one appearance with Rastafari dreadlocks, then appeared next with close shaven hair – he had to conform.

Though James wrote about the International Olympic Committee long before its modern commercial crassness, he would have understood present patterns perfectly. The IOC sees itself, on the one hand, as a multinational company devoted solely to the cause of sport without reference to politics and, on the other, practices, openly, politicized and patterned decision making.[21] James would have recognized the difference between the perceptions of the IOC and its realities, between its pronouncements and its practices. He would certainly have done so more cuttingly than some analysts who remain firmly bedazzled by Olympic superficiality.

He would have understood, too, the reasons for the International Cricket Council encountering difficulty dealing with match fixing, its largest ever problem. A complex matter, it has one core feature. The issue was ignored persistently because of the cultural distance between the leading countries. The ICC continues to believe that the global cricket's universal social practices are those of the Anglo tradition. This, despite touring players from earliest days commenting on crowd behaviour in the subcontinent and the Caribbean as very different from that at 'Home'. Put (perhaps too) broadly, Anglo crowds are largely passive watchers, those elsewhere bring to bear a more active culture. In those circumstances, gambling was natural. Current difficulties may be explained simply: if no problem is recognized, then no solution is required until, as happened with the Indian police inquiry, the issue moves from the sports to the civil arena.

James, then, was among the first to recognize the inextricable link between sport and politics, and the sophistication of his analysis remains. Once more, however, it could be that his linking of politics and the popular culture has not been taken up fully by later commentators on sports politics, again because the increasingly transnational nature of the work drives attention away from the cultural specificity that does so much to explain the link in the first place.

The Changes

One major limitation is James's largely static landscape. Surprisingly, given his analytical sophistication, the 'take' on evolution and change is not so sure as that on social relations through cricket. By 1963, he was writing about a cricket organizational form that had not shifted since the century's turn, whether it was the Caribbean regional cricket councils, the overarching regional Board or what was then the Imperial Cricket Council. James dealt with shifting relational patterns within an enduring structure. The patterns of power inside and between those bodies had shifted scarcely, either. His concern was with the struggle of the dispossessed inside the machine.

Given that, how useful is James in trying to analyze the modern game? At one level he would have a major problem. His characters are steeped in cricket's history and meaning. Telemaque, asked to express his disappointment, noted merely that these 'things' happen, with the 'things' redolent with the social context of the game. Moreover the characters, including James himself, 'knew' where they belonged even if they did not like the situation allotted to them. Culturally, the game had deep meaning from the smallest Caribbean community level through the collective West Indian psyche.

James might think the game has now been decultured in several ways. Steve Waugh is unusual in that he understands the game's culture and its place in Australian collective memory. Waugh's arrangement of a team visit to Gallipoli en route to England for the 2001 Ashes series might have linked cricket and warfare uncomfortably, but showed that he understood cricket not only as a game for several Australian generations, but also as a curious, largely inexplicable touchstone to national development. James would have understood that, but not the overemphasis on the commercial dimension.

He would have appreciated, especially, some post-colonial dimensions of the modern game. England captained by someone called Nasser Hussain and including Owais Shah and Uzzam Iqbal would have delighted him as at an earlier point did players like Basil D'Oliveira Roland Butcher, Norman Cowans and others. (It would be interesting to hear James on why the Caribbean migration impact upon English cricket now seems supplanted by the subcontinental one).

His analysis cannot explain the current traffic in players. Keppler Wessels, Graeme Hick, Andy Caddick and Andrew Symonds represent an ability to treat a game out of cultural dimension, in that they played for specific countries for reasons ranging from the economic to the opportunistic.[22] That is why contemporary observers have difficulty assigning meaning to contemporary cricket, because it is devoid of meaning and context (especially following the match-fixing scandals). If anything, reading James emphasizes that heartless state, simply by showing what really was at stake in the Caribbean game. An important side point is that the cultural passion for cricket continues most strongly in India and Pakistan and there are clear post-colonial reasons for that, as shown by writers ranging from Ashis Nandy to Emma Levine and, notably, Ramachandra Guha.[23]

That takes us to the modern Caribbean game specifically. Inevitably, after fifteen years of dominance, West Indies declined in the early to mid-1990s. Such is James's power over the critical view that the decline is regarded widely as both a playing problem and a social decay. What has been lost, it is thought, is a unifying purpose for cricket in the Caribbean.[24] Talented athletes eschew the game not just because of economic opportunities offered by American college sports, but also because cricket has lost its symbolism, its meaning. That has been traced to changing family patterns, global culture, lack of coaching and an array of other reasons.

Over all this hangs the spectre of change and, as I have suggested, James does not handle that well. His cricket was fixed in an era when the goal was the overthrow of a colonial regime. His successors work within a more complex world where Caribbean purpose, possibilities and plans are less clear-cut. The symbolic power of a Patrick Ewing or an Ato Bolden is not that they have gone to different sports, but that they have gone to different worlds from the one inhabited by James (even though he spent a long time in the United States – his lack of reference to American sports is striking or, at least, his devotion to the British one during that exile was telling). Even for James that is, understanding sorts from outside his 'host' culture proved difficult to interpret socially.

The Impact

The most immediate impact of *Beyond a Boundary* was that when scholars turned their attention to the social dimensions of cricket, they did so with necessary reference to James's textured take on the Caribbean. That impact was felt directly in the Caribbean. Arriving in Barbados in 1985, I was welcomed warmly by historians keen to support my work, for a reason curiously apart from the natural collegial atmosphere. One colleague commented that it was valuable to have an outsider investigate 'their' game, because that game took them to areas of the island's history too difficult to contemplate. They shared the global fear of having a game they loved produce unpleasant dimensions.

It was a variation on the theme that historians of sport encounter often: resentment at a 'sacred' social activity being subjected to critical inquiry with the risk that the foundations might be revealed as made of clay. In the Caribbean it was understood that the base was clay, but believed that the edifice was made of marble. It was time for the clay to be revealed. While James began the analysis, more work was required. For that very reason, however, the work produced has a patina of 'sameness'.

Powerful as the Jamesian code is, it has proved difficult to escape. Caribbean cricket accounts reflect strongly James's original typologies: intersections of colour, caste and class predominate, as do issues of stratification despite many aspects of the original typologies having passed. A good example comes in writings about the great Vivian Richards: by his own story and stories told by others, Richards exemplified the struggle for recognition and the parameters of power.[25] In Richards' case it is enriched by the references to Rastafari, but is still grounded in the Jamesian dialectic.

That is not to say that the dialectic is limited or passé. Newer work on Caribbean cricket subcultures, such as the Indian populations, invaluably refers to James (even though he ignored those sections). Nonetheless, newer Caribbean cricket 'problems' are proving difficult to confront because of the powerful history exercised by James.[26] That became evident during West Indies' 1990s playing slide. Much analysis concentrates on what might now be seen as the flimsy 'globalization' arguments: middle-class youth eschew the game for faster, more de rigueur activities such as windsurfing, while poorer classes turn to more potentially lucrative activities like basketball and athletics. Cricket is too slow and too inconclusive to attract contemporary youth.

The less visited and less palatable possibility is that the very social core that made cricket such a powerful force, and upon which James focused unerringly, has receded fast. It is not so much that slavery and its aftermath have been forgotten, but that the direct impacts upon social practice has been overlain by so many other forces, especially in Caribbean societies taking such different economic and political directions.[27] An increasing Caribbean problem, then, is that the cricket woes must be explained by the masters of the post-colonial regimes rather than blamed upon the pre-independence forces. That is an extremely difficult problem with which to grapple, and is not one where James is useful immediately: in a curious way, it is the parallel of the 1985 context where someone else might deal with it more readily.

In the non-Caribbean setting, James has been just as powerful and, in some ways, might just be a little more enduring than in the setting that produced his work. Since the Second World War, for example, Australia has become an increasingly multicultural community. Yet the evidence of that multicultural change has been almost non-existent in cricket. No Australian Aboriginal cricketer has yet played for Australia and none appear likely to do so immediately. Further, almost no Asian Australians appear currently in the first class game. In junior ranks there is an appearance now of non-Anglo names. The Jamesian analysis provides a good way into this paradox: cricket is a reflection and a manifestation of a particular 'world' that uses the game to help survive wider sweeping social changes. Tinkered with though it is, the playing form and ritual practices resonate with an earlier age atmosphere and social form that do not match automatically the cultural milieu in which a newer version of the Australian citizen is raised.

Curious reflections are possible in communities like Malaysia. While Malaysia has a cricket subculture, its strength and weakness is that the game has been dominated historically by the Indian community, more specifically by the Sri Lankan Tamil community, that came to the country as indentured labourers and who became prominent in industries such as the railways. Cricket was a marker for that community so that Chinese were drawn in rarely, and Malays became involved only where they could dominate socially and politically. That is almost quintessential James.

The same might be said of New Zealand where the English model and cultural setting, described so well by James, have persisted so strongly. Only recently has New Zealand turned to Australia rather than England for coaches, even though Australian cricket production methods have led the world for many years. New Zealand preferred 'English' coaches (one of mine was an 'Englishman' of Guyanese origin) in the face of a demonstrably failed English cricket culture. As James might have said, that indicates more about the culture of the production of the game than about the game itself.

Outside the cricket world, however, James has had a remarkably small impact upon the analysis of sports practice. In a way, that is a testament to the very power of his work, a curious point that may be explained thus. James's power lies in tying closely the game and the social milieu within which it arose. The inevitable logic must be, then, that the analytical power of such a view is bound by its social construct so, remove the construct and remove the power. Put more precisely, if James's model is applied to a game located in another social construct then its real meaning will be reduced. Baseball moves to a very different cadence as people like Roger Angell tell us.[28] Players like Ty Cobb, Babe Ruth, Jackie Robinson and Joe DiMaggio were constituted by worlds remarkably different from those of George Headley, Learie Constantine, Everton Weekes and Frank Worrell.

Conclusion

The measure of any work is within the power of its impact, and on that score there is no doubt that James's is the single most important analytical work on cricket. It is now aided by others such as Ashis Nandy on Indian cricket and Mike Marquesse on the decline of England,[29] but James started the process. What he showed was that a cricket culture can be explained fully only by deeply learned reference to the culture and location within which it is found. When read in association with Gramsci, Stuart Hall, Anthony Giddens and the like, it provides an enormously powerful understanding of the role of modern sport.

It will be apparent that his 'reading' of the Caribbean game, and its line into the 'game as we have transformed it' analytical framework, changed forever the way in which people would view that specific cultural form and cricket more widely – it provided the imperative to understand the culture as part of any attempt to understand the social implications of the game in that setting.[30] At the same time, applying the Jamesian cadence of cricket into a British colonial/post-colonial world has been much easier than putting it into other sports in different settings, even other colonial ones. Perhaps one of the strongest lessons has been the need to understand the locally specific in an age where the escalating tendency has been to 'read' the global. Curiously enough the globalization debate, represented by people like Tom Friedman and Sam Huntington, provides excellent reasons as to why the work of people like James must continue to be read.[31] He provides as an additional insight the power of perseverance and resistance within localized cultures, no matter the pressures upon them.

For my own part, I could not have had nearly as rich an understanding of the place of sport in many cultures around the world had I not read and re-read James Now, of course, therein lies a possible paradox of my own: if James has to be seen in the locally specific, then how can I have used his work in so many different settings? The answer is simple enough. Like all good and meaningful theoreticians, whether they work from within or towards a specific culture, James provides enormous insight into human behaviour, attitudes and ideals. He does not provide an analytical template, but he provides a way of seeing, and that is what can be applied more universally. Had it not been for James then, I would not have understood why I was so moved, almost every day for a year, as I passed by Frank Worrell's grave in the grounds of the Cave Hill campus of the University of the West Indies – it was a powerful and constant reminder of how cricket (for which read sport in general) had been and, in some locations, continues to be much more than a game.

Notes

[1] Buhle, ed. *C.L.R. James*; Stoddart, 'C.L.R. James'; Worcester, *C.L.R. James Apolitical Biography.*

[2] I was reminded of this a few years after my first reading of *Beyond a Boundary*. Malcolm Caldwell, radical English historian of, and commentator upon, Southeast Asia, gave a seminar at the end of a tiring Australian tour, and perked up only when the conversation turned to the fortunes of the Surrey County Cricket Club. He acknowledged freely the point that, as with James there was a contradiction between his Marxist position on Southeast Asian politics and his devotion to a conservative county cricket structure. Caldwell was murdered in Cambodia in 1978.

[3] Cardus, *English Cricket*; Stoddart, 'Barry Andrews Memorial Lecture'.

[4] Farred, 'The Maple Man'.

[5] Welsh, '(Un)Belonging Citizens, Unmapped Territory'.

[6] The conference was the 'Histories in Cultural Systems' meeting, 1991, organized by Greg Dening for the Humanities Research Centre of the Australian National University (Dening did not make the comment).

[7] At least one Caribbean radical now sees this view as a positive part of a trans-process by which West Indies made cricket their own: Tim Hector, 'Crisis in Society and Cricket – Women to the Rescue', http://www.candw.ag/~ jardinea/fthtm/ff990625.htm, 25 June 1999.

[8] James, *The Black Jacobins.*

[9] Guha and Spivak, eds, *Selected Subaltern Studies.*

[10] Macdonnell, *England Their England*; Parker, *The Village Cricket Match.*

[11] Cashman, ed. *The A–Z of Australian Cricketers.*

[12] Bassano and Smith, *The West Indies In Australia.*

[13] Two rare examples are Whiting, *You Gotta Have Wa* and Krich, *El Beisbol.*

[14] Roberts and James, *Crosscurrents.*

[15] Bosworth, *Italy and the Wider World.*

[16] Stoddart, 'Identity Spin'.

[17] Birbalsingh and Shiwcharan, *Indo-Westindian Cricket.*

[18] Manley, *A History of West Indian Cricket.*

[19] Contrast the recent sophisticated work of Rowe, *Sport, Media, and Culture* with his collaborative work with Geoffrey Lawrence – Rowe and Lawrence, eds., *Power Play.*

[20] An excellent Indian example may be seen in Guha and Spivak, eds., *Selected Subaltern Studies.*

[21] Jennings and Simson, *The Lords of the Rings.*

[22] All these players were born in one country but represented another, cutting away at a traditionally 'nationalist' sentiment underlying international cricket.

[23] Nandy, *The Tao of Cricket* to Levine, *Into the Passionate Soul of Subcontinental Cricket.* Wollen (1995/96) comments that Nandy, in his analysis of Indian cricket, attempts to combine a rejection of modernity with a commitment to a transformed future. I am indebted to Vinay Lal for alerting me to this range of work. Guha, *A Corner of a Foreign Field.*

[24] Stoddart, 'Cricket Matters'.

[25] Richards, *Hitting across the Line.*

[26] A good demonstration of this may be seen in Beckles, *The Development of West Indies Cricket.*

[27] Paget and Buhle, eds, *C.L.R. James's Caribbean.*

[28] Angell, *The Summer Game.*

[29] Nandy, *The Tao of Cricket*; Marquesse, *Anyone but England.*

[30] Stoddart and Sandiford, eds, *The Imperial Game.*

[31] Friedman, *The Lexus and the Olive Tree*; Huntington, *The Clash of Civilizations.*

References

Angell, R. *The Summer Game.* New York: Ballantine, 1984.

Bassano, B. and R. Smith. *The West Indies In Australia, 1930–1931.* Hobart: Apple, 1990.

Beckles, H. *The Development of West Indies Cricket. Vol. 2 – the Age of Global.* Kingston: University of the West Indies Press, 1998.

Birbalsingh, F. and C. Shiwcharan. *Indo-Westindian Cricket.* London: Hansib, 1988.

Bosworth, R. J. B. *Italy and the Wider World, 1860–1960.* London: Routledge, 1996.

Buhle, Paul, ed. *C.L.R. James: His Life and Work.* London: Allison & Busby, 1986.

Cardus, N. *English Cricket.* London: Adprint, 1945.

Cashman, R., ed. *The A–Z of Australian Cricketers.* Melbourne: Oxford University Press, 1997.

Farred, G. "The Maple Man." In *Rethinking C.L.R. James*, edited by G. Farred. Oxford: Blackwell, 1996.

Friedman, T. L. *The Lexus and the Olive Tree.* New York: Farrar, Strauss, and Giroux, 2000.

Guha, R. *A Corner of a Foreign Field: The Indian History of British Sport.* London: Picador, 2002.

Guha, R. and G. C. Spivak, eds. *Selected Subaltern Studies.* New Delhi: Oxford University Press, 1988.

Hector, Tim. "Crisis in Society and Cricket – Women to the Rescue." Review of Reviewed Item., no. (1999), http://www.candw.ag/~jardinea/fthtm/ff990625.htm.

Huntington, S. P. *The Clash of Civilizations and the Remaking of World Order.* New York: Simon & Schuster, 1996.

James, C. L. R. *Beyond a Boundary.* London: Hutchinson, 1963.

James, C. L. R. *The Black Jacobins.* London: Allison & Busby, 1980.

Jennings, A. and V. Simson. *The Lords of the Rings: Power, Money, and Drugs in the Modern Olympics.* London: Macmillan, 1992.

Krich, J. *El Beisbol.* New York: Prentice-Hall, 1990.

Levine, E. *Into the Passionate Soul of Subcontinental Cricket.* New Delhi: Penguin, 1996.

Macdonnell, A. G. *England Their England.* London: World, 1941.

Manley, M. *A History of West Indian Cricket.* London: Deutsch, 1988.

Marquesse. *Anyone but England*. London: Verso, 1995.

Nandy, A. *The Tao of Cricket: On Games of Destiny and the Destiny of Games*. New Delhi: Penguin, 1989.

Paget, H. and P. Buhle, eds. *C.L.R. James's Caribbean*. Durham: Duke University Press, 1992.

Parker, J. *The Village Cricket Match*. Harmondsworth: Penguin, 1978.

Richards, V. *Hitting Across the Line*. Sydney: Macmillan, 1991.

Roberts, M. and A. James. *Crosscurrents*. Sydney: Walla Walla and Mobitel, 1998.

Rowe, D. *Sport, Media, and Culture*. Buckingham: Open University Press, 1999.

Rowe, D. and G. Lawrence, eds. *Power Play*. Sydney: Prentice–Hall, 1986.

Stoddart, B. "C.L.R. James: A Remembrance." *Sociology of Sport Journal* 7, no. 1 (1990).

Stoddart, B. "Barry Andrews Memorial Lecture, Notes and Furphies." 1992.

Stoddart, B. "Identity Spin." *South Asia: Special Issue, Midnight to Millenium: Australia-India Interconnectedness* XXIII (2000).

Stoddart, B. "Cricket Matters: The International Game and Public Opinion." In *The Tenth Frank Worrell Memorial Lecture*. University of West Indies, 2003.

Stoddart, B. and K. Sandiford, eds. *The Imperial Game*. Manchester: Manchester University Press, 1998.

Welsh, S. L. "(Un)Belonging Citizens, Unmapped Territory." In *Not on Any Map*, edited by S. Murray. Exeter: University of Exeter Press, 1998.

Whiting, R. *You Gotta Have Wa*. New York: Vintage, 1989.

Wollen, P. "Cricket and Modernity." *Emergences* 7/8 (1995/96).

Worcester, K. *C.L.R. James Apolitical Biography*. New York: State University of New York, 1996.

INDEX